John George Phillimore

Private Law Among the Romans From the Pandects

John George Phillimore

Private Law Among the Romans From the Pandects

ISBN/EAN: 9783744772464

Printed in Europe, USA, Canada, Australia, Japan

Cover: Foto ©ninafisch / pixelio.de

More available books at **www.hansebooks.com**

8vo. cloth, 10*s*. 6*d*.

THE RESOURCES OF A NATION:

A SERIES OF ESSAYS.

By ROWLAND HAMILTON.

CONTENTS.

THE GENERAL CONDITIONS OF PROGRESS.
NATIONAL CHARACTERISTICS AND NATIONAL DEVELOPMENT.
RECIPROCAL RELATIONS OF FREE MEN. POLITICAL ECONOMY.
THE LAW OF INTERCHANGE. VALUE—DEMAND AND SUPPLY—RENT.
CONDITIONS UNDER WHICH POSSESSIONS ARE HELD. CAPITAL—CREDIT.
THE MEANS BY WHICH VALUE IS REPRESENTED. CURRENCY AND CIRCULATION.
REMUNERATION OF SERVICES. INTEREST. WAGES AND PROFIT.

8vo. cloth, 7*s*. 6*d*.

ON SOME

QUESTIONS OF INTERNATIONAL LAW:

By HISTORICUS.

Reprinted from *The Times*, with considerable Additions.

CONTENTS.

THE INTERNATIONAL DOCTRINE OF RECOGNITION.
THE PERILS OF INTERVENTION.
ON M. HAUTEFEUILLE 'DES DROITS DES NATIONS NEUTRES.'
THE LAW OF BLOCKADE.
NEUTRAL TRADE IN CONTRABAND OF WAR.
BELLIGERENT VIOLATION OF NEUTRAL RIGHTS.
THE FOREIGN ENLISTMENT ACT.
THE RIGHT OF SEARCH.
ON THE AFFAIR OF THE 'TRENT,' 1862.
THE TERRITORIALITY OF THE MERCHANT VESSEL.

AN APPENDIX, CONTAINING SOME ADDITIONAL LETTERS. 8vo. 1*s*.

PRIVATE LAW

AMONG THE ROMANS.

PRIVATE LAW

AMONG

THE ROMANS

FROM THE PANDECTS

BY

JOHN GEORGE PHILLIMORE, Q.C.

νῦν αὖτε σκοπὸν ἄλλον, ὃν οὔ πώ τις βάλεν ἀνὴρ
εἴσομαι, αἴ κε τύχωμι—πόρῃ δέ μοι εὖχος Ἀπόλλων.
Odyss. XXII. 7.

London and Cambridge.
MACMILLAN AND CO.
1863.

Cambridge :
PRINTED BY C. J. CLAY, M.A.
AT THE UNIVERSITY PRESS.

TO THE MEMORY OF

CLEMENT SWANSTON*,

LATE ONE OF HER MAJESTY'S COUNSEL,

AS A TRIBUTE TO GREAT ABILITIES, DEEP LEARNING,

SPOTLESS HONOUR, ENLARGED BENEVOLENCE,

AND INDULGENT FRIENDSHIP,

THIS VOLUME IS INSCRIBED BY

J. G. PHILLIMORE.

* The following passage from an old Italian commentator on the Pandects
describes Mr Swanston's character, and what I have myself experienced after
conversation with him, so exactly that I cannot help quoting it.

"Ea fuit clarissimi Salviani in adjuvandis meis opera, hominis qui morum
suavitate amabili consuetudine officiosâque diligentiâ, omnes omnino devin-
cit—seu verius qui totus ex candore modestiâ et facilitate concretus atque
compositus est, quique etiam a suis amatur ut qui maxime, sic quoad in-
dolem in studiis talem comperi de quo pronunciare merito possim quod nunquam ad eum accesserim quin semper recesserim doctior." BRENCKMANN,
Historia Pandectarum, Lib. IV. Cap. VI. p. 393.

PREFACE.

MY belief that some knowledge of the Roman system of Municipal Law will contribute to improve our own, has induced me to prepare the work I now offer to the public. As the diligent study of Homer and Euripides, of Cicero and Livy, of Dante and Bossuet, of Milton and of Shakespeare, would do more to refine the public taste, and to correct our antipathy to what is elevated and generous, whether in active life or speculative study, than any metaphysical inquiry into the principles of eloquence and poetry; so a familiarity with the works that formed Cujas and Doneau, Du Moulin, Pothier, and Montesquieu,—a knowledge of that social wisdom among Europeans unequalled, which has bound together so many successive generations, by ties that neither the sword of barbarous conquest could sever, nor the fraud of sacerdotal hypocrisy dissolve,—would do more to open the eyes of those whom habit or the desire of gain have not absolutely blinded to the deformities of our law, than any general or abstract dissertation on jurisprudence. We built our Chalcedon with Byzantium

b

before our eyes. This, however, is not the place to enter upon the reasons which alone among the nations of the West prevented England from sharing in the benefits of the Roman Law, and which have made every attempt to cultivate it among us, as if it had been the seed of some plant blown by the wind on an unfavourable soil, sterile and abortive.

The result, however, has been for our jurisprudence a coacervation of absurdities under the name of law in our books, such as are to be met with in the annals of no country where the Roman law has flourished, and for the character of those engaged in it as a profession a state of things down to the present century (for I desire particularly to be understood throughout this work as never speaking of my contemporaries, except when I allude to them directly), to describe which I will borrow the words of one of the most able as well as of the most eloquent men that ever took part in public life in England: "I might instance," says Lord Bolingbroke, "in other professions the obligations men lie under of applying themselves to certain parts of history, and I can hardly forbear doing it in that of the law, in its nature the noblest and most beneficial to mankind, in its abuse and debasement the most sordid and the most pernicious: a lawyer now is nothing more—I speak of ninety-nine in a hundred at least—to use some of Tully's words, 'nisi leguleius quidem cautus, et acutus, præco actionum, cantor formularum, auceps syllabarum.' But there have been lawyers who were orators, philosophers, historians; there have been Bacons and Clarendons. There will be none such any more till in some better age true ambition or the love of fame prevails over avarice, and till men find leisure and *encouragement* to prepare themselves for the exercise of this profession, by climbing up to the vantage-ground, as Lord Bacon calls it, of science, instead of grovelling all their lives below in a mean but painful application to all the little arts of chicane; till this happen, the profession of the law will scarcely deserve to be ranked among the learned professions." Such was the language of Bolingbroke; that of Swift is still more pointed. Burke, almost on his death-bed, says, in a letter to Lawrence, "our courts of justice seem in a league with villains of every description." And this state of things will last so long as attorneys are allowed to possess the exorbitant power they now enjoy, and instead of being subordinate to a class superior (or that society assumes to be superior) to them in education, are allowed to hold it in a state of comparative dependence, and a service that certainly is not perfect freedom. No stronger proof of their influence can be given than the fact that they actually threatened to ruin Mr Brougham if he persevered in bringing forward his schemes of Law Reform. Mr Brougham indeed said publicly, in answer to the threat, that if it was executed, he would sit in his chamber and take briefs without them. But though Mr Brougham, then in the zenith of his reputation, and the leader of a great party in the House of Commons, was beyond the reach of that powerful body, such is not the condition common ὀϊζυροῖσι βροτοῖσιν, who tread the rugged path of professional life; and so long as such power is vested in such a class, the attempts to pluck up the tares sown in the field of English law, during the night of the dark ages and long afterwards, by the enemies of all reason and all right, will be languid and unavailing. I say this, perfectly well knowing to what misrepresentation and abuse it will expose me, because the study of many years has satisfied me that I do well to be angry at the absurdities and abuses which contribute so largely to the profit of a handful of men, and to the moral and intellectual detriment of that class of the profession to which I belong. For what has been the result? No single great work on jurisprudence has ever been produced by any Englishman. At present, if a principle shews itself in our courts, it is like a cask in a rough sea, sometimes one part appears, sometimes another, never the whole. It is seen pitifully and imperfectly, instead of furnishing a sure standard and fixed rule by which all doubts may be brought to trial and against which all errors may be dashed in pieces. It has been a consequence of such a distempered state of things, that as the carefully cultivated ignorance of our judges prevented them from forming a reasoned opinion on any great question of jurisprudence, they have laid hold of some cant phrase as the basis of the conclusion at which they have arrived[1]. Such as, "Money has no ear-mark," "Equity must follow the law," "Christianity is part of the common law," "The law abhors a perpetuity,"

[1] Contradicting the maxim: " non ex regulâ jus fiat, sed ex jure regula sumatur."

and the like. For in spite of the most violent efforts, a velleity for the show of reason now and then
would force its way even among the patrons of fines
and recoveries, and the judges yielded to the necessity of having recourse to some articulated sound in
their barbarous and scanty vocabulary, that might be
mistaken for a principle or an idea, and serve to bind
together and explain the incoherent rubbish, to the
accumulation of which their lives and the lives of
their predecessors had been devoted. Then according to the quarter from which the current happened
to set, the judge endeavoured to transform himself
into various "miracula rerum"—into a patriot like
Judge Buller, when he said the writ of attaint (ex-
ploded in the days of the Tudors) was the dearest
privilege of an Englishman; a theologian like Lord
Kenyon, who probably had never opened a book in
any language but English after he was fourteen years
old, when he refutes all the arguments against the
doctrine and discipline of the Church of England in a
summing up of twenty minutes to a jury; a political
economist like Lord Tenterden, when he talked in a
strain of which a village nurse ought to have been
ashamed, about regrating and the precious metals;
a censor morum like Lord Eldon, when he deprived
one of the most gifted men in England, and a far
more scrupulous moralist than himself, or even perhaps than his friend the Duke of Cumberland, of all
control over his children; or a politician of the dark
ages, like almost all. Such occasions, however, were
not common. In general, they and their favourites
kept to their routine, which required about as much

intellectual activity as a turnspit is expected to shew
upon the wheel, where all he has to do is to lift up
his feet and put them down again. The wheel goes
round, and so did the law in the inevitable track
that had been made for it, as by the tinman beneficially in one case, by the attorney perniciously in the
other[1].

In this work my endeavour has been, avoiding
questions interesting rather to scholars and antiquari-
ans than to jurists, such as the Roman Criminal Law,
the different forms of marriage, the military testament, and the like, to select those parts of the Digest
which would best shew the grand manner in which
the Roman jurist dealt with his subject, as well as
those which most illustrate the principles by which
he was guided in establishing the great lines and
propositions of jurisprudence, such as the interpretation of wills and contracts, the authority given to
prescription, the protection of an occupier against
sudden violence (in which our law is to this hour so
shamefully deficient), and other topics, which every
lawyer must have frequent occasion to employ. It
is not however from the present age, or from those
in the eyes of whom literature or enlarged views, or
any knowledge of the jurisprudence of other countries
are crimes rarely expiated, who naturally struggle

[1] " Thomas, didst thou never see,
'Tis but by way of simile,
A Squirrel spend his little rage
In jumping round a rolling cage ?
Moved in the orb, pleased with the chimes,
The foolish creature thinks he climbs,
But here or there, turn wood or wire,
He never gets two inches higher."—PRIOR.

against any attempt to wrest from their hands the exorbitant power they now possess, or from the idols such men set up, that sound or rational ideas of legal regeneration are to be expected. On the contrary, next to the approbation of enlightened jurists, some of whom are happily to be found in the higher places of the profession, and one of whom now holds, "rarâ temporum felicitate," the highest rank in it, the hostility of such persons—legitimate descendants of those who in Queen Anne's time

> Shook their heads at Murray as a wit—

is the most infallible criterion of what is really beneficial to the commonwealth. Their enmity is the shade that pursues all that is not contracted or commonplace, and every aspiration to mend the condition of the profession to which you belong, or of the country in which you live. Montaigne, in one of his immortal Essays, has told us that to see a Venetian on horseback was no bad lesson of equitation, and in that point of view the efforts made against a course of liberal study by persons whose thoughts and observations, to use the words of Clarendon, "have been contracted within the limits of the books of that profession," or " within the narrower circle of the bar-oratory" have their use, "à nous amender, à reculons, par disconvenance plutôt que par convenance, par différence que par accord." The panegyrics pronounced by the champions of ignorance on those studying for the Bar might be answered, as South answered the fanatic who told him that " God did not stand in need of human knowledge ;" "Neither," said that accomplished writer, " does God stand in

need of human ignorance." Any other encouragement or assistance it would be absurd to expect from
the present age, the intellectual pedigree of which,
as every day almost and every department of public
life proves, dates most authentically from those
who preferred Fleming to Lord Bacon; until the
latter atoned for his transcendant genius by measure-
less corruption. We must not look for Guelphs
among the Ghibelines. But if ever the time shall
come in the history of this country when all men in
a certain station are ashamed of haranguing in favour
of the servile empiricism, which has made so many,
fit it may be for better things, mechanics instead of
jurists, masons instead of architects, and the law a
profitable trade instead of a noble science ; which has
given us Wrights, Norths, Wedderburnes, and Eldons,
instead of De Thous, Hôpitals, Molès, and Lamoi-
gnons ; and when incapacity to comprehend a principle is not looked upon as a mark of practical sense ;
if ever that time shall come, I shall be rewarded
far beyond my hopes, if my name is remembered
with kindness by those who trace the progress of
our institutions, not as that of one holding lucrative
office, and opposing education because the system
under which he obtained the patronage of an inferior and comparatively illiterate body must be perfect, but as that of one who, according to the measure
of his abilities, and without regard to immediate
interest, which he[1] was not too stupid to perceive,
was the first and ultimately the successful assail-

[1] "La vérité ne mène point à la fortune, et le peuple ne donne ni ambas-
sades, ni chaires, ni pension."

ant of Special Pleading. Let me close these remarks by a noble passage from a noble work : " C'est une étrange et longue guerre que celle où la violence essaie d'opprimer la vérité. Tous les efforts de la violence ne peuvent affaiblir la vérité et ne servent qu'à la relever davantage. Toutes les lumières de la vérité ne peuvent rien pour arrêter la violence, et ne font que l'irriter encore plus...la violence et la vérité ne peuvent rien l'une sur l'autre. Qu'on ne prétende pas que les choses soient égales, car il y a cette extrême différence...que la vérité subsiste éternellement et triomphe enfin de ses ennemis, parce qu'elle est éternelle et puissante comme Dieu même." Amen, and so be it.

TEXT-BOOKS CONSULTED.

LA SERVA. *Derecho Romano.* Madrid. Segunda Edicion.

SAVIGNY. *Obligationen recht.*

SAVIGNY. *System des heutigen Römischen Rechts.* Berlin.

VANGEROW. *Pandekten.* Marburg und Leipzig.

ARNDT. *Lehrbuch der Pandekten.*

PUCHTA. *Pandekten Vorlesungen.*

——— *Cursus der Institutionen.*

BRUNO. *Diritto Civile.* Napoli.

AVERANIUS. *Interpret. Juris.*

SALA. *Digestum Rom. Hisp.*

—— *Derecho Real de España.*

HAVBOLD. *Lineamenta Pandect.*

RICHERI. *Universa Civilis et Criminalis Jurisprudentia.* 3 Vols. Venice, 1846.

WARNKÖNIG. *Commentarii, &c.* 3 Vols. 8vo.

SCHILLING. *Römische Rechts Geschichte.*

MALEVILLE. *Analyse raisonnée de la discussion du Code Civil.*

CONTENTS.

CHAPTER I.

CHAPTER II.

CHAPTER VII.

CHAPTER VIII.

CHAPTER IX.

CHAPTER X.

CHAPTER XI.

CHAPTER XII.

CHAPTER XIII.

CHAPTER XIV.

CHAPTER XV.

CHAPTER XVI.

CHAPTER XVII.

CHAPTER XVIII.

CHAPTER XIX.

CHAPTER XX.

CHAPTER XXI.

CHAPTER XXII.

CHAPTER XXIII.

CHAPTER XXIV.

CHAPTER XXV.

CHAPTER XXVI.

CHAPTER I.

PRELIMINARY.

IF the law of a country is allowed to take the regular and natural course of progress, it usually passes through three periods, each of which has its own distinguishing peculiarity.

The first is the period of custom. Law is rude and simple as the notions of the people among whom it exists and who are the organs of its administration —it is the vehicle of their opinions, and the criterion of their refinement. To this stage of infancy succeeds a more various and complicated state of things. Law is split up into a number of elaborate distinctions, becoming more minute, frivolous and scholastic as subtlety increases and as the class supported by multiplying them, that is, by distorting and stifling truth, becomes more numerous, powerful, and indifferent to right. Such was the state of Roman jurisprudence long after Cnæus Flavius had published the forms which while kept hidden from the people were the main instrument of patrician ascendancy. This state of things is admirably described by Cicero in *Pro Murena*, and among us by a great master of style, Mr Justice Blackstone, in his famous judgment delivered against Lord Mansfield's view in

1

Perrin *v.* Blake, though such is the power of prejudice that he does not seem to be aware that his
argument is as severe a satire as man could utter
against the system it was intended to defend.

" Whatever their parentage," *i. e.* of these technical rules, " was, they are now adopted by the common law of England, incorporated into its body and
so interwoven with its policy that no court of justice
in this kingdom has either the power or (I trust)
the inclination to disturb them. The benefit of
clergy took its origin from principles of popery : but
is there a man breathing that would therefore wish
to abolish it ? The law of real property in this
country, wherever its materials were gathered, is
now formed into a fine artificial system, full of un-
seen connections and nice dependencies ; and he that
breaks one link of the chain, endangers the dissolu-
tion of the whole."

I say this is a bitter satire if we consider that
it was pronounced in the age of Burke, and more
than a century and a half after Lord Bacon flourished.
For the condition so described is but a phasis through
which the jurisprudence of an enlightened nation
must travel in its progress to a sound and rational
system. It is the consequence of increasing civility
and refinement which bring with them a multitude
of wants and exigencies unknown to those by whom
the early law was framed, and which are the result,
like much of the Roman Law, of collision amicable
and hostile with foreign countries, the knowledge of
their usages, and the relations arising from such
intercourse. With such objects and such multiplied

functions the law of a country must become complicated and prolix, till at last it grows to an uncouth
mass which no human industry can entirely master,
and which the people are utterly unable to comprehend.
In such a case the Lawyer of a free state is almost
absolute, for as his proceedings are carried on in a
technical phraseology, altogether unintelligible to the
mass of hearers, publicity is no check upon his proceedings[1]. In vain (and the present state of things
among us is a proof of the fact) are reports collected,
and treatises published on each separate head of law;
the power of the mind of the country over the law
is lost, and it is delivered up to those who have
every human motive to thicken the darkness and
aggravate the confusion:

> " Chaos umpire sits,
> And by decision more embroils the fray.
> ———— next him high arbiter
> Chance governs all."

The rights of men in such a state dwell upon
water, and the wave of the sea is their foundation.
Chicane is not the accidental infirmity but the
confirmed and settled habit of the law. To limit
the increase, or to acquire a knowledge of the dis-
connected mass is impossible, and as the difficulties
increase the intellect required to grapple with them
(as every volume of reports shews) diminishes.

[1] So a spectator at the trial of Al-
gernon Sydney, or Armstrong, or
College, or Lady Lisle, though he
might detect the fiendish wickedness
of the judge and counsel, must have
been unable to understand a great deal
of the injustice that was perpetrated.
So in civil matters till very late
periods; the forms of pleading enabled
a judge, if he was so disposed—and
such instances have been seen, in former times of course—to do gross and
grievous wrong without the knowledge
of the lay audience.

Nothing but a recurrence to first principles, a restoration of something like method and unity, in
other words codification, will raise the law to the
dignity of a science, or prevent inferior practitioners
of uncultivated and unphilosophical minds—chosen
by the favour of those whom they resemble—from
usurping the highest places in it and giving the tone
to those who make it a profession[1]. This brings us
to the third and final stage (which in some centuries
hence our practical country will perhaps arrive at), in
which this systematic unity is attained, in which the
facts, collected by experience and methodized by reason,
are embodied in a single volume, when law ranks
with the most liberal and dignified avocations, and
the lawyer is no more the mere *cantor formularum*
and *syllabarum auceps*. These three periods of original rudeness, subsequent confusion, and ultimate
system are clearly discernible in the Roman Law.
No people, as Hugo has remarked[2], ever were in
circumstances so favourable for moulding private
law, and carrying it to the highest point of con-
ceivable perfection as the Romans in the age of the
Antonines and Severus. Strange and mysterious
destiny of man, which imposes the sacrifice of some
blessings as the price of others, and seems to make
political freedom and the excellence of constitutional
right incompatible with enlarged and luminous principles in municipal legislation. Before I proceed to
explain the construction of the "Corpus Juris," I
must observe that from the middle of the twelfth

[1] "Le petit esprit étant parvenu à
faire le caractère de la nation." Montesquieu, *Gr. et Dec.*
[2] *Einleitung*, p. 2.

century it was the foundation of all instruction in law, throughout the south and west of Europe, our own country, as Selden in his notes to Fleta has shewn, down to the time of Edward the Second, not excepted. It was considered as a common law, from which even the consuetudines, coûtumes under the feudal system, were explained and filled up. And as it mitigated barbarity in the Middle Ages, it was by far the most important source from which, under a different state of things, those invaluable blessings to modern Europe[1], the codes of the eighteenth century, have been constructed.

Having premised so much, I come to the details. The history of Roman Law may be for our purpose conveniently divided into four periods. The first from the foundation of Rome to the enactment of the twelve tables A.U.C. 305, B.C. 449—infancy. The second from the twelve tables to the accession of Augustus A.U.C. 723, A.D. 31—youth. The third from the accession of Augustus to the death of Alexander Severus A.D. 235—manhood. And the last from the death of Alexander Severus to the reign of Justinian—decay.

Of these periods that which elapsed between the accession of Augustus and the death of Alexander Severus was the flourishing and glorious period of Roman jurisprudence. Excluded from the splendid functions of the statesmen and orators of the Republic, the Roman genius concentrated itself on the task of adjusting the eternal rules of justice to the infinite variety of human affairs, and for the first if not the

[1] And America. See Livingstone's *Civil Code of Louisiana.*

last time in the history of the species the names of
lawyer and philosopher were synonymous. Then
were composed those immortal works, the mutilated
fragments of which illuminated by reason, embellished
by the most exquisite propriety of diction, exalted
by the purest morality, have diffused order and
science over the rude efforts of Goths, Franks, Jutlanders and Vandals, and have been the guide and
ornament of every European country but our own.
England, as it was the last among the civilized
nations of the West to adopt the Gregorian Cal-
endar, repelled with jealous vigilance the encroach-
ments of light from the primæval darkness of her
law, and has preserved in all its shapeless deformity
the chaos accumulated by the successive contributions
of empirical mechanics, raised by proficiency in
chicane to stations where their ignorance and narrowness became public calamities, to whom all method was unknown and everything that resembled
principle unintelligible. Delighting in a barbarous
jargon which they transmitted from age to age, and
docile to the will of tyrant after tyrant, the English
lawyers were too often barbarous amid the polished,
and slaves amid the free[1]; while the Roman jurist,
trained in the schools of the Stoics and versed in the
noble idiom of his predecessors, asserted in a fault-
less style the sacred dictates of reason and of right,
and retained the virtues and eloquence of the Republic, while all around bore the marks of decrepi-
tude, corruption and servility.

[1] Livingstone, *Introd. Rep.* p. 56:
"This absurdity, worthy of Nero or
Caligula, continued to form a part of
English law till 1793."

The death of the Emperor Alexander Severus was followed by the most appalling anarchy. Sixteen Emperors perished by a violent death—nineteen pretenders to the empire carried desolation through the dismembered provinces—immense donatives[1] wrung from the exhausted inhabitants of a depopulated empire were the price of the disgraceful honours conferred by brutal soldiers on the minion of the day[2]. Such is the history of the fifty years of confusion which elapsed between the murder of Alexander Severus and the accession of Diocletian.

Two mighty events which had already exhibited themselves began rapidly to unfold the consequences with which they were pregnant during this period of disaster and dismay: these were the propagation of Christianity and the invasion of the barbarous hordes, whom the arms of the degenerate Romans were no longer able to restrain. The sublime doctrine of the unity of God struck at the root of Polytheism, and for an adherent of the ancient creed, whether he was so from conviction or belief in its expediency[3], toleration of that uncompromising and exclusive worship was impossible[4].

In the struggle between the ancient and modern creeds the Roman jurist arrayed himself on the side of the former, partly from respect for antiquity, partly from scorn for the character and attainments

---

[1] Salvian, *De Gubernatione Dei*, Lib. v. passim.

[2] In twelve hundred years France had 63 kings. In one hundred and sixty years, Casaubon remarks, seventy persons assumed the title of Cæsar in the Roman Empire.

[3] Montesquieu, *Dissert. Œuvres*, Vol. VII. p. 368.

[4] Symmachus, *Epist.* Lib. X. Ep. 54 Aurelian's letter to the Senate; Vopiscus, *H. Aug. Script.* Vol. II. p. 463, with note.

of the proselytes to the new theology, and partly because he saw that it tended to undermine the social structure already shaken by the fierce assaults of open violence. With the invasion of the barbarous hordes opens the dark and bloody page which records an almost total change in the modes of thought and habits of life among the inhabitants of Europe[1].

The separation of Church and State, slavish obedience to the authority of priests[2], confidence in the efficacy of external rites to procure everlasting happiness, claims to miraculous powers asserted as residing in the bones of illiterate fanatics or the persons of living mystagogues, idolatry under a new form, and addressed to beings and objects altogether contemptible—ostentatious professions of poverty and indifference to worldly honour reconciled to a fierce avarice and an indefatigable lust of power—the wretched

[1] As a specimen of the legislation produced under the influence of such counsellors, take Cod. 9. 8. 5. § 2: "Filii vero ejus quibus vitam imperatoria specialiter lenitate concedi-mus (paterno enim deberent perire supplicio, in quibus paterni, hoc est hereditarii, criminis exempla metuuntur) a materna vel avita, omnium etiam proximorum hereditate ac successione habeantur alieni, testamentis extraneorum nihil capiant, sint perpetuo egentes et pauperes, infamia eos paterna semper comitetur, ad nullos prorsus honores ad nulla sacramenta perveniant, sint postremo tales, ut his perpetua egestate sordentibus sit et mors solatium, et vita supplicium." And Cod. 1. 1. § 4, De Episcopali Audientiâ, 10. 9. 13. 1. 5, de Hereticis et Manicheis: "Hæreticorum autem vocabulo conti-

nentur et latis adversus eos sanctionibus succumbere debent, qui vel levi argumento a judicio catholicæ religionis et tramite detecti fuerint deviare.' l. 4, eod.: "In mortem quoque inquisitio extendatur." Arians, 5 eod., Nestorians, 6 eod., Eutychians, 8 eod., orthodox child of an heretical parent to succeed to all his property, 19 eod., conversion of a Christian, punished by confiscation of all the converter's property, 1. 7. 5. eod. ; if any one assail a converted Jew "cum saxis," "aut alio furoris genere," cum omnibus suis participibus concremandus, Cod. 1. 9. S. 3, Pagans, 1. 11. 8, condemned to the mines "post cruciatus corporis," right of sanctuary, Cod. 1. 12. 6.

[2] "Gagès pour ne rien faire." Mont. Œuvres, Vol. 1. p. 39.

intrigues of synods and court prelates and monks in lieu of the masculine qualities exercised in the senate and the camp—fear of the censure and respect for the authority of the Church exalted above all moral obligations—a complete surrender of the conscience and understanding to the dictates and legends of ecclesiastics, put forward as the chief if not the sole merit of a Christian—the most startling and incessant contrast between theory and practice, belief and conduct —the condemnation to never-ceasing torments of the wisest and most virtuous heathens because they were ignorant of events that happened long after their death—pride under the disguise of humility—temporal dominion growing up under the shade of spiritual authority[1]—great crimes and extravagant penances— impudent falsehoods justified in the cause of truth, rapine and eleemosynary foundations, rape and ascetic mortifications—gross materialism and seraphic ecstasies—exhortation changed into menace and abject entreaties into insolent command—a spirit sometimes inactive, sometimes full of scruples, almost always directed to comparatively selfish objects instead of the glowing patriotism that ennobled the very crimes of Greece and Rome[2]—above all the doctrine unequalled for its wickedness that the Almighty would for money become an accomplice in the foulest

---

[1] "Τὰ κατ᾽ οἰκονομίαν γραφόμενα." Athanasius cit. apud Daillet, De l'emploi des Pères.

"Une société de gens qui ne rendant jamais et recevant toujours attiroient insensiblement tout à eux." Mont. Œuv. I. 372.

[2] εἷς οἰωνὸς ἄριστος ἀμύνεσθαι περὶ πάτρης,

was the Roman's creed. The vulgar of course were slaves of superstition in Rome as in Belgravia.

Adrian says the Bishops at one time took to worshipping Serapis: "devoti sunt Serapi qui se Christi episcopos vocant." Vopiscus, H. Aug. Script. Vol. II. p. 720. 8vo ed. Lugd. Bat.

crimes—these were the distorted lineaments of
Christianity in the corrupt and mutilated shape it
wore for several successive ages, which were brought
out in bolder relief and became more distinctly visible as the long shadows of a polar night concealed
all that was refined and beautiful and really mag-
nanimous from the eyes of Europe, and which might
be traced by an attentive observer in the character
it assumed among the courtiers, bishops, ladies and
eunuchs who were so actively employed in moulding
creeds, practising childish ceremonies and contriving
the assassination of their rivals during the continuance of the Byzantine empire[1].

And when Diocletian[2] assumed the reins of government everything portended the evils that he
endeavoured for a while to avert by obliterating all
traces of republican forms, by multiplying the number of rulers, by replacing the ancient magistrates
with others of imperial origin, by tearing away the
mask of despotism and surrounding the throne of
the Cæsars with all the pomp and luxury of Asiatic
domination. Thus it became easy for Constantine to
transfer the seat of government to Constantinople,
to turn the Roman Senate into a local vestry, and
to make Christianity the religion of the state. He
and his successors took an active part in the go-

[1] "Les vices des âmes foibles et
des crimes réfléchis." Montesquieu,
p. 280, Vol. I.
"Deum," says Gravina, in a noble
passage that, though written by a
Roman Catholic, might be read with
advantage in the diocese of Oxford,
"velut in societatem criminum nefariè

vocantes, muneribus a rapinâ et fraude
atque alienarum opum usurpatione ve-
nientibus et motibus corporis, verbisque
nullo animi sensu pronunciatis ac men-
titis obsequiis placabilem ponunt."
p. 293, 4to ed.
[2] Montesquieu, *Gran. et Dec. des
Romains,* 17 ch.

vernment of the Church, convoked councils, interfered in arranging creeds, and provided for the support of the priesthood. They conferred large estates
upon the Church, and declared those estates inalien-
able. Pursuing to extremes a system which during
the time of persecution it had been wise if not
necessary for Christians to adopt, in defiance of all
reason, of the spirit and letter of Christianity, they
gave bishops jurisdiction[1] in matters merely secular,
a plague-spot that developed itself with fearful
rapidity throughout Europe. If to this power we
add that given to ecclesiastics of exterminating
heresies and heretics, we may form an idea of
the change which Constantine brought about, and
which gave an altogether different character to
social life in the countries subject to the Roman
legislation.

Jurisprudence shared the common fate. Not
only does Theod. II. in the edict publishing his
code complain "quod tam pauci ætate suâ proxi-
mâque extiterint qui juris civilis scientiam ditarentur
et soliditatem veræ doctrinæ receperint;" but Am-
mianus Marcellinus in the description he has given
us of the lawyers in his age, shews that jurisprudence had sunk to a condition of the most abject
ignorance and barbarity: "E quibus sunt ita rudes

[1] This Protestant and "Practical"!
country is the last in which, after the
most desperate resistance, this enormous abuse has been not exterminated,
but in some degree mitigated, in the
latter half of the 19th century. Singular commentary on the text in which
the great master of all Christians refused so much as to determine a controversy between two brothers as to a
piece of land, lest he should take upon
him the office of a judge. "I could
decide controversies," said Confucius,
"as well as another, but my duty is
to prevent men from having controversies."

nonnulli ut nunquam se codices habuisse meminerint,
et si in circulo doctorum doctoris veteris inciderit
nomen, piscis aut edulii peregrinum esse vocabulum
arbitrantur[1]." Yet selections made from the works
of writers who lived at this period were inserted
in the Pandects. They were Hermogenian, Aurelius, Arcadius, Charisius and Julius Aquila; the
first wrote "Epitomarum Juris libros sex," in the
order of the "Edictum perpetuum," which is supposed to have furnished the model on which the
Pandects were drawn up. As at this time the imperial enactments were the only source of legislation,
collections of them became almost indispensable.
Several such collections were made, called codes from
the caudex on which they were written. Of these
codes four were named after their authors, the Gregorian, Hermogenian, Theodosian, and that of Justinian[2].

The Gregorian and Hermogenian codes were the
work of two lawyers who digested into their compilations the constitution of the Emperors before Constantine, beginning probably, from the time of Adrian and
ending with that of Diocletian. These two compilers
lived in the time of Constantine and his son, and
the work of Hermogenian was subsequent to that of
Gregory, and intended as a supplement to it. Both
are stated by Gojarius, the compiler of the West
Gothic Breviary, to have the force of law[3]. The
next code[4] was that of Theodosius II., consisting of

---

[1] Amm. Marc. 30, 4.

[2] Schulting, *Jurisprud. Antiquit.*
683—718. Gothofred, *Prolegom. Cod.
Theod.* cap. I. p. 209. Hugo, *Lehrbuch d. G. des Rom. Rechts,* § 290.

[3] *Constit. un. Cod. Theodos. de Responsis prudentum.* Gothofred, *Cod.
Theod.* Tom. II. p. 32.

[4] The author is supposed to have been
the exconsul and exprefect Antiochus.

the constitutions from Constantine to Theodosius II. It consisted of sixteen books, the first five of which related exclusively to private law, and was by a special edict of Valentinian III., constituted the law of the Western Empire. It is only known to us through the Breviarium Alaricianum, or compilation made by the order of Alaric II.[1], after the battle of Poitiers, and promulgated at Toulouse[2]. The last eight books of the Theodosian code were published in 1550 by Du Tillet, the three preceding in 1566, by Argacius.

It is supposed that one great object of Hermo-genian and Gregory was to preserve the jurispru-dence that existed under the Pagan Emperors which the detestable hypocrite Constantine was anxious to obliterate. There he would have looked in vain for those anodynes of conscience, those palliatives of his enormous crimes, which the bishops among whom he presided were ready to minister[3]. A constitution I cite below furnishes abundant proof of his barbarous

---

[1] A.D. 506, "ordinante illustri Gojarico comite."
It contains extracts from the Codex Gregorianus, Hermogenianus, Theo-dosianus, the Receptæ Sententiæ of Paulus, the Responsa of Papinian, and the Institutes of Caius; it is often quoted, sometimes in the Canon law as "Lex Romana," or "Theodo-siana."

[2] A great part of the first five books of the Code were discovered by Closius and Peyron at Milan and Turin, Warnkönig, *Hist. du Droit Romain*, and have since been published by Wenck. De La Serna, *Derecho Ro-mano*, Vol. I. p. 87. Closius disco-

vered the "Gesta in Senatu urbis Romæ de recipiendo Theodosiano Co-dice." *ib.*

[3] Imper. Constantinus Aug. ad Maximum Præf. "Perpetuas pru-dentum contentiones eruere cupientes, Ulpiani et Pauli in Papinianum no-tas—qui dum ingenio laudem sec-tantur non tam corrigere eum quam depravare maluerunt—aboleri præcipi-mus." A.D. 321. See *Instit. de Nat. Juris et Gentium*, 8 and § 8. "Ut judici recedere ab eorum responso non liceret ut est constitutum," etc. De La Serna, *Derecho Romano*, Vol. I. 84, 87.

malevolence and presumption. In the year 428
Valentinian gave the clearest and most humiliating
proof of the utter and helpless incapacity to which
the rule of the sword sooner or later brings mankind by the decree De responsis prudentum. Five
jurists, Papinian, Paulus, Caius, Ulpian, and Modestinus were declared infallible; a majority was in
all cases decisive; when their opinions were equally
divided, that of Papinian was to prevail[1]. This law
in reality is to be attributed to Theodosius. It turned
the judge into an antiquarian, obliged to examine
manuscripts[2], and degraded his task still farther by
making his decision a simple question of arithmetic.
Justinian put an end to this thraldom[3].

The next code was that of Justinian, consisting
of his own laws and the rescripts of his predecessors. This work was undertaken in February
528, and brought to a close in the following April.
It was superseded by the "Codex repetitæ prælectionis." All citations from it were forbidden, and
it has not come down to us.

In the year 530 Justinian assigned to Tribonian
the task of compiling the Digest, which was to consist of extracts from the works and decisions of
ancient jurists. Tribonian was accordingly placed
at the head of a body consisting of twenty lawyers
and professors of jurisprudence. Ten years had been
allowed him to complete the work; but in less than
four years it was ready for publication, as Tribonian

---

[1] Serna, "Ley de citas," *Derecho Romano*, Vol. I. p. 84.
[2] Reckoning the decisions in Har-rison or Chitty's Digest is not an oc-cupation more illiberal
[3] *Const. de conceptione Digest.* § 6.

sought, says Gravina, an indulgent judge of his character, "potius ex celeritate gloriam, quam posteris utilitatem." The title of this work was "Digesta sive Pandectæ juris enucleati ex omni vetere jure collecta libri quinquaginta." They were published 16 December, 533.

As however the Digest was a work too extensive to be placed at once in the hands of pupils, Tribonian with the aid of two jurists composed the Institutes, which were published in November of the same year when the Digest was published, and received their ratification at the same time with the Digest, as authentic law.

In the year 534 Tribonian with four colleagues produced the work we now possess under the title of the *Codex repetitæ Prælectionis*.

From that time till the year 566, in which Justinian died, that emperor published a great variety of constitutions, adding to and derogating from the provisions of the Code. These are called Novellæ.

Tribonian is supposed, and often from venal motives, to be the author of the greatest number; he died in 546, and almost all are prior to that year.

The Digest is divided into seven parts and fifty books. The books are subdivided into titles, the titles into laws or fragments, the laws into paragraphs. The division into seven parts and the order observed was an imitation of the edict, adopted in all probability for the greater convenience of the forum[1].

---

[1] This is the opinion of Blume and of Hugo.

Considered as a scientific work the Pandects exhibit the deplorable condition of the age. It is destitute of all symmetry and even of convenient method. It contains contradictory laws and repetitions, and many passages of the ancient jurists cited not from the original works but from treatises into which they had been inserted. The powers conferred upon the compilers by their semibarbarous master over the precious works of the great masters of jurisprudence were excessive, and even these powers were transgressed. The writings of these illustrious teachers are mangled, torn from the context, and adulterated by stupid interpolations. The changes and additions so made are usually called *emblemata Triboniani*, and have excited the just indignation of succeeding jurists.

Before I proceed to lay before my readers in detail some of the more important doctrines of the Roman Pandects, it may be well to invite their attention to the reasons which render this branch of study indispensable to a jurist, and valuable to every purpose of liberal education. All writers whose opinions are entitled to any weight in such a matter, have agreed to recommend the study of the Roman Law not only as an admirable preparation for the duties of civil life, but as an inexhaustible mine of luminous argument, masculine sense, and uncorrupted equity[1].

---

[1] "Sunt quædam in Europa gentes, quæ non judicant res ex Romanis legibus, sed vernaculis. Et tamen, qui ibi res publicas gesturi sunt, fere Romanas leges apud exteros discunt, qui, ut accipio, interrogati, quid, quum nostrarum legum non sit apud eos usus, in his cognoscendis tantum operæ ponant, respondere solent: animam se spiritumque legum (sic enim loquuntur) excipere, hoc est æquitatis vim ac naturam hinc decerpere, ut de patriis legibus rectius judicent. Laudo prudentissimam vocem, qua significant omnia rectius perspexisse summos illos veros nostri juris auctores, et nemi-

"Dixi sæpius," says Leibnitz, "post scripta Geome-
trarum nihil extare quod vi ac subtilitate cum Romanorum jurisconsultorum scriptis comparari possit,
tantum nervi inest, tantum profunditatis .... nec us-
piam juris naturalis præclare exculti uberiora vestigia
deprehendas." In support of this last remark, and
to shew the tone and spirit of the civilians, I shall
quote some memorable passages from the work that
it has been my endeavour to illustrate. The reader,
when he places the passages I am about to quote in
contrast with the language of our statute-book, and
the sentiments of some judges as recorded in our reports and state trials, will decide whether some knowledge of the work in which they are contained might
not have been beneficial to those who compiled the one,
and to those who uttered the other; and whether men
who from mere ignorance, or vanity, or narrowness
of mind, or inveterate habit, or an invincible natural
antipathy to elevation and refinement not uncommon

nem satis instructum esse ad civitatem regendam, qui non in his cognoscendis tirocinium fecerit. Quid? quod
in his Juriconsultorum litteris bona
pars antiquitatis reliqua est? Veteres
mores sermonis Romani pleræque
figuræ, quas nisi hi explicarent in aliis
scriptoribus nonnumquam non aliter
atque in luto hæreremus, nec intelligi
optimorum auctorum plerique insignes
loci possent. Quod si historia, si aliæ
veterum litteræ nobis, ut debent, curæ
sunt, quum his passim lucem adferam
Jureconsulti vel a Grammaticis et
Rhetoribus eorum commentarios ad-
servari oporteret. Itaque nisi simul
*omnibus litteris bellum indicemus et
plane in belluas degenerare juvabit*, non
permittendum est, ut situ ac senio

Romanæ leges emoriantur." Me-
lancthon, *Oratio de Legibus*. Leibnitz,
Epist. 119: "Ego Digestorum opus
vel potius auctorum unde excerpta
sunt, labores admiror, nec quidquam
vidi, sive rationis acumen sive dicendi
nervos spectes, quod magis accedat ad
mathematicorum laudem ; mira est vis
consequentiarum." Schlosser, *über das
Studium des reinen Römischen Rechts*.
Hugo, *Civil. Mag.* Vol. I. pp. 33, 38.
"These remains of the Roman jurists
give us all that a judge requires to
qualify himself for his task."... "But the
journeyman who seeks not the path to
wisdom, but that in which he may
make most money in the shortest time,
must look for another road." *Ib.*

to prosperous mediocrity, endeavour to discourage such studies, are improperly described by Averanius[1], as the semibarbarous corrupters of youth.

Every one who desires that the student should possess competent notions of the objects of legal science—that his ideas of the subject should be coherent and systematic, not flung at random upon each other like a heap of stones, but bound together and forming part of a harmonious fabric, like the columns of a Grecian temple—that he should be able to pursue the subject into its smallest ramifications, and remark its finest varieties and shades of difference—that he should be a master of philosophical jurisprudence, and therefore never disposed to sacrifice the end to the means, avowedly promoting chicane—"that the law may be an art[2]!"—that he should be able to apply with the closest accuracy the rules of Logic to any doubt he may be called upon to solve—must begin the education of such a person with a complete system, containing comparatively few laws, but numerous rules for their employment and elucidation. Thus trained, the jurist, wherever the stage be laid on which he is called to tread—whether it be where

"Purpurea intexti tollunt aulæa Britanni,"

to frown down chicane among timeservers, pettifoggers and courtiers in England, cr among the "urbes

[1] "This want has given birth to a practice of extremely pernicious consequence; I mean the custom, by some so warmly recommended, of dropping all liberal education as of no use to students in the Law." "A lawyer thus educated in subservience to solicitors and attorneys will find, &c." Blackstone, Comment. Introd.

[2] Lord Hobart. Certainly not the "ars boni et æqui," but almost the exact definition of injustice.

Asiæ domitas," to mitigate the horrors of the yoke of
the rapacious stranger by an enlightened, stedfast and
impartial equity above the din of violence and extortion—let it be where it may—will perform his part
with grace and dignity; and where will he find a
system so complete, so long and so deeply meditated,
refined by such vast experience, and improved by
the application of so many centuries, as the Roman
Law?

I begin with the three great and well-known pre-
cepts laid down by Ulpian and placed in the front
of the pandects: "Juris præcepta sunt hæc—honeste
vivere—alterum non lædere—jus suum cuique tribuere[1];" to lead a stainless life, to hurt no man,
to give every one his due. In the same chapter
I find the doctrine that nature having made all men
kin, for man to lay a snare for man is wickedness.
"Quum inter nos cognationem quandam natura con-
stiterit, hominem homini insidiari nefas esse[2]."

Papinian says: "Beneficio affici hominem intersit hominis[3]." Man has an interest in contributing
to the weal of man. Ulpian says that not only the
person himself, but any man may appeal in behalf of
one who is led to punishment: "Credo humanitatis
ratione omnem provocantem audiri debere (et si ipse
acquiescit sententiæ) nec quærimus cujus intersit[4]."
Nay, he says even if the victim—probably this was
intended to save the Christians—should resist the
appeal: "Perire festinans—adhuc puto differendum
supplicium." From the law stamped on the heart

---

[1] II. 1. 1. 10. § 1.　　　　[2] Eod. 3.
[3] II. 18. 7. 7.　　　　[4] II. 49. 1. 6.

of man, "solis hominibus inter se commune," Pomponius deduces piety to God, submission to parents
and to country[1]; so rash[2] and hasty oaths are forbidden.
Respect is due to natural right and modesty
even where "serviles cognationes" are to be regulated: "Pater filiam non possit ducere et si ex servitute manumissi sunt et dubitetur patrem eum esse[3]."
The same rule applies in the case of affinity among
slaves: "Veluti eam quæ in contubernio patris fuerit
quasi novercam non possim ducere, et contra eam
quæ in contubernio filii fuerit patrem quasi nurum
non ducere," &c.   And as a fitting close I will cite
the noble passage of Papinian: "Whatever wounds
our reputation, piety, self-respect, that is, in one
word immoral, must be supposed for us impossible[4]."
   "Quæ facta lædunt pietatem existimationem verecundiam nostram et ut generaliter dixerim contra
bonos mores fiunt, ea nos facere non posse credendum est[5]."

[1] Π. 1. 2.
[2] Π. 12. 2. 13. 6. προπετωs μὴ
ὄμνυε.
[3] Π. 23. 2. 14. § 2.
[4] There is no such rule to be found
in Vesey junior, or in Meeson and
Wellsby, but much that encroaches
on it, e. g. Cornefoot v. Fowke.
[5] II. 28. 7. 15.
I may mention here that Tribonian,
taking a hint from the churchmen of
the day, affected great alarm lest Justinian, on account of his piety, should

be suddenly snatched up to Heaven.
Τριβωνιανος ἔφη περιδεὴς ἀτεχνῶς εἶναι
μή ποτε αὐτὸς ὑπὸ εὐσεβείας ἐs τὸν
οὐρανὸν ἀναληφθεὶς λάθοι. Procopius,
Hist. An. p. 84. Ed. Bonn, Corpus
Sc. Hist. Bz.
   Suidas tells the same story. Vol. II.
page 36. 1. 2. Ed. Gaisford. He says
also that he was an atheist, hated the
Christians in his heart, was governed
by an insatiable avarice, and that (like
Lord Bacon) he bartered justice for
money.

CHAPTER II.

GENERAL VIEW.

In this Chapter I have endeavoured to comprise the topics which, being in a certain degree common to every part of law, and necessary for just understanding of it, ought to precede a minute examination of details.

For the first topic I have selected the sources of Roman jurisprudence, the rules of law, and the method of their application. For the second, the persons for the sake of whom all legal rules exist, and the particular qualities by which they are distinguished; and for the third, the things the title to which is governed by legal rules, as well as the circumstances on which, in the intercourse of mankind, the law has impressed a peculiar importance.

All Law is natural or positive[1].

Nothing that Natural Law forbids can be commanded (so as to bind the conscience).

Nothing that Natural Law commands can be forbidden (so as to bind the conscience).

In this sense Natural Law is immutable.

Positive Law is established by the will of the legislator.

---

[1] *Inst. de Justit. et Jure*, § 3. Grotius, *de Jure Belli et Pacis*, I. § 1.

The "jus gentium" (international law) "solis hominibus inter se commune," is founded in part on natural, in part on positive Law[1]; it constitutes a principal part of public law.

Civil Law is written or unwritten[2]. It is public (emphatically national), that which binds the citizens of the state into one whole, and governs their relations to it[3]; or private, that which regulates the relations and prescribes the acts of individuals towards each other[4].

Much of the jus gentium was incorporated by the Prætorian law with the jus civile.

Ulpian has given this account of these expressions to denote the enactment, the repeal, and the modification, of a law :—

"Lex aut rogatur, i. e. fertur[5]; aut abrogatur, i. e. prior lex tollitur ; aut derogatur, i. e. pars primæ legis tollitur; aut subrogatur, i. e. adjicitur aliquid primæ legi ; aut obrogatur, i. e. mutatur aliquid ex primâ lege."

SOURCES OF LAW[6].

Gaius[7] thus enumerates the sources of Roman Law : "Lex, Plebiscitum, Senatusconsultum, Principum Placita, Edicta, Responsa Prudentium." Pom-

[1] II. 1. 1. 33.

[2] "Quod neque in totum a naturali jure vel jure gentium recedit, nec per omnia ei servit. Itaque cum aliquid addimus vel detrahimus juri communi, jus proprium, id est civile, efficimus." Ulpian, II. 1. 1. 6.

[3] The modern German writers use

Staats Recht, which is more accurate; our nearest word is Constitutional Law.

[4] *Inst.* 3.

[5] *Fr.* Ulpian. § 3.

[6] Savigny, *System*, 1. 109. Cic. *Top.* c. 5 ; *de Partit.Orat.* 37. Gaius, 1. 2—7.

[7] *Inst.* 1. 2. § 3—9.

ponius[1], in the exquisite sketch cited in the digest, gives a chronological view of the origin of Law, and comprises the causes of that origin in the following catalogue : " Lex prudentium interpretatio, legis actiones, plebis scitum, senatus consultum, principalis constitutio." Papinian says[2], " Jus civile est quod ex legibus, plebis scitis, senatus consultis, decretis principum, auctoritate prudentium, venit...Jus Prætorium est quod Prætores introduxerunt adjuvandi vel supplendi, vel corrigendi juris civilis gratiâ, propter utilitatem publicam, quod et honorarium dicitur ad honorem Prætorum sic nominatum." Here[3] then we find the division of Law into "jus scriptum" and "non scriptum." The "jus scriptum" being the law which derives its authority from a written instrument, in which description the Prætor's edict, even in those parts which are based on custom, must be included, so must the "responsa prudentium," as both became binding and ascertained, when they were incorporated with written law. But a custom did not become part of the jus scriptum because it was inserted by a jurist in his system ; for that insertion gave it no power that it did not possess before, and the origin of its authority was not to be found in any written edict.

A precise and settled contrast between two kinds of law is insisted upon by the Roman jurists in

[1] I. 2. 2. §'9.

[2] II. I. I. 7.

[3] Here the poverty of language leads often to equivocation. We must not confound the law which springs from " Natura " (Cic. Part. 37), which great writers have exhausted their eloquence to enforce, and of which some modern English writers, in the true spirit of the 19th century in England, dispute the existence, with either branch of the lex of the civilians, whether it be "jus scriptum" or "non scriptum."

the distinction they take care to make between
the jus civile and the jus gentium, as well as in
that between the jus civile and the jus honorarium[1].
The first of these distinctions arose from this state
of things. As intercourse between the Roman people
and foreign nations increased, it became necessary
to know and to apply the law of other states, in
the administration of Roman justice. The wider
the Roman dominion spread, the wider became the
views of their jurists, and in this way arose the
notion of a law common to the Romans with other
nations and with all mankind. So Caius tells us[2]:
"Quarundam rerum dominium nanciscimur jure
gentium quod ratione naturali inter omnes homines
peræque servatur; quarundam jure civili, id est jure
proprio civitatis nostræ." It was inevitable in such
circumstances, among such a people as the Romans,
that the narrow circle of municipal justice should
be enlarged, and that, to borrow Lord Bacon's meta-
phor, "the streams of justice," flowing through
different countries, and stained with the variation
of each soil through which they passed, should be
traced back to their fountains.

The common source of all law was found in the
common consciousness of right implanted in our
nature, "antiquius jus gentium cum ipso genere
humano proditum est[3]," from whence flowed as a
corollary that there was "id quod semper æquum
et bonum est:" at the same time particular institu-

---

[1] "Jus est civilis æquitas vel scriptis legibus sancita vel institutis aut
moribus recepta." Sallust. "Ars boni
et æqui." Celsus.

[2] II. 41. I. I. ib. I. I. 9.
[3] II. 41. I. I. Caius. "Man hath the
rule of right within." Butler's Sermons
on Human Nature, p. 30. Sermon 3.

tions and the rules applicable to them were common to the jus gentium and the jus civile. Such were the contracts by which the daily intercourse of mankind is for the most part carried on— emptio, venditio—locatio, conductio, &c.; such were many of the Delicta, inasmuch as they brought with them the duty of compensation—Delivery as the means of acquiring property, &c. On the other hand, marriage as between Roman citizens, the power of the father and the agnatio founded on it, some of the most important rights of property— mancipatio, usucapio, the verborum and literarum obligatio—the Delicta considered as the cause of punishment assigned by positive law and the whole law of inheritance belonged exclusively to the jus civile.

Yet most of these laws sprang from a common root, and were to be met with, though under different forms, in the law of other countries. Gradually institutions, analogous to those peculiarly the growth of Rome, were recognized even by the tribunals of that country. Thus, together with the marriage of the civil law, a form of marriage valid by the jus gentium, found its place. Together with the agnatio, a naturalis cognatio—together with property, "ex jure quiritium," that "in bonis"—together with the rigid form of the "Stipulatio," "Spondes Spondeo," other forms of contract more flexible, and of which foreigners might avail themselves. Even the law of inheritance, more than any other the creature of positive enactment, and adapted to the political object of the constitution, followed the same bias and law of development. Thus the improvement

and the triumph over the narrow and intensely selfish views of a caste, which the genius of Lord Mansfield, aided by the accumulated experience of centuries, could hardly succeed in effecting for a short time in a small part of English law, was achieved, seventeen centuries before his time, by the Roman genius for jurisprudence; and the opposition between the "jus civile" and the "jus gentium" became less and less with the increase of Roman knowledge and the progress of Roman domination.

We may collect from the Pandects that the jurists, from the works of whom they are composed, considered man in a threefold view; as an animal, i. e. a sensitive creature, as a being endowed with reason (particeps rationis[1]), and as a member of a particular society.

Considered in the first light, he was subject to the "jus naturale," the "jus" "quod natura omnia animalia docuit[2]." Ulpian tells us that he means by this rule, the law that all beings capable of pleasure and pain obey, submission to which is not a lesson of reason, but the dictate of instinct and the condition of their existence[3]. As a rational being, a mem-

---

[1] Cicero, *De Legibus*, 1, § 1.

[2] Suarez, Vol. v. p. 1. seq. Op. omnia, ed. Paris.

[3] So our great metaphysician: "Mankind has various instincts and principles of action, as *brute creatures have*, some leading most directly to the good of the community, and some most directly to private good." Butler, *Preface to Sermons*, p. 14.

The Stoics called these τὰ πρῶτα κατὰ φύσιν. Aul. G. *Noctes Atticæ*, 12. c. 5. "Sic est faciendum ut contra universam naturam nihil contendamus et eâ tamen conservatâ propriam sequamur." Cic. *De Off.* 1. 31.

"Quid enim aliud est natura quam Deus et divina ratio toti mundo et partibus ejus inserta." Seneca, *De Ben.* lib. 4. c. 7. A curious proof of the

ber of the great family of the human race, and framed
to hold some communion with those who share the
same nature as himself, he is subject to another law,
"quo gentes humanæ utuntur[1]," that is, the law without which the intercourse between human beings not
acknowledging any common superior, and therefore
between independent states, could not be carried on[2].
When the elements of discord that are kneaded up
in our nature obtain the ascendancy, recourse is had
to the jus gentium, often variously modified, to
palliate the consequences of such a state of things,
and to prevent the total disruption of all the ties
that bind human creatures to each other, to teach
men (as it has been happily expressed) "insanire
cum ratione." From the "jus gentium" also flow a
vast number of contracts essential to human intercourse—"ut emptio venditio," "locatio conductio[3],"
"societas," "depositum," "mutuum," "et alii innu-
merabiles."

Lastly, as the citizen of a particular state, man
is subject to the law established in that community,
by which positive and arbitrary rules are laid down,
and in the phrase of the Pandects the rules of

Stoical theory is to be found II. 9.
1. 11: "Cum arietes vel boves com-
misissent et alter alterum occidit,
Quintus Ennius distinxit ut siquidem
is periisset qui aggressus erat cessaret
actio, si is qui non provocaverat, com-
peteret actio,"&c. See also the distinction between matter and form, II. 32.
78. 4. "Ea materiæ potentiâ victa nunquam vires ejus effugiant," explaining
why "argentum" in a will included
plate, but "marmor" did not include

a statue.
[1] II. 1. 1. § 3. "Hinc descendit
maris atque feminæ conjunctio quam
nos matrimonium appellamus, hinc
liberorum procreatio, hinc educatio,"
&c.
[2] II. 1. 1. 9. "Quod vero naturalis
ratio inter omnes homines constituit
id apud omnes peræque custoditur
vocaturque jus gentium quasi quo
jure omnes gentes utuntur."
[3] *Inst.* 1. 2. § 2 ; II. 1. 1. 5.

the jus gentium are varied; sometimes abridged, sometimes relaxed, sometimes made more comprehensive, in short to the "jus proprium cujusque civitatis."

As instances where the positive law defines while it enforces the law of nature, we may appeal to the law regulating the relation of guardian and ward[1]. That the guardian shall watch over the interests of his ward is part of the law of nature. The precise limit of his responsibility is fixed by the civil law. That the borrower should take due care of the thing confided to him[2] is a precept of the law of nature enforced by the civil law. Again, the law of nature requires the parent to provide for his children; and, on the other hand, the law of nature allows a man to dispose of what belongs to him. To reconcile these two principles is the business of positive law.

The "jus civile" is again divided into written law, that is, law formally promulgated by the legislative authority; and unwritten law, that is, law "quod sine scripto venit," not originally sanctioned by formal promulgation in an edict, but the growth of custom arising from the interpretation of learned men; "jus quod sine scripto venit compositum a prudentibus," and which has become by tacit consent incorporated with jurisprudence[3].

A law may be considered either separately, or with reference to other laws, or with reference to

---

[1] II. 27. 3. 1.   [2] *Inst.* 3. 15. 2.

[3] "Ea quæ longâ consuetudine comprobata sunt ac per annos plurimos observata, velut tacita civium conventio, non minus quam ea quæ scripta sunt jura servantur." II. 1. 3. 35.

what it enjoins or forbids, or with reference to the persons subject to its control.

A law[1] considered abstractedly from other laws has the effect of annulling what is contrary to its behest, whether the letter or the meaning of the law be violated, and this whether a clause making an act it forbids null be annexed to it or not; and as the principal act is null, so is the accessory[2], and all intended for its support or corroboration, as the suretyship or pledge intended to enforce an unlawful contract.

An exception to this rule exists where the legislature has actually provided a remedy against the act it discountenances. For if the act was "ipso jure" null, the remedy would be superfluous, e. g. the "senatus consultum Velleianum" prohibited women from becoming sureties. But the suretyship was not a nullity, as the senatus consultum had provided the woman so bound with an "exceptio," which, if she pleased, she might employ.

So the "senatus consultum Macedonianum" cancelled[3] the debt of any money borrowed from an usurer by a "filius familias," "expectata patris morte," but if he chose when a "pater familias[4]" to pay the money, it could not be recovered. Again, it may be asked[5], how far a law may be set aside

[1] Cod. § 5. h. t.
[2] "Cum principalis causa non consistit ne ea quidem quæ sequuntur locum habent." II. 50. 17. 129.
[3] II. 14. 6. 1.
[4] II. 12. 6. 40.
[5] The principle is explained in this law, II. 2. 14. 7. 14. "Si paciscar ne operis novi nunciationem exsequar quidam putant non valere pactionem, quasi in eâ re prætoris imperium versetur. Labeo autem distinguit ut si ex re familiari opeis novi nunciatio sit liceat pacisci, ı de republicâ non liceat, quæ distinctio vera est."

by the consent of him whom it was enacted to protect. The answer is given by distinguishing between jus publicum, laws for a public, and laws for
a private object. The law belonging to the first
class could not be waved, "Jus enim publicum
privatorum pactis immutari non potest[1]." For instance, an agreement to wave the defence of a
"dolus malus" was nugatory. But the benefit of
a law belonging to the second class might be abandoned, "Quisque enim potest renunciari juri pro se
introducto."

This latter rule however was not applied in certain cases where it was the object of the legislature
to take care that certain classes of persons should
not have it in their power to injure themselves,
e. g. women in what related to their dower, wards,
minors, and prodigals[2].

Another question[3] on this head is, if an act is
absolutely null when the law inflicts a punishment
on the person committing it. It has been argued,
on the authority of a text of Papinian[4], that in such
a case the act punished was valid; but the sounder
view seems to be that it was not. First, because
there are many examples of different punishments
inflicted for the same offence, e. g. the thief was
liable civilly "in duplum," or "actione furti," "in

---

[1] II. 2. 14. 38; and with regard to
an agreement to waive the benefit
of the Falcidian Law, II. 35. 2. 15.
§ 1.

[2] "Is cui bonis interdictum est
stipulando sibi acquirit, tradere vero
vel promittendo obligari non potest, et
ideo nec fidejussor pro eo intervenire

potest sicut nec pro furioso." II. 45.
1. 6.

[3] Examples of merely penal laws
among the Romans. Ulpian, *Fragment.* tit. 1. princip. and §§ foll.

[4] II. 48. 19. 41. "Nec sane veri-
simile est delictum unum eâdem lege
variis æstimationibus coerceri."

quadruplum;" the "rapinæ reus," besides the quadruplum he was obliged to restore, was punished by
the Julian laws, "de vi publicâ et privatâ." Secondly,
it is a general rule that one general action[1] does not
destroy another for the same thing. Thirdly, the
nullity of the act can hardly be called a "pœna,"
but merely leaves matters as they were before the
act was done; and this gets rid of the objection
which rests on the passage of Papinian cited above;
and lastly, it may be remarked, that the object of
the legislature being to prevent the act, that object
is better attained by making it altogether as if it
had never happened, than by allowing it to exist,
while the doer is punished.

Another important division was that of *jus
publicum*[2] and jus privatum. Ulpian says the "jus
publicum" lay "in sacris, sacerdotibus, magistratibus." The parts of it were in his day, the jus pon-
tificum, jus augurum, jus flaminum, jus senatorium,
the law of wills. It concerns the relation of the
citizen to the state, and its institutions and policy.
Privatum "quod respicit ad statum et ad utilitatem
singulorum[3]."

---

[1] "Nunquam actiones præsertim pœnales de eâdem re concurrentes alia aliam consumit." II. 50. 17. 130. *ib.* 130. II. 47. 8. 2. § 1 : 47. 2. ult. *Inst. de Oblig.* 5. de vi bon. rapt.

[2] Pliny, lib. 8. *Epist. ad Aristonem.* II. 1. 9 ; II. 1. 2. § 16—§ 34. In. 10—21. Cujacius, Vol. III. p. 783.

Observ. lib. 27. 36. e.g. under the republic the Valerian and Porcian Law, the Laws regulating the division of the people into tribes, curiæ, classes and centuries, the laws concerning the comitia. Polybius, 6. 11—18. Tac. *Ann.* 1. c. 2. Hugo, *Lehrbuch*, p. 520.

[3] Cujac. *ubi supr.* II. 1. § 2.

CUSTOM[1].

The Romans defined custom "jus moribus constitutum." Consuetudinary law, according to their doctrine, indicated the tacit consent in its favour of the people among whom it was established, and was as binding therefore as written law. "Veluti tacita civium conventio non minus quam ea quæ scripta sunt jura servant in ea quæ longâ consuetudine comprobata sunt." But where a custom, introduced erroneously, had obtained the power of law, the parity of reason or principle of analogy did not apply "quod non ratione introductum sed errore primum deinde consuetudine obtentum est, in aliis similibus non obtinet."

Ulpian lays it down that in examining the validity of a custom it is most important to consider whether it had been established after litigation. "An etiam contradicto aliquando judicio confirmata sit." The word "etiam" is important, as it shews

---

[1] Suarez, Vol. VI. lib. 7. Hugo, *Lehrbuch*, ed. 9. p. 366. *Inst.* I. 2. II. I. 2. I. 3.

"Mores sunt tacitus consensus populi longâ consuetudine inveteratus." Ulp. *Frag.* § 4. II. 3. I.; II. I. 3. 35. "Sed et ea quæ longâ consuetudine comprobata sunt ac per plurimos annos observata velut tacita civium conventio non minus quam ea quæ scripta sunt jura servantur." 32. h. t. "De quibus causis scriptis legibus non utimur id custodire oportet quod moribus et consuetudine inductum est."

II. 4. 39. "Inveterata consuetudo pro lege non immerito custoditur, et hoc est jus quod dicitur moribus con-

stitutum." "Optima legum interpres consuetudo." II. I. 3. 37.

For an account of the influence of consuetudinary Law in Rome see Tacitus, whom I "dare be bold" to think a better teacher than Vico, or Niebuhr, who has copied him. *Ann.* 8. 26. "Ea res admonet ut de principiis juris et quibus modis ad hanc multitudinem infinitam ac varietatem legum perventum sit altius disseram." &c. II. h. t. 34.

Entick *v.* Carrington, one of the few judgments on a great question in our Reports that a Jurist may read without a blush. Wilson, *Reports*, Vol. II. p. 275.

that a custom might be valid if it had never been questioned, though if confirmed after dispute it was less vulnerable.

It was this principle[1] that enforced precedent and made "rerum perpetuo similiter judicatarum aucto-ritatem," equivalent to law in doubtful cases[2]. But the "consuetudo" must be "diuturna," "per annos plurimos observata[3]." The precise time is not fixed in the Pandects, and therefore the interpreters infer that it was left to the decision of the judge. "Cum dicit tempus nec adjicit diem sine 'dubio ostendit esse in judicantis potestate quem diem præstiterit." All things "moris et consuetudinis" were always taken to be included in contracts "bonæ fidei," though not specially mentioned. The law establish-ing this doctrine is a very pregnant one, and if from any hitherto inactive cause the judicial mind should expand and become less dark among us, will perhaps even in our courts be referred to by remote posterity with great advantage[4].

It is seldom that the maxims, "Specialia sem-per generalibus inesse[5]," or " In toto partem conti-neri[6]," are applicable to consuetudinary law. The maxim "In toto jure generi per speciem derogari[7]" is generally the rule for its construction.

---

[1] II. h. t. 38. 50. 17. 207. " Res ju-dicata pro veritate accipitur." II. 42. 1. 56; 32. 38. § 1.

[2] 33. h. t.

[3] 35. h. t.

[4] "Quia assidua est duplæ stipu-latio idcirco placuit etiam ex empto agi posse si duplam venditor manci-pii non caveat; ea enim quæ moris sint et consuetudinis in bonæ fidei judi-ciis debent venire." II. 21. 1. 31. § 20.

[5] II. 50. 17. 147.

[6] II. 50. 17. 113.

[7] " A jure scripto Romano mu-tuamur (inquit Molinæus) quod et æquitati consonum, et negocio de quo agitur aptum congruumque in-venitur: non quòd unquam fuerimus

"Rectissime receptum est[1]," says Julian, "ut leges non solum suffragio legislatoris, sed etiam tacito consensu omnium, per desuetudinem abrogantur." This law is directly contradicted by a law of Constantine, cited in the Code[2]. Various attempts have been made[3] to reconcile these contradictory enactments, the more remarkable as the barbarous interpolation, "suffragio legislatoris," in the first seems to shew that this insertion of the republican argument was intentional. The true solution of the difficulty is to be found in the inability of Justinian's venal lawyers to execute the mighty task they had undertaken, and to deal with the materials which the great jurists, from whose works the Digest was taken, had supplied. We are obliged to them, however, for their inconsistency in quoting a passage so strongly proving the liberal and masculine spirit which, while all around them was degraded, upheld the jurists of the empire[4].

---

subditi Justiniano magno aut successoribus ejus; sed quia jus illo auctore a sapientissimis viris ordinatum, tam est æquum, rationabile, et undequaque absolutum, ut omnium ferè christianarum gentium usu et approbatione commune sit effectum." Tit. *des Fiefs.* proem. n. 110. Molinæus.

[1] II. 50. 17. 80.

"Receptum est" is the common expression for consuetudinary law, whether established by popular usage, or the opinion of jurists: "quia receptum est," II. 5. 1. 12. § 2, "moribus inter nos receptum est ne inter virum et uxorem donationes valerent," II. 24. 1. 1. "cum jus potestatis moribus sit receptum," II. 1. 6. 8.

So the "bonis interdicere," II. 27. 10. 4. § 7; "Pupillaris substitutio," II. 28. 6. 2. So 23. 2. 8, "moribus introductum." So "jure civili receptum." Gaius, 2. 4. 3. Zimmern, 1. 5. 5. Compare II. 50. 17. 161, with 1. 3. 2. § 5. II. "receptum est quicquid a prudentibus probatum." Festus.

[1] L. 32. h. t.

[2] L. 2. Cod. h. t. "Consuetudinis ususque longævi non vilis auctoritas est, sed non usque adeo sui valitura momento, ut rationem vincat aut legem."

[3] Donellus, *Comm.* I. c. 10. Vangerow, 1. 28. Puchta, *Gen. R.* 81.

[4] To this proof of their superiority let me add the law (so opposite in its

Some eminent writers in Germany have conde-
scended to flatter the prejudices of the absolute
governments under which it was their misfortune to
live by arguing against codification, and representing
man as the mere creature of instinct, incapable of
constructing for himself a rational system of legislation. The head of this school, which has been
refuted not by reasoning only, but by practice and
experience, was Savigny. According to his argument, and that of his followers, the practice of tor-
ture to extort confession as it existed among conti-
nental nations, or of pressing to death as it existed
a quarter of a century ago in our own, ought to be
respected as a proof of the "internal life" and
"consciousness of a people[1]." Now in the first place,
to explain the origin of a law is in no way to pronounce an opinion on its justice. In the second
place, the notion of right and justice cannot be deduced from history and experience, because that
experience is contradictory. As human laws have
varied on the most important matters among the
most civilized nations, it is clear, that it is not to
them that we can appeal for the invariable standard
of what is right.

Lastly, if positive law be taken as the criterion of excellence, it must be assumed that man-

---

language to the doctrine of our ship-
money and prerogative judges), "non
puto delinquere eum qui in dubiis
quæstionibus contra fiscum facile responderit." II. 49. 14. 10.

[1] "There are people who hate every
man who endeavours to improve any
thing," says Leibnitz in his treatise
*Nova methodus discendæ jurispruden-
tiæ;* and he quotes examples of the
sufferers in such a cause, Valla, Ramus,
Galilei, Des Cartes, Harvey. He
would have added Turgot, Romilly,
and many others to the list, if he had
lived later.

kind has attained the utmost possible limit of perfection.

EQUITY[1].

The principles of equity are those to which the
judge must have recourse for the decision of every
question and the solution of every doubt. Whether
the matter at issue be great or small, whether it con-
cern the life of a citizen, or a point of merely technical procedure, every decision that is hostile to the
principles of equity, that cancels the "vinculum
æquitatis[2]," to use the emphatic words of Papinian,
is an unjust decision. To the immutability of her
everlasting decrees all positive rules must be subordinate. If, as in the case put in the Pandects,
the letter of the law be rigorously upheld, it must
be upheld because equity[3] requires it; if a defect
in the law is to be supplied, (as in another case[4],
registered in the same immortal page,) it must be
in obedience to the same grand and all-pervading
principle, "In omnibus quidem, maxime tamen in
jure, æquitas spectanda est[5];" over all cases and persons that supremacy is complete.

Little could those great lights of jurisprudence

---

[1] "Servare æquitatem quæ est
justitiæ maxime propria." Cic. _De
Off._ 1. 19.

[2] "Naturalis obligatio ut pecuniæ
numeratione ita justo pacto vel jurejurando ipso jure tollitur quod vinculum æquitatis quo solo sustinebatur
conventionis æquitate dissolvitur."

[3] II. 40. 9. 3. 12. § 1: "Quod quidem per quam durum est, sed ita lex
scripta est."

[4] II. 39. 3. 2. § 5: "Hæc æquitas
suggerit etsi jure deficiamur."

[5] "Premier objet du legislateur,
dépositaire de son esprit, compagne
inséparable de la loi, l'équité ne peut
jamais être contraire à la loi même.
Tout ce qui blesse cette équité, verita-
ble source de toutes les lois, ne résiste
pas moins à la justice." D'Aguesseau,
Œuvres, Vol. 1. p. 138.

imagine that the time would come when a nation
arrogating to itself exclusively the name of "practical," obstinately shutting its eyes and closing its
ears to their admirable lessons, would establish courts
to administer justice on principles ostentatiously and
professedly hostile to equity, disclaiming all sense of
her suggestions, and shaking off all notions of her
summons—courts clinging to the dregs and refuse of
barbarous legislation, in which the suitor, the case of
whom in a court of equity was too clear and plain
even for chicane itself to dispute, was defeated as a
matter of course[1]. Equally strange to them would
have been the meaning annexed by that nation to the
word equity, and the narrow, technical, harsh, contradictory, confused, pettifogging, vexatious doctrines
which under that name had been used to foment
litigation, and to take away the property, the liberty,
and in many cases the reason, of the miserable suitors
who had been tortured into an appeal to it. This
assuredly was not the beneficent and healing principle invoked by Paulus when he wrote the sentence
I have quoted. No proceeding like that which exhausted the patience even of such an age as that of
the Regency of George IV. was present to the mind
of Cicero, when in his panegyric on the great lawyer
of the Republic, he told the last of Roman senators,
"admirabilem Servii Sulpitii in legibus *æquitate*
interpretandis scientiam fuisse ait; cum non magis

[1] How could any enlightened notions of jurisprudence, or of equity,
the soul of law, prevail in a country
where such a device "in fraudem legis," as that of common recoveries,
was sanctioned by sworn judges on
the bench? Where is the law that
on such a principle might not be set
aside by judges sworn to administer
justice according to its provisions?

juris quam justitiæ consultus esset, et jus civile ad *æquitatem* referret[1]," or when he defined law to be "æquitas constituta iis qui ejusdem civitatis sunt ad res suas obtinendas[2]."

In all sciences there are certain first principles which are the basis of those who reason on them; and as in mathematics the common principles on which astronomy, mechanics, perspective, rest, are to be found in geometry, to which an appeal must always be made, so in arguments which arise on positive law, and in the discussion of particular cases, recourse must always be had to the principles of equity. Man has no more power over them than he has over the properties of the circle or the square[3]. Notwithstanding the sophistry of one or two great writers, and the foolish commentaries of modern sciolists, such principles exist in jurisprudence as well as in other sciences; and it follows that there are two kinds of laws, one subject to change, the other immutable. Such, for instance, are the rules laid down by Ulpian: "Honeste vivere, alterum non lædere, jus suum cuique tribuere;" and so with regard to the questions that arise from particular facts, some are evident and easy, others obscure, perplexed, and difficult. Now though the laws I have cited are immoveable, to which others might be added, and such as no time, or place, or event can alter, there depend on them others liable to fluc-

---

[1] Cicero, *Philipp.* 9.

[2] Cicero, *Top.* 2.

[3] In conformity with this doctrine of all jurists and philosophers, Ulpian says, II. 50. 16. 42 : "Probra quædam naturâ turpia sunt quædam civiliter, et quasi more civitatis." So Lord Coke says truly: "Things of the highest criminality are sometimes of the least disgrace."

tuation, and varying with the course of human
necessities, which make the application of eternal
law different in different ages and nations. Society
would perish as well in China as in France, if it were
declared to be law that men ought to do all the
injury possible to each other, to lead infamous lives,
to give no man his due, and in all cases to prefer
the interest of the individual to that of the common
weal. But whether a contract shall be committed
to writing before it can be enforced in a court of
justice, whether a will shall be attested by two only
or by a greater number of witnesses, whether a
prescriptive right shall be established after a period
of ten, twenty, or thirty years, these are matters on
which natural justice does not pronounce, and which
may be variously determined according to the policy
of the legislator and the evils against which it is
most essential for him to protect his fellow-citizens.
Yet the eternal principle remains, whether the interpretation be lax or strict, whether the law be
gentle or severe, whether its operation in this particular case be on the side of human sympathy,
or opposed to it, that what is equitable can never
break in upon the rules of justice, and that what is
just never can break in upon the rules of equity.
The extracts cited below from passages scattered
through the Digest shew the Roman jurists' notion
of equity[1].

[1] II. 33. 10. 1. § 2.
"Potentior est quam vox mens dicentis."
27. 1. 73. § 2. cit. infra.
16. 3. 31. § 2. "Bona fides quæ
in contractibus exigitur æquitatem

summam desiderat."
4. 4. § 1. "Non semper autem ea
quæ cum minoribus geruntur, rescin-
denda sunt. Sed ad bonum et æquum
redigenda sunt." &c.

LEGAL INTERPRETATION.

This topic naturally leads to the rules of legal interpretation. The gradual moulding and development of law, or as the French call it "jurisprudence[1]," was called by the Romans "interpretatio:" the result sometimes of opinions elicited by particular application and sometimes of discussion[2] on disputed points. Thus the "usucapio[3]" of the "bonæ fidei" possessor, the law of servitudes given to the "usucapio" of two years for houses, and several "legis actiones," were established. In every civilized country there will arise, generated from traditional usage and judicial construction, and general opinion, rules that float in the atmosphere of its tribunals, and which modify, circumscribe, or supply the place of positive legislation.

II. 39. 3. 2. § 5. "Hæc æquitas suggerit etsi jure deficiamur."

II. 5. 3. 40. cit. supra.

41. 1. 7. § 5. "Strictâ ratione," &c. "Sed vix est ut id obtineat." 50. 17. 192. § 1.

"In re dubiâ benigniorem interpretationem sequi non minus justius est quam tutius." 108 eod.

"Rapienda occasio est quæ præbeat benignius responsum."

17. 1. 29. § 4. "De bonâ fide agitur cui non congruit de apicibus juris disputare." 50. 17. 90.

"In omnibus, maxime tamen in jure, æquitas spectanda est."

"Hoc naturâ æquum est neminem cum alterius damno fieri locupletiorem." II. 12. 6. 14.

"Si licet hoc jure contingat, tamen æquitas dictat judicium se dari." II. 15. 1. 32.

[1] Portalis, *Discours Locré*, Vol. 1. p.

258. Domat. Vol. 1. p. 86.

[2] Cic. *de Or.* 1. 45.

"Herennius Modestinus et notando et disputando bene et optimâ ratione decrevit." II. 50. 4. 26. "Scævola respondit et in disputando adjiciebat." II. 28. 2. 19. So we find the expressions "plácet," "magis placuit," "dudum placuit," "post magnas varietates obtinuit," "hoc jure utimur," "inter omnes constat." The Twelve Tables were at first the framework of these elucidations, "His legibus latis," says Pomponius, after a narrative for which it is perverseness itself to substitute the scheme of an inhabitant of Berlin or Jena in the 19th century— "cœpit, ut naturaliter evenire solet, ut interpretatio desideraret prudentium auctoritatem, necessariamque disputationem fori." II. 1. 2. 5.

[3] Gaius, *Inst.* 2. 43.

To provide for every case that can possibly occur in the infinite variety of human affairs, is not only a vain, but, as the example of our statutes shews, a most mischievous and preposterous attempt, indicating complete ignorance of all that ought to be present to the mind of a legislator. When the legislator has laid down general rules, has contracted within certain limits the range of judicial interpretation, and has laid down in his code the clearly-defined text, to which every citizen in an ordinary case may apply for information as to his rights, his obligations, the course to be taken to obtain redress when he is wronged, and the liabilities to which he exposes himself by violating the rights of others, he has fulfilled his task[1]. " Neque leges, neque senatus consulta ita scribi possunt, ut omnes casus quandoque inciderint comprehendantur, sed sufficit ea quæ plerumque accidunt contineri."

The first division of rules is into those inspired by natural, and those dictated by positive law; those which are established because they are right, and those which are right because they are established[2]. That the keeper of a deposit should restore it belongs to the first, that a certain form should be observed to make a will or a donation valid belongs to the second class. All rules, whether natural or

---

[1] II. 1. 3. 10. And again, "Non possunt omnes articuli singulatim aut legibus aut senatus consultis comprehendi. Sed cum in aliquâ causâ sententia eorum manifesta est, is qui jurisdictioni præest *ad similia procedere* et ita jus dicere debet." 12 *ib.*

"Ruperit" includes "corruperit." II. 9. 2. 13.

"Novercæ et sponsæ personæ omissæ sunt sententiâ tamen legis continentur." II. 48. 9. 3.

[2] "Furtum, adulterium naturâ turpe est, enimvero tutelæ damnari, hoc non naturâ probrum est, sed more civitatis, nec enim naturâ turpe est, quod potest in hominem idoneum incidere." II. 50. 16. 42.

arbitrary, may again be divided into those which apply to all matters, those which apply to most, but not to all, and those which are limited to one, and have no relation to any other head of jurisprudence. The rule that equity is to be followed, is an example of the first class; that an agreement between two persons is a law to the contracting parties, is an example of the second, since it does not prevail in the case of wills[1]; and that a contract of sale may be set aside on the ground that one of the parties to it has been injured to an amount exceeding half the just value, is an example of the third.

No rule has any power on matters extrinsic to, or when distorted from, its proper spirit and application. "Quæ simul in aliquo vitiata est perdit officium suum[2]" are the words of Paulus, meaning not that the rule itself is impaired, but that if any circumstance is wanting to justify its application, "simul in aliquo vitiata est," its functions are at an end, "perdit officium suum." The fault is not in the rule; it is not vicious, for then it would be a rule no longer, but vitiated by an improper use[3].

Thus in the case put II. 28. 13. the testator by his will ordained, his wife being with child at the time of his death, that the child, if a boy, should have two-thirds of his fortune, and the mother one-third; and if a girl, that she should have a third, and his widow the rest. The widow brought forth a boy and a girl. There by a rigorous interpretation the

---

[1] Domat. 1. 78.
[2] II. 50. 161. § 1.
[3] A memorable and characteristic illustration of this was the argument from a *certiorari* in Mr Fox's East India Bill.

mother would lose all share in the succession, as the
event in which it was given to her did not take place.
But by an equitable construction (humanitate sug-
gerente) the estate was divided into seven parts, of
which the son had four, the mother two, and the
daughter one, "licet subtili juris regulæ conveniebat
ruptum fieri testamentum."

The necessity for interpretation arises when the
law, from a defective expression, is ambiguous or obscure; for, as a general rule, the maxim applies
"quum in verbis nulla ambiguitas est non debet
admitti voluntatis quæstio[1]." But there is another
case when interpretation is necessary, that is, when
the sense of the law, however manifest, would, if
applied indiscriminately, lead to unjust and shocking
consequences[2]. For instance, the "senatus consultum
de petitione hæreditatis" provided that the possessor
of an inheritance to which he was not entitled should,
after the suit began against him, restore every thing
as it was at the time the suit was instituted, to
the owner[3]. The strict construction of this rule
would make him liable for animals that might
happen to die during its continuance. But this Paulus denies: "nec enim debet possessor aut mortali-
tatem præstare aut propter metum hujus periculi
temere jus indefensum relinquere[4]."

[1] "Ut ait Pedius, quoties lege aliquid unum vel alterum introductum
est bona occasio est cætera quæ
tendunt ad eandem utilitatem vel
interpretatione vel certe jurisdictione
suppleri." 13 eod. See 4 eod. "Ex
his quæ forte uno aliquo casu accidere
possunt jura non constituuntur." 5 eod.

"Nam ad ea potius optari debet jus
quæ et persona et facile quam quæ
perraro eveniunt." 8 eod. "Jura non
in singulas personas sed generaliter
constituuntur."
[2] II. 1. 3.
[3] II. 5. 3. 25. § 5. § 7.
[4] Eod. tit. 40.

So if a debtor had been guilty[1] of "mora," he was liable for the thing due, though it might have ceased to exist. Strictly taken this rule would make him liable, if the "mora" had ever been incurred— though he had purged the "mora" by a subsequent offer to the creditor. Celsus denies that in such a case he is to be held responsible: "Celsus scribit eum qui moram fecerit in solvendo Sticho quem promiserat posse emendare eam moram postea offerendo— esse enim hanc quæstionem de æquo et bono in quo genere plerumque sub auctoritate juris scientiæ perni- ciose erratur[2]." The true principle is that no rule must be looked upon by itself, but as part of a great whole, and therefore the interpretation of it demands an inquiry whether it is not limited by other rules. As all justice partakes of a common essence, and therefore never can thwart, obstruct, or contradict justice, any more than truth can be opposed to truth, and every rule must be founded on justice, every one must have fixed and appropriate limits assigned by that universal reason on which all depend. The knowledge of this equity and the comprehension of its spirit, is the true basis of all legal interpretation.

EXAMPLES OF RESTRICTIVE INTERPRETATION.

Instances of the restrictive interpretation, besides those cited above, are to be found in the law pro- viding the libertus shall not be liable to the penal-

---

[1] "Si post moram promissoris bona decesserint tenetur nihilo minus perinde ac si homo viveret, et hic moram vide- tur fecisse qui litigare maluit quam restituere." II. 45. 1. 82. and 23. ib.

[2] II. 45. 1. § 3.

ties of suing his patron—if he repent and abandon
the action, if the patron though summoned does not
appear, or if the proceedings have been instituted
with the patron's assent—all these, though not specified in the edict, are to be considered as good grounds
of defence[1]. So a widow was forbidden to marry for
a certain time after her husband's death. The object
was to prevent doubt as to the offspring. Therefore
if she was delivered of a child after her husband's
death within the time fixed by law, she might marry
again immediately[2].

For the sake of the person (alimentarius) to
whom what was necessary for support or nourish-
ment had been left, an edict forbad an arrangement
(alimentorum transactio) by which for the sake of a
little present advantage (modico præsente) he might
be deprived of it, unless with the Prætor's sanction.
A question arose whether an arrangement that what
was due at the end of the year should be paid at the
beginning, or what was due yearly should be given
monthly, was valid without the Prætor's authority,
and Ulpian held that it was "quia meliorem[3] conditionem suam alimentarius tali transactione facit[4];"
and the purpose of the legislator was accomplished.

EXTENSIVE INTERPRETATION.

The extensive interpretation is that which includes
cases that the letter of the law strictly taken would
not comprehend—on the principle that what is done

---

[1] II. 2. 1. 11. See also 2. 15. 8. 6.
and 48. 3. 2. § 1.

[2] II. 3. 2. 11. 2.

[3] II. 2. 15. 8. § 6.

[4] II. 37. 14. 6. § 2. Compare L.
15 cod. 17. 1. 54. 47. 3. 2.

"in fraudem legis[1]" ought to be considered as done "contra legem," and that he acts "in fraudem legis" "qui salvis verbis legis sentontiam ejus circumvenit," or in the words of Ulpian, "fraus legi fit ubi quod fieri noluit, fieri autem non vetuit, id fit—et quod distat ῥητόν ἀπό διανοίας (dictum a sententiâ) hoc distat fraus ab eo quod contra legem fit."

Perhaps, however, the most striking instance of the application of this branch of the doctrine we are considering, is to be found in the rule of analogy of which we know the Roman jurists to have made such frequent use, as for instance, in producing so great a number of "actiones utiles;" and a little reflection will shew us that the employment of this principle does necessarily flow from the maxim quoted before, that to provide by name for every special emergency is a task beyond the compass of human legislation, whence the rule "ad similia procedere atque ita jus dicere" follows as a corollary. By this however is not meant a similarity of reason, but a similarity of fact, where the same reason is applicable; and in the words of the law commented on before, "ad eandem utilitatem."

It is important to bear in mind that no argument from analogy can prevail in cases of "Privilegia" and "jura singularia," inasmuch as "quod contra rationem juris receptum est non est producendum ad consequentias."

The maxim so frequently quoted, "Cessante ratione legis, cessat lex ipsa," is not in the full sense

<hr/>

[1] I. 3. 29. and 30.

[2] "Inquit lex ruperit, rupisse ver-   bum fere omnes veteres sic intellexe-
    runt, corruperit." II. 9. 2. 13.

tenable. Law is binding not from the reason by which it is justified, but from the authority by which it is established. The Roman law says, "nihil tam naturale est quam eo genere quidque dissolvere quo colligatum est[1]."

Grotius[2] asserts the principle, "cessante ratione, cessat lex," if the sole cause of the law ceases for ever, the intention of the legislator exists no more, and the law has expired. This doctrine he supports[3] by a law often quoted. Thus he says, "All laws grounded on a state of war cease without any formal repeal in peace." If however the cause is not absolutely and totally at an end, the question arises, whether to enforce it in the actual state of things would be incontestably at variance with the purpose of the legislator, in which the law has no more any binding power; and he appeals to the laws cited below[4]. For instance, he says the law forbids all citizens to mount the ramparts. A citizen nevertheless whose house is near them, and who hears the enemy, is bound to mount them, if it will contribute to repel the enemy : even however if the law is not at open variance with the intention of the legislator, there may be a question whether it imposes a general rule for a general object, or whether it considers that done which has not been done. The law, to prevent

---

[1] II. 17. 50. 17. 32.

[2] Toullier, 1. 121. Merlin, *Questions de droit. Tribunal d'appel.* § 5. Voet, tit. de Leg. § 43. Huber. eod. 9.

Grotius, *Inleydinge Tot de Hollandsche Geleertheyt*, B. 1. decl. 2. § 23.

[3] 26. 2. 30. "Duo sunt Titii, pater et filius, datus est tutor Titius nec apparet de quo sensit testator, quæro quid sit juris. Respondit, is datus est quem dare se testator sensit : si id non apparet non jus deficit sed probatio. Igitur neuter est tutor."

[4] II. 40. 4. 19. II. 1. 3. 29. 30. Arg. Tiraqueau, Indict. Pent. 1. 130—178.

bloodshed, forbids citizens to bear arms: this is
binding on the most peaceable inhabitant. But if
the law considers that done which has not actually
been done, e. g. when a person is obliged to marry
a woman because two witnesses prove a promise, he
who knows that no such promise has been in reality
made, is not bound "in foro conscientiæ," but upon
all other persons what has taken place is binding[1].

It is a main rule of interpretation that the whole
of a law should be considered, and the parts of it
carefully collated with each other. "Incivile est
nisi totâ lege perspectâ, unâ aliquâ particulâ ejus
propositâ judicare vel respondere[2]."

The "ratio legis," or final cause which has induced the legislature to enact the law, is a main
ingredient of rational interpretation. A good example is furnished by Modestinus[3]. The Emperor
Marcus had ordered that all lawfully chosen tutores
who wished to excuse themselves from undertaking
the office, should allege the grounds of their ex-
emption before a competent judge within fifty days,
if they lived in the same city with the judge or
within a hundred miles of it ; that those at a greater
distance should be allowed a day for every twenty
miles of distance, and thirty days over. The result
of a literal interpretation of this law would have
been that a person living at the distance of one
hundred and sixty miles from the spot, would have
thirty-eight days only within which to prefer his
claim[4], and therefore would be in a worse condition
than if he had lived on the spot; in which case he

---

[1] Grotius, *ubi supra.*   [2] II. 1. 3. 24.   [3] II. 27. 1. 13.   [4] 8 for 160 ; 30 over.

would have had fifty days. Therefore Scævola[1], Paulus, and Ulpian, coryphæi legum, held that fifty days should be allowed in all cases, and should be added to the thirty which the law gave to those who lived at a distance, and to the day for each twenty miles in such a case ; for, said they, "etsi maxime verba legis hunc habeant intellectum tamen mens legislatoris aliud vult."

There being in every law two things—the words used, and the signification those words were intended to convey—Celsus insists on the latter as the proper object of consideration : "Scire leges non est verba earum tenere sed vim ac potestatem." That it is not intended by this rule to enable the judge to play fantastic tricks in legislation, or to warp words from a meaning clear and unequivocal, is manifest from the law II. 40. 9. 12. § 1, to which Ulpian after quoting it adds "quod quidem perquam durum est— sed ita lex scripta est[2]."

The meaning of a doubtful law might be eluci- dated by the language of the legislator in subse- quent or previous enactments ; "non est novum ut priores leges ad posteriores trahantur[3]," and "Pos- teriores leges ad priores pertinent nisi contrariæ sint."

Again, in cases of doubt custom and the received opinion "jus quo civitas retro in ejusmodi casibus usa fuisset," and "the rerum perpetuo similiter

[1] Cervidius Scævola.
Compare this with the decision which made the statute of uses, penned, Lord Bacon tells us, with more care than any other law in the Statute- book, waste paper.

[2] II. 1. 3. 26, 27, 28. Bouhier, *Coutûme de Bourgogne*, 13 to 34.

[3] "Optima lex quæ minimum relin- quit arbitrio judicis. Optimus judex

judicatarum auctoritas" were established rules of interpretation[1].

EDICTA.

The simple rule which the Roman jurists followed, and which has prevailed in every country but our own, with regard to different actions, and therefore different jurisdictions, was to consider the interest of the suitor, the character in which he sued, and the object he sought to attain. It never occurred to them that two sets of maxims, distinct from and even contradictory to each other, should govern the case according to the court in which the proceeding was carried on—that in one and the same state of facts, one and the same object being sought, a Court of Equity was bound to do one thing, and a Court of Law another; that there should be one set of courts "not made for a righteous man[2]," and another set intended for him, "ce qui détermine la diversité des actions, c'est la competence des tribunaux, c'est l'objet auquel l'action se rapporte, c'est l'effet qu'on veut en tirer, c'est le fruit qu'on prétend en recueillir," said the illustrious D'Aguesseau[3].

The greater part of those subject to the Roman sway from the close of the second Punic war, indeed

qui minimum sibi." Bacon, De Aug. Sci. I. c. 3.

[1] II. cod. 37, 38. "Optima interpres legum consuetudo."

[2] The ipsissima verba of Lord Eldon in Cholmondeley v. Clinton, Bligh's Reports, Vol. IV. p. 95.

[3] Plaidoyer, 57. Vol. V. p. 415.

I might say from a much earlier period, was not entitled to the privileges of Roman citizens. Justice was administered by Roman magistrates among them, but the rules of the "jus civile," were not taken in a literal sense, applicable to their proceedings; they could not possess property, they could not contract obligations, they could not marry " ex jure quiritium." Hence there grew up a system according to which justice was administered to the peregrini, not according to the local law of Rome, but according to the jus gentium[1]. Over this law the Roman magistrate presided, and to mould and to develop it was the task of the Roman jurist. By it the intercourse between the Romans and the native of other countries, the citizen of other communities, was carried on. By the side of the law "ex jure quiritium" grew up the law "ex jure gentium ;" by the side of the "jus civile" the "jus honorarium," the Prætorian law resting in part on the same basis, but modified, expanded and refined by the application of more comprehensive principles. Losing thus

[1] Haubold, *Inst. Just. Rom. Privati*, p. 133. In the same Epistle of Cicero, *ad Att.* 6. 1. in which he gives some hints on the "jus Flavianum," which the fanatical followers of Niebuhr might study with advantage, he enters upon the account of his own Edict in Cilicia, which he divides into three parts ; the first, " Provinciale," that is, relating to matters entirely local, "de rationibus civitatum, de ære alieno, de usurâ, de syngraphis in eodem omnia, de publicanis ;" the second, to matters which could not otherwise be settled, "quod sine edicto satis commode transigi non potest, de hæreditatum possessionibus, de bonis possidendis," &c.; the third, "de reliquo jure," he has, he says, left blank, " ἄγραφον," meaning to adapt it to the edicts at Rome, "ad edicta urbana accommodat usum " ...... "itaque satisfacio omnibus." Hugo G. R. R. 430. Ed. 11. So the *Lex Rubria*, regulating the administration of justice in Cisalpine Gaul refers expressly to "eam stipulationem quam is qui Romæ inter peregrinos jus dicet in albo propositam habet."

4—2

its local and exclusive character it imbibed the
equity of the jus gentium, the two principles for-
tified and completed each the other; and when
the system came to the forming hands of the great
architects of the eighth and following centuries it
contained within itself all the materials for the
construction of the noble fabric which when the soil
of Europe was strewed with the shattered wrecks
of ancient wisdom became the fortress and sanctuary
of jurisprudence.

The instrument of this great work, and the means
by which all technical obstructions were removed
from the path of justice, were the edicts of the Prætors and the ædiles. "Eodem tempore," says Pomponius, " et magistratus jura reddebant et ut scirent
cives quod jus de quaque re quisque dicturus esset,
seque præmunirent, edicta proponebant quæ edicta
Prætorum jus honorarium constituerint. Honorarium dicitur quod ab honore Prætoris venerat." Or
in the words of Papinian, "Jus Prætorium est quod
Prætores introduxerunt adjuvandi vel supplendi,
vel corrigendi juris civilis gratiâ, propter utilitatem
publicam." In the year A.U.C. 687, the Tribune
Cornelius carried the Law "ut Prætores ex edictis
suis perpetuis[1] jus dicerent." Every Prætor might
prepare his edict, and of course much that had
been before propounded was transferred to the
edict of the succeeding year, " Edictum Tralatitium."

---

[1] The word "perpetuum" meant
that a controversy should be settled
on *principle* (not as it is in England)
as opposed to "prout res incidit:"
the perpetuum was applied to the word
Edict by the Cornelian Law. Dio
Cassius, lib. 36.

Pomponius 'tells us that Opilius, Cæsari familiarissimus, "primus Edictum. Prætoris diligenter composuit." But the final and most important of these changes was that made by Salvius Julianus[1], A.D. 131, who at the command of Adrian drew up another Edictum Perpetuum, in which whatever was of value in the edict of the Prætor Urbanus[2], or of the Prætor Peregrinus, or in the edictum ædilitium, was digested and made part of the permanent law of Rome. There is, however, no sufficient reason to maintain that this change was absolutely final, nor that the order of the edict underwent any violent or indeed material alteration.

Several clauses of the edict retained the name of their authors. These as enumerated by Hugo are

>Calvisiana actio,
>Carbonianum edictum,
>Cascellianum judicium,
>Faviana actio,
>Pauliana actio,
>Publiciana actio,
>Rutiliana actio,
>Salvianum Interdictum,
>The double Serviana actio.

---

[1] II. 37. 8. 3. "Propter id caput edicti quod a Juliano introductum est, id est ex novâ clausulâ." It gave the emancipated son a share in the succession.

[2] I am aware that Hugo G. *R. R.* 798, disputes this; he admits, however, that a contemporary of Justinian says that in his time (1) what was called in Latin the "Edictum perpetuum" was the Edict of Adrian. 2dly, That a considerable change was made in the Edict at this time. 3rdly, That Salvius Julianus was employed by him to digest the law. There is a learned work of Biener (Fred. Aug.), *de Salvii Juliani meritis in Edictum Prætorium recte æstimandis.* Lips.

Cicero[1], in one of the most beautiful passages of perhaps his greatest work, has given us the distinction between the edict of the Prætor and of the ædile. He says the latter related to the "mancipiorum venditio;" in this he says, as well as in the sale of an estate, "fraus venditorum omnis excluditur— qui enim scire debuit de sanitate, de fugâ, de furtis, præstat edicto ædilium[2]."

He remarks that whereas when he was a boy he learnt the law of the Twelve Tables by heart, every one when he was a man began their law with the Prætor's edict[3].

Perhaps there is nothing in which the extraordinary genius of the Romans for legislation displays itself more conspicuously than in the Prætor's edict and the rules according to which it was drawn up and regulated.

No method could be devised more effectually guarding against the caprice of a magistrate on one hand, and what Lord Bacon calls "the froward

---

[1] *De Officiis*, 3. 17.

[2] *De Legibus*, 1. 5: "non ergo a prætoris edicto ut plerique nunc, neque a 12 tabulis ut superiores, sed penitus ex intimâ philosophiâ hauriendam disciplinam putas."

[3] This is one of the weak parts of Gibbon's famous chapter. He was misled by Heineccius, in general a very faithful guide. Milman, the last commentator on Gibbon, knows little of Roman law, and nothing of jurisprudence. See Hugo, *Civ. Mag.* Vol. II. p. 461, on the process of Cisalpine Gaul, where he shews that the "fictiones" and "exceptiones," of which Heineccius complains as tricks, were considered so essential to the administration of justice that they were carefully inserted in the edicts for the provinces. The fictio was merely the means of preventing a dishonest defence—it ordered the judge to suppose that done which the suitor had no right (the substantial justice of the case considered) to deny. The exceptio was sometimes given by a positive law to guard against the rigour of the old Law. *Inst.* 4. 13. § 6: "quum ex multis causis exceptiones necessariæ sint, &c....quædam e legibus...vel ipsius prætoris jurisdictione substantiam capiunt.'

retention of custom[1]" on the other, than the scheme which obliged the judge before any case was brought before him[2] to announce to the suitor the rule by which it would be determined[3]. It cut off all pretext for indirect favour and supplication unless among those who were insensible to shame[4]. No king could forbid the Roman Prætor to deliver his sentence. No minister could alter the scroll in conformity with which that sentence under penalties more terrible to a Roman than loss of place or income was to be pronounced. No great Patrician could bias that impartial writing, transmitted with increasing authority from age to age, by flattering with his transient notice the wretched vanity of an upstart. No motive of inclination[5], no hope of future preferment, higher title, or of more lucrative office, could seduce from their plain meaning—no fears of Church or Court could intimidate into equivocation— the emphatic words, "Dabo. Non dabo—servabo— Prætor proponit—Prætor pollicetur;" liable to no

---

[1] The English system with curious perverseness reconciled both these evils; it allowed a judge to play fantastic tricks, and obliged him to perpetuate obsolete absurdity.

[2] Not in a jargon intelligible to lawyers only, nor in sentences scattered among a thousand volumes— but blazoned on the album that all might read. How many millions would have been saved to the community if any rule like the edict of the Ædiles as recorded in the 21st Book of the *Digest*, concerning the sale of moveables, warranty, &c. had been inscribed on the wall of the Common Pleas.

[3] "Ut scirent cives quod jus de quâque causâ quisque dicturus esset sequæ præmunirent." What Englishman could "præmunire" himself a few years ago?"

[4] The volume of Buckingham's applications to Bacon could never have been written under such a system. Cicero makes it the grossest crime of Verres that "in magistratu contra illud edictum suum sine ullâ religione decernebat."

[5] Whitelocke's *Memorials*, p. 66. *State Trials*, Vol. III. 157.

bribe, obnoxious to no solicitation. What could more ensure publicity, in the true sense of the words (for technical forms and a peculiar phraseology stifle publicity as much as closed doors), without which it is in vain to hope for decent honesty in judges, than the rule inscribed[1], "ubi de plano recte legi possit"? Thus the Roman, while he upheld great authority, provided for future exigencies. Solid and refined, durable, yet adapting itself to the ever-growing demands of society, his system, promulgated in such a way as to force a knowledge of its provisions on the people, contained in itself the means of constant improvement and renovation. The law remained flexible and elastic, while capricious decision was impossible. Pomponius expressly tells us that a large portion of the consuetudinary law, "quod sine lege vetustas comprobavit[2]," was engrafted on the Prætorian Edict.

The most distinguished jurists of Rome were thus every year employed to consolidate the jurisprudence of their country, and to keep the numerous subdivisions of it under the incessant control of prin-

[1] *U. D. P. R. L. P.* in tabulâ—in albo. Imagine, for instance, such rules as these written upon the wall of a Court of Equity :—I will deprive any one of whose theological opinions I disapprove of the education of his children. I will give money left to propagate the views of dissenters to the Church of England. I will make the grandchild of a rich man a beggar, by putting on the words of the testator a meaning he never dreamt of, and that no mind untainted by legal jargon could conceive. I will oblige a man to pay for a suit in which an attorney whom he never heard of, has engaged him without his knowledge or authority. If a first creditor on land can buy up the claim of a third creditor, I will take away the right of the second in his favour. I will take ten years to decide a case that a farmer from the plough might settle in an hour.—Would it not "startle" even the "dull night" of English routine and commonplace!

[2] II. 1. 3. 40 : and in turn it became the common law: "omnes prætores ita edixerunt."

ciple. The same spirit was thus infused through all its various members. To compose a well-digested edict was even in the time of Cicero deemed an object of generous ambition, and worthy of the rarest abilities. The Prætor was responsible for the errors he had committed. He might be accused by the Tribunes of having prepared a partial edict.

The value of the *jus honorarium* was limited to the time and place of the Prætor's jurisdiction. If a Prætor disapproved the principles laid down by his predecessor, he might omit them in the succeeding year; and this in the early ages of the Republic, before these doctrines had been thoroughly sifted, and had acquired by reiterated adoptions a binding force and hold on the public mind, was no doubt an event not uncommon. Hence we find in the older writers[1] the distinction between *lex* and *quod legis vicem obtinet,*—between the law and that which in this particular case is to be so considered. The Prætor could only declare what he would consider as law, subject among other restraints to the liability of its future application to himself. The task of restoring and improving the old law, of supplying its omissions and mitigating its harshness, was thus left to him with almost unlimited authority. And thus, from the yearly succession of Prætors, the Roman system was perpetually renovated and refined by an infusion of doctrines, the utility of which had made them current among the people, and by discarding others which experience had

---

[1] Gaius, IV. I. I. 8.

shown to be pernicious and ill adapted to the service of the Commonwealth.

The effect of this system was that a supply of actual opinions and customs were added to the Roman Law, and that Roman jurisprudence kept pace with the exigencies of the age and the progress of society. Obsolete doctrines were discarded (not by the ruin of some unhappy victim, in whose case they were for the first time questioned), and requisite alterations introduced. Improvement was always busy, and innovation always judicious. The law was constantly exposed to the salutary influence of public opinion; instead of stagnating into corruption and chicanery, it was governed by a salient active principle; it represented the wisdom of the age; it was not a dead letter but a living word, a merit well appreciated and happily described by the civilians when they use the phrase "*viva vox jura civilis.*"

RESCRIPTA.

The last form of written law[1] assumed among the Romans was that of the "principum" or "oratorum constitutiones;" under this name was comprised everything the ruler thought proper to establish.

The controversy as to the cause of this dreadful state of things, whether it was through the "Lex Regia[2]" or not, is of little value; "leges," "leges edictales," "epistolæ generales," "sanctiones," "con-

---

[1] Warnkönig, Vol. I. p. 16; Haubold, Lib. 4. c. 3. § 163. "Constit. Constant. M. et Theod. I. De abusu rescriptorum tollendo." *Cod. de Ll.* L. 12.

[2] II. 1. 5. 1.

stitutiones generales," are different names by which this exercise of authority is described[1]. "Mandata" were commands of the Emperor transmitted to the governors of the provinces; "Decreta," the sentences thus pronounced on appeal; "Rescripta," were the written answers of the emperors to those who asked for their opinion on questions of law. As the sphere of their influence extended they were constantly applied to by private persons, by women and soldiers more especially, to settle their doubts, or to grant them privileges. This is what Portalis has called with great propriety "la désastreuse legislation des rescrits."

The "rescripta" sent to corporations and municipal bodies were known by a name which has found its way into the public law of Europe as "pragmaticæ sanctiones[2]." The difference between the rescripta and the other heads of law that have been enumerated, is that the "rescripta" refer only to the particular case, and establish no principle, like the decisions of English judges. But with the decay of jurisprudence their number multiplied and their efficacy increased, till they became (as case-law among us and for the same reason—absence of judicial intellect) a principal part of Justinian's Codex.

The "Responsa Prudentum" were the opinions of eminent lawyers incorporated with Roman jurisprudence[3]. The splendid roll beginning with Q. M.

[1] *Inst.* 1. 2. Gaius, 1. § 5 : "imperatorem per legem imperium accipere." The discovery of this passage changed Hugo's opinion. G. *R. R.* Ed. 7. § 277.

[2] Cicero *ad Att.* 14. 3. "Tu si quid πραγματικὸν habes, scribes."

[3] Gaius, 1. 7—21 : "quibus permissum est jura condere." *Inst.* § 8. do J. N. et G. Zimmern. 1. 198. Gra-

Scævola, the teacher of Servius Sulpicius, ends with Hermogenian.   It contains five names of transcendent lustre: Gaius, who lived A.D. 169, under Marcus Aurelius, and Æmilius Papinianus, Julius Paulus, Domitius Ulpianus, and Herennius Modestinus, who flourished under Septimius and Alexander Severus, A.D. 211—222 [1].

PERSONS[2].

" Persona" was a word used to denote all who were entitled to civil rights in the Roman community; every thing to which an independent legal relation can be ascribed.

"Personæ" were either real or fictitious, public or private.

As the word "personæ" was used sometimes to denote not the individual, but the relation which he filled towards the commonwealth, the same individual might sustain several "personas," e. g. a

vina, 42. C. Th. *de resp. prud. Gothofred,* 1. 34.

[1] Hugo, *Civ. Mag.* Vol. v. p. 15, enumerates ten parts of the Prætor's Edict: 1. Præparatoria judiciorum; 2. de indiciis, *i. e.* de actionibus in rem; 3. de rebus, *i.e.* de actionibus in personam; 4. de dotibus, tutelis et furtis; 5. de bonorum possessione et testamentis; 6. de cautionibus quibusdam Prætoriis, vicem actionum gerentibus; 7. de delictis quibusdam; 8. de judiciorum fine sive executione, ut de missione in possessionem et re judicatâ; 9. de interdictis; 10. de

pignoribus, exceptionibus, stipulationibus Prætoriis, et aliis quibusdam rebus fortasse non satis certis.

[2] "Parum est jus nosse si personæ quorum causâ constitutum est ignorentur." *Inst. de Jur. Nat.* 14.

II. *De Statu Hominum,* L. 7. *ib.* 26 : " qui in utero sunt in toto pœne jure civili intelliguntur in rerum naturâ esse, nam et legitimæ hæreditates eis restituuntur, et si quæquam mulier ab hostibus capta sit, id quod natum erit postliminium habet :" as to imperfect births, see l. 14 *ib.* and II. de verb. signif. L.135. Cod. 6. 19. 3.

magistrate might act as father and magistrate in the emancipation of his sons[1].

"Personæ veræ" were born or conceived: "qui in utero est perinde ac si in rebus humanis esset custoditur quoties de commodis ipsius partus quæritur."

De la Serva in his excellent commentary on the Institutes, remarks that the use of the word "Persona" in Tit. 3, 1st Book of that work, is inaccurate, as the Romans did not apply the word "persona" to slaves. But may we not say, he adds, that in spite of the rigour of positive law (exigencias del derecho), it was sometimes "splendide mendax," and that with a generous inconsistency maxims and principles were allowed to filter into it that gave the lie to the absurd theory of servitude. For this theory, it should be remembered, the Roman jurist was no more responsible than St Paul. As a proof of this, it may be argued that neither Gaius nor Justinian rank slaves in the classes to which in strictness they belonged; and in a remarkable passage of the Digest[2], Paulus allows to them the rights arising from cognation and affinity. The terms person and individual are not convertible in law, for there are persons who are not individuals, as the state corporations (universitates), the fiscus, cities, (civitates), an inheritance, before it is accepted—and individuals who are not persons, as slaves. A person, in the sense of Roman law, may

---

[1] "Magistratum apud quem legis actio est et emancipare filios suos et in adoptionem apud se dare posse—Neratius ait." II. 1. 7. 4. *Instit.* 218. Hertius, 1. 3. 41.

[2] II. 23. 2. 14. § 2, § 3. Cassiodorus, 6. 8. Variorum Cod. 3. 6. "Servos qui personam legibus non habebant." "Servi nec personam habentes." Nov. Theod. 24. § 1.

be defined as a being, whether abstract or concrete, real or ideal, whether physically existing or the mere creation of law capable *of becoming the subject* of civil rights and obligations.

The creation of "universitates[1]" belonged to the legislative powers, and according to the vicissitudes of that authority in Rome was exercised first by a law, then by a senatus consultum, and finally by an imperial decree. "Universitas" was the general word by which the ideal unity of which I have been speaking[2] was denoted. These bodies might possess, contract, sue and be sued[3].

PERIOD OF BIRTH[4].

The child born after the 182nd day was recognized as a perfect birth. "Septimo mense nasci perfectum

---

[1] "Neque societatem neque collegium neque hujusmodi corpus passim omnibus habere conceditur, nam et legibus et senatus consultis et principalibus constitutionibus ea res coercetur." II. 3. 4. 1.

[2] *Inst.* Book 2. 1.

[3] II. 3. 4.

That the policy of Rome beheld with distrust any ἑταιρία, collegium, or unauthorized association among the subjects of the empire, is well known, and this was one cause of enforcing the laws against the Christians. A striking proof of this fact is to be found in Pliny, book 10. Ep. 43, in which Trajan refuses his assent to the establishment of a "collegium fabrorum" in Nicomedia, because he recollected "provinciam istam et præcipue eas civitates ab ejusmodi factionibus esse vexatas." Can we wonder that statesmen trained in such maxims saw with alarm associations governed by rules of their own, and professing a creed irreconcileable with theirs, diffused through every province and city of the empire? is it to be supposed that Trajan, Ulpian, and Sir Thomas More, were influenced by the motives of Philip the Second and Archbishop Laud?

[4] II. De rebus dubiis, 34. 5. 9. § 4.

"Si Lucius Titius cum filio pubere, quem solum testamento scriptum hæredem habebat perierit, intelligitur supravixisse filius patri et ex testamento hæres fuisse, et filii hæreditas successoribus ejus defertur nisi contrarium approbetur. Quodsi impubes cum patre filius perierit, creditur patri supervixisse nisi et hic contrarium approbetur."

"Cum pubere filio mater naufragio periit, cum explorari non possit, uter prior extinctus sit, humanius est credere, filium diutius vixisse." *Ib.* 22.

partum jam receptum est propter auctoritatem doc-
tissimi viri Hippocratis[1]."

THEY WERE LEGITIMATE OR ILLEGITIMATE[2].

Children born in matrimony but conceived before
were legitimate. If the birth of the child proved
that it must have been conceived before wedlock,
and the husband denied that any such intercourse
had taken place between him and the mother, the
burden of establishing that the child was legitimate
was flung on those who asserted it[3].

If the child was born within the time assigned
by law the husband of the mother was presumed to
be the father until the fact was shewn clearly to be
otherwise.   "Post decem menses natus non ad-
mittitur ad legitimam hæreditatem[4]."

---

[1] II. 25. 4. 1.   "Partus antequam
edatur mulieris portio est vel visce-
rum." "Partus nondum editus homo
recte fuisse dicitur." II. 35. 2. 9. 1.

II. 1. 5. "Qui in utero est perinde ac si in rebus humanis esset custoditur quoties de commodis ipsius
partus quæritur."

II. 15. "Non sunt liberi qui contra formam humani generis converso
more procreantur."

[2] Dig. 4. 4. 1. § 1 ; 10. 8. 4 ; 34. 1.
14. 1 ; 45. 1. 65. § 3. Inst. 1. 22. De
inutili Stip. 10. II. de reg. Juris, 3.

[3] II. de V. S. 101.

[4] II. de suis et leg. hær. 3. § 11.

II. de Statu hominum, 1. 5. 12.
Cocceius, Juris Contr. 1. 6. qu. 3.
II. De suis et Legit. hæredibus, "de

eo qui centesimo octogesimo secundo
die natus est Hippocrates scripsit justo
tempore videri natum."

This principle is recognized II. 48.
5. 11. 9 : "non utique crimen adulterii,
quod mulieri objicitur, infanti præjudi-
cat, cum possit et illa adultera esse et
impubes defunctum partem habuisse."

II. 22. 3. 29. 1.

" Si fingamus abfuisse maritum
verbi gratiâ per decennium, reversum
anniculum invenisse in domo suâ, placet nobis Juliani sententia hunc non
esse mariti filium :—non tamen feren-
dum, Julianus ait, qui cum uxore assi-
due moratus nolit filium agnoscere
quasi non suum, sed mihi videtur quod
et Scævola probat, si constet maritum
aliquandiu cum uxore non concubuisse

The mother's relation to the child was always the same, whether the child was legitimate or not. Marriage pointed out the father: "Mater semper certa est, etiamsi vulgo conceperit, pater est quem nuptiæ demonstrant[5]."

infirmitate interveniente, vel aliâ causâ, vel si eâ valetudine paterfamilias fuit ut generare non possit, hunc qui in domo natus est, licet vicinis scientibus, filium non esse," de his qui sui vel al. juris sunt. II. L. 3.

[4] II. de extr. cog. 13. 5. § 1. Donellus, 18. 5.

[5] *Coke Litt.* 244 a. Vol. II. Butler and Hargrave Ed. II. 2. 45. I doubt, though I have read accounts of the Council of Nice, if human absurdity ever went farther than the rule "intra quatuor maria." Notwithstanding however this powerful recommendation to the sympathies of our judges it has ceased to be part of our law. That the reader may judge of the wisdom of our common law and of those from the dicta of whom it emanated, I refer him to the case of Done and Egerton, Rolle's *Abridgment*, 1. 358. There Hobart, the same judge who justified a pleader's trick that "Law might be an art," laid down the rule in terms, that "if a husband was castrated, so that it is apparent that he could not by any possibility beget issue, and divers years afterwards his wife has issue, it should be lawful." The other three judges, strange to say, did not quite go this length; but they and the Chancellor were unanimous in holding "that if a married woman has issue in adultery, still if the husband be able to beget issue, and is within the four seas, it is *not* a bastard." It was also agreed (in a jargon well adapted to the matter) "that if a

woman elopes and lives in adultery with another, and during that time the issue is born in adultery, still it is a mulier by our law;" "but the husband must be within the four seas, otherwise it is a bastard." During all this time the wisdom and infallibility of the law and of judges, and of those by whom judges are made, was, as now, piously believed in by the routine-loving, purblind inhabitants of this "practical" and attorney-governed country. Coke, *First Instit.* 144. In the true genius of our law, the judges, being perhaps as a body the most unfit of all men who can read and write (not being clergymen) for such a purpose, usurped the functions of the legislature in inventing the rule, in mitigating and in taking it away. As Sir H. Nicolas says, "The law of Adulterine Bastards has thus undergone two important changes without the intervention of any act of the legislature." Pendrell v. Pendrell, Strange, 925. Buller's *Nisi Prius*, 268. Goodright and Saul, 43 *Resp.* 356; Morris v. Davis 5. Clarke and Finn, 234.

To complete this specimen of our capacity for legislation, I add this passage from Jenkins, *Cent.* c. 10. pl. 18: "If the husband be in *Ireland* for a year, and the wife in England during that time has issue, it is a bastard; *but* it seems otherwise *now* for *Scotland,* both being under one King." Could Rabelais go beyond this?

Ulpian says : If we suppose the husband to have
been absent (for the sake of argument) during ten
years, and at his return home to find a child of a
year old in his house, I adopt the opinion of Julianus, that the child is not the husband's son. However, Julianus says that he is not to be endured,
who being in constant cohabitation with his wife
refuses to acknowledge the son as his own. But
it seems to be law, and in this opinion Scævola
concurs, if it can be proved that the husband, from
supervening infirmity or any other cause, has not
cohabited with his wife, or was in such a state of
health as to make procreation impossible, that the
child born in his house, though with the knowledge
of the neighbours[1], is not his son.

The child born after ten months from the death
of the husband does not inherit[2].

The " vulgo concepti " were they who could not
name a father, or a lawful one[3].

With the deep knowledge[4] of human nature
which distinguishes the rules it has laid down, the
Roman law rejected the evidence of the married
mother to prove her offspring illegitimate, as well
because if she was actually cohabiting with her
husband, such a matter was hardly within her knowledge, as because the allegation of an act involving

[1] II. 2. 4. 6. Banbury Peerage case.
Nicolas *ad Bast.* p. 280, and the very
foolish protest in favour of the claimant, 531, with a weak speech on the
same side by Lord Erskine.
[2] II. 38. 16. 3. § 11.
[3] II. 1. 5. 23: qui et spurii appel-

lantur παρὰ τὴν σπορὰν. *Inst.* 1. 10.
12. Plutarch, *Quæst. R.* 103.
[4] II. 22. 3—29. § 1. 25. 3. 1. 7.
Cod. 4. 29. 14. Cod. 4. 7. 5. 2. 4. 30.
Cap. per tuas 10. extra de probationibus 2. 19. Richer, *Universa Jurisprudentia*, Vol. 1. p. 95.

the turpitude of the person making it was not to be credited. Little weight was to be placed on an assertion "ab iratâ." According to the code the asseveration even upon oath of both parents was not enough to prove their offspring illegitimate, unless corroborated by extrinsic evidence.

DEATH.

In questions when the actual period of death happened, the decision was regulated, in the absence of positive testimony, by the age of the person and the regular course of nature. If of two persons who had perished by the same catastrophe, it was necessary to decide which was the survivor—in a question between parent and child—the parent was taken to have survived the child, below, and to have died before the child, above, the age of puberty[1].

Age, soundness of mind and body, reputation, relationship, status civilis, are elements in describing the persona vera.

1. Age is divided by the time of puberty. The Roman law fixed twenty-five years as the age of majority.

2. Health of mind and body.

[1] *L. Journal,* 1860, Vol. III. page 65. "There is not in the English law any presumption, from age, sex, or other circumstances, as to the survivorship of one out of several persons who are destroyed by the same calamity." Wing *v.* Angrave, House of Lords, A.D. 1860.

[2] Callistrat. 1. 5. § 1—3. de extraordinar. cognit. (50. 13). "Existimatio est dignitatis illaesae status legibus ac moribus comprobatus, qui ex delicto nostro auctoritate legum aut minuitur aut consumitur." (§ 2.) "Minuitur existimatio, quoties manente libertate circa statum dignitatis poena plectimur sicuti quum relegatur quis vel quum ordine movetur, vel quum prohibetur honoribus publicis fungi; vel quum plebeius fustibus caeditur, vel in opus publicum datur, vel quum in eam causam quis incidit, quae edicto

3. Reputation. "Existimatio[2] est dignitatis illæsæ status." It consists in not being thought unworthy of those things which are usually given to persons in the class of which the citizen is a member.

The Roman law held as infamous[1],

" Qui in scenam prodeunt lucri causâ."

" Lenocinium exercentes."

" Mulieres liberæ corpore quæstum facientes."

" In adulterio deprehensi."

Corrupt judges.

Widows marrying "intra annum luctus," and those who married them[2].

Tutors and curators who before their accounts have been examined marry their ward, or marry her to their son[3].

They who betroth themselves to two persons at the same time[4].

Persons of full age fraudulently receding from a sworn agreement[5].

Persons guilty of certain offences[6], such as the crimen prævaricationis, expilatæ hæreditatis, sepulchri violati—of furtum, rapina, and injuria—adjudged by a formal sentence guilty of dolus in contracts

perpetuo infamiæ causa enumeratur." (§ 3.) "Consumitur vero quoties magna capitis minutio intervenit, id est, quum libertas adimitur; veluti quum aqua et igni interdicitur, quæ in persona deportatorum venit, vel quum plebeius in opus metalli vel in metallum datur."

[1] de his qui notantur infamiâ. II. 3. 2. 1. 2. de ritu nuptiarum, 23. 43. § 12.

[2] Altered by the Canon Law. c. 4.

4. X. de sec. nuptiis. Donellus, 18. 6. 18. II. 50. 13. 5. 1—3.

[3] L. Pen. Cod. de interdict. matr. 5.6.

[4] II. de his qui not. inf. 1.

[5] Cod. de transactionfbus, 2. 4. 41.

[6] Dig. 48. 1. 7. ib. 22. 47. 15. 3. § 1. ib. 12. 1. ib. 20. 2. de Stellion. Cujac. 10. 26. Donellus, 18. 8. Noodt ad Pandect. de his qui not. inf.

II. de his qui not. inf. L. 1. L. 4. § 5. L. 6. § 3. Cod. ex quib. caus. inf. inop. II. de publ. jud. L. 7.

bonæ fidei, such as depositum, mandatum, tutela, societas, a person accused of an infamous offence who compromised the accusation for money.

The "Levis notæ macula[1]" adhered to certain persons, as liberi histrionum, liberti, meretrices.

As to acts which though disgraceful were not specified by the law as infamous, the Digest says,

"Licet verbis edicti non habeantur infames ita condemnati, re tamen ipsâ et opinione hominum non effugiunt infamiæ notam[2]."

Persons connected by family ties were divided into those connected by consanguinity and affinity[3].

The degrees of consanguinity according to the Roman Law will be found in the passage cited below[4].

Cognati[5] were divided into agnati "per patrem cognati, ex eâdem familiâ," and cognati, in a narrower sense relations by the female side, "per feminas."

Agnati[6] sunt qui per virilis sexus personas cognatione juncti sunt.

[1] Heinecc. *Opusc. dissent. de levis notæ maculâ.* C. Th. de inoff. Testamento, L. 2. and 3. Cod. de inoff. Test. 27. II. 23. 2. 44.

[2] 12. 1. 2. 37. 15. 2. "Gravatam potius opinionem tuam quam infamia afflictam esse manifestum est."
II. 22. 5. 3. "Nec tamen res ex vulgi opinione testimanda sed ex factis turpibus quæ apud bonos et gratos viros existimationem onerant." Cod. ex quib. caus. inf. cir. 13.

[3] II. 28. 10. de gradibus et aff. *Inst.* 3. de grad. cogn. 3—6.
"Am not I consanguineous? Am not I of her blood?" *Twelfth Night.*

[4] II. de grad. et aff. 10. § 10. ib. 10. § 9. "Quoties quæritur quanto gradu quæque persona est ab eo incipiendum est cujus de cognatione quærimus," κ.τ.λ.

[5] Cujac. Obs. 9=18. According to the Canon Law the degrees of relationship are measured by distance from the common stock. Cap. ult. x. de consang. et affin. Boehmer, *Princip. Juris Canon.* § 389. Next of kin, Withy *v.* Mangles, 10. Cl. and Finn. 246.

[6] "quos agnatos Lex duodecim tabularum appellat." II. de V. S. C. 10. § 2. 195. § 2.

To this must be added a "ficta cognatio," by adoption in the Roman law, and that which was invented by the Church as a means of extending its influence, arising from the spiritual relation of the sponsor and the god-child.

Affinity was the connexion arising from marriage between one of the married persons and the blood relations of the other[1].

There are no degrees in affinity.

STATUS.

The Status of a Roman citizen consisted of three elements[2].

Libertas, civitas, and familia.

All men fell under the category of liberi or servi[3].

The "liberi" were divided into "ingenui" and "libertini." Into a detailed account of the rights which grew out of this state of things, such as the "jus patronatus," &c. it is happily not important to enter.

---

[1] II. de grad. et ad fin. 4. § 3. "Affines sunt viri et uxoris cognati... nomina sunt socer gener nurus noverca vitricus privignus privigna; viri frater levis viri soror, glos dicitur." Cap. 6. x. de eo qui cons. ux. x. de consang. et aff. "Omnes consanguinei viri sunt legitimi affines uxoris, et omnes consanguinei uxoris sunt viri affines legitimi."

[2] Toullier, 1. 133. "Status vox sumitur late vel stricte; late pro quâvis differentiâ secundum quam jus variat; stricte pro his tribus, libertatis, civitatis et familiæ." Huber *in Pan.* 1. 5. § 1.

[3] *Inst.* de libert. II. de statu hominum, 6. ib. 5. 1. and 3. ib. 25. de reg. juris, 207. manumissio, II. 40. 2. *Inst.* qui et quib. causis manumitt. The right of manumission was restricted by the law Ælia Sentia, and the law Fusia Caninia. Caii *Inst.* 1. 2. Ulpiani *Fragmenta*, 1. 24 and 25. Paulli *Recept. Sent.* 4. 14. *Inst.* de leg. Fus. Can. toll.

The civitas comprised the rights (public[1]),

Census, militiæ, suffragiorum, honorum, privati connubii, patriæ potestatis, testamenti factionis, tutelæ, usucapionis, gentilitatis, dominii legitimi, tutelæ.

The Peregrini were without these civil rights, and had only those "juris gentium."

Familia is used to describe all the agnati. "Communi jure familiam dicimus omnium agnatorum[2]." For though the father die, "tamen omnes qui sub unius potestate fuerunt, recte ejusdem familiæ appellabuntur, qui ex eâdem domo et gente proditi sunt."

The familia consisted of things as well as persons[3]. The res comprised the "sacra privata," and the slaves; thus there is a chapter[4] in the Digest headed "Si familia furtum fecerit."

Hence arose the division of persons into those "sui et alieni juris[5]."

Of these three elements of status, libertas might belong to a person who had neither civitas nor familia; civitas might belong to a person who had not familia, but not to a person without libertas—and familia could only belong to a person who had both civitas and familia.

Actions[6] in which the status of a person was

---

[1] Sigonius *de jure antiquo pop. Romani*, 1. c. 9.

[2] II. De Ver. Sig. 195.

[3] "Familiæ appellatio...et in res et in personas deducitur;" so the Law of the Twelve Tables said: "agnatus proximus familiam habeto." II. 50. 16. 195. 1.

[4] II. 7. 6. II. 10. 2. tit. familiæ

erciscundæ.

[5] II. 1. 6. 4. The law of the capitis deminutio will be found, II. 1. 16. ib. 5. *Inst.* quibus modis pat. pot. solvitur, 1. 12. 1. § 3. II. de reg. juris, 209. II. de interd. et releg. 4.

[6] *Inst.* 4. 6. 13. II. 40. 14. C. de adsert. toll. 7. 17. 1. 40. 14. L. 1. 5.

concerned were called Præjudiciales. They were affirmative, in which a person asserted his own status, or negative, in which he denied that of another.

To this head belonged

1. "Actio de libertate."
2. "Actio de ingenuitate."
3. "Actio de liberis legitimis vel illegitimis."

The actiones præjudiciales[1] were brought in the forum of the person whose status was impeached. The "res judicata" bound strangers to the suit[2].

No inquiry could be made as to the status of a person who had been dead five years[3].

The Roman lawyers called any change in the libertas, civitas, and familia, or the loss of any of them, "capitis diminutio."

The word was first applied to the community which lost a citizen, or the family which lost a member,—"capite minuebatur."

Afterwards it was transferred to the individual concerned, taking "caput" for the rights belonging to it; so they said of a man who had lost or changed his rights of freedom, citizenship, or family, that he was "capite minutus."

This diminutio capitis was of three kinds.

Maxima, Media, Minima.

Maxima, when the person concerned lost the "libertas" and "civitas."

Media, when he lost the "civitas," but remained a freeman[4].

---

[1] Cod. ubi caus. stat. agi debeat, 3. 22. 34. Si libertus ingenuus esse dicitur, 48. 14.

[2] II. de statu hom. 25.

[3] II. 40. 15. Ne de statu defunctorum post quinquennium quæratur.

[4] *Code Nap.* Art. 19. 21.

Minima, when he passed from one family into another to become the head of it, by emancipatio, or a member of it by arrogatio.

Thus did the Roman citizen belong not only to the great society of free men, whereby he became entitled to the rights of the "jus gentium," nor to the narrower community of Romans, whereby he became entitled to the "jus civile," but he stood also within the narrower precincts of the familia, that is in a certain relation not to his kindred generally, but to the agnati[1]; nay even if alone, the "status familiæ" was his—"emancipatus propriam familiam habet[2]," the basis[3] of substantial and precious rights, by which the "status civitatis" was made complete. Hence it is a corollary, that the status familiæ apart from the "status civitatis" could never be lost, but exchanged, and that the Roman citizen, the moment he ceased to belong to the paternal, became the member of another family, whether of a stranger or his own.

D'Aguesseau reproaches the Roman lawyers for not defining status: the fault is of course Tribonian's.

To the differences between human beings established by nature, others have been added by the usages of nations or the will of the legislator.

Such are those which exist between citizens and strangers, between magistrates and subjects, freemen and slaves; capable that is, or incapable, of exercis-

[1] "Jure proprio familiam dicimus plures personas quæ sunt sub unius potestate aut naturâ aut jure subjectæ, ut puta patremfamilias, matremfamilias, filiumfamilias, filiamfamilias, quique deinceps vicem eorum sequuntur ut puta nepotes, neptes et deinceps." II. 50. 16. 195. § 2.

[2] Vangerow, 1. 62. II. eod.

[3] e. g. inheritance.

ing public duties, entering into engagements, succeeding to property, &c.

PERSONÆ FICTÆ[1]—UNIVERSITATES.

Universitates, corporations, consist of a society of citizens united permanently for a public object. They exist by the sanction of the legislative authority. The Roman law recognised several purposes for which sometimes (under the name of collegia[2]) they might be established. "Religionis causâ coire non prohibentur dum tamen per hoc non fiat Senatus consultum quo illicita collegia arcentur." The Roman law allowed no citizen to be a member of more than one collegium[3]. The most important of these bodies were the "collegia Decurionum," the municipal authorities by whom the taxes were levied, and who were responsible for them through the Roman empire; offices which in its decline, notwithstanding a great variety of privileges and immunities[4], it became extremely difficult to fill. In these each member was responsible for his col-

---

[1] II. 3. 4. 7. § 2 = 48. 4. 1. § 1. sec. tit. ad municipalem de decurionibus, de albo scribendo, de muneribus et honor. de vac. et excus. munerum de administ. rerum ad civ. pertinentium, de operibus publicis. Cod. 10. 31—57.

[2] II. 47. 22. 1. § 1. Cod. de epis. et cler. 1. 3. 15. "Neratius Priscus tres facere existimat collegium." II. de V. S. L. 85.

[3] II. de colleg. 1. § 2: "non licet amplius quam unum collegium licitum habere; et si quis in duobus fuerit rescriptum est eligere eum oportere in quo magis esse velit."

[4] An account of these terrible burdens is to be found in Roth *de re Municipali*, the source of much of Mons. Guizot's work, and in Ritter's notes to the Theodosian Code. The severe punishments deno[r]....ed against those who avoided them by flying to the barbarians, &c., sufficiently prove their oppressive character. At first admission to the curia was confined to freemen of a certain order. Afterwards, as the necessities of the empire increased, the rule was relaxed, and

leagues. In other corporations, the individual was not responsible for the debts of the body, nor could he enforce the obligations due to it. "Si quid universitati debetur singulis non debetur, nec quod debet universitas, singuli debent." No measure was binding unless made by a certain proportion[1] (two thirds) of a collegium, nor could any member or officer be elected unless by a majority of at least two thirds.

FISCUS.

The Fiscus[2] was an artificial person possessing many peculiar rights described in the jura fisci, and comprising many functionaries. It managed all the revenue, including forfeitures, bona vacantia, &c. of the sovereign. At first it was distinguished "ab ærario populi," but this nominal difference came to a speedy end.

PIÆ CAUSÆ[3].

These comprised churches, hospitals, schools, eleemosynary foundations; the revenues set apart for which objects were administered by curators, and

---

what had been a privilege became a punishment for malefactors.

II. de decur. 3. § 2. 6. § 1—5. Voet. ad hoc tit.

II. de coll. et corp. L. 4. "Sodales sunt qui ejusdem collegii sunt. His potestatem facit lex pactionem quam velint sibi ferre dum ne quid ex publicâ lege corrumpant." Cod. de decur. L. 55. L. 60. L. 63.

[1] II. de decret. ab ord. fac. L. 2.

L. 3. "duabus partibus adhibitis." II. quod cujusque univ. nom. 3.

[2] Cod. de annonis et trib. 10. 16; de bon. vacant. 10. 10; de vectig. 4. 61. 3. 6; de Publican. 39. 4. 14. II. de jure fisci, 49. 14. 10. Cod. de privilegio fisci, 3. Fiscus semper habet jus pignoris. II. de jure fisci, 46.

[3] Cod. de episcopis et clericis et orphanotrophiis et xenodochiis, 1. 3. and 32. Nov. 120.

systematically plundered by bishops[1], who thereby acquired enormous wealth.

DOMICILE.

The domicile of a person is the spot on which that person has fixed his permanent residence, and which he has chosen as the abode[2] of his family and himself; to which when he has left it, he means in a short time to return; from which during the continuance of his absence he is a guest, a traveller, an inmate, or a stranger; and on the ending of his absence from which he is at home[3].

A domicile may be voluntary[4] or necessary. The choice of a voluntary domicile[5] may be established by express declaration, accompanied with an act, or inferred from circumstances and acts[6].

[1] These revenues drew down various persecutions on the church from the time of Decius. See Sarpi's admirable treatise.

[2] Brissonius *de verb. signif. Res, Pecunia. Inst.* 2. 1. 411. 2. 2. *Dig.* 1. 8. de divisione rerum. *Dig.* de V. S. 5. pr. 122. Heineccius du. R. 2. tit. 1. §§ 1—19. *Inst.* ejusdem 313 —321. 324, &c.

[3] D'Argentré has truly remarked that the beautiful passage, Code 10, contains "de veteris cujusdam juris consulti excerptis libris verba elegantiora." p. 25. C. B.

[4] D'Argentré makes will the essential ingredient of domicile. He says no lapse of time will make a domicile without the animus; and that Sforza the captive of Louis XII. never had a domicile in France; nor Zizim the

brother of the Turkish Emperor who was poisoned by the Pope at Rome; nor Regulus at Carthage. He allows a "legale domicilium," as of a priest in his parish. 26.

[5] Locre, 2. 228. "Ubi domicilium habeat existimatione animi esse existimandum." II. 50. 1. 27. 2. Cod. 10. 39. 7. Toullier, 1. 319. "Cives origo incolas domicilium facit." "Domicilium re et facto transfertur non nudâ contestatione." II. 50. 1. 20. 27. § 2. II. 50. 16. 203.

[6] Robinson, *Admiralty Reports.* The President, p. 280. "Sola vero domus possessio non valet ad domicilii constitutionem sine actuali habitatione." D'Argentré, 1630.

A mere intention to remove without some overt act, is not sufficient to constitute a change of domicile, being no more than a purpose residing in the breast of the party, and liable to change (something beyond a verbal declaration, some solid fact is necessary).

The mere possession[1] of a house or an estate does not constitute a domicile, neither has the resident a domicile in the place he inhabits for the prosecution of his studies.

That is a necessary domicile which is fixed or implied by law. The house of the husband[2] is the domicile of the wife—the house of the parent of the child forming part of his family[3]. The place in which he is obliged to dwell for the discharge of his duties is the domicile of the magistrate and public functionary[4]—that to which he is relegated of the relegatus[5].

A man may have more domiciles[6] than one. Generally speaking, every man may choose his domicile.

A domicile is lost by death, or the establishment of another inconsistent with it.

[1] "Sola Domus possessio quæ in alienâ civitate comparatur domicilium non facit." II. 50. 1. 17. § 13.

[2] "Vidua mulier amissi mariti domicilium retinet." 22. § 1. eod.

[3] Stare, status, état, state. "Locus ubi quis obeundi muneris causâ se sistit." Hotman. Comm. verb. jur. Tom. I. p. 930. Toullier, I. 135.

[4] "De eâ re constitutum est eam domum unicuique nostrum existimari debere ubi quisque sedes et tabulas haberet suarumque rerum constitutionem

fecisset." II. 50. 16. 203. 50. 1. 211.

[5] 50. 1. 27. 3. 50. 22. § 3. "Relegatus in eo loco in quem relegatus est necessarium domicilium habet."

"Cum domicilium dicimus simpliciter de eo intelligimus quod sibi quisque constituit." D'Argentré, p. 25.

II. 50. 16. 203. 50. 1. 27. § 1.

[6] II. 50. 1. 5. eod. 6. § 2. "licet difficile est."

"Difficile est sine domicilio esse quemquam." II. 50. 27. § 2.

"Roma communis Patria est." 33 eod.

If a person by his conduct lead any one dealing with him to suppose that he means to discharge the obligation in the place where it was contracted, he makes himself liable to the jurisdiction of the tribunals of that place. It would be hard, says Ulpian[1], that a man sailing to various places, or travelling through different countries, should be obliged to defend himself in all of them. But if he establishes, I do not say a domicile, but a little shop or place of barter, and has transacted business there, there he shall defend himself.

A person not in his domicile is said in the phraseology of the Roman law to be "absens[2]," a word employed sometimes in a strict, sometimes in a wider sense[3]. Various rules are established to guard the interests of such persons.

The analogy between the Furiosus (mente absens) and the absens, is often employed in the Roman law[4].

If there was a sufficient indication of will, residence of a single day was sufficient to establish a domicile. In the absence of such decisive proof, the

---

[1] II. 5. 1. 19. § 2. "durissimum est quotquot locis quis navigans, vel iter faciens, delatus est, tot locis se defendere, at si quo constitit non dico jure domicilii sed tabernaculam, officinam conducens, ibique distraxit vel egit, defendere se eo loci debebit." Savigny, 8. 222.

[2] II. 50. 16. 173. eod. 199.

[3] II. 50. 17. 124. § 1. "Furiosus absentis loco est."

"Prætor ait, 'dum ei qui abeat prius domum denuntiari jubeam,' abesse autem videtur qui in jure non est, quod et Pomponius probat...sed 'domum denuntiari sic accipere debemus, ut et si in alienâ domo habitet ibi ei denuntietur.'" II. 39. 2. 5. § 4.

[4] Cod. de Incolis, 2. Coûtume de Brétagne 449. "Et sera reputée residence propre le lieu où on est nourri, ou le lieu où l'on reside avec sa femme, ou le lieu où l'on a demeuré par l'espace de dix ans continuellement prochains, avant le décéds,"—taken, as D'Argentré remarks, from the Code and the Digest.

code held a presumption of it from a residence of ten years.

Temporary and accidental absence involves no change of domicile. They who on account of health, business, study, war, civil affairs, wander about the earth "domicilium non mutant," so long as they intend to return to the spot from which they set out. Ulysses during the whole twelve years he intended to return to Ithaca was never without a domicile[1].

The article of the custom of Bretagne, on which D'Argentré, from whom writers on the law of domicile have so largely borrowed comments, is this :

"Tous domiciliaires et estagers peuvent être convenus par devant le juge de leur demeurance—et est leur juge competent pour raison des crimes et contrats et en toutes actions personnelles dont la connoissance appartient au dit juge, si le convenu et adjourné n'est personne privilegiée." The framers of our custom, says D'Argentré, have done good service by including in a few rules the whole matter of a competent forum, the distinguishing marks of those who are to judge, and the limits of their authority scattered over the civil law, to preclude all doubt as to the person of the judge in litigated questions[2]. He goes on " in contractibus et delictis spectandus est domicilii judex et in personalibus actionibus quæ ex his oriuntur." D'Argentré says

---

[1] D'Argentré, 1630.

[2] Art. 9. D'Argentré, 24. How long will the supposed interest of a class suffocate this reason for a code among those who in questions of jurisprudence may still be called

"penitus toto divisos orbe Britannos"?

expressly that by domicile he means that of the person when he is sued[1]; and this is in strict conformity with the law of the Pandects[2].

COLLISION OF LAWS[3].

The rules of law govern the legal relations of men to each other; but what is the limit of their supremacy? As Positive Law is from its very nature subject to alteration, and not applicable alike to mankind, but to particular communities, and is liable to be changed in many of its qualities by the soil through which it flows, it is often necessary to define the precise limits of its authority. If different laws exist on the same matter, which is to prevail? We have not now to deal with the law which must be the same at Rome and Athens, which is eternal and universal, but with that which is successive and local. The law of the "forum domicilii" may be different from that of the "forum originis[4]," and that of the "rei sitæ" from either. The Pandects tell us that a contract is to be interpreted according to the custom of the country in which it is made[5]. So in the sale of an estate, the guarantee against eviction was to be given according to the custom

[1] p. 27. Eo tempore quo convenitur.
[2] II. 2. 1. 19.
[3] I refer the reader for information both on this and the former head to the excellent work of a very learned jurist and a very ill-used man, Mr Burge. "His saltem, &c."
[4] Savigny, *System*, Vol. VIII. "Est autem originis locus in quo quis natus est aut nasci debuit licet forte re ipsâ alibi natus esset, mater in peregrinatione parturiente." Voet. *ad Pand.* 5. 1, § 91.
[5] "Id sequamur quod in regione qua actum est frequentatur." II. 50. 17. 34.

of the country "in quo negotium gestum est[1]." The indelible character stamped by birth on the Roman citizen was shewn by the "stipulatio," "spondes spondeo[2]," &c.—a form in which none but a Roman citizen could contract—and by the distinction between the "Cives," the "Latini," and the "Peregrini." The first having the "connubium" and the "commercium;" the second, the "commercium[3]" without the "connubium;" and the third, neither. It is clear that these laws may pronounce a different decision—nay, that they very seldom would pronounce the same one on questions affecting

1. *Status.*
2. Right to immoveable property.
3. Right to moveable property.
4. Marriage.
5. Paternal authority.
6. Guardianship.

Hence the distinction of Statutes into Personal, Real and Mixed.

Personal being those the principal object of which is the person and his condition.

Real, the principal object of which is immoveable property.

Mixed, which affect both; according to some writers, neither; but the method and form of proceedings by which persons and things were affected, according to others.

---

[1] II. 21. 2. 6. rate of interest. II. 22. 1. 7.
II. 28. 1. 21. § 1. (will).
33. 7. 18. § 3.
30. 50. 3.

[2] Gaius, 3. 93. D'Argentré says the "domicilium originis nullo in usu fori est si aliud ullum est." p. 25.

[3] Voet. 2. 4. D'Aguesseau, 54. Plaidoyer, Vol. v. p. 281.

The general rules to be deduced on this subject are :—

1. Where the question turns on the status of a person, or his competence to perform certain acts, whether he is a minor or a major, the law of the domicile should prevail.

e.g. A Spaniard[1] is not of age and cannot make a will till he is twenty-five. He makes a will at the age of twenty-two in England. The will is invalid, and disposes neither of his property, nor of the moveable property belonging to him in England.

This opinion appears to me the sound one, and it is upheld by the great majority of writers. The Germans, whose learning is much more remarkable than their perception of legal analogy, dispute it, so does an American judge[2], on a very narrow ground, to which in all probability our courts would assent—though the weight of authority and argument is the other way. Nobody, as in the case put by the American judge, obliges the tradesman to sell his goods. To know the condition and rights

---

[1] "Menor se entiende el que no ha cumplido los 25 años aunque le falta muy poco tiempo para ello." Sala, *Derecho Real D'España*, Lib. I. tit. 8. p. 88. That it is the opinion of the Roman Law, appears II. 50. 16: "Assumtio originis quæ non est veritatem naturæ non perimit," κ.τ.λ. and eod. § 1: "Filius civitatem ex quâ pater ejus naturalem originem ducit non domicilium sequitur ;" and at this hour the marriage of a Jew is governed by his own law. Lindo *v.* Belisario, I.

Hagg. p. 231.
[2] The marriage of a Frenchman in a foreign country, if it was in violation of the Code Civil, 144—164, would be invalid; marriage there depends on a personal law not affected by change of domicile.

Burge, Vol. I. 131.
Huber, 2. 542.
Dalrymple *v.* Dalrymple.   *Consist. Reps.* Haggard.
Savigny, Vol. VIII. pp. 7, 168.
Kent, *Comment.* Vol. II. 454, 458.

of Caius with whom Titius contracts, is just as much
the duty of Titius as it is that of Caius to know his[1].

"Multo magis," says Huber[2], "statuendum est
eos contra jus gentium facere videri qui civibus
alieni imperii, suâ facilitate, jus patriis legibus contrarium, scientes, volentes impertiuntur."

D'Argentré lays it down that in the case of a
"prodigal" interdicted from the management of his
own affairs, the jurisdiction belongs to the judge of
the domicile.

The strong legal argument in favour of the last
rule is that several persons, each having a different
domicile, and a valid claim according to the law of
that domicile, may assert a right to the same estate.
In such a case, an appeal to the law of domicile
would leave the question undecided—for which law
must prevail? The Lex rei sitæ furnishes a simple
and decisive solution.

With regard to moveable property, it is considered as following the owner, as it appears to me
wisely, though Savigny[3] thinks it should be put on
the same footing as landed property, and follow
the law "rei sitæ." "Mobilia," say the writers on this
subject, "ossibus inhærent[4]," "mobilia veluti corpora situm mutantia domicilii legibus indicantur."

Of the three opinions that have been propounded,

[1] Pardessus, *Traité du Contrat de Change*, No. 361. *Des Lettres de Change*, I. 475.

[2] Félix, Vol. I. p. 185.

[3] Savigny, 8. 173.
So does the Bavarian Code. P. I.
c. 2. § 17.

[4] I. Félix, III.

2. D'Argentré, 1631, where he explains the passages that seem adverse
to this rule in the Pandects. 1629:
"dubitari non debet quin judicis aut
domini domicilii in mobilibus deferen-
dis potissimum omnium causa sit."
1630.

1st. That all the property of a deceased person ought to follow the law of his domicile;

2ndly. That all the property of a deceased person ought to follow the law "rei sitæ;"

3rdly. That the moveable property of a deceased person ought to follow the law of the domicile, and the immoveable that of the "rei sitæ;"—the third is that generally sanctioned by the opinion of the greatest writers, and the practice of the most civilized communities.

2. When a legal act is done, such as the preparation of an instrument, the rules requisite to make such an act or instrument valid, in the region where it is performed or drawn up, must be observed[1]. The maxim usually employed to express this rule is "locus regit actum[2]." And every one must be taken to have made the contract on the spot where he has bound himself to pay; "contraxisse unusquisque in eo loco intelligitur in quo ut solveret se obligavit." II. de ob. et act. 21. "Contractum autem non utique eo loco intelligitur quo negotium gestum est, sed quo solvenda est pecunia[3]." II. 42. 5. 3.

[1] "Contractus celebrati secundum jus loci in quo contrahuntur ibique tam in jure quam extra judicium etiam ubi hoc modo celebrati non valerent, sustinentur, idque non tantum de formâ sed etiam de materiâ contractus affirmandum est." Huber, Vol. II. 539.

"Qui in aliquo loco contrahit tanquam subditus temporarius legibus loci subjicitur." Grotius, 2. 11. § 2.

Hall and Campbell, Rep. Cowper.

Dalrymple v. Dalrymple, Haggard, Con. Reps.

Savigny has put the very question, Vol. VIII. p. 7, System des heutigen Römischen Rechts: "als Beyspiel zur Erläuterung kann die Handlungsfertigkeit dienen die nach dem Recht beurtheilt wird welches am Wohnsitz der Person gilt;" and 134 eod. he lays down what I think the just rule, that the law of the domicile must prevail.

[2] II. 21. 2. 6: "si fundus venierit ex consuetudine ejus regionis in quâ negotium gestum est pro evictione caveri oportet." II. 50. 17. 34: "regionis mos." Hertius de Collisione Legum.

[3] See particularly II. 5. 18. § 2.

The acquisition of landed property is determined by the laws of the country in which the land is situated.

For the rule "locus regit actum[1]" I have not been able to find any direct authority in the Pandects. There is an approach to it under the chapter "de operis novi nuntiatione[2]," requiring the "nuntiatio" to be made on the spot. The doctrine however is involved in the law requiring the wife to exact her dower where the husband was domiciled, not where the instrument appointing it is drawn up. "Ubi maritus domicilium habuit, non ubi instrumentum dotale conscriptum est." For the law adds, "that is not an instrument belonging to the class of those that require consideration of the place where they are made[3]."

The nearest approach however to the doctrine "locus regit actum" in the Roman law is in the code de testamentis, 6. 23. 9. A will had been made without regard to the rule of Roman law requiring the witnesses to be in the presence of the testator, "in conspectu testatoris," 9 cit., "sub præsentiâ ipsius testatoris," 30 eod. c., in answer to the demand of the heiress. The emperor says that the will is invalid unless by the special right of the country of the heiress, "si non speciali privilegio patriæ tuæ juris observatio relaxata est." It does not however appear that the will was made in that country.

The French Code in its original project contained

[1] Félix, 1. 150. Thémis, 2. 95. Zacharia. B. Novell. 11. 47. 1. § 1.
[2] II. 39. 1. 4. D'Argentré, p. 415,

ar. 97: "Instrumentum præsumitur falsum si non apponatur locus." He cites Cod. 10. 69, § 5.
[3] II. 5. 1. 65: Exceptio, &c.

this rule : "La forme des actes est reglée par les lois du lieu dans lequel ils sont faits ou passés." This was struck out, not because it was disputed, but because it was held so incontrovertible an axiom that the insertion of it would be superfluous.

The necessity for the application of such a rule must often be imperious. Savigny puts the case of a Prussian subject dying and desirous to make a will in France. The Prussian law recognizes no wills as valid but those made with the aid of a court of justice. The French law gives no power of the kind to its courts of justice. The result must be, that but for the application of such a principle the will would be invalid[1]. The reasons assigned by Rodenburg, of whose work the principal part of that of Boullenois is a translation, and Voet, for this rule, are— First, the difficulty for an individual possessed of property in various countries to make a will according to the form prescribed in each of those countries. 2ndly, the impossibility in which the testator might be, of complying with the rule prescribed in his domicile or the place where his goods are situated. 3rdly, the importance of upholding a solemn act, done in good faith. 4thly, the unavoidable ignorance of the majority of mankind in such matters. Voet says the same rule applies here that caused the Romans to ratify the testamentum militare[2]. Mr Burge, in his excellent Treatise[3] says, "With respect

---

[1] Code Louisiana, Art. 10.
Félix, 152.
Story, 474.
[2] "Est omnium Doctorum sententia, ubicunque consuetudo vel statu-

tum locale disponit de solemnitate vel formâ actus, ligari etiam exteros ibi actum illum gerentes." Dumoulin, Consult. 43.
[3] Vol. I. p. 26.

to those laws which are called mixed laws, all deal-
ings, contracts, wills, and other instruments, which
are made in the manner prescribed by the law of
the place in which they are entered into and made,
are in every other place deemed valid and effectual.
But neither personal, real nor mixed laws will be
allowed to operate on, or control the title to real
or immoveable property, in opposition to a prohibitory law of a contrary tendency prevailing in the
place in which that property is situated."

The exceptions are,

1. Where the person from whom the act eman-
ates has left his country to elude a positive prohibition of the law[1] ; for fraud cancels everything.

2. Where there is a special prohibition to use
other forms than those prescribed by the law of the
domicile in the particular case, e.g. the case of
landed property in England.

3. The case of Ambassadors.

4. Where the form prescribed by the law of
the place in which the act is done contradicts the
public law (the jus publicum) of the domicile.

To judge, say the authors of the *Répertoire de
Jurisprudence*[2], whether a statute be real or personal, we must not look to the remote effects of it ;
otherwise as there is no personal statute which does
not produce some effect on property, and no real
statute that does not in some way affect persons,
we must say that there is no statute which is not real

---

[1] See the case of Brook and Brook,
lately decided in the House of Lords.

[2] Autorisation Maritale, § 10, No. 2.

Puissance Paternelle, § 7. 425.   Effet
retroactif, 3. § 2. art. 5. no. 3.

and personal at the same time.... What then is to be done? we must fix on the principal, direct and immediate object of the law, and leave the consequences aside. If the principal, direct and immediate object of the statute is to govern the condition of the person, the statute is personal—its effect on property is a distant consequence of its personality; if, on the contrary, the principal, direct and immediate object of the law is to regulate the condition of the property, the statute is real, the effect it has on persons is but the remote consequences of its reality[1].

RIGHT—PRIVILEGIUM.

Right is the power of a person to exercise his will in some visible way, and to call upon the community of which he is a member to assist him when impeded in its exercise : to every right there must be a corresponding duty to act, or to forbear on the part of others.

Law is that expression of the will of a state by which particular actions are prohibited, commanded, permitted, and protected by public authority.

The law may confer a right upon an individual which, according to its ordinary rules, would not exist, and which is inconsistent with its tenor. This is called a privilegium[2], in the strict sense, and it

[1] Félix, 1. 48.

[2] "Privilegium specialiter civitati datum." II. 50. 1. 17. § 5. A. Gell. *Noct. Att.* 10—20. "Leges præclarissimæ de 12 tabulis tralatæ duæ: quarum altera privilegia tollit...ad- mirandum tantum majores in posterum providisse : in privos homines leges ferri noluerunt : id est enim privilegium : quo quid est injustius? quum legis hæc vis sit, ut sit scitum in omnes!" &c. Cic. *de Leg.* 3. 19.

is confined to the individual "non egreditur perso-nam[1]."

In a wider sense, the privilegium is "jus singu-lare[2];" which constitutes an exception (like the pur-veyance of our Norman kings, or the " privilegium militum" among the Romans) to the common law. This is defined " quod contra tenorem juris propter aliquam utilitatem auctoritate constituentium intro-ductum est[3]."

Privilegia in the restricted, as well as in a wider sense, may be divided into affirmative and negative personæ rei, and causæ[4].

RES—THINGS.

Every visible object of law, not described by the word person, falls under the category of thing. In a more limited sense the word "res" comprised any thing that *could* be inherited. The res that actually formed part of an individual's estate, were called bona—and the word pecunia was also constantly applied to denote them all : " Pecuniæ nomine non solum numerata pecunia, sed omnes res etiam soli

---

[1] II. 15. 1. 1. § 2: "plane ex his (constitutiones) quædam sunt persona-les nec ad exemplum trahuntur."

[2] So the laws by which magistrates in England are protected against Spe-cial Pleading.

De Privileg̈iis, 5. 33. in 6 to 5, 7. Clem. 5. 7. II. 42. 5. 12. and 17.

[3] II. 1. 3. 16: "Quod contra ratio-nem juris est non est producendum ad consequentias." 14 eod. "in his quæ contra rationem juris constituta sunt non possumus sequi regulam juris."

II. 29. 1. 2: "propria atque singula-ria jura (de militis testamento)." II. 49. 14. 37. Savigny, *Sys.* 1. 61—66.

[4] II. 43. 20. 1. § 43: "datur (jus aquæ ducendæ) interdum locis, inter-dum personis, interdum prædiis ; quod prædiis datur extinctâ personâ non extinguitur, quod datur perso-nis cum personis amittitur." II. 50. 17. 196: "privilegia quædam causæ sunt, quædam personæ ; et ideo quæ-dam ad hæredem transmittuntur, quæ causæ sunt." 68 eod.

quam mobiles et tam corpora quam jura continentur," in commercio—extra commercium, in patrimonio—extra patrimonium.

Res *alicujus* vel *nullius*—either common to all,
or the property of individuals, of the state, or of
public bodies.

Res privatæ.   Whatever could belong to an
individual.

Property of the state.   " Publica sunt quæ populi
Romani sunt," flumina, hortus, ripæ.

Res universitatis[1].   Such were the theatres,
public walks, pastures, &c. belonging to towns—
collegia. *Communes*, aer, aqua profluens, littora, in
littore inventa.

Res nullius[2].   Such as belonged to the first occupier.   They are of two kinds.   Such as never have
belonged to any one, and such as have ceased to
belong to a former owner.   " Thesaurus est vetus
quædam depositio pecuniæ cujus non extat memoria
ut jam dominum non habeat, sic enim fit ejus qui
invenerit quod non alterius sit[3]," and

---

[1] *Inst.* § 6. de rer. div. "Universitatis sunt non singulorum quæ in civi-
tatibus sunt, theatra, stadia, et si quæ
alia sunt communia civitatum."

[2] " Feræ igitur bestiæ et volucres et
pisces et omnia animalia quæ mari
cœlo et terrâ nascantur, simul atque ab
aliquo capta fuerint, jure gentium statim illius esse incipiunt." *Inst.* de
rer. divis. § 12.   II. de acq. rer. dom.
I. I. de usu et hab. 7. 8. 22. § 1.
  II. de usucap. 41. 3. 37. § 1.

II. de bon. poss. sec. tab. 37. 12. de
legat. 30. 96. § 1.
  This doctrine, founded on reason
and equity, is altogether irreconcilable
with our game-laws, and the commentaries upon them sometimes delivered
by our judges.   A judge is bound to
uphold and administer the law as he
finds it, however impolitic; but he is
not obliged, as so many think, to talk
nonsense in its defence.

[3] II. de acq. rer. dom. 31. § 2.

DIVINI JURIS.

Res sacræ[1], ut ædes sacra.

Res religiosæ.   Sepulchra.

Res sanctæ[2] (veluti muri et portæ quodam modo divini juris sunt).

Justinian allowed the property of the church to be sold to redeem captives, to assist the poor in time of famine, or to discharge a pressing debt. The Canon law[3] forbad the alienation of such property, "nisi ob necessitatem, causâ cognitâ et cum decreto superioris."

Again, res were divided into corporeal, and incorporeal.

Incorporeal were creatures of the law, "quæ in jure consistunt, sesicut hæreditas, ususfructus, usus, et obligationes[4]," that is, servitudes.

The term "res incorporales[5]" was not only employed to denote things actually incorporeal, e. g. rights, and the legal means of enforcing them—but

[1] II. de rer. divis. I. ju. "divini juris."

Inst. de rerum div. § 8.

II. 45. 1. 83. § 5.

Cod. de Sc. Ecc. 1. 2. 21. 17. 23.

Novell. 120. 10. 7.

Cic. *pro Domo.*

"Purus locus dicitur, qui neque sacer, neque sanctus est, neque religiosus, sed ab omnibus hujuscemodi nominibus vacare videtur." II. de religios. 2. § 4 : "religiosum autem locum unusquisque suâ voluntate facit dum mortuum infert in locum suum." II. de divis. rerum, 6. § 4.

[2] "A sagminibus. Sagmina sunt herbæ quas legati populi Romani ferre

solent. Κηρυκεῖα." "Ut leges sanctæ sunt." II. de divis. rer. 8. 9. § 3. Cic. *de n. Deorum,* Lib. 2. § 2.

[3] Tit. 10. de rebus ecc. alien.

[4] *Inst.* 2. 1. 1 et 2.

[5] *Inst.* de rer. divis. § 1.

II. 12. 1. 2. § 1 : "mutui datio consistit in his rebus quæ pondere, numero, mensurâ constant ; quoniam eorum datione possumus in creditum ire, quia in genere suo functionem recipiunt per solutionem quam specie, nam in cæteris rebus ideo in creditum ire non possumus, quia aliud pro alio invito creditore solvi non potest."

Cujac. Obs. 11. 37.

things tangible, of which only the class, or the value, or the quantity, was under consideration. It was also used to denote an universitas rerum, an artificial whole (though consisting of tangible parts), such as an inheritance, a flock of sheep, peculium, a library. These latter were called universitas facti[1], because they were made a whole by the will of an individual. The inheritance was " universitas juris," because it was always considered a whole by the law.

Corporeal were moveable and immoveable. Some moveable things[2] had a peculiar signification[3] in the language of the Roman law.

e.g. Merx meant any article used in commerce.

Tignum, any material used in a building.

Vestis, any article used as a covering to the body.

Ruta cæsa[4] (eruta e terrâ et cæsa) things severed by any means from the soil, or object of which they had formed a part, and not yet applied to any other purpose.

---

[1] II. 5. 5. 50.
II. de verb. S. 178. § 1. L. 208. L. 222. II. de usurp. et usucap. 30. II. de petit. hæred. 22. II. 49. 7. 20. 10. ib. 1. II. 6. 1. 56. *Inst.* de leg.: "Si grex legatus fuerit et postea ad unam ovem pervenerit quod superfuerit vindicari potest."

[2] "Mercis appellatio ad res mobiles tantum pertinet." II. de v. S. 66. 207 ib.

"Tigni appellatione continetur om-nis materia ex quo ædificium constat, vineæque necessaria." II. de tigno juncto, 1. § 1. de v. S. 62.

"Vestis appellatione tam virilis quam muliebris et scenica, etiamsi tragica sit aut citharœdica sit, significatur." II. de v. S. 227.

[3] Gaius, 2. 21.

[4] "Spectant huc eruta e terrâ arena arbores cæsæ," &c. II. 18. 17. 18. ib. 33. 7. 12. § 23. ib. de v. S. 245. ib. de reg. juris, 242.

IMMOVEABLES—PRÆDIA RUSTICA ET URBANA.

Of immoveables, some are such in a real, as lands, houses, &c., others in a legal sense. Such are things[1] so annexed to what is immoveable as not to be severed from it without substantial injury. Things which are essential to the enjoyment of immoveable property, "ea quæ perpetui usus causâ in ædificiis sunt," and things declared immoveable by the policy of the law.

Jus was used in the sense of a power conferred by law—a right; it might be enforced by action, by interdicta, sometimes by exceptiones: it was "in rem[2]," and the action by which it was enforced was called vindicatio; or in personam, when it was called condictio.

Res were also divided into fungibiles[3], "quæ ipso usu consumuntur," and non fungibiles, "quæ usu non consumuntur[4]," into principales and accessoriæ; into the various kinds of fructus naturales, such as the wool of sheep; industriales and civiles,

---

[1] II. de act. erat. Lex 13. § ult.: "ea esse ædium solemus dicere quæ quasi pars ædium vel propter ædes habentur." ib. 17. 3. ib. 38. 2. ib. 18: "dolia in horreis defossa." Ib. ib. Ib. 17. § 7: "Labeo generaliter scribit ea quæ perpetui usus causâ sunt in ædificiis sunt ædificii esse, quæ vero ad præsens non esse ædificii."

[2] II. de pactis, 2. 1. 57. § 2. § 44. 5. 1. 3.   7. 9. 5.
4. 3. 4. § 34=4. 3. 2. § 2.
Can. cap. 8, de concess. præbend. 6. ib. cap. 40.

[3] *Inst.* 2. 4. § 2.

[4] "Quare huc non pertinent partes rei quas integrantes vocant, scilicet quod unam faciunt substantiam, veluti partes domus fundi." II. 48. 1. 49.

"Scapham non videri navis esse respondit nec quidquam conjunctum habere, nam scapham ipsam per se parvam naviculam esse, omnia autem quæ conjuncta navi essent, veluti gubernacula, malus, antennæ, velum, quasi membra navis esse." II. 21. 2. 44: "Fructus pendentes pars fundi videntur." II. de rei vindic. 44.

such as rent, interest, income; pendentes, perceptos, such as crops; percipiendos[1], exstantes et consumtos; and impensæ[2], which were necessariæ, utiles, voluptuariæ.

(1) Necessariæ, "quæ si factæ non sint res aut peritura aut deterior futura sit," "velut aggeres facere, flumen avertere, ædificia vetera fulcire, itemque reficere."

(2) Utiles[3], that improved the property—"veluti pecora prædiis imponere, veluti balnea exstruere."

(3) Voluptuariæ[4], that added to its beauty— "quæ speciem duntaxat ornant, non etiam fructum augent, ut sunt viridaria[5], et aquæ salientes," &c.

Onera rei, burdens, on the discharge of which its possession was conditional; such as payment of a debt, of a legacy, surrender of a submission to an easement. Besides, res were divided into "res mancipi," and "nec mancipi," a distinction obliterated by Justinian; and into dividuæ and individuæ.

There are three classes of things[6], says Pomponius, one comprising what the Greeks called ἡνωμένον, single objects, as a man, a stone, &c.; a second consisting of things combined into one body, as a house, a ship, &c.; a third, of things actually different, but comprised under one appellation, as a flock, a legion, a people.

---

[1] II. 22. 1: "cum re emptor fruatur æquissimum est eum usuras pretii pendere." II. 44. 4. 17. II. de usur. 6. § 1.

[2] II. de v. S. 19. II. 25. 1. 1. § 1.

[3] II. de v. S. 79. § 1. II. de impens.

in res dot. fact. 4. § 1.

[4] II. de v. S. 79. § 2. II. de impens. in res dot. fact. 7.

[5] Gaius, 2. 15—27. Ulpiani *Frag.* 19. § 1.

[6] II. 41. 3. 30.

LEGAL TRANSACTIONS—NEGOTIA [1].

Legal transactions are manifestations of will directed to an effect that the law will establish. They may be uni-lateral, when they are the expression of a single will; bi- or pluri-lateral, when the consent of two or more wills is necessary to their existence. Among the most important of the former may be ranked Testaments. The latter are called "pactio," "conventio."

Again, negotia may be divided into negotia juris civilis, juris gentium, actus legitimi.

Stricti juris, and bonæ fidei [2].

Onerosa [3], gratuita, lucrativa [4].

Inter vivos, and mortis causâ.

To constitute such a transaction there is required —the capacity of the parties to it, and sometimes of others; a legal purpose; a sufficient declaration of that purpose.

This may be express or tacit [5], in words, in writing or by signs; by direct or indirect [6] expressions,

---

[1] II. 4. 2. quod metus causâ gestum est.

II. 4. 3. de dolo malo.

II. 44. 4. de doli et metus exceptione.

II. de legat. 3. 2.

[2] "Et solo nutu pleraque consistunt." II. de obl. et act. 52. § 9. II. 46. 2. 17: "nutu etiam relinquitur fidei commissum." II. de obl. et act. 38: "placuit non minus valere quam scriptura quod vocibus linguâ figuratis significaretur."

[3] II. 11. 45. 8. 5: "non tantum verbis ratam haberi posse, sed etiam actu."

[4] De reg. juris, 48. *Inst.* de inu-

til. stipul. 3. 20. 10. Cod. 4. 38. 2. II. 28. 1. 20. 4. Cod. 6. 22. 9. can. 7. c. 15. qu. 1.

[5] "Labeo ait, si patiente vicino opus faciam, ex quo ei aqua pluvia noceat non teneri me actione aquæ pluviæ arcendæ." II. 39. 3. 19. "Is qui tacet non utique fatetur, sed tamen verum est eum non negare." II. 50. 17. 142. Savigny, 3. § 130.

[6] II. 31. 69. jur.

32. 11. § 4: "sufficiunt tibi vineæ et fundus" is equal to "contentus esto illâ re."

II. 23. 12. 7. § 1. 21. 2. 12.

II. 24. 3. 2. § 2. 19. 2. 13. 11.

from which the intent may be collected[1]. The mere signification of the will is not sufficient in all cases, unless certain forms are observed : such as presence of witnesses[2], registration, &c. Sometimes the law supposed assent[3].

The basis of these negotia of circumstances which impress a character on transactions[4] that demand judicial interference is the will. This leads to the consideration of obstructions to its exercise; such are violence[5] (vis), intimidation (metus), fraud (dolus malus), and errour (error).

The essence of all civil affairs is the declaration of will[6]. This is either really made, or, from motives of equity and policy, supposed by the legislator to be made. A real declaration may either be express, by word or writing, or implied[7] from some act.

It follows, that transactions performed by persons unable to give their consent are invalid. Minority[8],

---

II. 1. 7. 5: "vel consentiendo vel non contradicendo." II. 24. 3. 2. § 2.

[1] II. 46. 8. 5. 20. 1. 26. § 1. 146. 12 and 16.

"Recusari hæreditas non tantum verbis sed etiam re potest et alio quovis judicio voluntatis." II. 29. 2. 95.

"Si passus sim aliquem pro me fidejubere vel alias intervenire mandati teneor." II. 17. 1. 6. § 2.

II. 19. 2. 13. 11: "taciturnitate reconduxisse in ipso anno quo tacuerunt." II. 21. 2. 12. II. 36. 1. 37. jur.

"Nemo dubitat recte ita hæredem nuncupari posse 'hic mihi hæres esto' cum sit coram qui ostenditur." 28. 5. 58.

[2] *Inst.* de cont. vend. 3. 23. 4. 21.

Cod. de fid. *Inst.* 4. 21. 17.

[3] II. 20. 2. 6. pr.
    II. 3. 3. 35. 30.

[4] "Negotium sæpissimè idem est quod Græcè πρᾶγμα seu χρῆμα aut res Græcè et Latinè desideratur in omni neutrali adjectivo." Sanctius, L. 4. de Ellipsi Minerva.

[5] II. 35. 1. Savigny, 3. 116—142. Arndt, p. 72. Leibnitz, *Op.* Vol. IV. pp. 3, 92—158.

[6] II. 45. 1. 100. 125. *Inst.* de v. 6. 3. 15.
    Inst. 28. 3. 16.
           28. 7. 10. 1.
           28. 5. 77.

[7] II. 12. 1. 37—39.

[8] II. 46. 2. 9. 1. II. 12. 6. 18.

madness, disease, excessive intoxication, violent pas-
sion, were grounds, on which acts that would have
been binding on persons not so affected might be
set aside.

Ignorance[1] (which includes error) is either ignorance of fact, or ignorance of law. Ignorance of fact
is either ignorance of what has been done by yourself, or by another person. Ignorance of what has
been done by yourself, was, generally, no defence[2]; but allowance was made for weakness of
memory[3].

Ignorance[4] of what had been done by another
was a good defence, unless the ignorance was so
crass as to be inexcusable.

FRAUD—DOLUS MALUS[5].

This either vitiated all proceedings tainted with
its effects, or gave rise to an action[6], unless it has
been condoned after full knowledge. Labeo[7] defined

[1] "Non videntur quo errant consentire." II. de reg. Juris. 116.
[2] II. 16. 1. 7: "fidejussor nullam
replicationem habebit, quia facti non
potest ignorantiam prætendere." II.
42. § 10. 5. § 1, sub fin. "quia alieni facti ignorantia tolerabilis error
est."
[3] II. 12. 6. 22.
[4] "Sed facti ignorantia ita demum
cuique non nocet si non ei summa negligentia objiciatur ; quid enim si omnes
in civitate sciant quod ille solus igno-
rat, et rectè Labeo definit, scientiam
neque curiosissimi neque negligentis-
simi hominis accipiendam, verum ejus
qui eam rem diligenter inquirendo no-

tam habere possit." II. 23. 1. 2. ib.
9. § 2.
[5] "Sive ab initio dolo malo factum
est, sive post pactum dolo malo aliquid
factum est, nocebit exceptio." II. de
pactis, 7. 11.
[6] II. 19. 1. 13. 4.
[7] II. 4. 3. 1. § 2. ib. 44. 4. 1. § 3.
ib. 2. 14. 7. § 9: "Dolus malus fit
calliditate et fallaciâ, et ut ait Pedius,
dolo malo pactum fit quoties circum-
scribendi alterius causâ aliud agitur,
et aliud agi simulatur." II. 4. 3. 1.
§ 3: "non fuit contentus Prætor dolum dicere, sed adjecit malum, quoniam
veteres dolum etiam bonum dicebant,
et pro solertiâ hoc nomen accipiebant."

dolus malus to be " omnem calliditatem, fallaciam, machinationem ad circumveniendum, fallendum, decipiendum alterum adhibitum."

The dolus malus might either affect the substance or the incidents of a contract ; e. g. it might either induce a person to sell, who but for the fraud would not have sold at all[1]—in hoc ipso ut venderet circumscriptus—or it might induce a person to buy at a higher price than he would otherwise have given, what he was however resolved to purchase[2].

Wherever a civil wrong had been sustained for which there was no specific remedy, an action lay " de dolo[3]."

Violence was "majoris rei impetus qui repelli non potest[4]." " Nihil consensui tam contrarium est quam vis et metus[5]."

Intimidation[6], such as was required to set aside an act, was more than could be caused by mere suspicion or persuasion, or reverence for authority domestic or external ; "metus accipiendus non quilibet timor sed majoris malitatis." It must be such as the person urging it (age, sex and character considered) might rationally entertain[7].

L. 16. II. de min. 25. ann.: "Hoc sensu in pretio emtionis et venditionis naturaliter licet contrahentibus se circumvenire usque ad dimidium."

[1] II. de pactis, 1. § 2.

[2] 19. 1. 13. 4.

[3] II. Stellionatus, 3. § 1 : "quod in privatis judiciis est de dolo actio hoc in criminibus stellionatus persecutio, ubicunque igitur titulus criminis deficit illic stellionatum objiciemus." See the Law, 21. 1. 14. § 9: "Si venditor nominatim exceperit de aliquo morbo

et de cætero sanum esse dixerit aut promiserit standum est eo quod convenit...nisi sciens venditor morbum consulto retiarit, tunc enim dandum esse de dolo malo replicationem."

[4] II. 4. 2. 1 et 2.

[5] II. de reg. juris, 116.

[6] II. quod metus causâ, 9. 6 eod. 5 eod. e. g. " servitutis, stupri, cruciatus, mortis, aut verberum, carceris, concussionis bonorum vel majoris partis."

[7] " Quis sit justus metus ex affectu

Violence might be condoned, and there were cases in which intimidation was legitimate; "veluti si a magistratu metus ordine juris injectus est[1]," "jure licito." It mattered not who was the author of the violence if the person against whom the action was brought was a gainer by it[2].

The natural ingredients of a contract (naturalia) were those annexed to its character by law, and therefore presumed to belong to it; but these ingredients might usually be eliminated (where the policy of the state did not forbid such a proceeding) by the will of the contracting parties; but when the will was impotent[3], as in the case of a testator binding himself not to change his testament, the original character of the contract prevailed[4].

The accidents of a contract were those circumstances which did not affect its substance, and might be engrafted upon it at the pleasure of the persons making it. Such were (1) conditions, (2) time, (3) object (modus), (4) motive, (5) description.

CONDITIONS[5].

The will requisite to give effect to a transaction may be absolute or conditional. The will which depended on the condition referring to a past or

metuentis intelligi debet, cujus rei disquisitio judicis est."

[1] II. eod. tit. 3. § 1. Fox's Speech on the Westminster Scrutiny.

[2] II. quod metus causâ, § 14: "In hâc actione non quæritur utrum is qui convenitur an alius metum fecerit, sufficit enim hoc dicere, metum sibi illatum vel vim et ex hâc re eum qui convenitur, etsi crimine caret, lucrum tamen sensisse."

[3] Averanius, 4. c. 12. n. 12—27.

[4] II. 32. 22.

[5] II. de contrah. temp. 36. II. 28. 3. 16.

present event, was either void or absolute, according
to the existence or non-existence of the event ; and
although the person expressing the will was ignorant of it, "nec placuit instar habere conditionis
sermonem qui non ad futurum sed ad præsens
tempus refertur etsi contrahentes rei veritatem
ignorent."

"Quum[1] ad præsens tempus conditio confertur
stipulatio non suspenditur," "quamvis contrahentes
conditionem ignorent."

The will subject to a future condition which
must certainly happen, was absolute.

A contract subject to an impossible condition
"si digito cælum tetigeris" was void: a bequest subject to such a condition was absolute.

Immoral conditions, or conditions supposing an
indecent or calamitous event, as that a freeman
should become a slave, were impossible, "nec enim
fas est hujusmodi casus expectare[2]."

A condition[3] implied by the nature of the trans-

---

[1] Averanius, c. 22, Vol. I. p. 178,
ad L. I. II. de leg. 2, reconciles the
apparent difference between Ulpian
and Modestinus, who says (nonnunquam de cond. et dem.), "si Mævius
voluerit Titio darem is an invalid
bequest," which is true, whereas
Ulpian says, de legatis L. I. in princ.
II. de legatis 2, that such a bequest is
valid in substance but in a different
phrase.

[2] "Quoties fundus in diem addicitur
utrum pura emtio est, sed sub conditione resolvitur : an vero conditionalis
sit magis emtio, quæstionis est : et
mihi videtur verius interesse quid actum sit ; nam si quidem hoc actum est

ut meliore allatâ conditione discedatur,
erit pura emtio, quæ sub conditione
resolvitur : sin autem hoc actum est ut
perficiatur emtio, nisi melior offeratur
erit emtio conditionalis." II. 18. 2.
2. § pr.

[3] II. 35. 1. 99.
       23. 3. 68.
       35. 1. 107.
Sometimes they are called "conditiones juris," "multum interest conditio facti an juris est, nam hujusmodi
conditiones, si navis ex Asia venerit,
si Titius consul erit, impedient hæredem circa adeundam hæreditatem
quamdiu ignoraret eas impletas esse.
Quæ vero ex jure venient in his nihil

action, " quæ tacite inesse videntur," as marriage in
the case of a promised Dos, did not make it conditional.

Conditions may be affirmative[1], "si in Capitolium
ascenderit," or negative, "si in Capitolium non ascenderit."

They may be casual, depending on accident.

Potestative, on what it is in the power of one
of the contracting parties to accomplish; or mixed,
depending partly on their will, and partly on the
will of a third person.

Suspensive, or resolutory[2], as the existence of the
transaction is to begin or to end with a future event;
e.g. payment of money in a certain time, absence of
a higher offer.

Conditions inconsistent with the essence of the
transaction to which they were annexed[3], as "I will
pay you if I please," made the transaction void,
"nullius momenti faciet actum."

---

amplius exigendum quam ut impletæ
sint." II. 35. 1. 21. II. 21. 1. 43.
10.

II. 35. 1. 19. 1: "Hæc scriptura,
si primus hæres erit damnas esto dare,
pro conditione non accipienda; magis
enim demonstravit testator quando
legatum debeatur quam conditionem
inscruit, nisi forte hoc animo fuerit testator, ut faceret conditionem."

   [1] II. 35. 1. 67. pr. 35. 78. § 1.
      35. 1. 7.
      28. 5. 4.
      28. 7. 28.
      45. 1. 7.
      29. 4. 1. § 8.
   Code Nap. 1169. 1171.
   [2] II. 18. 2. 2.

18. 3. 1.
41. 4. 2. § 3.
18. 1. 3.
[3] II. 44. 7. 8.
   50. 17. 77. Frag. Vat. 329.
The Canon Law says: "si conditiones contra substantiam conjugii in-
serantur, puta, si dicat alteri, contraho
tecum si generationem prolis evites, vel
donec inveniam aliam honore vel facul-
tatibus digniorem, aut si pro quæstu
adulterandam te tradas matrimonialis
contractus caret effectu, licet aliæ conditiones appositæ in matrimonio si
turpes aut impossibiles fuerint debeant
pro non adjectis haberi propter ejus
favorem."

   Cap. 7. 4. 5.

Until the event contemplated according to the rational interpretation of his will by the imposer of the condition happened, it was pending[1] (pendet conditio); when it took place, the condition was at an end, " deficit conditio."

Negative conditions ceased[2] when the event on the non-happening of which the transaction depended became impossible.

Sometimes the condition, though not literally fulfilled, was looked upon as accomplished :

When it had been prevented by him whose interest it was to prevent it[3]:

When the person whose co-operation was necessary towards it[4], and for the sake of whom it had been established, refused his co-operation.

Sometimes when events, over which the person charged with it had no control, made its fulfilment impossible ; as the condition of a will being that he should emancipate Stichus[5], if Stichus died after the testator's death.

Modus[6], is the assigned object of a particular

[1] II. 50. 17. 213.
   20. 1. 13. 5.
   44. 7. 42: "is cui sub conditione legatum est pendente conditione non est creditor, sed tunc cum extiterit conditio," &c.
   II. 40. 9. 27. Savigny, 3. 149.
[2] II. 18. 6. 8: "Quum semel conditio extitit perinde habetur ac si illo tempore quo stipulatio interposita est sine conditione facta est."
[3] "Jure civili receptum est, quoties per eum cujus interest conditionem non impleri fiat quominus impleatur, perinde haberi ac si impleta conditio esset." II. 50. 17. 161.

[4] II. 28. 7. 11. 23.
   31. 34. § 4.
   36. 2. 5. 5.
   35. 1—14. 31. 78.
[5] II. 30. 54. 2: "quia per te non stetit quominus perveniat ad libertatem."
   II. 9. 2. 23. § 2.
   33. 20. pr.
   29. 5. 3. 31.
[6] II. de condit. et dem. 35. 1. 17. 4. eod. 8: "nec enim parem dicemus eum cui ita datum sit, 'si monumentum fecerit,' et eum cui datum est, 'ut monumentum faciat'."

transaction; if a legacy be bequeathed to Titius, provided he erect such a tomb, it is left " sub modo."

Causa, is the reason which induced any one to do a particular act, e.g. leave a particular legacy, "Falsam causam legato non obesse verius est quia ratio legandi legato non cohæret."

Demonstratio, is the specification of a particular thing or person, inserted in a written instrument, in order to guard against mistake. If, therefore, the thing or person can be ascertained, without the specification, an error in it is immaterial, as the purpose it is intended to answer is accomplished. Hence the maxim, " Falsa demonstratio non nocet," "nam demonstratio plerumque vice nominis fungitur, nec interest falsa an vera sit, si certum sit quem testator demonstraverit[1]." But the transaction became invalid if the false specification made the object or intention uncertain[2], or proved the " causa negotii," the motive which had caused it, erroneous, in a particular sense; as if Caius, erroneously believing Titius his son, made him his heir[3].

He who bought from a ward[4] was bound to shew that the guardian assented to the contract; but as

---

[1] II. de cond. et dem. 34. cod. 17. 1: "Igitur et si ita servus legatus sit: Stichum coquum Stichum sutorem do lego, licet neque coquus neque sutor sit, ad legatarium pertinebit, si de eo sensisse testatorem conveniat."

[2] "Si quis legaverit ex illo dolio amphoras decem, etsi non decem sed pauciores inventi sunt non extinguitur legatum, sed hoc tantum modo accipit quod invenitur." II. 31. 8. § 2.

[3] Cod. de hæred. instit. l. 4: "Si pater tuus eum quasi filium hæredem instituit quem falsâ opinione ductus suum esse credebat, non instituturus si alienum nosset, isque postea subditus esse ostensus est, auferendam ei successionem Divorum Severi et Antonini placitis continetur;" and see II. de cond. et dem. 72. § 1, which shews that a mistaken recital of a legacy never given did not aid the supposed legatee.

[4] II. 6. 2. 13. II. de verb. oblig. 30: "Sciendum est generaliter si quis se scripserit fidejussisse videri omnia solenniter acta."

a general rule, it was presumed that every condition made necessary by law to the validity of a contract had been observed.

DOCTRINAL INTERPRETATION OF WRITTEN INSTRUMENTS.

1. If the words are clear, but the intention of him who employed them doubtful, the words are to be followed : "Cum in verbis nulla ambiguitas est non debet admitti voluntatis quæstio[1]."

2. If the words are equivocal, but the intention of him who used them clear, the intention, not the words, is to be followed.

Where the words are unintelligible, the task of interpretation ends[2].

If any ingredient essential to the validity of an act was disputed, the person insisting on the act was bound to prove it as against a stranger, e. g. the purchaser from a ward was bound to prove the assent of the guardian to the purchase[3].

If by the course of events, an act originally contemplated as legitimate and possible, became, during the interval preceding the promise and accomplishment, and without the fault of the promiser, unlawful or impossible, the obligation was extinguished[4].

---

[1] II. 32. 25. § 1. et eod. 68: "non aliter significatione verborum recedi oportet quam cum manifestum est aliud sensisse testatorem."

[2] II. 32. 69. 1.

[3] "Qui a pupillo emit probare debet tutore auctore lege non prohibente se emisse." II. 6. 2. 13. § 2. For the exception see II. 45. 1. 30: "Sciendum est generaliter quod si quis scrip-serit se fidejussisse videri omnia solenniter acta."

[4] But so much as remained possible or lawful was to be done nevertheless, e. g. if a flock had been left and all had perished but one sheep, the sheep was to be given, II. 30. 1. 22. The area was to be given if the house was burnt, II. de solut. 98.

This is the meaning of the rule which was long disputed, and much qualified by the Roman jurists,
"ea quæ initio recte constituta sunt resolvuntur si
inciderint in eum casum a quo incipere non potuis-
sent[1];" but this does not hold universally, "non
tamen in omnibus hoc verum est," says Paulus[2].
Hence the apparently conflicting rule, "non est
novum ut quæ semel utiliter constituta sunt durent,
licet ille casus extiterit a quo initium capere non
potuerunt." Thus, a man makes a will, and then
loses his senses;—his will is valid. The same doctrine
applies to marriage and other contracts. Again, by
the Roman law a donation to a wife was invalid;
but that to a concubine, or even a meretrix, was
good[3]. If a man married his mistress, the gift made
to her when she was his concubine continued to be
valid. This law bears very much on the doctrine
of prescription, "nec enim committi, aut mutari,
quod recte transactum est, superveniente delicto potest." The rule "quod ab initio vitiosum est non
potest tractu temporis convalescere," applies to contracts where the origin must always be considered[4].
It did not, however, apply to marriages, which though
originally invalid, might if, when the impediment to

---

[1] II. de v. ob. 98. in fin. Of this
there is a curious illustration in our
history. Lord Bolingbroke after his
attainder married a French lady. She
had a large sum of money in the hands
of an English banker: he laid hold of
this pretext to keep it, alleging that
he durst not pay the money to Lord
Bolingbroke, and it was with great
difficulty that the money was wrested
from him. The whole argument is
admirably stated in Averanius, Lib. 4.
c. 22, Interpretationum Juris.

[2] II. de verb. oblig. § 2. L. penult.

[3] II. de donat.inter vir. et ux. l. 1. 2.
eod. 38. II. de donat. 5. II. de cond.
ob temp. causam 4. "donationes in
concubinam collatas non posse revo-
cari convenit, nec si matrimonium inter eosdem postea fuerit contractum,
ad initum recidere." II. 39. 5. 31.

[4] II. 45. 1. 83. § 5. sacram, &c.

their validity was removed, the parties persevered in their intention, become valid[1].

DAMNUM[2]—HARM.

Generally speaking, the word damnum meant any harm whatever. In a narrower sense it was held to mean any diminution of the loser's patrimony: "Damnum et damnatio ab ademptione et quasi de minutione patrimonii dicta sunt[3]."

No redress was given to the author[4] of his own loss. Loss from an extrinsic cause was either casual, or the result of a lawful or of an unlawful act.

Casual loss[5] (casus fortuitus) was that arising from causes which no human strength or foresight could avert. Unless by special compact, no person was responsible for it. The danger of such accidents was termed "periculum[6]."

---

[1] e. g. the governor of a province could not contract a valid marriage with a resident in it; but if he did contract such a marriage, and ceasing to be governor persevered in his engagement, the marriage became valid: "etsi contra mandata contractum est matrimonium in provinciâ, tamen post depositum officium si in eâdem voluntate perseverat, justas nuptias effici." II. 23. 3. 65.

[2] "Damnum pati videtur qui commodum amittit quod consequi poterat." II. 43. 8. 2. 11. "Si libero nocitum sit, ipsi perpetua erit actio; sed si alius velit experiri annua erit hæc actio, nec enim hæredibus jure hæredi-

tario competit quippe quod in corpore libero damni datur; jure hæreditario ad successores transire non debet, quasi non sit damnum pecuniarium, nam ex æquo et bono oritur." II. 9. 3. 5. 5.

[3] II. 31. 2. 3.

[4] "Quod quis ex culpâ suâ damnum patitur non intelligitur damnum sentire." II. de reg. 7. 203.

[5] Vis major: vis divina: fatum: ex incendio, furto, rapinâ, hostilitate. II. locati 25. § 6: 33 in fine 59. II. de minor. 11. 5. II. de damni infect. 24. § 4. Prousteau. Meermann, Thes. Vol. III.

[6] de peric. et comm. rei venditæ, I. 14. II. commod. 5. § 14. eod. 10.

The Twelve Tables mention dolus, to this culpa was opposed ; culpa included casus.

Dolus malus has been already mentioned. In every transaction, and under all circumstances, the person against whom it could be proved was responsible to the sufferer, nor could he be exonerated from his liability by an express contract, "illud nullâ pactione effici potest ne dolus præstetur[1]."

DAMNUM ARISING FROM CULPA.

Culpa is neglect of due care without the intention of inflicting loss.   It occurs when that has not been done which ought to have been done, and that has been done which ought not to have been done; in strict legal[1] language it is opposed to "dolus."

There are various degrees of culpa[2],—lata, media[3], and levissima: "lata culpa est nimia negligentia non intelligere id quod omnes intelligunt[4]."

The "levis culpa[5]" is mentioned Π. 30. 47. § 5, "Culpa autem qualiter sit videamus non solum ea quæ dolo proxima est verum etiam quæ levis est."

§ 1. Π. de nautico fœnore 4. Π. naut. et caup. 3. § 1, 4. Π. depositi 1. § 35. Meermann, *Thes.* Vol. IV. 51. Schweppe, 3rd Ed. p. 464. *Römische Rechtsgeschichte.*

[1] Π. 2. 14. 27. § 3.

[2] "Magna negligentia culpa est, magna culpa dolus." Π. de v. S. 226.

[3] "Utrumque genus culpæ varie appellatur, veluti negligentia, desidia, segnities, incuria, nimia securitas, imperitia, inertia, infirmitas, imprudentia, simplicitas, rusticitas, ineptia." Π. ad L. aq. 8. et 30. § 3.

[4] I am aware that the Germans have abused their leisure by raising unprofitable subtleties on this division of the culpa. It is a vain logomachy, but I think the passages I have cited bear out the old view. Muhlenbruch, p. 343.

[5] "Generaliter quotiescunque non fit nomine pupilli quod quivis paterfamilias idoneus facit non videtur defendi." Π. 26. 7. 11. And see the remarkable passage which might have been quoted over and over again in our courts. Π. 9. 2. 30. § 3.

The levissima, II. 9. 2. 44, " In lege Aquiliâ et levissima culpa venit."

The rules as to the responsibility for the " culpa " varied according to the nature of the contract[1].

1. Where the chief benefit fell to the share of one of the parties, he was responsible for every degree of " culpa[1]," the other for the " culpa lata " only.

2. Where the benefit was equal, and in cases arising from the right of holding and enjoying the property of another, any degree of culpa made the person guilty of it (civilly of course) responsible[2].

3. From partners[3], and from a husband in the administration of his wife's dower, that degree of care only was required, which they were in the habit of applying to their own affairs.

4. A person who undertook the management of another person's affairs, although he derived no benefit from his employment, was responsible for any degree of culpa. But they who were forced to undertake such a task, such as the tutor, or curator, were only bound to apply the same care which they employed in the administration of their own affairs.

---

[1] II. 13. 6. 5. § 2: "in contractibus interdum dolum solum interdum et culpam præstamus dolum in deposito nam quia nulla utilitas ejus versatur apud quem deponitur, merito dolus versatur solus, nisi forte et merces—accessit tunc enim...etiam culpa exhibetur...sed ubi utriusque utilitas vertitur, ut in emto, ut in locato, ut in dote, ut in pignore, ut in societate, et dolus et culpa præstatur—commodatum autem plerumque solam utili-tatem continet ejus cui commodatur, et ideo verior est. Quinti Mucii sententia existimantis et culpam præstandam et diligentiam."

[2] II. 44. 7. 1. § 4: "ille qui mutuam accepit...exactissimam diligentiam custodiendæ rei præstare compellitur, nec sufficit ei eandem diligentiam, adhibere quam suis rebus adhibet, si alius diligentior custodire potuerit."

[3] Inst. 3. 25. 9.

The heirs of such persons were responsible to the extent of the property of the deceased, for the dolus, and such degrees of culpa as would have made him liable.

The burden of proving the culpa lay on the person alleging it[1]. But if the defendant, admitting the loss of the thing for which he was responsible, declared that the destruction of it was not owing to any fault of his, it lay upon him to disprove his liability.

Mora, or unlawful delay, is connected with the topic of dolus and culpa; it is the neglect to perform a particular action within the time required by law.

The creditor who refused to receive payment[2], and the debtor who failed to make it, were "in morâ." If there was a valid reason, justa causa for the delay[3], the person who would otherwise have incurred the consequences of mora was exonerated from them.

The "mora" began sometimes from the mere operation of law, whence the well-known maxim "dies interpellat pro homine[4]," sometimes from the particular act of the adverse[5] party. It was, how-

---

[1] Cod. de pub. 13. Cod. de edendo 4. Cod. de pign. act. 5. II. 19. 2. 9. § 4. II. de probat. 19.

[2] "Nisi forte per promissorem steterit quo minus suo die solverct aut per creditorem quo minus acciperet, etenim neuter eorum frustratio sua prodesse debet." II. mandati 37. "Si ea obtulerit creditori et ille sine justâ causâ ea accipere recusavit." II. 72.

de solut.

[3] "Non enim in morâ est is a quo pecuniæ propter exceptionem peti non potest." "Sciendum non omne quod optimâ ratione fiat, moræ adnumerandum." II. de usur. 21.

[4] Donellus, Comment. 16. c. 2. § 2. Noodt, de fœnore et usuris, Lib. 3. c. 10.

[5] "Mora fieri intelligitur non ex re

ever, rather a question of fact than law[1]. "Mora[2]" might be purged by the debtor's offer to pay "ante ritem contestatam[3]," by the tacit indulgence of the creditor, by his express permission, by novation, by payment[4].

The consequences[5] of "mora" were, that the risk (periculum) of the thing in question fell upon the person guilty of it; that the debtor became liable for profits and interest, that he was liable for the penalties of a stipulation; on the other hand, the debtor, after giving due notice to the creditor, might obtain payment for the keep of a slave whom the creditor had refused to receive, and by abandoning or

sed ex personâ, id est si interpellatus opportuno loco non solverit." Voet, Comment. ad Pand. Lib. 22, tit. 1. § 25.

[1] "D. Pius Tullio Balbo rescripsit an mora facta intelligatur neque constitutione ullâ neque Juris auctorum quæstione decidi posse cum sit magis facti quam juris." II. de usuris 32.

[2] "Stichi promissor post moram, offerendo purgat moram certe enim doli mali exceptio nocebit ei qui pecuniam oblatam accipere noluit." II. de verb. oblig. 73. § ult.

[3] "Si insulam fieri stipulatus sum et transierit tempus quo potueris facere quamdiu litem contestatus non sum posse te facientem liberari placet, quodsi jam litem contestatus sim nihil tibi prodesse si ædifices." II. eod. 84.

[4] "Si Stichum dari stipulatus fuerim et cum in morâ promissor esset, quo minus daret, rursus eundem stipulatus fuero desinit periculum ad promissorem pertinere, quasi morâ purgatâ." II. de nov. 8. "Novatione factâ non committitur stipulatio." ib. 15.

[5] "Si mora per mulierem fit quo minus dotem reciperet dolum malum duntaxat in eâ re maritus præstare debet." II. 24. 3. 9. "Illud sciendum est cum moram emtor adhibere cœpit jam non culpam sed dolum malum tantum præstandum a venditore." II. 18. 6. 17. "Si post divortium res dotales deteriores factæ sint et vir in reddendâ dote moram fecerit omni modo detrimentum ipse præstabit." II. 24. 3. 25. § 2. "Stipulatus sum Damam aut Erotem servum dari quum Damam dares ego quo minus acciperem in morâ fui mortuus est Dama an putes me ex stipulatu actionem habere? Respondit...non...nam ...si per debitorem mora non esset quo minus id quod debebat solveret, continuo eum debito liberari." II. 45. 1. 105. "Si per emptorem steterit quo minus ei mancipium traderetur pro cibariis per arbitrum indemnitatem posse servari...dixerunt." II. 19. 1. 38.

II. 4. 2. 14. § 11.

II. 45. 1. 135: "si non multo post obtulisset," &c.

depositing, or pouring away (as in the case of wine in casks) the article in his possession, exonerates himself from all responsibility. If both buyer and seller had been guilty of "mora[1]," he who had last been guilty of mora, things remaining as they were, if the other was willing to perform his part, incurred its responsibilities. "Si per emtorem mora fuisset deinde cum omnia in integro essent venditor moram adhibuerit... æquum est posteriorem moram venditori nocere[2]."

ID QUOD INTEREST—THE DIFFERENCE[3].

Whatever damage entitling you to a legal remedy you suffer from the unjust conduct of another man, whether it be because he has not done what he ought to have, or he has done what he ought not to have done, went under the name of "ejus quod interest;" so we read, "Id quod interest non solum ex damno dato constare sed ex lucro cessante[4]."

LEGAL VALUE OF FACTS.

Everything arising from human will and intention falls under the head of facts; and in that sense they are opposed to accident. That which is done by a being destitute of reason, by a maniac, or one

---

[1] II. 19. 1. 51.

[2] II. de peric. et comm. rei vend.17. apud Meermann, *Thesaur.* T. 3.

[3] Matth. Magnus de eo quod interest, Lib. 2. Donellus, Comment. Lib. 26. "Sensu generali quidquid amisimus facto alterius injusto cujusque restitutionem petere jure perfecto possumus." II. ratam rem haberi, l. 13. "In tantum competit in quantum mea interfuit, id est quantum mihi abest quantumque lucrari potui." II. ad Leg. Ag. II. de damn. infec. II. 4. § 7.

[4] Cod. 7. 47.

intoxicated, is considered the effect of accident[1]. Mere
thoughts and intentions followed by no act are held
as nothing in law: for "cogitationis pœnam, nemo
patitur[2]," our intentions are so far important as they
are revealed by an act, to which they give signification[3]. No law commands what is impossible[4]. The
chief division of acts is into those which are and
those which are not lawful. Under the head of
unlawful are comprised not only acts done against
law, or in fraud of law, but all that are contra
bonos mores, and against the rights of others: no
one can profit by an unlawful act, and every one is
liable to compensate the injury he has inflicted upon
another.

Of those which are lawful, the physical act is
the main ingredient, sometimes the legal character.
Possession belongs to the first class; and as this is
of great importance in Roman law, I will now
proceed to the consideration of it.

[1] "Impune puto admittendum quod
per furorem alicujus accidit quomodo
si casu aliquo sine facto personæ id
accidisset." II. 26. 61. II. 48. 16.
1. § 3: "incipit quærere qua mente
ductus ad accusationem processerit,"
&c. "Inconsultum calorem calumniæ
vitio carere," eod. § 5.

[2] II. 48. 19. 18.

[3] II. 50. 16. 54: "sane post veterum auctoritatem eo perventum est ut
nemo ope videatur fecisse nisi et consilium malignum habuerit, nec consilium habuisse noceat nisi et factum se-
cutum fuerit." II. 50. 16. 218: "verbum facere omnem omnino faciendi
causam amplectitur." "Nemo ex suo
delicto meliorem conditionem suam
facere potest." II. 50. 17. 134. § 1.

[4] II. 28. 7. 16. eod. 20: "ἀδύνατος
conditio pro non scriptâ habenda est."
II. 45. 1. 26. § 61.
47. 15. 5.
47. 2. 12. § 1.

CHAPTER III.

POSSESSION.

THE difficulty of defining possession arises from the simplicity of the notion: it is hard to use words which do not obscure an idea that is intelligible to every one; and accordingly elaborate treatises have been written on the subject much to the benefit of their authors, and very little to the improvement of jurisprudence.

Every one understands that when he enters his friend's house on a visit he is not taking possession of it[1]. Every one understands when he leaves his town-house for his summer-house, that he does not abandon the possession of the former. Every one understands that possession may be one thing, and the right to possession another. Every one perceives that cases may be put in which the physical occupation of Caius is the possession of Titius[2], and

---

[1] II. 41. 2. Donellus, 5, &c. Savigny, *Recht des Besitzes.* II. 43. 1. *Inst.* 4. 13. II. 43. 16, 43. 17, 43. 26, 43. 31. "Qui jure familiaritatis amici fundum ingreditur non videtur possidere, quia non eo animo ingressus est ut possideat licet corpore in fundo sit." II. 41. 2. 1. As to the traditio "longa manu" and "brevi manu," see II. hœc tit. 1. 21. and II. 41. 1. 9. § 5. II. 6. 2. 9. § 1. II. 12. 1. 9. § 9. II. 21. 2. 62. II. 18. 1. 94. "Non est enim corpore et actu necesse apprehendere possessionem, sed etiam oculis et affectu et argumento esse eas res quæ propter magnitudinem ponderis moveri non possunt, ut columnas, nam pro traditis eas haberi si in re præsenti consenserint et vina tradita videri cum claves cellæ vinariæ emtori traditæ fuerint." Savigny, *Recht des Besitzes*, 14—18.

[2] "Possessio per procuratorem ignoranti quæritur." II. 41. 2. 49. § 2.

that in a legal sense[1] (as in the case of peculium in the Roman law, or of a distant inheritance which has fallen to him) Titius may possess property of the existence[2] of which he is unconscious, and therefore that the maxim, "adipiscimur corpore et animo neque per se animo, aut per se corpore," though of general use is not of universal application. It is so far true that the grasp of a maniac[3] does not make him possess the thing he holds, and that the wish or intention of a miser does not give him possession of the property of his neighbour.

There were under the Roman system[4] two rights peculiar to civil as distinguished from natural possession; one the right given to the possessor of claiming the protection of the interdicts to maintain or restore possession[5]: "interdicta quæ possessionis causam habent:" to obtain which nothing beyond the fact of possession and the animus possidendi were requisite[6].

"Alium possessorem ministerio meo facio." "Procurator alienæ possessioni præstat ministerium." II. 41. 2. 18.

[1] "Quæsitum est cur ex peculii causâ per servum ignorantibus possessio acquireretur—Dixi utilitatis causâ—receptum." II. 41. 2. 44. § 2.

[2] See II. 41. 2. 15. 40: "quod servus vel procurator vel colonus teneat dominus videtur possidere, et ideo his dejectis ipse dejici de possessione videtur etiamsi ignoret eos dejectos per quos possidebat." II. 43. 16. 1. 22. "Procurator, si quidem mandante domino rem emerit, protinus illi adquirit possessionem." 41. 2. 42. § 2. II.

[3] "Furiosus et pupillus sine tutoris auctoritate non possunt incipere possidere, quia affectionem tenendi non habent, licet maxime corpore suo rem contingant; sicuti si quis dormienti aliquid in manu ponat." II. 41. 2. 1. § 3.

Savigny, *Recht des Besitzes Thémis,* Vol. III. p. 44. Warkönig, 244. Vol. I.

[4] "Possessio plurimum facti habet." Papinian, II. 46—19, and see the law Peregre profecturus, II. 41. 2. 44. "Possessio non tantum corporis sed et juris est." II. de acq. et amitt. poss. 49. § 1.

[5] II. 43. 1. 2. § 2: "Omnis de possessione controversia aut eo pertinet ut quod non possidemus nobis restituatur, aut ad hoc ut retinere nobis liceat quod possidemus." II. 43. 17. 1. § 4.

[6] "Separata est causa possessionis et usucapionis; nam vere dicitur quis

The other right[1] was that of usucapio, or exchanging by lapse of time a precarious for a permanent title. For this another element was requisite[2], i. e. "bona fides."

For these purposes possession was distinct from property, and the possessor, however weak his title, was protected[2] against a wrong-doer: "Adversus extraneos vitiosa possessio prodesse solet[3]."

The Roman lawyers were careful to keep the right of the possessor distinct from that of the right to the property. The English law has confounded both—absurdly. Before the question as to the property was decided, the Roman magistrate[4] settled the preliminary point on whom the burden of disproving the argument from possession was to be cast, and who was to enjoy the benefit of the presumptions which it furnished. Ulpian gives the instance of a widow dispossessed forcibly of an estate given to her by her husband during the marriage. The gift was invalid, but the widow had a right to

emisse, licet malâ fide, quemadmodum qui sciens alienam rem emit pro emptore possidet licet usu non capiat." II. 41. 4. 2. § 1. *Inst.* de usucap. 2. 6: "Jure civili constitutum fuerat ut qui bonâ fide ab eo qui dominus non erat, quum crediderit eum dominum esse, rem emerit...is eam rem si mobilis erat anno ubique, si immobilis biennio tantum in Italico solo usucapiat, ne rerum dominia in incerto essent."

[1] "Sa bonne foi lui tient lieu de titre." Domat. L. 3. § 3.

[2] "Quod ait Prætor in interdicto, nec vi, nec clam, nec precario alter ab altero possidetis, hoc eo pertinet ut si quis possidet vi aut clam aut precario, *si quidem ab alio prosit ei possessio*, si vero ab adversario suo, non debeat eum propter hoc quod ab eo possidet, vincere—has enim possessiones non debere proficere, palam est." II. 43. 17. 1. § 9.

[3] II. 41. 2. lex ult.: "nihil commune habet proprietas cum possessione." II. de poss. a. vel arm. 12. § 2: "Proprietas et possessio misceri non debent." lex ult. eod. Savigny, *Recht des Bes.* 2—4.

[4] Ordonnance 1667. tit. 38. art. 4 et 4. The pétitoire could not be brought forward till the possessoire had been decided.

the interdict for restitution: "Si maritus uxori do-
navit, eaque dejecta sit, poterit interdicto uti[1]."

The interdicts framed to establish[2] disputed possession were two: the one, the "uti possidetis," which
applied to immoveable; the other, the "utrubi,"
which applied to moveable property. "If," says the
Digest, "the litigants claiming property do not agree
which ought to enjoy the advantage of possession,
'possessoris commodo[3],' it must be determined by the
interdict." The interdict "uti possidetis" could not
be brought after a year from the time when the right
to bring it first occurred.

The interdicts "recuperandæ possessionis" lay
against him who had acquired possession, vi, clam,
or precario. They were therefore three. The interdict de vi[4] lay where there had been violence, whether by acts or atrocious threats. It applied to
things moveable and immoveable. It must be
brought within the year for the recovery of possession, but might be brought afterwards for the profits.

By it the person ejected was restored to his original possession, and obtained damages for the injury
he had sustained.

The interdict "de clandestinâ possessione[5]" lay

[1] II. de vi et vi armata, 1. § 10.

[2] II. 43. 17. uti possidetis. II. 43.
31. Utrubi Cod. 8. 6. Savigny, R. des
B. 37. 39. Gaius, 4. 150. Rates apud
399 = 499. Meermann, 7. 495 = 539.

[3] II. 43. 17. § 2. 3: "intra annum
quo primum experiundi potestas fuerit, agere permittam." II. de a. v. arm.
pot. 1. II. de v. S. 156.

[4] "Unde tu illum vi dejecisti aut

familia tua dejecit de eo, quæque ille
tunc sibi habuit, tantummodo intra
annum—post annum de eo, quod ad
eum qui vi dejecit pervenerit—judicium dabo." II. de vi et vi armatâ, 1.
Cicero pro Cæcin. 31, 32.

Possession of minerals in the tenant
though property in the lord. Keyse
v. Power, 2 Ell. and B. 144.

[5] "Clam possidere eum dicimus qui

against him who had furtively obtained possession
without the knowledge of his adversary.

The third interdict, "de precario," lay against a
holder at will who refused to give up what he had
been suffered to possess: "Quod precario ab illo
habes, aut dolo malo fecisti ut desineres habere, qua
de re agitur illi restituas:" II. de precario, l. 2.   It
might be brought after the year.   By it the holder
was answerable for all the loss[1] sustained by the
proprietor in consequence of his refusal to deliver it
to him.

Such is the general outline of a branch of law
which has much engrossed the attention of the German writers.   Paulus states truly that it is the root
of property: "Dominium rerum ex naturali possessione cœpisse[2]."   The forty-fourth law of the 41. 1.
chapter of the Digest illustrates the subject most
scientifically[3].   So does the law declaring that if
the creditor holding a pledge lets the pledge to the
owner of it, the creditor is still the possessor: "Cum
et animus mihi retinendi sit et conducenti non sit
animus possessionem apiscendi," in which the question is made to turn altogether on what in the

---

furtive ingressus est possessionem ignorante eo quem tibi controversiam
facturum suspicabatur et ne faceret
timebat." II. de a. v. a. poss. 6. Cujacius, Obs. 9. 33. Brissonius *de
Form.* 3. c. 12. Niebuhr, 2. 370.

[1] "Plane post interdictum editum
oportebit et dolum et culpam et omnem causam venire, nam ubi moram
quis fecit precario omnem causam
debebit constituere." II. eod. 3. 5.

Possessio—jus possessionis *animus*

sibi habendi.

Effects of possessio, by the Civil
Law.   1. Usucapio.   2. Interdicta.

Genera summa : *civilis ;* possessio
(simpliciter). Possessio *naturalis.*

Other divisions of possessio :
  bonæ = malæ fidei,
  veræ = quasi,
  justæ = vitiosæ,
  separate = joint.

[2] II. 41. 2. 1. 1—3.

[3] II. 13. 7. 37.

schools is called the *subjective* element, which should be compared with Papinian's law as to the inefficacy of the right of Postliminium to restore an interrupted possession, because "possessio plurimum facti habet[1]." In the following remarks the reader will find the topic examined in more detail.

Possession contrasted with property is a question of fact, as the latter is of law; but a fact which "*plurimum ex jure mutuatur,*" is mainly qualified by law.

It became necessary for the Romans to lay down accurate rules concerning it on account of the "usucapio" given by the civil law, by which possession ripened into property, and of the interdicts granted by the Prætor for the protection of the mere possessor.

The mere corporeal detention of an object did not necessarily constitute possession.

He was the possessor who held the thing "corpore et animo," ψυχῇ δεσπόζοντος, in the words of Theophilus. The "fur" and the "prædo" might possess[2]. But as the "animus" of the owner was wanting, neither the "usufructuarius," nor the "superficiarius[3]," nor the "conductor," nor the "commodatarius[3]," nor the "depositarius[4]," nor the "procurator[5]," nor the "qui ex edicto Prætoris in pos-

---

[1] II. 4. 6. 19.

[2] The passage which seems to contradict this, II. 47. 2. 1, only says that the malæ fidei possessor could not bring the "furti actio," which gave the double value. This is perfectly consistent with what I have stated, and indeed is a corollary from the admirable law, II. 50. 17. 134: "nemo ex suo delicto meliorem causam suam facere potest."

[3] II. 13. 6. 8. 10. 37. 11.

[4] II. 42. 1. 12.

[5] 43. 16. 1. § 22: "quod servus vel colonus vel procurator tenet dominus videtur possidere," &c.

sessionem missus est," could possess. But the interdict was granted, "singulari jure," to the "creditor
pignoratitius[1]," the "emphyteuta[2]," to him "apud
quem[3] res deposita est," if it was so agreed; to him
" qui precario[4] rem rogavit," unless it was otherwise
covenanted.

Savigny, in his celebrated treatise, divid:ng possession into naturalis and civilis, draws this distinction between them.

Possessio civilis, he says, is the possessio which
ripens by means of the usucapio into property.

Possessio naturalis is followed by no such consequence.

There are two kinds of the possessio naturalis:
either it is such a possessio as elicits the interdicta
in its defence, possessio per eminentiam; or it is not,
and then, according to the view I take, it is possessio
in a more narrow and ordinary sense.

The Possessor civilis is he who unites corporeal
apprehension or detention with the animus domini.

The Possessor naturalis is he whose detention is
a merely physical act, not qualified by any such
legally recognized intention: e. g. if the thing be
extra commercium, if he hold in another name as
colonus, &c., in this case there is only the "res
facti quæ jure civili infirmari non potest[5]." The conclusive passage against the view of Savigny is,
"Quod vulgo respondetur, causam possessionis ne-

[1] II. 41. 4. 12.
　　41. 3. 16.
[2] II. 2. 8. 15. § 1.
[3] II. 16. 3. 17. 1.

[4] II. 43. 26. 4. § 1.
　　43. 26. 6. § 2.
[5] II. 41. 2. 1. § 4. Vangerow, Vol.
1. p. 269.

minem sibi mutare posse, sic accipiendum, at ut possessio non solum civilis sed etiam naturalis intelligatur; et propterea responsum est neque eum apud quem res deposita aut cui commodata est lucri faciendi causâ pro hærede usucapere posse."

The common doctrine that no one can alter the origin of his possession is to be understood as applying not only to civil, but natural possession; and therefore it is laid down that neither the holder of a deposit, nor he to whom a thing has been lent, "lucri faciendi causa," can have the right "usucapere pro hærede." The argument arising from this text is rendered irresistible by the passage cited below, which seems to me irreconcilable with the view of Savigny[1].

He is ejected, says Ulpian[2], who possesses, whether civiliter or naturaliter, and in either case may apply for the interdict "de vi." If the wife be ejected from an estate given to her by her husband[3], she may (though the gift be invalid) obtain this interdict: not so the colonus.

The wife, the natural possessor, holding in her own name, could, because there was no true possessor in whose name it could be obtained, against a mere wrong-doer.

The colonus, being neither natural nor civil pos-

---

[1] II. 41. 3. 33. § 1, and see Gans' scholia on Gaius, p. 265.

[2] II. 43. 16. 1. § 9, 10. Vangerow, 1. 273.

[3] II. 43. 16. 1. § 10. So Paulus says, if I order the vendor of a thing I have bought to give it to my wife, and he delivers possession of it in conformity with my direction, he is exonerated "quia licet illa jure civili possidere non intelligatur certe tamen venditor nihil habet quod tradat." II. 24. 1. 26.

sessor, could not, because the landlord, the true possessor, was the person to obtain it.

This appears to me to illustrate my position. So
a slave[1] could not have the "animus domini,"
therefore not the civilis possessio, of his peculium;
but he might have the naturalis possessio of it.

It may be said, perhaps, to evade the difficulty,
that when a legal representative takes possession of
an object for Caius, without his knowledge, Caius
must be supposed to have a general will to ratify
the act.

The "colonus," the "inquilinus," the "depositarius," are "in possessione," but they do not possess,
for the "animus sibi habendi" is wanting to them.

The "possessio corpore[2]," says Pomponius, may
be in one man, and the "possessio animo" in another,
at the same time.

Thus, although possession and property were, as
we should bear in mind, fundamentally different
ideas in the Roman law, yet that law did not, as
ours has done, leave the idea of possession loose and
fluctuating, but imparted to it altogether, as far
as it could, legal relation and character. "Possessio," says Papinian, "non tantum corporis sed juris
est[3]."

The slave—the captive—the person who had
undergone the "maxima capitis diminutio," could
not have the "animus domini;" neither could the
"infans," or the "furiosus," unless with the consent

---

[1] II. 45. 1. 38. 7: "quamvis civili
jure servus non possideat tamen ad
naturalem possessionem hoc referen-
dum est."

[2] II. 43. 26. 15. § 4.

[3] II. 41. 3. 49. § 1.

of the tutor or curator[1]. The "pupillus" might, if it was for his benefit.

The object of possession must be corporeal; it must be the whole, where the parts have no independent existence, as in the case of moveables, "in re mobili"..."nunquam enim pro diviso possideri potest[2]."

Part of an estate might be taken into possession, in the name of the whole. Actual contact with the object was not necessary[3]; it might be symbolical; "vina tradita videri quum claves cellæ vinariæ emtori traditæ fuerint;" it was enough if the power of dealing with the object was given[4]; "manu longa tradita." Sometimes the will of the original owner, without any delivery, was sufficient to transfer possession of a thing actually in the custody of another[5].

The will to possess must have a definite object.

"Incerta pars nec tradi nec usucapi potest[6]."

"Incertam partem rei possidere nemo potest[7]."

More than one person could not at the same time possess the same thing[8].

---

[1] "Infans possidere recte potest si tutore auctore cœpit nam judicium infantis suppletur auctoritate tutoris." II. 41. 2. 31. § 2.

[2] II. 6. 1. 8, otherwise in the case of land.

II. 41. 4. 26.
    41. 3. 23.
    41. 3. 30. 1.

[3] 41. 2. 1. § 21. So "claves honor" gave the "merces" therein lying to the buyer. II. 41. 1. 9. 6.

[4] "Pecuniam quam mihi debes aut aliam rem si in conspectu meo ponere te jubeam efficitur ut et tu statim libereris et mea esse incipiat," &c. II. 46. 3. 79.

[5] II. 41. 1. 9. § 5.
II. 12. 1. 9. § 9.
II. 50. 17. 76.
II. 41. 2. 34.

[6] II. 41. 2. 26.

[7] 41. 2. 3. § 2.

[8] II. 4. 1. 2. 3. 5.
II. 13. 6. 5. § 15.
II. 43. 17. 3.
II. 43. 26. 15. § 4.

On the other hand, the mere naked fact of possession gave the possessor certain rights, "justa
enim an injusta possessio sit in hoc interdicto," the
uti possidetis, "nihil refert—qualiscunque enim possessor *hoc ipso quod possessor est* plus juris habet
quam ille qui non[1] possidet[2]."

So the "Prædo" stood in the light of a possessor; "qui interrogatus possideat responsurus sit
quia possideo; nec ullam causam possessionis possit dicere[3]." Whether the possession was just or
unjust turned upon the "causa." Of unjust possession there were three causes: clam—vi—precario.
The possessio which became property through the
usucapio, required a "justus titulus," a "bona fides"
in the possessor, and a thing capable of "usucapio."
This "possessio ad usucapionem" was called "civilis
possessio," and opposed to the "naturalis possessio[4]."
There might be several "causæ[5]" of possession.
But the possessor could not change the causa;
"nemo sibi ipse causam possessionis mutare potest[6]."

The result of what we have been considering
leads us to the conclusion that the differences be-

[1] II. 43. 17. 2.
      41. 2. 36.

[2] But the malæ fidei possessor
could not bring the "furti actio,"
which gave the double value of the
thing. II. 47. 2. 1: "sed nemo de
improbitate suâ consequitur actionem," which taken with 50. 17. 134.
§ 1, is, I think, in this way reconcile-
able with the other passages I have
cited.

[3] II. 5. 3. 11. 1.
      12. 13.

[4] II. 43. 16. 1. § 9: "Dejicitur is

qui possidet sive civiliter sive naturaliter possidet."

II. 10. 4. 3. 15: "Sciendum est
adversus possessorem hâc actione (ad
exhibendum) agendum, non solum
eum qui civiliter sed et eum qui
naturaliter incumbat possessioni."

[5] "Nec enim sicut dominium non
potest nisi ex unâ causâ contingere
ita et possidere ex unâ duntaxat causâ
possumus." II. 41. 2. 3. 4.

[6] II. 41. 2. 3. § 19: for the expla-
nation of the rule, see II. 41. 3. 33.
§ 1.

tween "dominium" and "possessio" are, first, that possession, though in its effects a consequence or question of law, is considered in itself a question altogether of fact. Secondly, the mere will of the owner did not in all cases displace the "dominium," e. g. if the person to whom a gift was made was unable or unwilling to accept it.

In the mean time, if the reader will refer to the remarkable law of the Pandects, 6. 1. 9, he will see how careful the Roman jurists were to guard against all these subtleties (which would have been so eagerly laid hold of and encouraged in our courts, as a means for exasperating chicane and protecting violence) from interfering with substantial justice. Ulpian says, "It shall be the duty of the judge in this action," the rei vindicatio, "to ascertain the fact, an reus possideat," then he enumerates several instances in which it might be said that the person having the physical power to give up or retain the thing, did not technically possess it. "But I," said Ulpian, "am of opinion that the thing may be effectually claimed from all who hold it, and in the power of whom it is to give it up," "ab omnibus qui tenent et habent restituendi facultatem peti posse,"—admirable words, which sweep away all the cobwebs under which chicane conceals its desire of trifling with truth and right[1].

---

[1] So the "ad exhib." II. 10. 4. 3. § 15.

Contrast this with the pettifogging which at once restored all the quibbles about the legal estate that had ruined so many families in eject-ment. "The trust estate shall not," said Lord Mansfield, "be set up in an ejectment to defeat the title of the cestui que trust in a clear case." Doe v. Pott. Douglas, 700. That it should have been necessary to lay down such

On the contrary, possession resting on fact ceases where the will is withdrawn. Thus Paulus tells us that the husband ceases to be the possessor of any thing he has given to his wife, though such gifts were by the Roman law void, "quoniam res facti jure civili infirmari non potest[1]."

It follows that "dominium" might be acquired without possession, for if an inheritance was accepted by the heir, all the hereditary rights accrued to him, but not possession: "Possessio tamen nisi naturaliter comprehensa ad nos non pertinet[2]." An exception was made in favour of the "usucapio," which the heir was allowed to take up and to complete, "quia possessio[3] defuncti quasi juncta descendit ad hæredem et plerumque nondum hæreditate aditâ completur."

Possession is natural or civil; natural, the physical detention of an object without the right or animus of the owner; civil, the detention sometimes not physical of a thing ex justâ causâ, and with the "animus domini[4]."

---

a rule in the latter half of the 18th century in England shews the sad condition of our jurisprudence. Still more characteristic of our narrowness is it that immediately after Lord Mansfield's death it became law again, that the trust estate should be set up for "that sole purpose." Our folly in matters of jurisprudence is almost incredible; I do not mean the folly of the "scorticanti," but of the larger half into which the species is divided, the "scorticati."

[1] II. 41. 2. 1. § 4.
[2] II. 41. 2. 23.

[3] II. 1. 9.
II. 4. 1. 3. 2. 3. 3, "naturalis possessio."
II. 43. 18. § 9, 10: "Dejicitur is qui possidet sive civiliter sive naturaliter."
[4] II. 41. 2. 10. 1. In the eye of the law the "animus domini" does not exist, whatever may be the purpose of the holder; e.g. if the thing be "extra commercium," a deposit. Vangerow, Vol. 1. p. 270.
II. 43. 16. 1. 9. § 10.
24. 1. 26.
"Saltus hybernos æstivosque ani-

The character of the will is described by Theophilus as ψυχὴ δεσπόζοντος διαφορὰ τοῦ κρατεῖν καὶ τοῦ νέμεσθαι αὕτη, ὅτι κρατεῖν ἐστι φυσικῶς κατέχειν, νέμεσθαι δὲ τὸ ψυχῇ δεσπόζοντος κατέχειν[1].

PRESCRIPTION[2].

The chief advantage which the Roman law gave to the "bonâ fide" possessor was the power of acquiring a title by prescription.

Prescription is the right which after undisputed possession of a thing for a time fixed by law, makes the thing so possessed our own. "Adjectio dominii," says Modestinus, "per continuationem possessionis, temporis lege definiti." Π. de usucap. 3.

The true basis of prescription is the perishable nature of man and all that belongs to him. It is necessary for the security of such a being that there should be a period when continued enjoyment should be the proof of right, and when the death of witnesses or the loss of documents should not impair his title to his estate, or deprive him of the means to resist an antiquated demand. "Usucapio fundi," says Cicero, "finis solicitudinis ac periculi litium." "It exists," says Gaius, § 44, "ne rerum dominia divitiis in incerto essent." "Usucapio rerum," says Neratius, "constituta est ut aliquis litium finis esset."

mo possidemus quamvis certis temporibus eos relinquamus." Π. 41. 2. 3. 11. Ad 29. Just. § 4. 2. 3. § 29. *Basilik.* 50. 2. 61.

[1] "Aliud est possidere, aliud in possessione esse; denique rei servandæ causâ, legatorum, damni infecti, non possident sed sunt in possessione custodiæ causâ."

νομή ἐστι φυσικῶς ἡ τοῦ πράγματος κατοχή· κατὰ δὲ τοὺς νόμους ἐστι ψυχὴ δεσπόζοντος κατοχή. Syn. *Basilic.* edit. secund. p. 431. cit. apud Vangerow, p. 270.

[2] "Humano generi patrona prescriptio." Cassiodorus. "Vetustas quæ semper pro lege habetur variorum minuendarum scilicet litium causâ." Π. 39. 3. 2.

Arbitrary in its term, it is fixed in its principle, for it rests upon the same basis with society itself; that compromise between occasional wrong and general right which is inseparable from the condition of a finite being. Therefore we may dismiss altogether the trivial topics in support of it which were urged in the decline of Roman jurisprudence[1], and which attorney-made judges, strangers to that and every other branch of knowledge, have with wonted perverseness picked up at second hand, and repeated to shew their learning, such as "vigilantibus non dormientibus," &c., and place this most beneficent doctrine on its real foundation. It may be worth our while to consider for a few moments its history among the Roman people.

Under the old Roman law[2] there were only certain things called "mancipi," which were capable of usucapio. Of these, moveables acquired the right in one year, and immoveables in two. This was the Law of the Twelve Tables.

The Prætor's edict extended this principle under the name of "longi temporis præscriptio" to incorporeal rights, and "res nec mancipi." The term which guarded the "bonâ fide" possessor was ten years "inter præsentes," and twenty years "inter absentes." After the lapse of that period he obtained a valid exceptio against any one who claimed the property.

If the possessor, after the prescribed time had

---

[1] Which is in the original Cod. 40. 7. 2: "ut sit aliqua inter desides et vigilantes differentia;" a reason worthy of Tribonian and Baron Dunce.

[2] "Usus authoritas fundi biennium, cæterarum unum annuus usus est."

elapsed, lost the property, an "actio utilis" was given to him for its recovery. "Justus Titulus" and "bona fides" were required to give the possessor the benefit of this principle.

This doctrine was partially changed under Constantine, but in the year 424, under Theodosius II., a law was enacted[1], which, with slight modifications, was embodied in the Code. The Code extended the same rule of prescription to all parts of the empire, and added a law that henceforth a thirty years' prescription should be sufficient in all cases, with the exception of the action "finium regundorum," a limitation that was afterwards abolished. By another law of Justinian, the thirty years' prescription was reiterated, in spite of "verbosa quorundam interpretatio," as the law for all suits but the "hypothecaria actio," against which forty years were requisite[2]. The law of Justinian made three years' possession a good title, "firmum jus," to moveables.

It appears from this historical summary that all suits were at first imprescriptible. That the principle of prescription having been applied to some, was gradually extended to all. Hence the phrase, "perpetua actio," which at first meant an imprescriptible action[3], came to signify an action that might be brought within thirty years.

In order to found a title on prescription, the

[1] Savigny, *System,* Vol. v. p. 278.
Cod. Theod. l, 11. de act. certo tempore, fin. 4. 14.
Cod. de præscript. 30. 7. 39. 3.
[2] *Basilika,* 10. 4. αὐτοκινητὰ διὰ τριετίας, Meermann, *Thes.* 5 = 65.
Donellus, 5. 4. *Instit.* h. t.

Cod. 7. 40. 1. § 1. The Lawgiver complains that the law had been revived in many cases, "iteratis fabulis sæpe recreata."
L. Un. C. de usucap. transformandâ.
[3] Inst. de perpetuis, 4. § 12.

possession ought to be a possession "animo domini," bonâ fide, continued, peaceable, and founded on a "justus titulus,"—"animus domini," that is, the possessor must hold it as his own, not as an assignee, or trustee, or mortgagee. A man[1] may possess a thing bonâ fide, though he purchases it, "a non domino," even if he knew the vendor not to be the owner, if there was reasonable ground that he had the right to dispose of it, as in the case of a "procurator," or a "tutor :" " Bonæ fidei emtor esse videtur qui aut ignoravit eam rem alienam esse aut putavit eum qui vendidit jus vendendi habere."

The "bona fides" then is the reasonable belief of the possessor that he has acquired the property of the thing he possesses : thus if my agent purchase an estate for me without my knowledge, although I become the possessor of it immediately, while I am so ignorant, that possession cannot be the origin of a title by prescription : "Si emptam rem mihi procurator ignorante me, meo nomine apprehenderit, quamvis possideam eam non usucapiam." II. de usucap. 47.

The purchaser[2] of a thing which he knew did not belong to the vendor when he purchased it, though he has possession, has not such a possession as will found the usucapio. The possession founded on an error in fact might be the foundation[3] of a prescriptive title[4], but possession founded on an error

---

[1] II. 50. 16. 109.

[2] "Separata est causa possessionis et usucapionis; nam vere dicitur quis emisse sed malâ fide, quemadmodum qui sciens alienam rem emit pro emptore possidet licet usu non capiat."

II. pro empt. 2. § 1.

[3] "Qui a quolibet rem emit quam putat ipsius esse bonâ fide emit." De contrah. empt. 27. II. 11.

[4] "Nunquam in usucapionibus juris error possessori prodest."

in law could not[1]. "Bona fides" was so essential
that any one believing, though erroneously, that his
possession was not such as to give rise to the usucapio, could not prescribe for what he so possessed.

The Roman law was satisfied if the "bona
fides" existed at the commencement of the possession, "initio possessionis[2]," says Papinian. "Si eo
tempore quo res mihi traditur putem vendéntis esse
deinde cognovero alienam esse perseverat per lon-
gum tempus capio[3]."

The avarice of the dignified[4] ecclesiastics which
as soon as they could usurp power became the
scandal and scourge of Christendom, introduced a
very important change in this doctrine. Gratian
quotes it in the terms of the Roman law. But two
decretals, one in the time of Alexander the Third,
and the other in the time of Innocent the Third,
require a continued "bona fides," i.e. they require
that during the whole time of the possession it never
should come to the possessor's knowledge that the
origin of the property he held was unlawful. To
say nothing of the condition of Europe when these
decrees were promulgated, which must have rendered them a source of almost interminable litiga-

[1] "Siquis id quod possidet non
putat sibi per leges licere usucapere
dicendum est etiam si erret non procedere tamen usucapionem." II. de
usucap. 32. § 1.
[2] II. 44. § 4. dict. tit. Cod. de
usucap. transf. 7. 31. lex usuc.
Richeri, § 662 sq.
[3] II. de acq. rer. dom. 48. § 1.
Julianus gives a very wide definition
of the bonæ fidei emptor, which has
puzzled interpreters a good deal. II.

22. 1. 2. 5. § ult.
[4] Novell. 18. 2.
Cod. 24. de sacrosanctis Eccl. Justinian extended the time of prescription as against the church to 100
years. In 491, 40 years had been
fixed on. The abuses were so enormous that Justinian was obliged to
restore the old law. Nov. 131. c. 6.
The most efficacious of all laws made
to check the rapacity of the church was
that drawn up by D'Aguesseau, 1749.

tion, as two-thirds of the soil of the continent had probably at one time or other belonged to the Church, it is easy to imagine the application of such a rule, and its tendency to increase the scandalous possessions of the clergy[1].

The onus[2] of proving Dolus lay on the person asserting it, "quamvis in exceptione."

CONTINUANCE[3].

The time required, as we have seen, was various. Three years were required to give a title to moveables; ten years (inter præsentes), twenty years (inter absentes) to immoveable property. The "præsentes," according to Justinian's rule, were those who lived in the same province, the "absentes," those who lived in another. It was not necessary for the possessor to hold all the time by his own title, he might profit by a derivative one, the heir might profit by the testator's possession, the buyer by the seller's, the donee by the donor's.

Possession might be interrupted by natural (as

[1] Savigny, *System*, 5. 328. Another useful doctrine was that prescription did not run in times of heresy against the Church: "In præscriptione contra ecclesiam Romanam schismatum tempora non numerantur." c. placuit. 1. c. cum vobis. 14. c. de quarta. 4. c. auditis. 15.c. 1. ne sede vacante quid &c.

"Bona fides per totum præscriptionis tempus necessaria est." c. ult. hic. c. possessor 2. de reg. juris in 6.

"Romana ecclesia tribunalem præscriptionem contra ecclesiam non admittit." Cap. 4. x. de Præsc. Nov. 111.c. 1. Nov. 131. c. 6. x. de Præsc. 2. 24. 8.

"Unde oportet ut qui præscribit in nulla temporis parte rei habeat conscientiam alienæ." Trin. 3. cap. ult. de Præscript.

[2] II. 22. 3. 18. 1.
Cod. 2. 21. 6.

[3] II. 44. 3. 14. § 1. "Plane tribuuntur accessiones possessionum his qui in locum aliorum succedunt."

II. 41. 2. 13. §9: II. 41. 3. 14: "Id tempus venditoris prodest emtori quo antequam venderet possedit." ib. 14: "de accessionibus possessionum nihil in perpetuum neque generaliter definire possumus, consistunt enim in sola æquitate."

opposed to legal) and by legal causes. Naturaliter[1], by violence of man, or of natural agents, streams, or the sea, &c.; nor does it signify whether the possession was forcibly interrupted by the real owner or not[2]. Civil interruption[3] takes place when steps are taken to recover by legal means from the holder of the thing in question. Such is citation, "litis contestatio[4]."

JUSTUS TITULUS[5].

Justinian enumerates the following causes of a "justus titulus," i. e. of that title which might lead the possessor of another man's property to suppose it his own.

1. Pro emptore[6], purchase. 2. Pro soluto[7], payment. 3. Pro hærede[8], supposed heir. 4. Pro donato[9], gift. 5. Pro derelicto[10], thing abandoned by the owner. 6. Pro legato[11], bequest. 7. Pro dote[12], dower. 8. Pro suo. "Pro suo possessio[13] talis est

[1] "Naturaliter interrumpitur possessio cum quis de possessione vi dejicitur vel alicui res eripitur." II. de usucap. 5, the excellent law "sin vi dejectus est perinde habendus est ac si possideret." de acq. poss. II. 27. applies only to the spoliator.

[2] Ib. "nec eo casu quicquam interest is qui usurpaverit dominus sit necne." II. de reg. juris, 45. II. de usucap. 21: if the possessor gave the thing possessed to the real owner as a pledge or a deposit or a lease, the possession was interrupted, "neque pignus, neque locatio, neque emtio rei suæ consistere potest."

[3] Cod. de ann. except. l. 2. Cod. de acqu. poss. l. 10. *Coutûme de Paris*, 1. 13: "quiconque a joui et possédé sans inquiétation."

[4] There is an old writer on the Canon Law who says Adam could not have been turned out of Paradise unless he had been summoned to account for his conduct.

[5] Instit. hoc tit. §§ si quis a non Domino.

[6] II. 41. 4.

[7] Cod. 41. 5.

[8] II. 41. 5.

[9] 41. 6. [10] 41. 7. [11] 41. 8.

[12] 41. 9. 7. 26. 7. 28. 7. 29.

[13] 41. 10.

"Pignori rem acceptam usu non capimus quia pro alieno possidemus." II. 41. 3. 13.~ "Id quod quis cum suum esse existimaret possederit usucapiet etiamsi falsa fuerit ejus existimatio." It must however be "probabilis error," II. 41. 10. 5. § 1. "justa causa erroris," II.41. 4. 11.

cum dominium nobis acquiri putamus et ex eâ causâ possidemus." Π. pro suo 1.

It matters not to the "justus titulus" whether the owner, from whom the thing is acquired, be owner from a lucrative or an onerous title, by donation or purchase. But he must be owner, and not entitled to the possession, or entrusted with it, for a particular purpose, consistent with, or implying the fact that another is the proprietor, as in the case of the "precarium," "locatio[1]," &c.

Things which could not legally be possessed could not be prescribed for; such were things sanctæ, sacræ, religiosæ, publicæ, and "liberi homines[2]."

The "memoria operis facti[3]" might be proved by hearsay.

Certain things were withdrawn from the operation of the rule as to prescription, "peculium adventitium," Cod. 6. 60. 1. Property belonging to children of a first marriage, Nov. 22. 24. Fundus Dotalis, Π. 23. 5. 16. Cod. de jure Dotium, 5. 12. 30. These are of less importance, but to them[4] must be added stolen things, according to a law of the Twelve Tables, and the Lex Atricia (about A.U.C. 560). But the produce[5] of the things stolen were not exempted

---

[1] Π. 43. 16. 1. § 9.
    41. 2. 3. 18. 6. § 1. 10. § 1.
[2] "Usucapionem recipiunt maxime res corporales, exceptis rebus sanctis sacris publicis populi Romani et civitatum, item liberis hominibus." Π. 41. 39. Cod. 7. 22. 3. Inst. de usucap. et longi temp., præscript. 1. § 1. Cod. 7. 39. 6.
[3] Π. 22. 3. 28: "quum omnium hæc est opinio nec audiisse, nec vi-

disse quum id opus fieret, neque ex iis audiisse qui vidissent aut audiissent."
[4] Inst. 2. 6. 2. 3.
    Π. 41. 3. 4. § 6—33.
    50. 16. 215.
Gaius, 2. § 45. 49. A. Gell. N. Att. 17. 7.
[5] Π. 41. 3. 4. § 19. 1. 10. § 2. 1. 33.
    45. 1. 26.
    47. 2. 48. § 5.

from usucapio, unless in the hands of the thief. The young of human beings and of animals stolen were however res furtivæ, even though the mother had borne them in the house of a bonâ fide possessor.

This inherent vice in possession was however purged away, if the thing came back to the possession of the owner. It was not sufficient if it had come[1] to the hands of his representative without his knowledge.

Or if, having been stolen from the temporary holder, as a procurator, or a creditor, it came back to his possession.

This happened when it was so far in his possession, "ut avelli non possit[2]."

Or if it was in his power to recover it, "si rei vindicandæ potestatem habuerit."

Or if by a lawful transaction the owner transferred the property to the actual possessor.

To this list must be added, "res vi possessæ[3]," not "amissæ[4]." If a malæ fidei possessor[5] of moveables sold them, he was guilty of theft.

According to the lex Julia repetundarum[6], nothing given in violation of that law to the governor of a province could be prescribed for.

---

[1] II. 41. 3. 4. § 6. 12. 21. 49.
In. 2. 6. 8.
4. 1. 12.
II. 41. 4. 7. § 3. 7.
47. 2. 8. 4. 20. § 1.
50. 16. 215.
[2] II. 41. 34. § 12.
41. 47. 7.

II. 47. 2. 6.
[3] Gaius, 2. 45. Inst. 2. 6. § 2.
II. 41. 3. 33. § 2.
[4] 41. 3. 22. § 4. eod. 33. § 2.
[5] Inst. 2. 6. § 3.
[6] II. 48. 11. 8. 8. § 1.
41. 4. 48.

Neither could materials[1] belonging to one man, and worked up into the building of another, so long as the building stood.

By the Twelve Tables[2], the five feet on each side of the boundary line were withdrawn from usucapio.

If the law prohibited alienation[3], it prevented usucapio: "si res talis sit ut eam lex aut constitutio alienari[4] prohibeat, eo casu Publiciana non competit, quia his casibus neminem prætor tuetur—ne contra leges facias."

---

[1] II. 41. 1. 7. § 11.
  41. 3. 23. § 2.
[2] Cic. *de Legibus*, 1. 21.
  Cod. 3. 39. 6.
[3] II. 23. 5. 16.

[4] II. 6. 2. 12. § 4.
  But see "si ab eo emas quem prætor vetuit alienare, *idque tu scias*, usucapere non potes." II. 41. 3. 12.

CHAPTER IV.

GENERAL VIEW.

DE DOMINIO[1].

THERE were before Justinian three kinds of dominium: 1st, Nudum jus Quiritium; 2dly, the Dominium naturale, in bonis; 3dly, the Quiritarium junctum naturali.

In order to constitute the dominium Quiritarium[2] it was requisite that there should be "jus commercii" in the owner; 2dly, that the thing itself should be "in commercio;" 3dly, "acquisitio civilis." Acquisitio civilis was of two classes, inter vivos and mortis causâ. Inter vivos was twofold: 1st of "rerum mancipi," which was by "mancipatio[3];" 2dly, of rerum "nec mancipi[4]," which might be by Traditio: in jure cessio, usus, or usucapio.

ACQUISITIO MORTIS CAUSA.

Legatum vindicationis—legatum præceptionis—caducum.

[1] II. 6. 1. De rei vind.
6. 2. De Publicanâ in rem actione. Haubold, p. 278.
Heineccius, *Ant. R.* lib. 2. tit. 1. § 19, 20, 22—25. Lib. 4. tit. 6. § 24, 25.
Hugo, *Lehrbuch d. g. d. R. R.* p. 148. ed. 9.
[2] L. Jab. 3. Varro, *de Re R.* 2. 10.

Niebuhr, 2. 119.
Ulpian. *Frag.* 19. § 2—17.
[3] Gaius, *Inst.* 2. § 119—122.
[4] II. 15. 1. De Peculio.
II. 41. 1. De acquirendo rerum Dominio.
II. 41. 3. De usurpationibus et usucapionibus 41. 4—10. Pro emtore.
Inst. 2. 1. 2. 6. 2. 9.

Vis—rei vindicatio.

The requisites for this kind of property were a "res quæ est in commercio;" adquisitio, by the methods of acquiring property pointed out above originating from a person not the owner, "a non domino."

Natural: occupatio, Traditio, rei mancipi (irregular transfer) longi temporis possessio: fideicommissum. Vis: Publiciana in rem actio. Exceptio rei' venditæ et traditæ.

Increase common to the Dominium Quiritarium and naturale: 1, per accessionem; 2, per fructus.

Justinian's[2] alteration will be found in the reference below.

The peculiar actions to which the Dominium gave rise were; 1, rei vindicatio; 2, Publiciana in rem actio; 3, actio communi dividendo; 4, actio ad exhibendum.

The right of property[3] is not absolute, but modified by the exigences of the state in which it exists, and by the institutions of which it is upheld.

---

[1] II. 6. 1. de rei vindic.
II. 6. 2. de Public. in rem actione. Hugo, Lehrbuch, ed. 9. p. 148. eod. 763. Heineccius, Ant. T. R. lib. 2. tit. 1. § 19. lib. 4. tit. 6. §§ 24, 25.

[2] "De nudo jure Quirit. tollenda." Cod. l. un. Ulpian. Frag. 1. § 16. Meermann, Thes. 7. p. 7. 46.

[3] Cod. Mandati, l. 21. "Dominium est jus utendi et abutendi re suâ quatenus juris ratio patitur." Abutendi in this passage is not to be translated abuse, but to consume or wear out by use, e.g. burning wood, and is employed in opposition to "uti," which means only to use a thing salvâ rerum substantiâ.

Examples of such limitations are to be found in some of the most luminous and instructive chapters of the Roman law, under the head, Actiones de tigno juncto, aquæ pluviæ arcendæ.

Property can only then be said to be limited when the owner is prevented from doing something with it, or obliged to suffer interference with it.

The "cautio damni infecti" is rather a duty imposed on the proprietor than a limitation of his right.

The fundamental maxim on this head is, "Qui jure suo utitur neminem lædit." This principle is clearly recognized in the laws of the Digest, allowing the intercepting of subterranean springs, and erection of buildings[1].

Sometimes, however, though very rarely, the "animus[2]" with which an act is done determines its legality.

---

[1] Acton v. Blundell, 12 M. and W. 324.

Dickinson v. the Grand Junction Company, which of course unsettles the principle laid down in Acton v. Blundell, Excheq. 7. 282, may be referred to by the student of English Law; but the jurist will consult II. 39. 2. 24. 12. "in domo meâ puteum aperio, quo aperto venæ putei precisæ sunt, an tenear? ait Trebatius, non teneri me damni infecti; neque enim existimari operis mei vitio damnum tibi dari in eâ re in quâ jure meo usus sim;" and 26 eod. See Wright v. Howard, Leach, v. C. 1. S, and S. 203. Broom, *Comm. on E. Law*, page 707. Selwyn, *N. P.* last ed. 1139. "Denique Marcellus ait," (Marcellus was not a Puisne Judge,) "cum eo qui in suo fundo fodiens vicini fontem averterit nihil posse agi." Those two lines and a half are worth to suitors a volume of the vacillating ambiguous trash heaped up in our reports; in which, the moment a gleam of principle appears, it is darkened by hundreds of doubts, exceptions, qualifications, "about it, Goddess, and about it," expressed in the style of our reported judgments.

[2] II. 39. 3. 2. 9. "Idem Labeo ait, si vicinus torrentem, ne aqua ad eum perveniat, et hoc modo sit effectum, ut vicino noceatur, agi cum eo aquæ pluviæ arcendæ non posse . . . quæ sententia verior est: si modo non hoc animo fecit, ut tibi noceat, sed ne sibi noceat." I have discovered no other law based on this principle in civil matters.

Whatever was a natural consequence of the exercise of the right of property on one spot of ground, must be submitted to by the neighbour without any distinct servitude[1], e. g. the vapour of a cheese factory.

If the public road became impassable from a sudden accident, "fluminis impetu vel ruinâ," the neighbour must allow a passage over his land[2].

To this head must be referred the law "de glande legendâ[3]," glans being used for every kind of fruit, as "tignum" is for every kind of material used in building. "Glandis nomine omnes fructus continentur," regulating the right to gather fruit fallen on a neighbour's land; and the law "de arboribus cædendis," by which, if a tree overhung the house of a neighbour, he might cut it down; and if it overhung his land, trim it up to fifteen feet from the soil[4].

DOMINIUM[5], SPECIAL.

Dominium, in the strict sense of the Roman law, was the exclusive right to the complete enjoyment of an external object. This included the right, not only to use (utendi) but to destroy (abutendi) that object.

[1] II. 8. 5. 8. § 5 : "sed et interdictum uti possidetis poterit locum habere si quis probibeatur qualiter velit, suo uti."

[2] II. 8. 6. 14. § 1.

[3] II. 43. 28. L. un.

[4] II. 43. 27. 1.

[5] Theophilus, *Paraphrasc*, uses the words ἐν νόμου δεσποτείᾳ. Theophilus, 5. § 4. and Varro, *de R. R.* 2. 10. n. 4,

dominus legitimus.

II. 6. 1. Heineccius, *A. R.* 2. tit. 1. Lib. 4. tit. §§ 24. 25.

II. 6. 1. Hugo, *Lehrbuch*, p. 148 sq. 433. 763-sq. 932. Ed. 9.

II. 10. 1. Finium Regundorum.

39. 2.

43. 9. 27. 43. 28. 47. 3. Hein. *Inst.* § 337.

In the early age of Roman jurisprudence there was but one kind of dominium, that which entitled the owner to a "vindicatio ex jure Quiritium." Afterwards there was recognized a twofold dominion, that "ex jure Quiritium," "legitimum," to which the word dominium was more emphatically appropriated, and that which a man was said to have "in bonis[1]," which the Prætor gave an action to recover. Gradually the two kinds of property were assimilated, and in the time of Justinian all difference between them was swept away[2].

Dominium therefore is that right which gave rise to the "actio vindicandi," its object.

Dominium may be plenum[3], as described above, or minus plenum, i.e. the naked property severed from the enjoyment.

"Recte dicimus[4] eum fundum totum nostrum esse etiam cum ususfructus alienus est quia ususfructus non dominii pars sed servitutis sit."

The thing which is the object of "dominium" may cease to be, for its owner, either naturally, i.e. when it is worn out, consumed, or worsened; or civilly, i.e. by alienation.

Alienation may be either by an act which takes

---

[1] "δεσπότης βουστάσιος." Theoph. *Inst.* 5. § 4.

[2] Cod. de nudo jure Quirit. toll. 7. 25.

[3] II. 23. 3. 78, de jure Dotium. II. 7. 4. 2. "Si duobus separatim alternis annis ususfructus relinquatur continuis annis proprietas nuda est: quum si legatarium unum substituas, cui alternis annis legatus sit ususfructus, plena sit apud hæredem pro-prietas eo tempore quo jus fruendi legatario non est. Quodsi ex duobus illis alter decedat, per vices temporum plena proprietas erit."

[4] II. de v. S. 25. Inst. de usu. 2. 3. "Cum finitus fuerit totus ususfructus revertitur scilicet ad proprietatem, et ex eo tempore nudæ proprietatis dominus incipit plenam in re habere potestatem." *Inst.* 2. 4. § 4.

place between the living, or by the testament of the dead. It may be for a time, or irrevocable.

As the right of property in a thing is that which gives the right of excluding all others from its enjoyment, it is an essential consequence of it that two persons cannot have this right over every part of the same thing: "Celsus ait, duorum in solidum dominium esse non potest." П. Commod. 5. § 15.

But it is possible that several persons may have a joint property in a single object, i. e. each of such persons may possess not a tangible share, but a share recognized by law in a single object: "Plures[1] in uno fundo dominium juris intellectu non divisione corporis obtinent."

The person entitled to this intellectual share is entitled[2] to his portion of its profits, may alienate it, or require that it shall be changed into a material one; on the other hand, he cannot, without the assent[3] of his co-proprietors, dispose of the common object, or any of its parts.

The modes[4] of acquiring dominion by the Roman law were natural, i. e. by the law of nations, or civil, i. e. such as were the creation of the Roman Civil Law.

---

[1] П. de leg. 66. 2. "Unusquisque portionem habet pro indiviso." П. 10. 3. 6. 1. "Communem rem habent." П. 10. 1. 4. § 6. "Communis est (servus) pro partibus indivisis." 45.3. 5.

[2] П. 17. 2. 68. Cod. de commun. divid. 3. 37. 5. П. 10. 3. "Communi dividendo." L. 15. 20. 27.

[3] "Sabinus in re communi neminem dominorum jure facere quidquam invito altero posse—unde manifestum

est prohibendi jus esse, in re enim pari potiorem causam esse prohibentis constat." П. 10. 3. 28.

[4] П. 41. 1. 1. Inst. 2. 1. 11. Theophilus, 2. 1.

De acq. rer. d. 1. § 1. "Omnia igitur animalia quæ terrâ, mari, cælo, capiuntur, id est, feræ bestiæ, et volucres, pisces, capientium fiunt." Cod. 5. § 2. "Feras bestias quas vivariis incluserimus, a nobis possideri, sed

The natural modes of acquiring dominion were[1]:
Occupation. The apprehension[2] of an object not
appropriated, with the intention of making it our
own. Under this head may be ranged the right of
the hunter to wild animals which he had captured.
The right of the finder to the thing found. The
right to the goods of an enemy.

Delivery[3]. The act by which a thing is transferred to us for the purpose of giving us the property
therein. To make a valid delivery, the person delivering must have the right and the will[4] to transfer

eos pisces qui in stagno sunt aut feras quæ in silvis circumseptis vagantur a nobis non possideri quoniam relictæ sunt in libertate naturali." Inst. de rer. div. § 13. "Nec interest quoad feras bestias et volucres utrum in suo fundo quisque capiat an in alieno." II. 47. 10. 13. § ult. II. 8. 3. 16.

Gaius, de acq. dom. 3. "Quod nullius est id ratione naturali occupanti conceditur. Nec interest quod ad feras bestias et volucres utrum in suo fundo quisque capiat an in alieno. Plane qui alienum fundum ingreditur venandi aucupandive gratiâ potest a domino si is providerit jure prohiberi, ne ingrederetur." How much guilt and misery would have been spared if this plain rule of natural justice, laid down by benighted heathens, had not been utterly and savagely repudiated by Christian legislators in England. See moreover, and carefully consider, the admirable law "in laqueum." II. 41. 1. 55.

[1] De a. r. d. 31. § 1. "Thesaurus est vetus quædam depositio pecuniæ, cujus non extat memoria, ut jam dominium non habeat, sic enim fit ejus qui invenerit quod non alterius sit." Inst. de rer. div. § 39. "At si

quis in alieno loco, non datâ ad hoc operâ sed fortuito invenerit, dimidium domino soli concessit et dimidium inventori." Cod. 10. 15. L. 11. II. de jure fisci, 3. § 10. Bynkershoek, *Obs.* 2. § 4. p. "Quæ ex hoste capiuntur jure gentium statim capientium fiunt." II. de a. r. d. 5. § 7. II. de capt. et postlim. 49. 15. 20. § 1. Cujac. *Obs.* 4. 9, "publicatur ager ex hostibus captus." II. h. t. 20. 1. Distinction between hostis and prædator. II. 50. 16. 118. eod. 234. II. 41. 2. 1. § 5, 6, 7, 8, 9, and 20. II. 1. 5. 4.

[2] "Apprehensio etiam oculis et affectu fieri potest." II. 41. 2. 1. § 21.

[3] "Traditio nihil aliud transferre debet vel potest ad eum qui accipit quam est apud eum qui tradit." II. de a. r. d. 20. "Nunquam nuda traditio transfert dominium sed ita si venditio aut aliqua justa causa præcesserit propter quam traditio sequetur." II. eod. 31. Theophilus, 2. 1. 40.

[4] II. de obl. et act. 58. II. de acq. vel amitt. poss. 34. "Neque impedit translationem dissensus dantis et accipientis, circa causam dandi et accipiendi, dummodo obligatio certa præcesserit in tradente." II. de a. r. d. 9. Inst. de rer. div. 46.

the property; the person receiving it must have the power and intention to receive.

Delivery might be real or symbolical[1], "veluti clavium traditione."

Perception of the produce of the thing.

The *bonâ fide* possessor of what belonged to another was entitled "pleno jure" to the produce[2] of it. This right vested at the moment when the produce was severed from the thing producing it. "Julianus ait, fructuarii fructus tum fieri quum eos perceperit, bonæ fidei autem possessoris mox quum a solo separati sunt[3]." This right included natural produce as well as that which the skill and labour of the possessor had been employed to create[4].

The produce not gathered did not become the property of the possessor: "Dominus de fructibus ab eo *consumtis* agere non potest."

Accession. This might happen from the gradual deposit of alluvial soil by a river suddenly leaving its channel, or it might happen from the act of man, such as from building or planting on the soil. The Rule of Roman Law[5] was "omne quod inædificatur

---

[1] Π. de pecul. 8. Π. de adq. amitt. poss. 3. 1. Π. 18. 1. 74. Π. de a. r. d. 9. § 6. Π. 46. 3. 79. "Pecuniam quam mihi debes aut aliam rem si in conspectu meo ponere te jubeam, efficitur ut et tu statim liberaris et mea esse incipiat, nam tum quod a nullo corporaliter ejus rei possessio detineretur adquisita mihi, et quodammodo longâ manu tradita existimanda est." Inst. de rer. div. "Interdum etiam sine traditione nudâ voluntas domini sufficit ad rem transferendam." Vinerii *Select. Quæst. rit.* 1. 40.

[2] de usuris. 25. Π.

[3] Π. 7. 4. 13. Π. de furtis, 49. § 6. "ex furtivis equis nati statim ad bonæ fidei emptorem pertinebunt."

[4] "Bonæ fidei emptor non dubie percipiendo fructus etiam ex alienâ re, interim suos facit, non tantum eos qui diligentiâ et operâ ejus pervenerunt, sed omnes, quia quod ad fructus attinet loco domini pæne est." Inst. de rerum div. 35. Π. de usucap. 4. 19. Π. fin. reg. 4. § 2.

[5] Π. 47. 3. 1. de tigno juncto. Π. de a. r. d. 60. Π. rer. vindic.

solo, solo cedit[1]." By the law of the 12 Tables the
proprietor of a tignum (which word was used to
denote every species of material) used in another
man's building could not claim the restoration of the
tignum itself, but double its value as a compensation.
So the rule was "plantæ quæ terræ coalescunt[2], solo
cedunt; eâdem ratione frumenta quoque quæ sata
sunt solo cedere intelliguntur."

The property in letters (licet aureæ) passed to the
owner of the paper[3] on which they were written. For
painting it was established "tabulam picturæ cedere."
So where[4] one thing was united to another in such
a manner as to be inseparable from it without the
destruction of one or both (confusio, commixtio[5]),
e. g. purple woven into a garment, a jewel set in
gold, mulsum made of one man's wine and another
man's honey, the property became joint, or went to
the *bonâ fide* owner of the principal thing, who was
bound to make compensation[6] to the other owner.

---

23. § 6. "lex 12 tabularum neque
solvere permittit tignum furtivum
ædibus vel vineæ junctum, neque vin-
dicare, quod providenter lex effecit
ne vel ædificia hoc prætextu diruantur
vel vinearum cultura turbetur."

[1] II. de a. r. d. 7. § 10.

[2] Inst. de rer. divis. II. de a. r.
d. l. 9. "Arbor radicitus emta et in
alio posita, priusquam coaluerit, prioris domini est—ubi coaluit agro cedit."
II. de a. r. d. § 2. II. 10. 3. 19.
II. de a. r. d. 7. 13.

[3] Inst. de rer. divis. § 31.

[4] "Si armario vel navi tabulam
meam vel ansam scypho junxeris, vel
emblemata phialæ, vel purpuram ves-

timento intexeris, aut brachium statuæ
coadunaveris." II. de aur. arg. leg.
7. § 2. "Si tuum scyphum alieno
plumbo plumbaveris, alienove argento
ferruminaveris, non dubitatur scyphum tuum esse et a te recte vindicari." II. de a. r. d.

[5] "Si quid quod ejusdem naturæ
est ita confusum est atque commix-
tum ut diduci et separari non possit,
non totum sed pro parte esse vin-
dicandum (Pomponius scribit), ut puta
meum et tuum argentum in massam
reductum est, erit nobis commune."
II. 6. 1. 3. § 2.

[6] II. de rei vindic. 23. § 4. "In
omnibus istis in quibus mea res per

In some cases the owner of the property incorporated "agere potest ut separentur."

Another[1] kind of the accessio was called "specificatio," when the materials belonging to one man were wrought into a new form by another. The Sabinians held the property to be in the owner of the raw material, the Proculians held it to be in the workman. Justinian laid down the rule that if the materials could be restored to their original form, as in the case of a silver vessel, they should belong "domino materiæ," if they could not "eum esse dominum qui fecerit."

METHODS OF ACQUIRING PROPERTY BY THE CIVIL LAW.

The Civil Law gave the right of property in specific and separate objects, "res singulares," or in an assemblage of objects considered as a whole, "per universitatem," *e. g.* a flock.

The means[2] to enforce the right of the proprietor to a specific corporeal object was called "rei vindicatio," *i. e.* a real action which the owner might bring against the possessor of such an object.

It lay against the possessor by the civil as well

prævalentiam alienam rem trahit, meamque efficit, si eam rem vindicem, per exceptionem doli mali cogar pretium ejus quod acceperit dare."

[1] Inst. de rer. div. § 25.

II. de a. r. d. 25. L. 27. § 1. "Si ære meo et argento tuo conflato aliqua species facta sit, non erit ea

nostra communis, quia quum diversa materia æs atque argentum sit ab artificibus separari et in pristinam materiam reduci solet." II. 41. 1. 12. § 1.

[2] II. 6. 1. "In rem actio competit ei qui aut jure gentium aut jure civili dominium acquisivit." 23. eod.

as against the possessor by the natural law,—against any one, in short, who detained the thing and had the restitution of it in his power. It lay against the heir, unless he had ceased to be the possessor of it, or "quatenus locupletior factus est[1]," and against him who before the "lis" was "contestatus," had fraudulently got rid of the possession, "sed et is qui ante litem contestatam dolo malo desiit possidere."

The action[2] lay against the supposed possessor, who undertook to defend the action, though he was not in fact the possessor; but a recovery against him did not bar the owner's right of action against the true possessor[3]. So, 1st, "is qui liti se obtulit," 2, "qui dolo desiit possidere," were considered as possessors.

It might be brought for an uncertain share in an object if it was not in the suitor's power to know the precise share to which he was entitled. "Incertæ[4] partis vindicatio datur, si justa causa interveniat."

A Special Law[5] forbade the "vindicatio" to be

---

[1] II. de r. v. 27. § 1. "meum est ...cujus vindicandi jus habeo." eod. 49. § 1.

"Puto autem ab omnibus qui tenent et restituendi facultatem habent peti posse." II. de r. v. 9. c. 52. eod.

"Per hanc actionem non solum singulæ res vindicabuntur, sed posse etiam gregem vindicari. Pomponius scribit: Idem et de armento, de equitio, cæterisque quæ gregatim habentur dicendum est." eod. 1. 3.

"Pro possessione dolus est." II. 50. 17. 131.

[2] II. de r. v. 25. "Is qui se ob-

tulit defensioni sine causâ rem non possideret, nec dolo fecisset quo minus possideret ; non est absolvendus."

[3] "Si is qui obtulit se fundi vindicationi damnatus est nihilominus a possessore recte petitur, sicut Pedius ait." 7 eod. II. de hæred. petit. 13. § 14.

[4] 76. II. de r. v. "justam habet ignorantiam legatarius...Itaque talis dabitur actio."

[5] "Lege speciali prohibita est vindicatio tigni alienis ædibus juncti." 23. 6. eod. The owner had an "actio de tigno juncto," in which he reco-

brought for a "tignum" used in the building of another man.

If the defendant repudiated the possession, the thing was delivered to the claimant[1].

The thing sought must have an independent existence: if it was part of another thing, the remedy was by an action "ad exhibendum[2]."

PUBLICIANA IN REM ACTIO[3].

This action lay in behalf of the *bonâ fide* possessor of a thing[4] to which he had not acquired a prescriptive title, and to which he could establish an indefensible right on other grounds, against a mere wrong-doer, who was not allowed to take advantage of these defects in the quasi owner's title. It was an equitable action, and in all other respects but those mentioned resembled the "rei vindicatio[5]."

It might be answered by the "exceptio dominii" and by the "exceptio bonæ fidei possessionis[6]."

Of two bonâ fide purchasers of the same thing from one who was not the owner, he to whom it

---

vered double the value of the thing used, unless he chose to wait for the downfall of the fabric. II. 47. 3.

[1] "In rem actionem pati non compellimur, quia licet alicui dicere se non possidere, ita ut si adversarius possit convincere rem ab adversario possideri, transferat ad se possessionem per judicem, licet suam esse non approbaverit."

[2] "Armamenta navis singula erunt vindicanda, scapha quoque separatim vindicabitur." II. 6. 1. 3. § 1. II. 4. 23. § 5.

[3] "Si quis id quod traditur ex justâ causâ, non a domino et nondum usucaptum petet, judicium dabo." Cicero *pro Cluentio*, 45. *Instit. de act.* 4. II. 6. 2.

[4] "Nam si usucaptum est habet civilem actionem, nec desiderat honorariam." II. 6. 2. 1. 1.

[5] "In Publicianâ actione omnia eadem erunt quæ et in rei vindicatione diximus." II. 6. 2. 7. § 8.

[6] Eod. 16. 17. II. 17. 1. 57. Cujac. 10. 6. obs. Savigny, *System*, 7.

had been delivered had the best right to the Publiciana: "magis Publicianâ uti possit[1]."

EMPHYTEUSIS[2].

Emphyteusis was a right to occupy and enjoy the land of another, on condition of the payment of a yearly sum. The person having such a right was termed "emphyteuta."

The right might be conferred by will, by convention accompanied with delivery, by prescription.

The "emphyteuta" had the right to the produce. He might change, so long as by so doing he did not worsen the character of the farm. He might hypothecate or altogether alienate his right, subject to the condition of offering to the owner of the soil the opportunity of preemption.

Unless prohibited by the terms of the contract, he might transmit his right to his heirs, and he was entitled to the benefit of the "actio Publiciana" against the wrongful occupant, even though he should happen to be the landlord[3]; on the other hand, the

---

[1] II. 6. 2. 9. § 4. "Et Julianus scribit...ut siquidem ab eodem non domino emerint potior sit cui priori res traditą est—quod si a diversis non dominis melior causa sit possidentis."

[2] *Inst.* 3. 25. II. 6. 3. Cod. 4. 66. The right originally arose from the permission to occupy lands of the estate, on condition of planting them, ἐμφυτεύειν.

Burmann *de Vectig. Poss. Rom.* c. 1. 2. 3, hence the notion was transferred to lands of the sovereign and of private persons. "Non efficiuntur domini." II. 39. 2. 15. § 26.

Novell. 120. c. 1. § ult. Cod. de pactis 5. 14. 22. c. 6. § 2. Voet, *Comm. Pand.* h. t. *Inst.* de loc. cond. 3. 25. § 3. By the Nov. 7. c. 3, in emphyteusi ecclesiasticâ, succession was limited to the grandson.

The Emphyteusis, superficies and pignus are servitudes; but as the first two are forms of enjoying property peculiar to the Roman law, I have placed them in this chapter.

[3] "Adeo adversus dominum ipsum, ita tamen si vectigal solvatur." II. 6. 3. 1. § 1. II. de Public. in rem actione, 12. § 2.

owner was entitled to all the rights he had not parted with to the emphyteuta, to the yearly sum paid by the emphyteuta, to the jus protimeseôs, and to a fine settled at the fiftieth part of the value on alienation (this was called laudemium in the Latin of the middle ages).

This right terminated by efflux of time.

By the death without heirs of the emphyteuta.

By adverse prescription.

By the dereliction of the property.

By the expulsion of the emphyteuta.

By the non-payment of the rent.

By fraudulent sale concealed from the owner.

By a substantial deterioration of the property through the fraud or violence of the emphyteuta.

DE SUPERFICIEBUS[1].

This right was very similar to the emphyteusis; the word superficies was used to denote not the surface of the soil only, but any building erected on the soil of another. The property of such a building was in the owner of the soil; but the tenant erecting it, "superficiarius," had a peculiar right called "superficies:" it was that of acting as the owner of the building on payment of a yearly ground rent. His rights were protected by a special interdict, "exemplo uti possidetis[2]."

---

[1] II. 43. 18. Savigny, *Recht des Besitzes*, §§ 8, 23, 47.

II. 43. 17. 3. § 7 : "vel cœnaculum alienis ædibus injunctum."

II. 18. 1. 32.

II. 6. 1. 75. Savigny, *Recht des Besitzes*, § 9. 4. § 23. Toullier, *Droit Civil François*, 3. 103.

[2] "Si non solvit expelli potest." II. 20. 4. 15. 6. 1. 74. II. 7. 4. 1. II. 20. 1. 13. § 3. II. de acq. rer. d. 60. II. de solut. 98. II. de serv. Præd. un. 13.

The chief limitations of property in the Roman law may be thus summed up :—

1st. The owner was bound to allow boughs of trees 15 feet from the earth to overhang his soil. Π. 43. 27. de arboribus cædendis.

2ndly. He was bound to allow his neighbour three days to carry away fruit that had fallen on his soil. Π. 43. 27. de glande legendâ.

3rdly. He was bound to allow a party-wall to make a "venter" in his house short of half a foot. Π. 8. 5. 17.

4thly. In the event of the highway becoming impassable, "fluminis impetu," or "ruina," to allow a passage across his land. Π. 4. 6. 14. § 1. 11. 7. 12.

5thly. Not to block up the natural channel through which the water escaped from his neighbour's land. Π. 39. 3.

6thly. To repair his own buildings if they were in such a state as to threaten injury to his neighbour, and to remove what else might cause reasonable apprehension. Π. 39. 2. and 8. 5. 17. 2.

7thly. He could not take away materials that had been worked up in buildings, &c., but might recover double the value of them. Π. 47. 3. de tigno juncto.

CHAPTER V.

REMEDIES AGAINST WRONG.

I MAY refer the reader to the Commentaries of Gaius for an account of the manner in which the Roman guarded the suitor against the danger of technical error, instead of digging pitfalls, like those who created and upheld the system of special pleading, as it existed among us on all sides, and sometimes in the midst of the path he was obliged to tread blindfold. Never has there existed a system so thoroughly vicious in all its parts, or leading so surely to the triumph of chicane, as the system of pleading which prevailed in England till within these few years; and to their familiarity with, and obstinate maintenance of which, so many lawyers owed their elevation. All I propose now to do is, to lay before the reader a concise view of the chief heads into which the Roman actions were divided.

ACTIONS[1].

The best definition of an action is that it is the

---

[1] Schilling, Vol. II. p. 336.   Cod. 4. 10.
Instit. 4. § 6.   Donellus, Vol. VI.
Dig. 44. 7.   Gaius, *Instit.* 4. 11—33.

right of enforcing what is due to the Plaintiff, by the judgment of a legal tribunal.

" Jus persequendi in judicio quod sibi debetur[1]."

The word was early used to denote the formula employed in suits[2], and was from thence transferred to denote the forms of process[3].

It had a general and special signification[4]. In a special sense, it meant the actio personalis, as contrasted with the actio in rem petitio, and the persecutiones.

The Plaintiff was the "actor," "qui agit"—sometimes the "petitor."

The Defendant, the "reus"—"is unde petitur"—"qui convenitur"—"fugiens"—ὁ φεύγων.

It was necessary to prove not only that the act complained of was actionable, but that it gave the Plaintiff a right of action, and against the Defendant. The Plaintiff, if successful, recovered not only the "corpus[5]," but the "causam rei," in other words, all he would have had connected with the thing sued for, if the cause of complaint never had arisen.

---

[1] II. c. 59. de obl. c. art.

[2] Hostilianæ actiones. *De Orat.* I. 57.

[3] Cic. *ad Att.* I. I. *de Orat.* I. 41. II. de origin. juris. I. 2. 2. § 6. l. 7.

[4] II. 50. 16. 178. § 2. "Actionis verbum et speciale est et generale, nam omnis actio dicitur sive in rem sive in personam sit petitio, sed plerumque actiones personales solemus dicere, petitionis autem verbo in rem actiones significari videntur, persecutionis verbo extraordinarias persecutiones puto contineri, ut puta fidei commissorum et si quæ aliæ sunt quæ non habent juris ordinarii executionem," 28 h. t. "Actio in personam infertur, petitio in rem, persecutio in rem vel in personam rei persequendæ gratiâ."

[5] "Nec enim sufficit corpus ipsum restitui sed opus est ut et causa rei restituatur, id est ut omne habeat petitor quod habiturus foret, si eo tempore quo judicium accipiebatur restitutus illi homo fuisset." II. 6. I. 20. II. 22. I.

In doubtful cases, favour was for the Defendant[1].

Considered in their origin, "actiones" were "civiles" or "honorariæ."

"Civiles" was the name given to the oldest "Legis actiones," either because they were established by positive law, or because they were adapted to the words of the law[2].

Honorariæ included the Prætoriæ[3] actiones[4], and the ædilitiæ actiones[5].

Again, they are divided into "actiones directæ," and "actiones utiles:"

"Actiones directæ" being originally and immediately given for a definite case;

"Actiones utiles" being actions moulded in analogy to "actiones directæ" in cases to which these latter were not applicable. This relation of the utilis to the directa actio is indicated by the word "quasi;" for instance, the "quasi Serviana actio[6]," "quasi Publiciana[7]," "quasi Calvisiana vel Faviana[8]," sometimes by the expression "exemplo," or "ad exemplum[9]."

The object of the "utilis actio" was to complete

[1] "Favorabiliores rei potius quam actores habentur." II. 50. 17. 125.
Gaius, 4. § 57. II. 42. r. 38.
[2] Gaius, 4. § 11. Pomponius, II. r. 2. 6, describes them as legitimæ actiones.
[3] II. 36. 1. 63. § 9.
[4] 46. 1. 63. § 9. 31. h. t. "Quas Prætor ex suá jurisdictione comparatas habet." I. 4. 12. Many of these Prætorian actions were named after their author, e.g. Publiciana, Serviana, actio. Some from the occasion on which they were given, "injuriarum

actio;" some from the persons affected, "exercitoria," "institoria actio;" some from the object, "tributoria."
[5] Cod. 4. 58. Such were the "redhibitoria," the "quanti minoris," or "æstimatoria." II. 21. r. 47. § 2. 44. § 1. § 2. h. t.
[6] Inst. § 7. and § 31. h.t. II. 16. 1. 13. § 1.
[7] 6. 1. 70.
[8] 38. 5. 13.
[9] II. 7. 1. 17. § 3. "utilis actio exemplo Aquiliæ," 36. 45. § 21.

the remedy intended by the "directa actio," and supply any defect that had escaped the legislator; sometimes to enlarge or mitigate the antient law[1].

In so far as these "utiles actiones" supplied facts in reality wanting, but not essential to the justice of the case, though required for the "actio directa," they were called "fictitiæ actiones[2]."

The Prætor, in the flourishing state of Roman Jurisprudence, granted an "utilis actio" "cognitâ causâ[3]." The effect of the "utilis actio[4]" was the same with that of the "directa." The object of these actions was to prevent technical wrong, to secure substantial justice, to take care that "æqui-tas[5]" was forthcoming to the suitor for the sake of the common weal.

Actions are again divided with reference to their cause and object into "in rem" and "in personam[6]."

In the widest sense, the "actiones in rem" in-cluded the "actiones præjudiciales," to ascertain the

---

[1] Gaius, 2. § 253. I. 2. 23. § 4. 4. 3. 16. 1. 3. § 202. § 219. II. 4. 6. 43. II. 19. 5. 21. "Quoties deficit actio vel exceptio utilis actio vel exceptio est." II. 48. 23. 3. "Utiles actiones necessariæ non erunt cum et directæ competunt." The object was in that to improve the law and make it more liberal, just the opposite to that of our judges in their decision on the statute of uses.

[2] Ulpian, 28. 12. Gaius, 4. § 38. "actio utilis," "in quâ fingitur." Theophilus, 4. § 12. 2. 23. § 4. οὐτιλίας ἀγωγὰς...πλαγιαστικὰς, oblique.

[3] II. 43. 18. 1. "Si qua alia actio de superficie postulabitur causâ cognitâ dabo."

[4] "Nec refert directâ quis an utili

actione agat .... cum utraque actio ejusdem potestatis est eundemque habet effectum." II. 3. 5. 47. § 1.

[5] A very different thing from the "Equity" contained in Vesey. I. II. 13. 5. 5. § 9 : "utilitatis gratiâ." 13. 4. II. : "quia *iniquum erat*, non posse stipulatorem ad suum pervenire ideo visum est utilem actionem in eam rem comparare." II. 19. 51. Just the reason why our law would have refused it ; otherwise, as Lord Hobart wisely said, "How could the Law be an art !" Hugo, *Re. G.* 657. 1. "utilis," II. 17. 1. 37, is used in the common not the technical sense.

[6] II. 19. 3. 2 : "Hæc actio utilis est etsi merces intervenit."

"'status'" of an individual; but in a more restricted and usual sense, "actiones in rem" are those actions by which a person asserts his claim to possess a corporeal object, "In rem actio est per quam rem nostram quæ ab alio possidetur petimus et semper adversus eum est qui rem possidet[1]." These were called vindicationes or petitiones.

"In personam[2]," or "personales actiones," are actions brought against some person who is bound to give us some thing, or to perform some act. Such obligations may arise not only out of the lawful, but out of the unlawful acts, of the defendant[3]—and are as various as the different kinds of obligation. The word by which the classical Jurists describe these actions is "condictio[4]."

In a more limited sense, it means an "actio in personam," which is to enforce a "dari oportere." If it is intended to obtain a specific quantity, or one of a class of objects, it is called "certi condictio," or "condictitia actio[5] per quam certum petitur[6]," or in the opposite case, "incerti condictio[7];" if the

[1] Gaius, 4. 5. I. h. t. § 15: "appellamus in rem quidem actiones vindicationes." II. 39. 1. 9. 25. h. t. 20. 1. 16. § 3.

[2] II. 25. pr. h. t. Gaius, 4. § 2.

[3] "Quædam ex contractu, quædam ex facto...sunt. Ex contractu actio est quoties quis sui juris causâ cum aliquo contrahit....Ex facto actio est quoties ex eo teneri quis incipit quod ipse admisit, veluti furtum vel injuriam commisit vel damnum dedit." II. 25. § 1. h. t. "Agit unusquisque aut cum eo qui ei obligatus est vel ex contractu vel maleficio." I. § 1. h. t.

[4] Gaius, 4. § 5: "appellantur—in

personam—actiones quibus dari fierive oportere intendimus, condictiones." II. 25. h. t. § 2: "in personam quæ condictio appellatur."

[5] Festus : "condictio in diem certum ejus rei quæ agitur denuntiatio." I. h. t. § 15: "condicere est, denuntiare priscâ linguâ." Gaius, 4. 18: "Actor adversario denunciabat ut ad judicem capiendum die 30 adesset."

[6] II. 12. 1. 9. § 1. Gaius, 4. § 19. Theoph. 3. § 15. II. 25. 2. Gaius, 4. § 33.

[7] II. 45. 1. 75 : 7. 5. 1. § 1 : 8. 2. 35. 12. 7. 3.

action was to recover a certain quantity of money (certa pecunia numerata), its particular name was "actio si certum petatur;" if not for money, it was called "triticaria," or "triticaria condictio[1]."

Many of these condictiones had their peculiar names indicating their origin, "condictio sine causâ," "condictio causâ datâ, causâ non secutâ," "condictio ob turpem causam," "ei debiti," &c.

If a personal action arose out of a new law which had not given to it any precise or specific definition, it was called "condictio ex lege," or "ex lege condictitiâ[2]."

Actions were divided into universal, which sought the collective whole, as the hæreditatis petitio[3];

Generales[4], which had for their object several rights and obligations bearing a certain relation to each other; and

Speciales[5], which related to a single object, or to a number of objects included under the same species.

They were divided into private, which concerned private interests, and popular, in which the public were protected[6].

In popular actions the prætor might, if several appeared as plaintiffs, select one fittest; and the person who had an interest was preferred, "is cujus interest," to others.

---

[1] II. 13. 3.

[2] "Si obligatio lege nova introducta sit, nec cautum eadem lege quo genere actionis experiamur, ex lege agendum est." II. 13. 2. l. un.: "condictio quæ ex lege descendit." II. 48. 5. 28.

[3] II. 6. 11.

[4] II. 17. 2. 38. II. 39. 3. 1. 17.

[5] II. 6. 1. 73. & 3. 6. 1. § 1.

[6] "Eam popularem actionem dicimus qua suum jus populus tuetur." II. 47. 23. 1.

Women and wards, unless their interest was concerned, could not bring them.

With reference to the relation in which the parties stood to each other, actions were divided into simplicia and duplicia judicia. All that were not duplicia were simplicia. The duplicia were three: "familiæ erciscundæ," "communi dividendo," and "finium regundorum." In any one of these three either of the litigants might be Plaintiff or Defendant, and might be compelled to fulfil certain obligations towards the other. "Judicium communi dividundo," "familiæ erciscundæ," "finium regundorum," "tale est ut in eo singulæ personæ duplex jus habeant agentis et ejus quorum agitur[1]." Sometimes these were called "mixtæ actiones[2]." In general he was considered Plaintiff who took the first step in the suit; if both began at the same time it was decided by lot[3].

Actions in a similar point of view were divided into "directæ," and "contrariæ[4];" "directæ" being those which went immediately to the main object of an obligation, whence they are sometimes called "principalis actio," and "rectum judicium;" "contrariæ" being those instituted for counter and collateral claims arising out of the same obligation, e. g. compensation.

When the obligation was direct, and springing necessarily from the contract, both litigants had a "directa actio;" a "contraria actio" only arose for

[1] II. 10. 1. 10.　10. 2. 2. § 3.　10.
3. 2. 1.
[2] 44. 7. 37. 1.
[3] II. 10. 3. 2. 1.　II. 5. 1. 13.
[4] II. 13. 6. 17. § 1.　18. § 4.　I. 4.
16. 2.　II. 4. 4. 28.　II. 6. 2. 14.　13.
6. 18. 2. 4. 18.　27. 41. § 2. § 4—8.

the defendant when the obligation was accidental and subordinate—as when other obligations had been contracted by the defendant for the plaintiff, for which the latter made no allowance ; of which kind instances repeatedly arose in the tutela, negotia gesta, &c.

A most important division[1] of actions with regard to the power of the judge was into those "bonæ fidei" and those "stricti juris." The latter class contained those actions in which no latitude was given to the judge. The former, called by Cicero "arbitria," those in which he was enjoined by the formula from which he derived his authority, to decide "ex fide bonâ," "ut inter bonos agier oportet," "quantum," or "quod æquius melius ;" in such cases, the judge gave the plaintiff all the profit to which he had an honest right, and to the defendant the benefit of every honest defence. Hence the saying of Scævola[2], that such cases were the test of a great judge, "in his magni esse judicis statuere quid quemque cuique præstare oportere." And hence the pointed and concise expression "bonæ fidei judicio exceptiones insunt[3] ;" words that outweigh cartloads of our reports[4]. By far the majority

---

[1] I. h. t. § 28. II. 13. 6. 3. § 2. Cic. pro Rosc. Com. 4. Top. 17. Theoph. 4. 6. § 30 : "de bonâ fide agitur cui non congruit de apicibus juris disputare." II. 17. 1. 29. § 4. Seneca, de Ben. 3. § 7. Gaius, 4. § 163.

[2] This is a conclusive proof of the opposite ideas different nations annex to words which in dictionaries are put as synonymous. The Roman notion of equity was as opposite to that of an

English lawyer (still more of our English suitors) as Heaven is to Hell.

[3] II. 18. 5: 3. 24. 3. 21. 30. 84. § 5

[4] If our word equity had the usual meaning that belongs to the idea in civilized countries, it would seem odd that this is precisely the class of cases to which it does not apply, and that it is reserved for plaintiffs and defendants of comparative opulence. "Bonæ fidei sunt hæc ex emto vendito (not of

of actions, those especially "quibus vitæ societas continetur," belonged to this class. The "stricti juris" applied to unilateral obligations where only one person was bound, e.g. "stipulatio," "literarum obligatio;" to the same class belonged personal actions, where the formula ran "dare oportere," and "condictiones," in the narrowest sense. In these cases equity was as much due to the litigants, as in those "ex fide bonâ;" but equity prescribed a different form of proceedings. The Romans were not such gross barbarians, as to confine equity to one set of courts, and exclude it from another—that they left to those descendants of Jutlanders who were to sit on the bench of justice[1] in the southern part of this island.

There remains to be mentioned another class of actions called "arbitrariæ." In these, whether real or personal, the judge is empowered to pronounce an "arbitrium" provisionally for the plaintiff, and if it be not complied with, to impose upon the defendant the payment of such a sum as the equity of the case demands[2].

---

land only) locato conducto," "negotiorum gestorum," "mandati," "depositi," "pro socio," "tutelæ," "depositi pro socio," "tutelæ," "commodati," "pignoraticia," "familiæ erciscundæ," "communi dividundo," "præscriptis verbis quæ de æstimato proponitur, et ea quæ ex permutatione competit," and "hæreditatis petitio."

[1] "Quod ob rem datur ex bono et æquo habet repetitionem." II. 12. 6. 6. 5. § 4: this was "stricti juris." 10. 66. eod.: "hæc condictio ex bono

et æquo introducta:" see 25. 2. 25, where the law of nations is appealed to; even in penal actions the same "æquum" is invoked. II. 12. 1. 9. 1.
  II. 9. 3. 5. 5.
    47. 10. 11. 1.
    47. 12. 10.
  Cujacius, *Observ.* 22. c. 14.
  [2] Gaius, 4. § 163. I. § 31. h.t.: "quasdam actiones arbitrarias appellamus .... in quibus nisi arbitrio judicis is cum quo agitur actori satisfaciat, vel uti rem restituat vel exhibeat

With reference to the method of procedure, actions were divided[1] into " vulgares actiones," " judicia prodita," and " in factum actiones." The " vulgares actiones " were moulded according to formulæ[2] which made technical mistake impossible, just as ours till within these few years made it inevitable. The formulæ were either " in jus conceptæ," when they set forth a ground of complaint according to the Civil Law, or " in factum conceptæ," when the " factum " was at the beginning of the formula[3].

The " in factum actiones[4]" included the

   1.   Prætorian[5].
   2.   The Præscriptis verbis actiones[6].
   3.   The utiles[7].

These are not to be confounded with the " formula in jus," and the " formula in factum concepta," of which an account, invaluable to the jurist, is given by Gaius, 4. § 45, 46, 47. It is curious to contrast the anxious care of the Roman legislator to make every pleading subservient to substantial

---

vel solvat vel servum dedat condemnari debet." 4. 3. 18. § 1. 68. 10. 1. 4. § 3. II. 4. 2. 4. 13. 4. 2. "Arbitraria actio utriusque utilitatem continet actoris et rei." § 3.

[1] II. 19. 5. 1 : "Nonnunquam evenit ut cessantibus judiciis proditis et vulgaribus actionibus quum proprium nomen invenire non possumus facile descendamus ad eas quæ in factum vocantur." 2 eod.: "nam quum deficiunt vulgaria atque usitata actionum nomina præscriptis verbis agendum est." 11 eod.: "quia actionum non plenus numerus esset ideo plerumque actiones in factum desiderantur, sed

et eas actiones quæ legibus proditæ sunt si lex justa ac necessaria sit, supplet Prætor in eo quod legi deest."

[2] 1. h. t.   II. 38. 5. 46.
[3] Gaius, 4. §§ 45, 46.
[4] II. 1. h. t.
[5] II. 2. 14. 7. § 2.   II. 12. 2. 11. § 1. 44. 7. 13. and II. 2. 14. 1. 1. & 2. & 13. § 1. & 16. & 22. & 24. Gaius, 4. § 132. Cod. 2. 14. 6.
[6] II. h.t. 2—4. II. 16. 3. 1. § 9. 43. 26. 2. 2.   10. 3. 23.
[7] II. 9. 2.   53. 11. II. h.t.

The formulæ were abolished by Constantine.

Cod. 2. 58. 1.

justice, with the equal anxiety to promote an opposite object in the pages of Meeson and Wellsby[1].

JUDICIA, ORDINARIA AND EXTRAORDINARIA[2].

The characteristic of the "ordinaria judicia"
was, that the magistrate within whose jurisdiction
the suit was brought, instructed the process, pointed
out and enforced the legal rules applicable to it—
and having done this, named a private judge, to
whom (subject to these directions) the determination
of the case was entrusted.

When the magistrate himself, without the intervention of a private judge, investigated and decided
the case, he was said "extra ordinem jus dicere,"
and the "judicium" was "extraordinarium." In
the time of Diocletian and Maximian this was
established as the general rule, and the naming of
a private judge became exceptional. Thus the "solitus judiciorum ordo" was gradually abolished, and
the old system inverted.

Besides this, judgments were divided into those
which "legitimo jure consistunt," "legitima judicia,"
such as arose in Rome or within a mile[3] of Rome

[1] See Reeve, *Hist. of English Law,*
Vol. III. p. 89.

[2] I. 3. 12. 1. Savigny, *Geschichte
des R. R,* Vol. I. p. 101. Theophilus,
3. 12 : ἡνίκα τὰ δικαστήρια ὀρδινάρια
ἦν, τουτέστιν ἡνίκα ἐκινεῖτο ἐν μόνῳ τῷ
καιρῷ τοῦ κονβέντου . . . σήμερον δὲ τῶν
δικαστηρίων ἐξτραορδιναρίων ὄντων καὶ
ἐν παντὶ καιρῷ γυμναζομένων.
I. 4. 15 : "quoties extra ordinem

jus dicitur qualia sunt hodie omnia judicia," "tunc locum habebat quando
judicia ordinaria in usu erant sed cum
extraordinariis judiciis posteritas usa
est." I. 3. 12.

[3] Gaius, 4. 103—105. *Pro Rosc.
Com.* 5. Gaius, 4. 109.
II. 4. 6. 31. II. 27. 7. 9. § 2. Gaius,
4. 110.

between Roman citizens and those "quæ imperio continentur." To the last class belong the "recuperatoria judicia," those in which the single judge or one of the litigants was a peregrinus, and those which arose between Roman citizens at a greater distance than a mile from Rome.

ACTIONES PERPETUÆ ET TEMPORALES.

In the old Roman Law[1] the "Perpetuæ actiones" were those which were not destroyed by prescription; and this was usually the case with those founded in the Civil Law. "Actiones temporales," or "temporariæ," were those which must be instituted within a certain time. Theodosius[2] made a law that all actions must be begun within thirty years from the time when the cause of action first existed, with some exceptions in favour of "actiones hypothecariæ," "actiones" for the "fundi patrimoniales" of the ruler, and "actiones" for the claims of the Church or benevolent institutions. From this time actions, the right to bring which continued for thirty years, were called perpetuæ; and those which expired in a shorter time were called temporales.

EXCEPTIONS. DEFENCES[3].

To enter into any detail upon this subject would be beyond the scope of this undertaking. Many

---

[1] Gaius, 4. 110. But see II. 48. II. 2. II. 5. 2. 8. § 17.

[2] Theoph. c. 4. 14. Symmachus,

Ep. 10. 52. II. 44. 3. Cod. 7. 39.

[3] *Inst.* 4. 13. II. 44. 1. Gaius, 4. 115.

of the "exceptiones" were furnished to protect the
Defendant against the injustice which would be the
consequence of a literal application of the law.   The
"exceptio" took the Defendant out of the category in
which the "intentio" or charging part of his adversary's statement had placed him.   If, for instance,
the Plaintiff had agreed not to sue the Defendant,
bound to him by a former covenant, the Defendant,
admitting the existence of the obligation, excluded
himself from the effect of it by the exceptio of the
"pactum conventum."   Thus Ulpian says, "exceptio
est quasi quædam exclusio, quæ opponi actioni cujusque rei solet, ad excludendum id quod in intentionem
condemnationemve deductum est."

   They were perpetual[1] and temporary, or dilatory
and temporal.   Some of the most important are
the "exceptio rei judicatæ[2]," the "exceptio doli[3]," and
the "exceptio metus."   The "exceptio doli" was established that no one should turn the law into an
occasion of profiting by his own evil act, against
natural equity, "ne cui dolus suus per occasionem[4]
juris civilis contra naturalem æquitatem prosit."
The "exceptio doli" was "in personam;" that of
"metus," "in rem."   Every "exceptio in factum"
gave rise to a "doli exceptio."   For *he* was guilty

---

[1] II. 44. 3. 3.

[2] Eod. 2.

[3] Eod. 4.   Eod. 4. § 1.

[4] II. 44. 4. 2. § 1: "non sufficiet ei,"
i.e. the Defendant, "ostendere in re
esse dolum aut in alterius dicat dolo
factum ; eorum personas specialiter debebit enumerare dummodo hæ sint
quarum dolus noceat," it must be the

"dolus malus actoris ;" the Prætor did
not say, Find for the Plaintiff, "si in
eâ re nihil dolo malo factum est;" but,
"si in eâ re nihil dolo malo *actoris*
factum est:" on the contrary, the
"metus exceptio" ran, "si in eâ re
nihil metus causâ factum est."   II.
44. 4. 4. § 33.

of "dolus" who sought to obtain that which the Defendant had a valid reason to refuse, "quod quâcunque exceptione elidi potest petit," unless he was ignorant of the circumstances—"nisi talis sit ignorantia in eo ut dolo careat[1];" for even if originally ignorant, he has no right, when the facts are made known to him, to persevere. In the "bonæ fidei judicia" the exceptio doli was not specified in the formula, but taken for granted: "In bonæ fidei judiciis inest exceptio doli[2]."

The Principles of Roman Law as to the "exceptiones" were,

First. That the Defendant was bound to prove the "exceptio[3]:" "Reus in exceptione actor est."

Secondly. That the Defendant by pleading the "exceptio," did not admit the Plaintiff's charge: "Non utique existimatur confiteri de existimatione adversarius, quocum agitur qui exceptione utitur[4]."

Thirdly. That the Defendant might avail himself of different "exceptiones[5]:" "Nemo prohibetur pluribus exceptionibus uti quamvis diversæ sunt[4]."

Fourthly. That though the "doli mali actio" must be brought within a certain time, the "doli mali exceptio" was perpetual, because the Plaintiff could choose the time to sue, but the Defendant could not choose when he should be sued[6].

[1] II. eod. 2. § 5.
Gaius, 4. 119.
[2] II. 24. 3. 21. 30. 84. 5. 18. 1.
68. 1. 18. 5. 3.
[3] II. h.t. l. 1.
[4] 9. eod.
[5] 8. eod.
[6] 44. 4. 5. § 6: "Non sicut do

dolo actio certo tempore finitur, ita etiam exceptio eodem tempore danda est, nam hæc perpetuo competit, cum actor quidem in suâ potestate habeat quando utatur suo jure, is autem cum quo agitur non habeat potestatem, quando conveniatur."

I now propose to lay before the reader an account of the Preventive Remedies furnished by the Roman Law. This will involve the consideration of the peculiarly Prætorian jurisdiction, under which will fall the Obligationes ex Delicto, and the law of Servitudes. We shall then examine the law of Contracts and of Inheritance.

CHAPTER VI.

PREVENTIVE REMEDIES[1].

INTERDICTS.

MOST of the particular interdicts will be considered under their several heads, in the particular matters to which they relate. But it may be useful to prefix an account of this peculiar and most salutary branch of prætorian jurisdiction.

Originally they consisted in certain formulæ, but they may be defined as proceedings by which the Prætor forbids or commands some action.

They applied, says Ulpian, to divine and human things. To divine, as those " de locis sacris aut religiosis;" to human things, sometimes in the case of private or public property, " de his quæ sunt alicujus;" sometimes in the case of what was the property of no one, " de his quæ nullius sunt." Those relating to property were either when the property was public or private.

Public: " de locis publicis, de viis, deque fluminibus publicis."

Those affecting private property might relate "ad universitatem," as the interdict " quorum bonorum;"

---

[1] II. 43. 1.

or particular things, as the interdictum "uti possi-detis," "de itinere actuque."

There were three kinds of interdicts, "exhibitory," "prohibitory," and "mixt," which were both prohibitory and exhibitory.

The exhibitory interdicts were those which ordered the production of a particular thing. The prohibitory those by which a particular act was forbidden. Some edicts related to what was present, as the "uti possidetis;" some to what was past, as those "de itinere actuque et aquâ æstivâ." Some, as has been stated, were double, some were simple; some were annual, some perpetual. Some are given directly against the principal, others called noxales, on account of the delicta of those under our power—as when they have broken down or destroyed any thing, or raised a new work, "clam" or "vi[1]."

The produce of what the interdict enabled the litigant to recover, could only be what had accrued from the day that it was sued for. The interdict had no retroactive operation.

INTERDICT "QUORUM BONORUM[2]."

By this interdict the person whom the Prætor had sent into possession of property demanded restitution of that property from those who actually possessed, or who were supposed to possess it, as heirs or possessors.

It applied to the "universitas," and not to par-

[1] Π. 43. 1. 5. "Interdicta noxalia sunt quæ ob delicta eorum quæ in nostrâ potestate sunt dantur."
[2] Π. 43. tit. 2.

ticular things. It did not reach the debtors to the inheritance, but merely the possessors of the property to be inherited. The person who applied for it was bound to prove that he had a right to the possession; therefore if Caius demanded possession of property as the son of Titius, he was bound to prove that he was so.

QUORUM LEGATORUM [1].

This was given to obtain possession, and to enable the heir to recover what a legatee has taken as a legacy without the consent of the heir. The Prætor assisted the heir after he had given the requisite security against the letter of the law.

It lay only against the possessor who claimed what was sought to be recovered as legatee or fidei commissarius, not against him who claimed by a "donatio mortis causâ."

It was given to the heir and to the possessor and to their heirs and successors, but only, as has been said, after security [2] had been given.

With the characteristic wisdom of the Roman Law, it lay not against the possessor only, but against him "qui dolo desiit possidere," that is, who had purposely deprived himself of the power to restore what was sued for.

Though neither the "usus" nor the "ususfructus" could, strictly speaking, be said to be possessed,

---

[1] II. 43. 3. "Ut quod quis legatorum nomine, non ex voluntate hæredis occupavit, id restituat hæredi; etenim æquissimum prætori visum est unumquemque non sibi ipsum jus dicere, occupatis legatis, sed ab hærede petere."

[2] "Satis datum sic arbitror, si sic satis datum sit ut legatario vel ipso jure acquisita sit idonea cautio, vel per mandati actionem acquiri possit, et tunc interdicto locum fore." Eod.

but to be held[1], the interdict lay for them as it did for a servitude.

"NE VIS FIAT EI QUI IN POSSESSIONEM MISSUS EST[2]."

This was given to protect the person whom the Prætor had directed to take possession of property for the purpose of safe custody[3] until his claim upon it was decided, or the cause for which he was authorised to take possession had ceased.

It mattered not for the purpose of the interdict whether the person against whom it was sought had prevented the person seeking it from taking possession by fraud, or expelled him from that possession by violence.

DE TABULIS EXHIBENDIS[4].

This interdict was exhibitory. It lay against the person possessing or fraudulently ceasing to possess, "qui dolo desiit possidere," any testamentary writing of a deceased[5] person[6]; "ad omnia quæ causam testamenti continent," "ad omnem omnino scripturam testamenti sive perfectam sive imperfectam:" it mattered not if it was invalid, if a subsequent will had been made, if it was said to be forged, or made by him who had not "testamenti factionem," nor if the will had been in part or

[1] "Quod neque ususfructus neque usus *possidetur* sed magis *tenetur.*" Eod.
[2] II. 43. 4.
[3] II. 42. 4.
[4] II. 43. 5. "Exhibere, hoc est

materiæ ipsius apprehendendæ copiam facere."
[5] Eod. 1. 2.
[6] § 10. "quia verba prætoris *reliquerit* fecerunt mentionem."

totally "deletum sine dolo." It lay against the "ædituus" or "tabularius" to whom the care of the will had been entrusted.

The object of it was to compel the witnesses of the will to attest their signatures[1] before the Prætor, —if they would not attend voluntarily, they might be coerced; any one might apply for it who took an interest under the will, and the "condemnatio" was "quanti interfuit," the amount of his interest.

---

[1] And then the preposterous use of written evidence in courts of Equity is imputed to the Roman law!

CHAPTER VII.

OBLIGATIONS ARISING FROM DELICTA[1].

GENERAL REMARKS.

"DELICTUM" is the intentional violation of a general law. Every one who commits such an act is liable to repair the damage he has occasioned, and to suffer the penalty inflicted by law. This liability, civil as well as penal, attaches to each offender, nor does the punishment of one exonerate the rest, "si cum uno agatur cæteri non liberantur[2]."

By the Roman Law "delicta" were divided into public and private. This division is marked by the different power of accusation, as it is extended to every citizen or limited to the injured person, by the different tribunals, under the jurisdiction of which such offences fell, by the character and method of applying the punishment inflicted. Any Roman citizen might prosecute a public "delictum;" on the contrary, the sufferer alone could institute proceedings for a "privatum delictum." Private delicta were tried in the same manner, and before the same

---

[1] De la Serva, *Curso del Derecho Romano*, Vol. II. p. 383.

[2] II. 9. 2. 11. § 2. So II. 26. 7. 55. 1. "Quamvis unus," sc. tutor, "duplum præstiterit, nihilominus etiam alii tene-antur; nam in aliis furibus ejusdem rei pluribus, non est propterea cæteris pœnæ deprecatio quod ab uno jam exacta est."

judges, as a civil obligation. Public delicta were subject to their own forms of proceeding, and tried by other judges. In private delicta the penalty was employed for the benefit of the person injured. In public delicta the punishment was corporal, or a fine paid to the treasury.

The opinion of Ortolan and Du Caurroy, that a criminal intention was not requisite in all cases to establish a "delictum privatum" cannot be maintained. Their argument is that the Lex Aquilia inflicts the same punishment on an injury occasioned by negligence as on an injury which is intentional. But if we observe that the Aquilian Law punishes not delicta only, but negligence also, inflicting the same penalty, but not attributing the same character to its consequences, as in cases of delicta, we shall reject a theory that is inconsistent with the spirit of the Roman Law. To this it may be added, that however the acts of imprudence punished by the Aquilian Law, if considered separately, infer no wrong intention, yet they are the result of other voluntary acts done in violation of law, and of the precautions enforced by law to guard against evils, and thus are impressed with some portion of the character of delicta.

The private delicta[1] enumerated in the Institutes are furtum[2]—rapina—damnum—injuria. The Digest treats of several others, as "de tigno juncto," "arborum furtim cæsarum," each having its origin in the law of the Twelve Tables: the "servi corrupti[3]:" the action for an injury inflicted "dolo malo"

---

[1] Gaius, § 182. L. 3.   [2] II. 47. 3 = 7. h. t.   [3] II. 11. § 3.

in a crowd[1]—in these actions the condemnation for the first year was "in duplum," afterwards "in singulum:" the action "quod metus causa[2]:" the action against those who took advantage of a fire, a falling down of buildings, a shipwreck, a naval fight, to appropriate property—actions the condemnation of which was for the first year "in quadruplum," afterwards "in simplum."

PREVENTIVE REMEDIES.

Obligations arising from "delicta[3]" and "quasi delicta."

Delicta interfering with the exercise of public rights.

The doctrines of the Roman Law[4] on this subject relate,

1.   To the protection of a "locus sacer :" "Ne quid in loco sacro fiat."

An interdict lay against the person who violated this rule.

2.   To the protection of a "locus publicus[5]." If any thing was done to injure a "via publica," any one might obtain an "interdictum prohibitorium[6]" against the wrong-doer.

---

[1] II. 47. 84. "Hoc autem edicto tenetur non solus qui damnum in turbâ dedit, sed et is qui dolo malo fecerit ut in turbâ damni quid daretur, sive illo venerit sive non fuerit præsens...dolus enim malus etiam absentis esse potest."

[2] II. 47. 9.

[3] II. 43. 6. to 43. 15.

[4] "In muris itemque portis et aliis sanctis locis aliquid facere ex quo damnum aut incommodum irrogetur, non permittitur." II. 43. 6. 2.

[5] II. 43. 8. "Ne quid in loco publico vel itinere fiat." "Viam publicam eam dicimus cujus solum publicum est...viæ privatæ solum alienum est, jus tantum eundi et agendi nobis competit." 2. § 21. h. t.

[6] "Hoc interdictum perpetuum et populare est." 2. 34. h. t.

But the rule applied only to the " viæ rusticæ :". the " urbicæ" were under the care of the magistrate[1].

An " edictum restitutorium" lay against one who continued such an injury[2].

3. To protect the navigation of public rivers : " Ne quid in flumine ripâve ejus fiat quo pejus navigetur," or " quo statio iterve navigio deterior sit[3]."

4. To prevent the course of a river from being changed[4].

5. For the protection of "aqua ex castello[5]."

6. For the protection of the public " cloaca[6]."

7. To prevent the burial of a corpse or the building of a tomb on the property of another against his will[7].

8. " Operis novi nuntiatio[8]."

One of the most refined and admirable parts of Roman jurisprudence.

The " operis novi nuntiatio" is the extra-judicial act by which any one apprehensive of injury from walls newly begun may prevent their continuance, till his right has been decided, with the privilege of compelling his adversary, who perseveres after such a notice, to restore every thing to the state in which it was at the time the "nuntiatio" was given, however the question of right may be decided[9].

The operation of this remedy was not retrospec-

[1] II. 2 = 24. h. t.

[2] 2. 35. h. t.

[3] II. 43. 12.

[4] II. 43. 13.

[5] 43. 20. i. e. " ex eo receptaculo quod aquam publicam suscipit."

[6] 43. 23. 1. § 15. § 16. 2. II. 11. 8.

[7] "Hoc interdictum prohibitorium esse palam est." II. 11. 8. § 4.

[8] II. 39. 1. II 43. 25. Cod. 8. 11.

[9] II. 39. 1. 20. § 3. "Prætor ait quod factum est restituas...neque interest quid factum sit an non, sive jure factum est, sive non jure factum est, interdictum locum habebit."

tive: "Adversus futura opera inductum est, non adversus præterita."

There were three grounds on which the "operis novi nuntiatio[1]" could be applied for—

Natural: when any thing was fixed in a building of our own, or erected on our soil.

Public: when any right established by law was violated.

Impositious: i. e. to guard what had been imposed.

When any one having imposed a servitude on his buildings did what interfered with the enjoyment of it[2].

The "nuntiatio" could only be employed for injuries connected with the soil, "opera solo conjuncta." Ulpian says he makes an "opus novum" "qui aut ædificando aut detrahendo aliquid pristinam faciem operis mutat[3]."

Again, the remedy lay,

"Damni depellendi causâ," "ut damni infecti caveatur[4]."

"Publici juris tuendi gratiâ[5]," in which case any citizen of age might apply for it: in other cases the right was limited to him "ad quem res pertinet[6]."

---

[1] II. 39. 1. 5. § 9.

[2] Whether this extended to all servitudes is the subject of much discussion. Gluck, Vol. x. p. 221, in spite of the large expression of Ulpian, II. 43. 25. § 3: "Jus habet novum opus nuntiandi qui aut dominium aut servitutem habet." The passage in the text is "ædibus suis," which would exclude the servitude "prædiorum rusticorum," and this view is

farther borne out by the L. 14. h. t.

[3] 1. § 12. h. t.

[4] II. 39. 1. 17. II. 43. 24. 1. 7.

[5] "Nam reipublicæ interest quam plurimos ad defendendam suam causam admitti." II. h. t. 3.

[6] 1. 20. 4. h. t. "Quem in locum nuntiatum est nequid operis novi fieret, quâ de re agitur, quod in eo loco antequam nuntiatio missa fieret, aut in eâ causâ esset ut remitti deberet, fac-

Whatever was done after the "nuntiatio" was illegal.

It was a peculiarity of the "nuntiatio," that it was "in rem," not "in personam;" wherefore it availed against a madman or an idiot[1].

It must be made on the spot, "eo loci ubi opus fiat." It need not be given to the master; if given to any one "qui in re præsenti fuit domini operisve nomine," it was sufficient, though a slave, a wife, a boy, or a girl[2].

If the person who complained of the work, complained only of a portion of it, he was bound to specify the exact portion of which he complained, and define the limits within which the work might be carried on.

The "operis novi nuntiatio" was only valid for him in whose name it was given[3]: "Morte ejus qui nuntiavit extinguitur nuntiatio."

The right, however, acquired by the violation of the "nuntiatio" was not extinguished by the death of the person who used it[4].

As to the defendant, the proceeding being "in rem[5]" was valid against his heirs—with this distinction, that in case of transgression he might be compelled to restore the plaintiff to his original condition, at his own expense, which was the penalty of his

tum est, id restituas." II. 43. 24. 7. § 2. "Qui ante remissionem nuntiationis, contra quam prohibitus fuerit, opus fecerit, duobus interdictis tenebitur, uno quod ex operis novi nuntiatione competit, altero, quod vi aut clam," &c.

[1] 10. h. t.

[2] 39. 1. 5. § 22. 4. "Sufficit enim in re præsenti operis novi nuntiationem factam esse, ut domino possit renuntiari."

[3] 8. 6. h. t.   5. 6. h. t.

[4] 20. § 6. h. t.

[5] 8. 7. h. t.   23. h. t.   But this is irreconcileable with II. 4. 7. 3. § 3. Meermann, *Thes.* 6. p. 781.

fault; but if he died, the heir was not liable for the
penalty, but only obliged to allow the plaintiff to
destroy what had been done, to furnish "patientiam
destruendi operis[1]," unless in so far as he was a
gainer by the transgression of the law[2].

If the spot belonged to several, the "nuntiatio"
was valid against all; but if one of several proprietors transgressed, he alone was liable to the interdict,
the others being only bound to the "patientia." The
"nuntians" was bound to take recorded evidence of
the state of the work when he made his protest, "ut
appareat quid postea factum sit[3]."

An "exceptio" prevailed against the interdict
when after the "nuntiatio" an agreement[4] had been
settled between the parties, unless the "nuntiatio[5]"
had been "publici juris tuendi gratiâ," in which no
such agreement could be valid; or if the work was
such as to admit of no delay, the defendant might
apply to the judge to determine "an talia opera
fuerint ut contemni nuntiatio deberet[6]:"—again, the
"nuntiatio" had no effect where the defendant was
engaged in an act expressly sanctioned by law, e. g.
repairing a "rivus."

[1] 22. h. t.
[2] 20. § 7, 8. h. t.
[3] L. 8. cod. tit. § potest. § et probari. "Ut probari possit quid postea
ædificatum sit modulos munire debet
is qui nuntiat, qui ut sumantur con-
feranturque Prætor decernere solet."
[4] 1. § 10. h. t. "An danda sit
conventionis exceptio, et ait Celsus
dandam."
[5] II. 2. 14. 7. § 14. "Si paciscar,
ne operis novi nuntiationem exsequar,

quidam putant non valere pactionem,
quasi in eâ re Prætoris imperium versetur: Labeo autem distinguit, ut si
ex re familiari operis novi nuntiatio
sit facta, liceat pacisci; si de republicâ,
non liceat: quæ distinctio vera est."
[6] II. 39. 1. 5. § 13. "Proinde si
quis cum opus hoc morâ periculum
allaturum esset nuntiaverit opus novum, dicemus apud judicem quæri
debere an talia opera fuerint ut contemni nuntiatio deberet."

As to the manner of extinguishing the "operis novi nuntiatio," before Justinian the rule was, that it expired in a year, and could not be renewed unless the nuntians had procured a sentence within that time in favour of his "jus prohibendi." Justinian abolished this rule[1].

Another cause was, the remission of a competent judge[2].

If the defendant wanted to exonerate[3] his work from the "operis novi nuntiatio," he applied to the proper judge for a "remissio," and this was given at once unless the nuntians swore, "se non calumniæ causâ opus novum nuntiare[4]," or the "cautio de rato" was not given by him who had given the "nuntiatio procuratorio nomine[5]."

In other cases a petitory suit was instituted in which the nuntians was plaintiff, and therefore sustained the "onus probandi." The nuntians by adopting this mode of action renounced all possessory remedies[6], and therefore Ulpian[7] gives the person whose right is encroached upon a caution against adopting this form of remedy, unless in cases where the soil beyond all doubt belonged to the defendant, recommending in other cases recourse to the interdict "quod vi aut clam," or the "uti possidetis."

[1] Cod. h. t. l. un.

[2] II. 43. 25. l. un.

[3] 39. 1. 5. § 17.

[4] 5. § 14. h. t.

[5] 5. § 18. h. t.

[6] 5. § 10. h. t. Basil 58. 80. Gr. 1. § 3, ὁ παραγγέλλων γίνεται ἐνάγων. 1. § 6. h. t.

[7] 5. § 10. h. t. "Melius esse eum per Prætorem vel per manum, i. e. lapilli jactum prohibere, quam operis novi nuntiatione; cæterum operis novi nuntiatione possessorem eum faciemus cui nuntiaverimus: at si in suo quid faciat quod nobis noceat, tunc operis novi denuntiatio erit necessaria."

II. 5. § 17. 8. § 2. § 4. 12; 20. § 1; 21. h. t. II. 43. 25. l. un. § 2. II. 46. 5. 2. § 1. 46. 5. 1. § 6.

Cap. ult. X. de novi op. nunt. 5. 32. Greg. 9. II. 46. 5. 1. 6. 8. § 3. h. t. Cod. h. t. l. u.

Another cause was "stipulatio ex operis novi nuntiatio," that is, where the defendant gave the "cautio.
de demoliendo," a promise that if defeated he would
replace every thing as it stood at his own expense.

Lastly, the death of the nuntians, or his loss of
all interest in the property concerned.

OF PROHIBITIONS[1] AND THE INTERDICT "VI" OR "CLAM."

Closely connected with the "operis novi nuntiatio" is the "prohibitio," and the interdict "quod vi
aut clam," founded upon it.

If any person interested in the land forbad another from altering its condition, and the "prohibitus"
notwithstanding persevered, the "interdictum quod
vi" obliged him to restore every thing to the state
in which it was when the prohibition was signified
to him.

The right of the "prohibitus" did not come into
question : if he persevered he violated the law, as in
the case of the "nuntiatio." "Parvi refert utrum
jus habuerit faciendi an non, sive enim jus habuit sive
non ; tamen tenetur interdicto propter quod vi aut
clam fecit ; tueri enim jus suum debuit, non injuriam
comminisci."

No particular form was requisite to signify the
"prohibitio[2]." The simplest act was sufficient, so
entirely different from the English Law was Roman
Jurisprudence.

---

[1] II. 43. 24.

[2] "Prohibitus intelligitur quovis prohibentis actu: id est, vel dicentis se prohibere, vel manum opponentis, la-

pillumve jactantis prohibendi gratiâ.' 20. § 1. h. t. 1. § 6. h. t. "Vi factum id videtur esse quâ de re quis cum prohibetur facit." II. 50. 73. § 2.

The "prohibitio" was a wider remedy than the "nuntiatio." It comprised "opera in solo facta," i. e. all changes of any kind that affected the property; not merely buildings: "qui arbores succidit utique tenebitur et qui arundinem et qui salictum... item et in vineis succisis, et si quid circa arbores fiat[1]." So, loading rich soil with a pile of manure, digging a trench into which the ox of the "prohibens" has fallen in a public wood, destroying a house, taking the tiles from one, polluting a well-spring, ploughing in certain cases, might be among the objects it was to prevent.

The remedy lay not for the owner only but any one who had an interest, "quia ego sum cujus interest[2]." The rule that the "nuntians" made the defendant for the purposes of the proceeding a "possessor," is inverted in the case of the "prohibens[3]." Therefore not the "prohibens," but the "prohibitus," became the plaintiff. But if the heir of the "prohibitus," "ignorans causam præcedentem," continued what his predecessor had begun, the interdict could not be used against him[4]. The edict applied to the possessor however innocent, for it ran, "quod vi aut clam factum est[5]," not "quod vi aut clam fecisti," as Ulpian remarks.

The liabilities are concisely summed up by Paulus[6]. He "qui vi aut clam fecit," if the possessor, was obliged to allow and pay for the removal of what he had

---

[1] 7. § 5. § 6. § 7. § 8. h. t.   7. § 5. 13. § 3. § 4. § 7. h. t.   II. 47. 7. 11.

[2] 13. § 4. § 5. h. t. 11. h. t.

[3] II. 39. 1. 5. § 10.

[4] 20. § 3. h. t.   [5] § 13. h. t.

[6] 16. § 2. h. t. "In summâ qui vi aut clam fecit, si possidet patientiam et impensam tollendi operis qui fecit nec possidet impensam, qui possidet nec fecit patientiam tantum debet."

done—if the doer, but not the possessor, to pay for
it; if being sued he was the possessor but not the
doer, to allow it.   The same principles that apply to
the interdict "quod vi" hold good when an "opus
clam factum" is in question.   Ulpian has given the
definition of the "clam," "clam facere videri Cassius
scribit eum qui celavit adversarium, neque ei denun-
tiavit, si modo timuit ejus controversiam, aut debuit
timere."   The Roman Law discouraged chicane as
much as violence.

"CAUTIO DAMNI INFECTI[1]." SECURITY AGAINST ANTICIPATED INJURY.

There were cases in which though a person had
sustained a very positive injury, he could recover
no compensation.   If an old house fell upon that to
which it was contiguous, not only could the owner
of the house injured recover no damages from the
owner of the first house, but he could not compel
him to carry away the rubbish if he chose to abandon it:
" si modo omnia quæ jaceant pro derelicto habeat."

In order to guard against[2] such an occurrence
the person endangered might demand security from
the owner and maker of the "opus" by which he
was menaced, for indemnification against the apprehended injury.   If on account of "angustiæ temporis[3]," or absence on behalf of the commonwealth,
injury had happened before the "cautio" had been
required, the person injured might obtain] "cautio
de damno præterito."   The person from whom the
cautio was sought might exonerate himself by giving

---

[1] II. 39. 2. 6.   [2] 7. h. t.   [3] 9. pr. h. t.

up the property, or opus[1]; if he did neither, the plaintiff might be put in possession of the "ædes," at first without ousting the defendant, "missio in possessionem ex primo decreto[2]." If this was ineffectual, the property was considered as derelict, and passed to the plaintiff, who might instead, if he preferred such a course, suppose the cautio had been given[3].

AQUÆ PLUVIÆ ARCENDÆ ACTIO[4].

This was also a remedy against anticipated wrong, "damnum nondum factum;" after the completion of a work however, "opere tamen jam facto," from which damage was apprehended. It lay whenever in consequence of any work changing the natural current or drain of "aqua pluvia," i. e. water descending from the sky, whether it mixed with other water or not, there was reason to fear injury to the land of him who employed it. It lay against the owner, not against the "usufructuarius[5]," for the restoration of the original drain, and not for compensation that had accrued "ante litem contestatam."

It might be answered by shewing that the "opus" was done by public authority[6]; that it had existed[7] from time immemorial; that it was a servitude to which the land of the plaintiff was bound to submit; and that it had been done "patiente vicino[8]," with his tacit assent.

---

[1] 7.

[2] 15. § 11—20. h. t.   15. § 16. h. t.

[3] 13. § ult. h. t.   II. 43. 4. 4. § 2.

[4] II. 39. 3.

[5] An "utilis actio" lay against the fructuarius.   II. 22. § 2. h. t. 3. § 4.

[6] h. t.   II. 5. 6. § 6. 7.   11. § 3.   22. § 2. h.t.

[6] 2. § 3. 22. § 1. h. t.

[7] " Si tamen lex agri non inveniatur vetustatem vicem legis tenere."

[8] 19. h. t.

ACTIO AD EXHIBENDUM[1].

The object of this action was to compel the possessor of any moveable, to produce it for the inspection of any one who had a just and probable cause (of the existence of which cause the judge was to determine) for demanding to see it. Several admirable maxims of Roman jurisprudence are contained in the chapter dealing with this subject. For instance, he who had fraudulently ceased to possess the thing in question, "qui dolo desiit possidere," was treated as the possessor. And again, in answer to one of those cavils which are the scandal of human reason, and which our law has so anxiously encouraged, I find this noble passage: "non oportere jus civile calumniari, neque verba captari, sed quâ mente quid diceretur animadvertere conveniri[2]."

I cannot end my remarks[3] on this head without observing that this law contains the rule from which our doctrine of Habeas Corpus was taken, probably through the medium of some canonist. The passage is as follows: "Si liber homo detineri ab aliquo dicatur, interdictum adversus eum qui detinere dicitur de exhibendo eo potest quis habere[4]."

Where the defendant did not admit[5] the possession, or where, though the equity existed, there were technical obstacles to this form of proceeding, there lay a suppletory "actio in factum[6]." To this head

---

[1] П. 43. 5. *De tabulis exhibendis.* П. 10. 4.

[2] П. 10. 4. 19.

[3] П. 43. 29. de homine libero exhibendo.

[4] П. 10. 4. 13.

[5] "Æquitas exhibitionis." П. 10. 4. 3. § 14.

[6] П. 10. 4. 3. § 14. П. 43. 5.

may be referred the interdicts[1] " de liberis exhibendis," and "de uxore exhibendâ." These were pre-
paratory to the interdict "ad ductionem," which ran
thus: "Si L. T. in potestate L. T. est quo minus
eum L. T. ducere liceat—vim fieri veto[2]."

To this head may be referred the "editio actionis[3]," and the "editio instrumentorum," which made
technical tricks, error and surprise, as nearly impossible under the Roman system, as under ours, till
within these ten years, it was inevitable.

DE GLANDE LEGENDA[4]. DE ARBORIBUS CÆDEN-
DIS[5]. DE MIGRANDO[6].

We have seen that in certain cases the owner
of land on which the moveable of another is to be
found can be compelled "ad exhibendum." There
are however in certain cases specific remedies by
which the same object may be more speedily and
more certainly attained.

The interdict "de glande legendâ" compelled the
proprietor of the soil on which the fruit belonging
to another had fallen, to allow the owner of that
fruit to pick it up every third day[7].

The interdictum "de arboribus cædendis" enabled
any one, injured by a tree overhanging his house or
land, to get rid of the nuisance, in the first place, by

[1] Π. 43. 30.
[2] 43. 30. 3.
[3] Π. 2. 13. The plaintiff could take
his adversary to the "album" and
show him the clause he meant to use.
[4] Π. 43. 28.
[5] Π. 43. 27. 1.
[6] Π. 43. 27. 32.
[7] "Glandis nomine omnes fructus
continentur." § 2. h. t.

extirpation, in the second, by lopping up to fifteen feet from the soil, in conformity with the law of the Twelve Tables.

The interdictum "de migrando" enabled the inquilinus[1] who had paid his rent, or who owed no rent, or who wished to remove any thing not liable to be distrained for the rent, to do so without opposition from the landlord[2].

DE CLOACIS[3].

This interdict enabled any part-owner of a "cloaca," on giving "cautio damni infecti," to repair it on his neighbour's premises.

In like manner, every one who had a servitude "itineris actusve," might make such reparations as the road required by the interdictum "de itinere actuque reficiendo[4]."

The plaintiff, in addition to the right, was bound to shew the exercise of it "nec vi nec clam nec precario," in the preceding year, and also to give security "de damno infecto[5]."

FOR THE REMOVAL OF A CORPSE[6].

The person on whose land or in whose monument a corpse had illegally been deposited, had an

---

[1] Not the colonus.

[2] II. 43. 32. Every case in which the landlord would have a right is guarded against by the edict. It is really astonishing (were it not for the profound ignorance of Englishmen on all subjects of jurisprudence) that with such an example before our eyes Special Pleading should have so long prevailed, and to a certain degree should still prevail, in this country.

[3] II. 43. 23.

[4] II. 43. 19.

[5] 43. 19. 3. § 11—16. 4, 5.

[6] II. 11. 7. 2. § 1—7.

"actio in factum" against the person who placed it there, to compel him to remove it, or pay the value of the land.

OBLIGATIONS ARISING FROM DELICTA. THEFT. FURTUM[1].

"Furtum" is the fraudulent removal of a thing from the place in which it was for the sake of profit, either from the thing itself, or its use or possession, in violation of the law of nature.

I refer to the passages in the note[2] to justify the translation I have given as exhibiting the intended definition of "furtum."

From the word "contrectatio" it is inferred that "furtum" could not be committed of immoveables[3]. Thus the mere entry into a chamber for the purpose of theft did not constitute the "furtum[4]." But he who received money to pay the debt of Titius to Caius, and instead of doing so[5] paid his own debt to Caius, was guilty of "furtum."

---

[1] *Inst.* 4. § 1. II. 47. 2: "Furtum est contrectatio rei fraudulosa, lucri faciendi gratiâ, vel ipsius rei vel etiam usus ejus possessionisve, quod lege naturali prohibitum est admittere."

[2] II. 41. 2. 3. § 18: "Si rem apud te depositam furti faciendi causâ contrectaveris desino possidere. Sed si eam loco non moveris, et inficiandi animum habeas, plerique veterum et Sabinus et Cassius recte responderunt, possessorem me manere *quia furtum sine contrectatione fieri non potest*, nec animo furtum admittatur." II. 10. 4. 15: "Thesaurus meus in tuo fundo est, nec eum pateris me effodere: *cum eum loco non moveris*, furti quidem—nomine agere recte non posse me Labeo ait."

[3] II. 47. 2. 25: "verum est, quod plerique probant, fundi furti agi non posse." Gaius, *Inst.* 2. § 51. against the opinion of the Sabiniani.

[4] "Qui furti faciendi causâ conclave intravit nondum fur est, quamvis furandi causâ intravit." II. 47. 2. 21. § 7.

[5] "Julianus scripsit, si pecuniam quis a me acceperit ut creditori meo solvat, deinde cum tantam pecuniam eidem creditori deberet, suo nomine solverit, furtum eum facere." II. 47. 2. 52. § 16.

The criterion of the crime was unlawful gain, wherefore a man might be guilty of a furtum of what belonged to himself[1].

The taking unlawfully the "hereditas" of another "ante aditam hæreditatem[2]," was not a furtum, but constituted the "crimen expilatæ hæreditatis," and fell under the cognizance of the "præses provinciæ." Neither could married people have the "actio furti" against each other[3]. The injured person had his "actio furti" against the wrongdoer for four- or two-fold compensation, as the furtum was "manifestum" or "non manifestum[4]."

DOLI ACTIO[5].

This action, where there was no other remedy, lay for the reparation of intentional and illegal injury. It gave a right to complete compensation if brought within two years, but if brought later, only to the gain which the defendant had obtained from his dolus. As it was a "famosa actio," it could only be brought where the damage amounted to two aurei, and not against persons whom the plaintiff

---

[1] II. 47. 2. 15. § 1: "Dominus qui rem subripuit in quâ ususfructus alienus est, furti usufructuario tenetur." So he might commit a furtum "rei pignoratæ," 19. 6. 54. § 1. h. t.; or if he lent to another what he had received for his own use: I quote the passage, which is a remarkable one: "Ex quo satis apparet furtum fieri si quis usum alienæ rei in suum lucrum convertat, nec movere quem debet quasi nihil lucri sui gratiâ faciat. Species enim lucri est ex alieno largiri et beneficii debitorem sibi acquirere." 66. "Si is qui rem pignori dedit vendiderit eam, quamvis dominus sit, furtum facit; sive eam tradiderit creditori sive tantum obligaverat." II. 13. 1. 16.

[2] II. 47. 19. 2.

[3] II. 25. 2.

[4] II. 47. 2. 27. § 50=2—8. 21. 9. 34. 52. 54. § 4. eod.

[5] II. 4. 3. II. 50. 17. 47. 4. 3. 18. 1. § 1. 4. 6. 7.

was bound to hold in reverence. In this last case an "actio in factum" for the recovery of the unlawful profit lay in its stead.

Analogous to the "actio doli" is the "actio quod falso tutore gestum esse dicatur[1]."

The action against the person who had imposed upon another, by assuming the authority of a "tutor," although he was not tutor: "In eum qui, cum tutor non esset, dolo malo auctor factus esse dicetur, judicium dabo, ut quanti ea res erit tantam pecuniam condemnetur[2]."

SI MENSOR FALSUM MODUM DIXERIT[3].

This was an action against the "mensor agrorum," who, like an English barrister, could bring no action for his fees, but received an "honorarium," and gave his labour "beneficii loco." It could only be brought in cases of "dolus malus," "visum est enim satis abundeque coerceri mensorem, si dolus malus solus conveniatur ejus hominis qui civiliter obligatus non est." Therefore neither want of skill nor negligence were actionable. "Lata culpa[4]" was tantamount to "dolus."

He who purposely hindered another from appearing[5] at the proper time before a court of justice.

He who fraudulently[6] prevented one "in possessionem missus" from taking possession.

He who by the alienation of any disputed pro-

---

[1] II. 27. 6.
[2] II. 27. 6. 7.
[3] II. 11. 6.
[4] II. 11. 6. 1.
[5] II. 2. 10.
[6] II. 43. 4. II. 4. 7.

perty[1] made it more difficult or less beneficial for another to recover his right.

These persons were all liable to an action "in factum."

In the last case, if the wrongdoer was the plaintiff, he had an "exceptio."

The measure of damages in this case was the injury sustained in consequence of the change by the aggrieved party[2], e. g. "si res fuerint usucaptæ ab eo cui alienatæ sint."

To this head belongs the "Actio Pauliana[3]."

If a debtor alienated his goods to the injury of his creditors, the Actio Pauliana, an "actio in factum" (sometimes an "interdictum fraudatorum" attended with very much the same consequences) was given to them. This action supposes an "alienatio in fraudem creditorum" as its foundation. This might be by paying before the money[4] was actually due, or any act that might prevent the creditors from receiving their share in the distribution of the bankrupt's property. It lay against the alienee, whose privity to the fraud, if he had received the property as a gift, it was not necessary to prove; but if he parted with it to a third alienee, who was bonâ fide,

[1] This is one of the most refined and salutary parts of Roman jurisprudence: it is the grand maxim, so opposite to all the ideas of those who made the mass of incoherent exceptions which is called law among us, "ne cujus deterior causa fiat ex alieno facto." Could such a monstrous injustice as "tacking" have existed in a court of equity, if our judges who created and supported it had ever heard of such a principle?

[2] 3 h. t. = 4.

[3] "Quæ in fraudem creditorum facta sunt, ut restituantur." 4. 2. 8. Cod. 7. 75.

[4] 10. 12. eod. tit. "nam prætor intelligit fraudem etiam in tempore fieri."

such last-mentioned alienee was not liable "si cui donatum est non esse quærendum an sciente eo cui donatum gestum sit, sed hoc tantum an fraudentur creditores[1]."

"[2]Qui a debitore, cujus bona possessa sunt, sciens rem emit, iterum alii bonâ fide ementi vendidit, quæsitum est an secundus emptor conveniri potest : sed verior est Sabini sententia, bonâ fide emptorem non teneri, quia dolus ei tantum nocere debeat qui eum admisit."

The object of the action was the recovery of what had been alienated with its profits, so far as might be necessary to satisfy the creditor—nor could the alienee recover what he had given from the creditors. The action lay for a year "ex die factæ venditionis," and afterwards, for the profit made, for a reason that will seem surprising to the readers of our law, "iniquum enim prætor putavit in lucro morari[3], eum qui lucrum sensit ex fraude."

It lay against the heirs whose inheritance had been increased by the fraud of the deceased[4].

ACTIO SERVI CORRUPTI[5].

This actio lay against the seducer or corrupter of a slave, "quo cum deteriorem faceret," or the harbourer of one who had run away. With its usual discrimination and humanity, the Roman Law does not hold him responsible who did this "vel humanitate, vel misericordiâ ductus, vel aliâ probatâ et

---

[1] 6. § 10. h. t.   25. pr. h. t.
[2] 9. h. t.
[3] II. 42. 8. 10. 24.
[4] 10. ult. 11 h. t.
[5] II. 11. 3.

justâ ratione." It applied to one who made a bad slave worse, as well as to one who made a good slave bad[1].

CALUMNIA[2].

The person who has received money to abstain from harassing another by an unrighteous lawsuit, or to do any litigious act, may be compelled to refund four times the sum he has received if the action "in factum" be commenced for it within the year, and the sum itself, if he be sued afterwards.

The action lay in the case of criminal as well as in that of civil proceedings[3].

He who gave money to another "ut negotium faceret[4]" to a third person, could not recover the money so given, but the right of action was given to the third person : "ei dabitur petitio propter quem datum est ut calumnia ei fiat." Therefore if Caius received money from Titius to bring a suit against Paulus—and from Paulus not to bring it—he was liable in two actions to Paulus.

Money's worth[5], the release from an obligation, the loan of money without interest, the sale or hire of a thing for less than its real value, was tantamount to money—nor did it matter whether the money was given to the corrupt person or to another for his benefit. Neither did it matter whether the money was paid before or after the judgment[6].

---

[1] "Immo et si erat servus omni modo fugiturus, vel furtum facturus, hic vero laudator hujus propositi extitit, tenetur, non enim oportet laudando augeri malitiam."

[2] Π. 3. 6.

[3] 1. h. t.

[4] 3. § 3. h. t.

[5] 2. h. t.

[6] 1. § 2. h. t.

The action[1] did not lie where there was a "bonâ fide transactio:" "Neque enim transactionibus est interdictum sed sordidis concessionibus."

The case of Lord Bacon was also provided for[2]: "Si igitur accepit ut negotium faceret, sive fecit sive non fecit tenetur, et qui accepit ne faceret etsi fecit tenetur." So lofty was the morality of the Roman Jurist (heathen as he was) even amid the universal degradation of a race steeped to the lips in servitude —so careful was he to block up every loophole to prevarication and every avenue of guilt, and so striking is the contrast furnished by his rules, to the anxiety with which our law long provided every possible defence that low cunning could suggest for the rapacity, violence, and extortion, to which our judges shewed for so long a period so strong a sympathy[3].

RESTITUTIO IN INTEGRUM[4].

This was the immediate interference of the magistrate to replace the suitor in a situation from which he had been inequitably and to his prejudice removed: "Integri restitutio est redintegrandæ rei vel causæ actio[5]."

To prove the utility of this chapter[6] of juris-

---

[1] 6. § 3.

[2] This is the defence put forward by those who in our day have been transported by their admiration for Lord Bacon's glorious intellect to vindicate his bottomless corruption ; but the defence, scandalous as it is, cannot be supported. Lord Bacon sold injustice as well as justice, as he himself plainly says.

[3] See the case of Arne and Huggins,

in the State Trials, disclosing crimes almost incredible, which, thanks to the judge, were perpetrated with impunity.

[4] II. 4. 1—7. Cox, Reports, 1. 333. Donellus 21. 4—14. P.Williams 3. 315. Glück, 5. 392. Pothier, *Pandector. Inst.* Vol. III. p. 196. Domat. 2. 267. Code civil. 1674. 1334 seq.

[5] *Pauli sententiæ.*

[6] Ulpian 1. de Integ. rest. "Integri

prudence would be superfluous; it is self-evident.
Under this head the Prætor relieves men who have
erred or been imposed upon, be it from fear, be it
through craft, be it from age, be it from absence.

It was eminently the creature of Prætorian law,
and could be employed[1] only where in cases no help
could be obtained in the ordinary course of justice.
It was granted by the Prætor after a careful investigation of the circumstances of the case: "Omnes in
integrum[2] restitutiones causâ cognitâ a Prætore pro-
mittuntur, scilicet ut justitiam earum causarum ex-
aminet an veræ sint, quarum nomine singulis sub-
venit."

Though the chief heads were enumerated[3], the
effect of this salutary principle was not confined to
them: "Item inquit Prætor, si qua alia mihi justa
causa videbitur, in integrum restituam." This clause,
the law goes on to say, is necessary: "Multi enim
casus evenire potuerunt qui deferrent restitutionis
auxilium nec singulatim enumerari potuerunt; ut
quoties æquitas restitutionem suggerit ad hanc clau-
sulam erit descendendum[4]."

Like most Prætorian remedies, it must be invoked within the year, "annus utilis," only that
"propter capitis diminutionem" was "perpetua."

---

restitutionem Prætor tribuit ex his causis quæ per dolum, metum, et status permutationem, et justum erro- rem, et absentiam necessariam, et in- firmitatem ætatis, gesta esse dicuntur." Pauli Rec. Sent. 1—7. 2. What would the authors of this jurisprudence have thought of the decision in "Taltarum's" case?

[1] II. 4. 4. 16. "Si communi auxilio et mero jure munitus est non debet ei tribui extraordinarium auxilium," &c. 4. 2. 21. § 3.

[2] II. 4. 1. 3.

[3] II. 4. 1. 1. § 1. "Verba edicti ta- lia sunt." II. 4. 1. 29. § 6.

[4] II. 4. 5. 26. § 9. Constantine ex- tended the privilege. L. 2. Cod. Theod.

The remedy extended not only to the persons themselves who required it, but to their successors : "Omnium qui ipsi potuerunt in integrum restitui successores in integrum restitui possunt, et ita sæpissime est constitutum[1]."

It was granted not only against the person who had done the wrong, or taken the advantage, but against any possessor of the object the restitution of which was required ; no man therefore, says Paulus, whom the Prætor has promised to restore "in integrum" is excluded from what he claims[2].

It was not granted where the loss sustained was trifling[3], "propter satis minimam rem vel summam," with the exception of that "ex causâ doli;" for the person against whom in such a case a judgment had been given was infamous[4]. Where there was a case of "lucrum cessans[5]," it was open to all. But it did not apply where the gain sought would be caused by the loss of another, or by his punishment[6]. Minors might have recourse to it, though they had not sustained actual loss, "sed etiam cum intersit eorum litibus et sumtibus non vexari[7]."

A minor could not take advantage of this re-

---

de integri restit. Justinian enlarged the time to four years, without distinction of age or place. L. ult. Cod. de temporib. in integrum restit.

[1] II. 4. 1.

[2] "Nemo videtur re exclusus quem Prætor in integrum se restituturum pollicetur." Paulus ad edict. 7. 15. eod. "Is qui actionem habet ad rem restituendam, ipsam rem habere videtur." II. 50. 17. 14.

[3] II. 4. 1. 4.

[4] II. 4. 3. 25. II. 4. 3. 1. § 4. "Quoniam famosa actio non temere debet a Prætore decerni."

[5] II. 4. 4. 7. § 6. "Hodie certo jure utimur ut et in lucro minoribus precurratur." II. 4. 6. 27. "Sive quid amiserit sive lucratus non sit."

[6] "Non cum et lucri faciendi causâ ex alterius damno vel pœnâ auxilium sibi impertiri desiderant." II. 4. 6. 18.

[7] II. 4. 4. 6.

medy merely because a transaction in which he had engaged, and in which a prudent man would have engaged, had, from any sudden or unforeseen cause (an earthquake, or an inundation), turned out unprofitably[1]. But where the "lubricum ætatis" had been the cause of loss, as if he had accepted an inheritance burdened with debt, or exposed to many contingencies[2], the minor might obtain restitution[3] to his former state.

Assistance[4] was given to the minor only when he was "captus contractibus," not when he was "delinquens." Only if he incurred, by an error in the course he ought to have adopted, and by denying instead of confessing, the "damnum dupli," he might be relieved against this part of his loss[5].

If the minor hastily, "juvenili levitate ductus," rejected an inheritance, and applied for restitution while everything was "in integro," "omnimodo audiendus est;" but if he waited till the inheritance was sold, and the transactions concerning it closed, to take advantage of the labours of him on whom it had devolved, "repellendus est[6]."

If the minor could procure relief "mero jure et communi auxilio," this extraordinary remedy[7] was

---

[1] II. 4. 4. 11. § 4. 15. "Item non restituetur qui sobrie rem suam administrans occasione damni non inconsulte accidentis, sed fato, velit restitui...neque enim ætatis lubrico captus est adeundo locupletem hæreditatem, et quod fato contingit cuivis patrifamilias quamvis diligentissimo possit contingere." 5. eod.

[2] "Multis casibus obnoxiæ," "districte probandum est in rebus quæ fortuitis casibus subjectæ sunt non esse minori adversus emptorem succurrendum,"."nisi aut sordes, aut evidens gratia tutorum vel curatorum doceatur." Eod. 7. § 8.

[3] Eod.   [4] II. 4. 4. 9. § 2.

[5] The Canon Law puts churches and eleemosynary endowments on a level with minors. X. h. t. 1. 3. 6. De rebus Eccles. 3. 13. 11

[6] 24. § 2. eod.   [7] Eod.

not granted to him, as if he made a contract "sine tutoris auctoritate, nec locupletior factus est."

He could not be "restitutus in integrum" if he had given liberty to a slave[1], and "injuriarum judicium semel omissum repeti non potest[2]."

If the minor when he came to full age[3] ratified what had been done, he could not take advantage of this remedy; but if his acts when of full age were the necessary consequence of what he had done as a minor, he might do so[4].

This chapter of the Pandects is especially recommended by D'Aguesseau[5] to the student who wishes to make himself a great magistrate: "Si le jeune homme......veut le devenir, la matière des contrats et des obligations sera celle à laquelle il s'attachera d'abord dans l'étude du droit, en y joignant celle des restitutions en entier, qui est aussi fondée sur les premières notions de la justice naturelle, et qui est d'un usage continuel au Châtelet."

ABSENCE.

This head of relief applies to those who were absent "reipublicæ causâ," "sine dolo;" e. g. all soldiers "qui discedere signis sine periculo non possunt:" not on leave of absence, but "dum domum vadit aut redit."

---

[1] "Adversus libertatem." Eod. 11. § 9.

[2] 37. eod.

[3] "Si quis major factus comprobaverit quod minor gesserat, repetitionem cessare." 3. § 1. eod.

[4] "Minor miscuerat se paternæ hæreditati, majorque factus exegerat aliquid a debitoribus paternis; mox desiderabat restitui in integrum: quo magis abstineret paternâ hæreditate contradicebatur ei, quasi major factus comprobasset quod minori sibi placuit, putavimus tamen restituendum in integrum initio inspecto." 3. § 2. eod.

[5] Vol. XV. p. 102.

Any one not a soldier who by order of the council had been present on a military expedition where he had been killed—"hæredibus succurrendum."

"Medici militum."

"Qui provinciis præsunt."

Any one specially ordered by the ruler to exercise the functions of judge or assessor in his native province, "puto enim reipubl. causâ abesse."

"Procurator Cæsaris."

"Qui missi sunt ad gratulandum principi."

The absence "reipublicæ causâ" lasted so long as the duty was to be fulfilled or the function exercised. Time was allowed for return; but if any one "deflexerit suæ rei causâ," that was not to reckon in his favour—illness and inclement weather were to be excused, "habebitur ratio humanitatis—sicuti haberi solet et hiemis et navigationis et cæterorum quæ casu contingunt."

But magistrates resident at Rome were not absent "reipublicæ causâ."

Nor the farmers of taxes.

Nor those employed to draw up the Acta Præsidum.

They must be absent "coacti et non sui commodi causâ," "sine dolo malo."

CHAPTER VIII.

LAW OF SERVITUDES AND USUFRUCT[1].

RIGHTS IN THE THING.

WHERE the natural liberty that otherwise would belong to the proprietor is abridged, and his power over what belongs to him is subjected to a right existing for the benefit of another, the property so burdened is no longer free, and is therefore said in the Roman Law to be servient, servire, and the liability is called by the Roman Law a servitude, and in ours an easement. The essential characters of a servitude according to the Roman Law were, first, that it imposed no active duty. This is over and over again stated in the Pandects. Such a duty might exist, but would not be a servitude. It compelled the owner to abstain himself from doing what otherwise would be lawful, or to allow others to do what otherwise would be unlawful: "Servitutum non ea natura est ut aliquid faciat quis, ... sed ut aliquid patiatur vel non faciat[2]." Secondly, it

---

[1] *General Texts.*
"Illud etiam verum puto quod Ofilius scribit: si fundus tuus vicino serviat, et propterea aquam recipiat, cessare aquæ pluviæ arcendæ actionem, sic tamen, si non ultra modum noceat. Cui consequens est quod Labeo putat: si quis vicino cesserit, jus ei esse aquam immittere, aquæ pluviæ arcendæ eum agere non posse." II. 39. 3. 2. § 10.

La Serva, Vol. I. 271. *Der. Rom.*

[2] II. 8. 1. 15. § 1. II. 8. 5. 6. 2. 11. II. 8. 5. 8. 2.

could exist only over the property of another: "Nulli enim res sua servit[1]." This is a corollary from the definition that it is a dismemberment of property[2].

Thirdly, there could be no servitude of a servitude; therefore a legacy[3] of an usufruct in a right of way, an aqueduct, &c. was invalid.

A servitude[4] might be personal—due to a person, as to the usufruct of an estate, or real, due from one thing to another; as the servitude to which particular buildings or land were subject in town or in the country, e.g. "oneris ferendi, tigni immittendi, protegendi fluminis vel stillicidii."

A real might be turned into a personal servitude[5], "si testator personam demonstravit cui servitutem præstari voluit."

A servitude[6] was not to be extended beyond reasonable limits: it was to be enjoyed "civiliter." An absolute right granted to Titius of walking at

---

[1] II. 8. 2. 26.

II. 8. 2. 27. "In re communi nemo dominorum jure servitutis neque facere quidquam invito altero potest neque prohibere quo minus faciat—nulli enim res sua servit."

II. 33. 2. 1.

II. 7. 1. 15. "Proprietatis dominus, ne quidem consentiente usufructuario, servitutem imponere potest."

[2] What litigation and ruin would have been averted if this simple principle had been applied sooner to outstanding terms of years in our system.

[3] "Nec usus nec ususfructus itineris, actus, viæ, aquæductus legari potest, quia servitus servitutis esse non potest." II. de usufr. 2. leg. 1.

[4] De servit. 1.

II. 8. 4. 12. e. g. "Cum fundus fundo servit...ædificia quoque fundis et fundi ædificiis eâdem conditione serviunt."

[5] II. 8. 3. l. penult.; and in the case "itineris, actus, viæ, pascendi, aquæ haustus." *Passage of Spanish Sheep from one part of Spain to the other.* Jovellanos.

[6] II. 8. 1. 4. § 1. "Si cui simplicius via per fundum cujuspiam cedatur, vel relinquatur, in infinito videlicet per quamlibet ejus partem ire, agere, licebit—*civiliter* modo, nam quædam in sermone tacite excipiuntur; non enim per villam ipsam neo per medias vineas ire agere sinendus est, cum id æque commode per alteram partem facere possit minore servientis fundi detrimento."

his pleasure over the land of Caius did not enable Titius to walk over the vines of Caius, or into his drawing-room, or to inflict wanton mischief on his property.

Fourthly, it could not exist unless it was for the benefit of somebody[1] (unlike the fantastical and wantonly vexatious[2] devices of the barbarians who established the feudal law); so a stipulation with another person that I shall not use a particular road of my own farm, is of no avail, "quod nihil vicinorum interest non valet[3]."

The grant of a servitude tacitly[4] carries with it the allowance of all that was in reason necessary for its enjoyment: "Si iter legatum sit quo nisi opere facto ire non possit, licere fodiendo, substinendo, iter facere, Proculus ait[5]."

The owner of the servient object was not bound to keep it in repair. The right to a servitude was indivisible[6].

---

[1] "Quoties nec hominum nec prædiorum servitutes sunt quia nihil vicinorum interest non valet, veluti ne per fundum tuum eas, aut ibi consistas, et ideo mihi concedas jus tibi non esse fundo tuo uti, frui, nihil agitur." II. 8. 1. 15; but see 19. eod. "Quædam enim deberi habere possumus etiamsi nobis utilia non sunt."

[2] Fowling was for that reason excluded, II. 8. 3. 16: οὐκ εὔλογον ἀκόντων τῶν δεσπότων ὑμᾶς ἐν ἀλλοτρίοις χωρίοις ἰξεύειν, said Divus Pius.

[3] "Qui habet haustum iter quoque habere videtur ad hauriendum." II. commun. præd. 11. § 1.

[4] II. 8. 4. 11. 1: "tacite hæc jura sequuntur."

[5] As a general rule; but the owner of a wall supporting the beam of another man as a servitude might be bound to repair it according to the better opinion. "Evaluit Servii sententia in propositâ specie, ut possit quis defendere jus sibi esse cogere adversarium reficere parietem ad onera sua sustinenda." II. eod. "In omnibus servitutibus refectio ad eum pertinet, qui sibi servitutem adserit, non ad eum cujus res servit." II. si serv. vind. 6. § 2.

[6] II. 8. 1. 11 and 17.

REAL SERVITUDES[1].

The word servitude used by itself generally denotes a real or prædial servitude.

In real or prædial servitudes there are two invariable objects: one to which, and another from which, a right is due. The first is called the dominant, the second the servient "prædium." A real servitude was a burden imposed on one prædium for the benefit of another prædium.

"Neratius ait, nec haustum pecoris, nec appulsum, nec cretæ eximendæ, calcisque coquendæ, jus posse in alieno esse, nisi fundum vicinum habeat[2]."

They must exist for the benefit of the dominant land[3]; and the right to them cannot be detached from it, or extended beyond its exigencies[4]. They may be not only for substantial profit, but for delectation; as the right of bringing water not only to irrigate the pasture, but to improve the landscape. But they could not be established for merely personal objects independent of the estate, "ut pomum decerpere liceat, ut cœnare, ut spatiari in alieno possimus[5], servitus imponi non potest." They were bound to have a constant and perennial cause; wherefore the right of bringing water from an artificial pond or reservoir could not be granted, "omnes

[1] "Patientia pro traditione." II. de servit. 4.
[2] II. d. s. p. 2. 5. § 1.
[3] II. d. s. p. 2. 5. § 1. cod. 7. § 1. "In rusticis prædiis impedit servitutem medium prædium quod non servit."
[4] De s. p. 2. § 24. "Hoc jure utimur ut etiam non ad irrigandum sed pecoris causâ vel amœnitatis aqua duci possit." II. de aq. quot. 1. § 11.
[5] II. 8. 3. 5. § 2. "Neratius dicit ut maxime calcis coquendæ et cretæ eximendæ servitus constitui possit, non ultra posse quam quatenus ad eum ipsum fundum opus sit."

autem prædiorum servitutes perpetuas causas habere
debent et ideo neque ex lacu[1], neque ex stagno con-
cedi aquæductus potest." Servitudes were either
continuous, exercised without interruption, or discon-
tinuous, i.e. exercised at intervals.

The prædium in respect of which the servitude
was due might be urban or rustic. The prædium
urbanum had relation to the superficies[2], the prædium
rusticum to the soil[3]. Some servitudes were called
rustic because they belonged to a prædium rusticum,
such as iter, actus, via, aquæductus, which if they
had been annexed to a prædium urbanum would be
called urban.

As instances[4] of urban servitudes we may name
the servitude "oneris ferendi," when the wall or
pillar of one man sustained the weight of the building of another. The owner of the servient building
might exonerate himself by relinquishing the property.

The servitude "tigni immittendi[5]," of receiving in
the wall the beam of another house and allowing it
to remain.

"Tigni projiciendi[6]," of allowing the beam to

---

[1] II. d. s. p. u. 28. "Stillicidii
quoque immittendi naturalis et perpetua causa esse debet."

[2] Inst. de serv.
II. de serv. 1. 3.
II. commun. præd. 1. "Prædiorum
urbanorum servitutes hæ sunt quæ
ædificiis inhærent, ideo urbanorum
prædiorum dictæ, quoniam ædificia
omnia urbana prædia appellamus etsi in villâ ædificata sunt."

[3] This is the view of Vinnius on a

matter much disputed: it agrees with
II. 8. 1. 3. "Servitutes prædonum
aliæ in superficie consistunt."

[4] De s. p. u. 33.

[5] Eod. 8. 2. "Ut tigna suscipiat."
Compare 14. eod.

[6] II. de v. s. 242. § 1. "Inter projectum et immissum hoc interesse, ait
Labeo, quod projectum esset id quod
ita proveheretur, ut nunquam requi-
esceret."

project over part of another house without resting on it.

"Altius non tollendi[1]," when the occupier of one house was forbidden to raise his building, lest this might affect the enjoyment of another.

"Ne luminibus officiatur[2]:" this was almost identical with the preceding one.

By the "luminum servitus[3]" the neighbour was obliged to receive the light from our windows[4].

The servitus "stillicidii" or "fluminis[5]" was twofold; "recipiendi," by which the neighbour was obliged to allow the water to drop from our roof upon his land.

"Non recipiendi," by which he was to keep the water collected on his roof from falling upon our land.

The "stillicidium" was the word used to denote water falling in separate drops.

The "flumen," that which flowed in a continued current. Besides these, there were the "cloacæ[6]," "latrinæ," "fumi immittendi[7]."

---

[1] De s. p.u. 2. Instit. de serv. § 2. II. de s. p. u. "Si inter te et vicinum tuum non convenit ad quam altitudinem extolli ædificia quæ facere instituisti oporteat, arbitrium accipere poteris." 24. eod.

[2] "Hoc maxime adepti videmur ne jus sit vicino altius ædificare atque ita minuere lumina nostrorum ædificiorum." 17. eod. Planting a tree might be forbidden on the same ground. "Nam et arbor efficit quo minus cœli videri possit." Eod. 2. "Interdum dici potest eum quoque qui tollit ædificium vel deprimit luminibus officere, si forte κατ' ἀν-

τάκλασιν vel pressurâ quâdam lumen in eas ædes devolvatur."

[3] "Luminum servitute constitutâ id acquisitum videtur ut vicinus lumina nostra excipiat." II. de s. p. u. 4.

[4] "Lumen, id est ut cœlum videatur, et interest inter lumen et prospectum, nam prospectus etiam ex inferioribus locis est, lumen ex inferiore loco esse non potest." II. d. s. p. u. 16.

[5] II. 8. 2. 17. § 3. eod. 20. Inst. 1. de servit. II. 8. 2. 28. Theoph. Parap. § 1. Inst. de serv.

[6] II. 43. 23. 1. § 4.

[7] II. si serv. vind. 8. § 5.

The servitudes "prædiorum rusticorum" were iter, actus, via, aquæductus ; "iter" was the right of a man to passage[1]; "actus," the right to drive cattle or a vehicle; "via," was the right of driving, riding, or walking on an ascertained and measured road, set out by public authority. The "iter" did not include the "actus," but the "actus" did include the "iter," and the "via" both. The "aquæ-ductus[2]" was the right of passage for running water through the field of another. Besides these, the principal servitudes were the "aquæ haustus," the "pecoris ad aquam appellandi," the "pascendi," "cretæ lapidisque eximendi," "arenæ fodiendæ," "calcis coquendæ."

Real servitudes might be established :—

By the will of private individuals, signified either by covenant or by testamentary disposition ; to which, in affirmative servitudes, may be added a quasi traditio and acquiescence: "Si de usufructu agatur tradito Publiciana datur, itemque servitutibus urbanorum prædiorum per traditionem constitutis vel per patientiam ... item rusticorum[3]." A servitude might be granted by implication, as if a right was granted, which, unless the servitude was granted also, would be useless : "Usufructu loci legato etiam accessus dandus est, quia et haustu relicto iter quo-

[1] II. 8. 3. 1. eod. 7. "Viæ latitudo ex lege duodecim tabularum octo pedes in porrectum habet, in anfractum, id est ubi flexum est, sedecim." II. d. s. p. R. 8. "Quâ vehiculum ire poterit, alioquin iter erit non via." 23. eod. 13. § 2.

[2] II. 43. 20. 4. II. 8. 3. 10. eod. 21. eod. 22. II. 39. 3. 17. § 1. Inst. de servit. 2. 3. 2. II. 8. 3. 20. § 3. II. 43. 20. 1. § 13. II. 8. 3. 1. 1.

[3] Dig. 6. 2. 11. § 1.

que ad hauriendum præstaretur[1]." It might be limited to time, place, and particular modes of enjoyment[2]. Nobody but the owner (including by that word[3] the superficiarius and emphyteuta) could impose or acquire a servitude.

A joint owner[4] could not impose a servitude without the assent of his coproprietor. The real owner could not impose a servitude[5], even with the consent of the beneficial holder, unless it was such as clearly not to injure him: "Veluti si talem servitutem concesserit jus sibi non esse altius tollere."

A servitude might be established by the decision of a judge, in cases of necessity, e.g. if a road was destroyed by an inundation[6], "vicinus proximus viam præstare debet." And by prescription[7], "siquis diuturno usu et longâ quasi possessione jus aquæ ducendæ nactus sit, non est ei necesse docere de jure, quo aqua constituta est, veluti ex legato, vel alio modo, sed utilem habet actionem ut ostendat per annos forte tot usum se, non vi non clam non precario."

Servitudes[8] are lost by the lapse of the time for

---

[1] Dig. 8. 2. 10.

[2] "Modum adjici servitutibus posse constat, veluti quo genere vehiculi utatur—vel non agatur, veluti ut equo duntaxat—vel ut certum pondus vehatur, ut grex ille transducatur, aut carbo portetur." II. de servit. 4. § 1. § 2.

[3] In these cases the Prætor supplied the law in behalf of the actual owner—when the property came to the real owner the servitude ceased. "Servitutes quoque Prætoris jure

constituentur, et ipsæ ad exemplum earum quæ ipso jure constitutæ sunt utilibus actionibus petentur, sed et interdictum de his utile competet." II. 43. 18. 1. § 9.

[4] II. 8. 1. § 2.

[5] "Ne quidem consentiente fructuario." II. de usufruct. 15. § ult.

[6] II. serv. quom. amitt. 14. § 1.

[7] II. si servit. vindic. 10.

[8] II. quemad. servit. amittun. II. de s. p. urb. 30. II. de s. p. urb. 20. § 2. 31.

which it was agreed they should exist, or from a supervening cause, such as express compact, destruction of one of the estates, or by the blending of the two estates by non user, for ten years, for the present, and twenty years for the absent; there being during that time full opportunity of its enjoyment.

PERSONAL SERVITUDES.

Servitudes are called personal, which are created for the benefit of a person, and cease to exist when he does. They are four :—

Ususfructus, usus, habitatio, jus operarum servilium.

Ususfructus is the right of enjoying the property of another without impairing it substantially: "Ususfructus est jus alienis rebus utendi fruendi, salvâ earum substantiâ." From corporeal objects, which the very act of using did not consume, to which it was at first confined, it was afterwards extended to objects of all kinds, security being given to the heir for the value of such as were of a consumable nature[1]. This latter right was called "quasi ususfructus."

Thus the ususfructus nominum[2] might be bequeathed.

[1] "Senatus censuit ut omnium rerum quas in cujusque patrimonio esse constaret, ususfructus legari possit—quo senatus consulto inductum videtur ut earum rerum quæ usu tolluntur vel minuuntur possit ususfructus legari." II. 7. 5. I. "Utilitatis causâ senatus censuit posse etiam earum rerum (quæ ipso usu consumuntur) usumfructum restitui, ut tamen eo nomine hæredi utiliter cavetur." Inst. de usufructu, § 2.

[2] "Post quod omnium rerum ususfructus legari poterit. An et nominum ? Nerva negavit, sed est verius quod Cassius et Proculus existimant, posse legari." II. de us. earum, &c. L. 3.

The usufruct was created by the spontaneous act of private men, by will[1], by contract, by law, as the right of the father in the "peculium adventitium" of the son; by the sentence of the judge, when of two litigants, the property in an estate is assigned to one, and the usufruct to another[2], by prescription[3].

The rights of the usufructuary[4] were the fruits and profits of the thing enjoyed : such as the wool, milk, and offspring of animals, the skill of a slave, the produce of mines and quarries[5] which he was entitled to dig, if it was for the benefit of the estate. He was entitled to the loppings of wood, but not to cut down forest-trees, unless for works of necessity. But he did not become the proprietor of a treasure found on the land, nor of the child of a slave, nor of alluvial land. He was entitled to all the means requisite for the enjoyment of the property, such as a right of way to the land, and to all the remedies necessary for the protection of the property which the owner could employ, such as the "cautio damni infecti," the "novi operis nuntiatio." He might sell or hire his own rights to others, but he could only sell the property to the owner[6].

The quasi usufruct gave the rights of an owner,

---

[1] Inst. 2. 4.

[2] Dig. 16. 6. 1.

[3] Ib. 10. 3. 6. 10. 2. 16. 1.

[4] Ib. 7. 1.

[5] Ib. 7. 1. 13. § 5.

[6] "Finitur usus si domino proprietatis ab usufructuario cedatur cum cedendo extraneo nihil agitur." Inst.

§ 3. "Diximus usumfructum a fructuario cedi non posse nisi domino proprietatis, et si extraneo cedatur, id est ei qui proprietatem non habet, nihil ad eum transire sed ad dominum proprietatis reversurum usumfructum." II. de jure dotium, 23. 3. 66.

enabling the beneficial holder not only to alienate and worsen, but to consume the property.

The duties[1] of the usufructuary were to preserve in its integrity that of which he enjoyed the usufruct. Thus he was bound to keep buildings in repair, watercourses open; to feed cattle and slaves ; to maintain the numbers of a flock, by supplying it with offspring ; to supply dead or decaying vines and trees by others. He might open windows or embellish rooms, but not change the character of the house he inhabited, nor extirpate fruit-trees, nor destroy dwellings, nor sell[2] the "instrumenta" of the farm, nor let out to hire garments of which he had the use, nor employ dresses for the stage, otherwise than on the stage. So he was bound to employ slaves in their proper functions ; if he sent a librarian to manage a farm, or turned an actor into a bath attendant, "abuti videbitur proprietate ;" neither could he by improving the property increase the risk or burdens of the proprietor.

The expense incurred for the sake of produce fell on him alone ; so did that of repairs, which he could only escape by abandoning his right as usufructuary ; a right however that did not belong to the usufructuary who had injured the property. He was not obliged to restore buildings that had fallen down from age ; if he did, he might demand compensation.

---

[1] Dig. 7. 1. 15. § 3. "Generaliter Labeo ait, in omnibus rebus mobilibus modum eum tenere debere ne suâ feritate vel sævitiâ ea corrumpat." Dig. 7. 1. 44. 7. §§ 2, 3. ult. 45. "Sicut impendia cibariorum in servum cujus ususfructus ad aliquem pertinet, ita et valetudinis impendia ad eum respicere naturâ manifestum est." 68, 69. "Fructuarius causam proprietatis deteriorem facere non debet—meliorem facere potest."

[2] Dig. 9. § 7.

He was bound to discharge the burdens inherent in the property.

The usufructuarius[1] was obliged to find security that he would fulfil his obligation; until he did so the proprietor might take the produce of the thing, unless he was himself to blame for the delay. The fiscus gave no security, "quia non solet fiscus satisdare[2];" neither could security be required from the father "in peculio adventitio."

The proprietor might waive his right to exact security.

The right to usufruct[3] was destroyed by the lapse of the appointed time; by the happening of the condition on which it was to cease; by the death of the usufructuary; by the "maxima" or "media capitis diminutio[4]" of the usufructuary; by merger, e.g. if the usufructuary acquired the right to the property himself, or ceded his right to the proprietor[5]; by the destruction, or substantial change of the thing enjoyed, e.g. if the usufruct of a field were bequeathed to a man, and it became a lake; subject however, in the last case, to the revival of the usufruct, if the property recovered its original character; by non user, of ten years between the present, of twenty between the absent.

Fruits gathered[6] belonged to the usufructuary and his heirs; not gathered, to the proprietor.

---

[1] Ib. 7. 9. 1. § 3. § 7. Ulpian says that both sides will do well to make an inventory: "Ut inde possit apparere an et quatenus rem pejorem legatarius fecerit."

[2] Dig. 36. 3. 1. § 18.

[3] Dig. 7. 4. 15. 16.

[4] Cod. de usufructu, 16. § 2.

[5] " Rei mutatione interire usumfructum placet." Dig. 7. 4. 5. § 2.

[6] Dig. 7. 4. 13. "Si fructuarius messem fecit, et decessit, stipulam quæ

The last fruits from what produced fruit continuously were divided *pro ratâ* between the usufructuary and the proprietor. But the fruits from what produced fruit at certain intervals went altogether to the usufructuary, if his right ceased after the fruit was gathered; if it ceased before, to the proprietor.

Besides[1] the method of enjoyment which has been explained, the Roman Law recognized a "quasi ususfructus," an inferior species, that is, the bare naked use of the property of another for a time, severed from all profit, "sine fructu," "boni viri arbitratu[2]."

Thus the "usus" might be in one person, the "fructus sine usu" in another, and the property in a third[3]. This right varied with the nature of the thing to which it applied: if the use of a slave, or a house, or a picture were bequeathed to any one, the rights of the usuarius were coextensive with those of the usufructuarius, except that he could not let nor lend them[4]. If the usus of flocks and herds belonged to any one, he was not entitled to their young, or their wool, or their milk[5]. He might use the sheep to manure, and the oxen to plough. Sabinus allowed the usuarius of land to take "quod ad victum

in messe hæredis ejus esse Labeo ait— spicam quæ terrâ teneatur domini fundi esse." § 26. § 58.

[1] Dig. 7. 8. 1. § 1.

[2] Warnkönig, *Comment.* I. p. 449.

[3] "Poterit autem apud alium esse usus, apud alium fructus sine usu, apud alium proprietas." Dig. 7. 9. 14. § 3.

Ib. 8. "Neque locabunt neque con-

cedent habitationem sine se."

Ib. 12. "Neque vendent usum."

[4] See a beautiful passage, De finibus, I. § 4.

[5] Labeo allows the legatee of a usus a little milk: "Modico lacte usurum puto, neque enim tam stricte interpretandæ sunt voluntates defunctorum." 7. 9. 14. 12.

14

sibi suisque sufficiat," which Nerva denied. But Ulpian adopts the former opinion, "aliquanto enim largius cum usufructuario agendum est pro dignitate ejus cui relictus est usus."

The "usus" of a wood was equal to the usus-fructus of it, as otherwise the usuarius would derive no benefit from it[1].

The "usus[2]," unlike the "ususfructus," was in-divisible. "Usus pars legari non potest, nam frui quidem pro parte possumus, uti pro parte non pos-sumus."

Justinian[3] declared the right of inhabiting a house to be a servitude, which had been a moot point among older writers. The "operæ servorum" constituted another servitude[4], which it is not neces-sary to examine.

PIGNUS [5].

The "pignus[6]," pledge, is the right given to a creditor in the admitted property of another for his security; it is also used to signify the thing so given.

It was "contractus juris gentium, nominatus, bonæ fidei, re perfectus, quo res a debitore creditori traditur et obligatur, ut magis in tuto sit creditor, et cum creditori fuerit satisfactum, tum eadem species, integra et non deteriorata, debitori restituatur."

---

[1] 7. 9. 14. 22.
[2] Dig. de usu et habit. L. 19.
[3] Cod. 3. 33. 13.
[4] Dig. de oper. serv. 7. 6.
[5] I take the Pignus among the Ser-vitudes rather than among the Con-tracts. According to the arrangement of Vangerow, "Pignus est res omnis pro debito creditori obligata." Inst. de Act. 4. 6. § 7; Donellus, 14. 2. 10; Donellus, Appendix, Vol. xv. 433, "De pign. et hypo."
[6] II. 20. Pothier, *Pandect.* h. t.

It gave an "actio directa" to the debtor against the creditor for the restoration of the thing pledged, and "contraria," for the creditor against the debtor to recover the money laid out in its preservation.

There are two kinds of pignus, the one when the actual possession of a moveable thing pledged is delivered to the creditor, which is the specific notion of pignus; the other, later in date, when the thing pledged was immoveable[1] and possession is not transferred, which was called *hypotheca*[2]. Another important division was into the pignus that was special, referring to certain distinct particular objects, and that which was universal, comprising all the debtor's property, what he had acquired and what he might acquire. From this last were exempted, however, property which it was illegal to pledge, e. g. dotalia and fidei commissa, and property which it was not to be supposed the debtor would pledge, e. g. the things of every-day use, such as garments, furniture, or objects to which he was bound by ties of affection, such as natural children, concubine, &c.

The word "pignus" comprised both kinds of pledge. Delivery was not essential to the validity of it: "Pignus contrahitur non solâ traditione sed etiam nudâ conventione, etiamsi non traditum est[3]." Neither was any particular form of words necessary to establish the pignus. Any words from which the consent of the person bound could be inferred were

---

[1] "Proprie pignus dicimus quod ad creditorem transit; hypothecam cum non transit possessio ad creditorem."

[2] "ὑποτιθέναι, hypotheca."

II. 13. 7. 9. § 2; but see II. 20. 1. 5. § 1.

[3] II. de pigner. action. l. 1.

sufficient : "Sicuti est in his obligationibus quæ consensu contrahuntur[1]."

Neither was a written document necessary, if the fact could otherwise be proved[2]: "Ideo et sine scripturâ si convenit ut hypotheca sit et probari poterit, res obligata erit de quâ conveniunt."

The "pignus speciale" might include "universitatem rerum," e. g. an inheritance as well as a distinct and particular object. The pledge of a particular object included the produce, and any accession it might receive; it did not comprise what was purchased by the sale of those fruits, nor, in the absence of an express stipulation, the peculium, of a slave, nor the thing which had undergone complete transformation, as a ship made out of mortgaged wood; but so long as the thing could be recognized, the pledge adhered to it. Thus if a house was turned into a barn, or if a man built on mortgaged land, the mortgage continued.

There were *four kinds of pignus:*—

Two from the act of the magistrate—the Prætorium[3] and the Judiciale[4].

Two from the consent of the proprietor—one by will[5], the other by contract.

Any one competent to the management of his property might *pledge* what belonged to him. The ward could not without the sanction of his guardian.

If property was pledged by a stranger, with the consent of the owner[1], or if having been originally pledged without his knowledge, the owner afterwards assented to it, the pledge was valid. If he who pledged the property of another[2], the creditor at the time of the pledge supposing it to belong to the debtor, afterwards acquired possession of the thing so mortgaged, the pledge was valid. So if the owner of the thing pledged by a stranger[3] connived at the fraud, or consented tacitly to the pledge[4].

If, however, Titius pledges my property without my consent, and makes me his heir, I am not bound to ratify the pledge[5].

Any thing not excepted specially by the law might be pledged. The exceptions were:

Free men, things sacred, things in dispute, "res litigiosæ," wife's dower, the arms of soldiers, the hope of the remuneration given to athletes, the utensils, living and dead, of husbandry.

The effects of the pignus[6] were, as to the debtor,

That the debtor retained the property of the thing pledged, and the right to its produce.

[1] "Aliena res pignori dari voluntate domini potest, sed et si ignorante eo data sit, et ratam habuerit, pignus valebit." II. de pign. act. l. 20.

[2] "Rem alienam pignori dedisti, deinde dominus ejus rei esse cœpisti—datur utilis actio pigneratitia creditori." II. 13. 7. 41.

[3] You may recover, says the code, 8. 16. l. 2. si aliena res pig. "si non sciens hoc agi in fraudem creditoris ignorantis dissimulâsti."

[4] "Si quis fidejubeat, quum res illius a debitore pro quo fidejussit pignori data sit, bellissime intelligitur,

hoc ipso, quod fidejubeat, quodam modo mandare res suas esse obligatas." in quib. caus. pign. II. 20. 1. l. 5. § 2. ib. 26. § 1. "quum suâ manu (in the name of another) pignori domum suam futuram sciens scripserat, consensum ei obligationi dedisse manifestum est."

[5] II. 13. 7. § 41.

[6] II. curia Stell. 3. 2. "Si is qui rem pignori dedit vendiderit eam, quamvis dominus sit, furtum fecit, sive eam tradiderit creditori sive speciali pactione tantum obligaverat."

That he had also the power of selling it; but if he sold it without the knowledge of the creditor to whom it was pledged, he was guilty of "stellionatus," and liable to an action "furti."

As to the creditor,

That he might not only keep[1] but sell[2] the thing pledged in satisfaction of his debt.

This right[3] remained so long as any portion of the debt was unpaid at the proper time[4].

If the creditor sold without any right[5], he gave no title to the purchase; if he sold in conformity with his right, but "malâ fide," or without observing the form of law, the debtor had an "actio pigneratitia," for the loss sustained against him; or an "actio ex vendito" against the buyer, if he was privy to the fraud.

A debtor[6] might make it part of the contract that the thing pledged should not be sold, but after the creditor had thrice summoned him to pay, the thing pledged, in spite of the agreement, might be sold[7].

The pledge[8] might be the contract called in the

---

[1] II. 13. 7. 9. § 5.   ib. 10.

[2] 20. 5.   "venditionem ob pecuniam solutam et creditam recte facit."

[3] "Quamdiu non est integra pecunia creditori numerata," &c.   6. Cod. dedisti pign.

[4] "Si annuâ, bimâ, trimâ," &c. "sed omnibus pensionibus præteritis, etiamsi una portio soluta non sit, pignus potest venire." II. 13. 8. § 3.

[5] Cod. dedisti pign. 1. 8.   Cod. si vend. pign. ag. l. 2.   Cod. dedisti pign. l. 7. and 8.   Cod. si vend. pign. ag. l. 1. and 4.

[6] "Quæritur, si pactum sit a creditore ne liceat debitori hypothecam vendere vel pignus, quid juris sit? et certum est,...ut pactioni stetur." II. dedisti pign. 7. § 2.

[7] "Ubi vero convenit ne distraheretur, creditor si dietraxerit furti obligatur, nisi ei ter fuerit denunciatum ut solvat et cessaverit." II. 13. 7. 4.

[8] II. de pign. 11. § 1. in quib. caus. pign. 68.   "Cum debitor gratuitâ pecuniâ utatur, potest creditor de fructibus rei sibi pignoratæ ad modum legitimum usuras retinere."

Roman Law ἀντίχρησις. That gave the creditor the power of appropriating the profit of the thing pledged, as interest for the unpaid debt; e.g. of occupying a house or land until the obligation was discharged.

The "lex commissoria," or the clause that if the debtor did not pay within a given time he should forfeit all property in a right to the thing pledged, was declared illegal[1].

The claims of creditors, where the same thing had been pledged to several, were marshalled on the following principles : in the absence of any special privilege,

If the claims were simultaneous, each had a right "in solidum" to the thing in question—subject, however, to the rule "melior est conditio possidentis."

If the claims were not simultaneous, the maxim "qui prior est tempore potior est jure" prevailed.

A more remote creditor might oblige the senior creditor to give up his right on paying the principal and interest; but he could not worsen the condition of an intermediate creditor, or violate the maxim "qui prior est tempore potior est jure," by a mean contrivance of chicane.

PRIVILEGED CREDITORS[2].

The Romans divided privileges into privileges of the person, and privileges of the cause[3]. The privi-

---

[1] "Placet infirmari eam (lex commissoria) et in posterum omnem ejus memoriam aboleri." Cod. 8. 35. 3.

[2] Π. 49. 14. 28.

[3] Troplong, *Droit civil expliqué. Privileges et hypothèques*, Vol. I.

Π. 50. 17. 196. "Privilegia quædam causæ sunt quædam personæ, et

lege of a debt incurred for funeral expenses of him whose estate was liable for the debt is an instance of the first. The privilege of the fiscus, of the second. All privileges, however, in a certain sense, were personal, as they could only give the right to personal action, and not to one in rem; from this it followed that the hypotheca came before the personal privilege. "Restat ut adnotemus," says Cujacius[2], "creditores hypothecarios anteponi creditoribus chirographariis,id est qui debitores personali tantum actione obligatos habent, etiamsi creditores chirographarii sint antiquiores...sive habeant privilegium causæ sive privilegium temporis; nam eos excludunt hypothecarii creditores optimâ ratione, quia habent actionem hypothecariam, quæ est actio in rem, in quam plus cautionis est quam in personam." Cujacius has stated the order of rights given by the simple "hypotheca" with great precision: "Prioris temporis hypotheca firmior est, posterioris infirmior, quia in id tantum efficax est, quo summa pignoris excedit summam prioris sortis[3]." Hence the maxim so plainly just, "qui prior tempore potior jure." To consider the matter more in detail.

Creditors were privileged with reference to the especial favour with which the law considered certain persons or certain rights.

To the first class belonged the fiscus[4]: secondly, the wife and children claiming her dowry.

ideo quædam ad hæredem transeunt quæ causæ sunt, quæ personæ sunt ad hæredem non transferuntur."

[2] Recit. Solenn. Cujacius on qui potior in pignore, &c. c. 7.

[3] Cujacius, Paratitla on c. qui potior in pignor.

[4] L. ult. Cod. h. t.

To the second[1], those who had spent money in recovering, saving, or keeping in repair the thing pledged (supposing them to possess the jus pignoris), or (by a law of the emperor, A.D. 469) he who could support his claim by an authorized instrument[2], "qui instrumentis publice confectis nititur," or one attested by the hands of three or four men "integræ opinionis."

The possessor of the thing pledged might, if he paid the debt to the creditor suing for its recovery[3], stipulate that he should succeed to his rights.

In the absence of any special convention the law implied a pledge[4],

In the goods belonging to the tenant, taken into a house of which the rent was in arrear.

In the produce of land in favour of the landlord.

In favour of him who had spent money in rebuilding and repairing a house, on the house itself.

In favour of wards and minors on all things purchased with their money.

In favour of legatees, or those in a similar condition to legatees, on the property burdened with their legacies.

In favour of the wife for her "dos," "paraphernalia," and the "donatio propter nuptias."

The pledge was cancelled—

By payment of the debt for which the property had

---

[1] II. 20. 4. 5. "Interdum posterior potior est priori, ut puta si in rem istam conservandam impensum est, quod sequens credidit, veluti si navis fuit obligata et ad armandam vel reficiendam eam credidero;" 6. and

7. "Et si in cibaria nautarum fuerit creditum, sine quibus navis salva pervenire non poterat."

[2] Cod. h. t. c. 11.

[3] 20. 4. 5. § 7.

[4] Donellus, L. 15. c. 50. § 6.

been pledged[1]; whether "ipso jure," as by payment, or a valid "exceptio," which prevented its recovery.

By the remission of the creditor, which might be expressed by a formal covenant—or tacit, as if he gave up to the debtor[2], or bequeathed to him the instrument proving the debt.

If he consented to the sale of the thing pledged[3].

If he consented that the thing pledged to him should be pledged elsewhere, without insisting on his prior right[4].

If he consented to accept another security for his debt[5].

By the destruction of the thing pledged[6].

By the lapse of time[7].

The remedies of the creditor were[8]—

The "actio hypothecaria :" this was "in rem," by which he recovered possession of the thing pledged[9]. At first the legislator gave the "actio Serviana" against the colonus for the rent : afterwards it was extended to other pledges, and was called the "quasi Serviana."

It lay against the debtor and his heirs if he had more than one "in solidum."

It lay against the "possessor," real or fictitious, of the thing pledged.

---

[1] II. quib. mod. p. solut. 8. § 1. Cod. de pign. 24.

II. 20. 66. 11. § 2. 11. § 1. II. de pign. act. 9. § 3.

[2] II. de pact. 3. de liber. leg. 1. Cod. de remiss. pig. II. 20. 6. 4. § 1.

[3] II. 158. de reg. juris. "Creditor qui permittit rem venire, pignus dimittit." "Si voluntate creditoris alienatus fundus est, inverecunde applicari sibi cum creditor desiderat."

II. 20. 6. 8. § 6.

[4] II. 20. 6. 12. pr.

[5] II. 20. 6. 6. § 1. 20. 6. 9. § 3.

[6] II. de pign. act. 21. Ib. 35.

[7] Ib. 31. Cod. 8. 24. § 1.

[8] Donellus, L. 15. c. 50. 13. II. 20. 1. 17. 44. 7. 25. II. de pign. 13. § 4. 18. § 5. Inst. de act. § 7.

[9] II. de pign. 16. § 3. 22. Comm. Div. 12. § 7. quibus mod. pec. solv. 12. § 1. de servit. 16.

If the creditor was deprived against his will of the possession of the thing, it lay before the debt for which the pledge had been given was due.

It did not lie against a debtor of the debtor, unless the "nomen" of the former had been pledged.

In this action the onus of proof lay on the plaintiff, who was bound to shew that the thing sued for had been given in pledge at a time when it was "in bonis" of the debtor[1]. He was bound also to shew the possession of the defendant, unless the defendant was the debtor, in which case he was only bound to prove that the thing had been pledged to him.

The possessor against whom this action lay was bound to give up the pledge, or to pay the debt.

The possessor[2] might defend himself by the "exceptio,"

1. "Excussionis," i.e. the plea that sufficient means had not been taken to obtain the money from the principal debtor.

2. "Præscriptionis," i.e. for a bonâ fide possessor ten years, "inter præsentes;" twenty, "inter absentes."

The possessory remedies were the Interdictum Salvianum, against the colonus[3]; Quasi Salvianum against any other person who had pledged the property in question.

The "actio Pigneratitia[4]" lay "in personam creditoris," on behalf of the debtor for the recovery of the pledge when the debt was paid.

---

[1] II. de pign. 16. § 3. Eod. 21. § 1.   pign. 24.
[2] II. de cond. indeb. 20. qui pot. in   [3] II. 44. 33. Cod. 8, 9.
pign. 19. Cod. de fidei, 2. and 5. de   [4] Cod. 4. 24. 2. II. 13. 7.

CHAPTER IX.

LEGAL NATURE OF OBLIGATIONS[1].

THE doctrine of obligations may be considered as falling under two categories, general and special. The general one is that which explains the ground upon which all obligations rest, the special one is that which explains the precise form into which the general law has cast itself in any particular instance.

The number of special obligations must of course multiply with the inventions of men, and the exigencies of society; but though it may be impossible to refer each as it arises to any established name, it will be governed by the general rules which control the obligatio, subject to its own individual object, and the analogy it bears to those already in existence.

"Obligatio" is the legal relation which gives one person, the creditor, a right to a particular act by another, the debtor: "Obligationum substantia non in eo consistit ut aliquod corpus[2] nostrum vel servitutem nostram faciat, sed ut alium nobis obstringat ad dandum aliquid vel faciendum vel præstandum."

---

[1] *Inst.* 3. 13. П. 44. 7. Cod. 4. 10.   [2] П. 44. 7. § 3.

So long as the system of "Formulæ" was in use, this was manifest from the "intentio," which was "ea pars formulæ quâ actor desiderium suum concludit," and was framed "in personam," e. g. "si paret A. A. N. N. sestertium decem millia dare oportere[1]." So the Digest[2] tells us, "creditores accipiendos esse constat eos quibus debetur ex quâcunque actione vel persecutione."

The object of the creditor of an "obligatio" being to enforce an act, the act must be, abstractedly speaking, possible, "impossibilium nulla obligatio[3]:" abstractedly speaking, because an impossibility personal to the debtor is no excuse[4]. "Si ab eo stipulatus sim qui efficere non potest, quum alii possibile sit, jure factam obligationem Sabinus scribit."

The act must be lawful[5].

It must have a pecuniary value[6], and a value to the creditor[7], unless there be a moral duty, or a motive of affection concerned[8].

---

[1] "In rem" would have run "si paret, fundum ex jure quiritium dicti Agerii esse;" and see Gaius, 4. 2. 3.

[2] Π. 50. 16. 10.

[3] Π. 50. 17. 185.

[4] Π. 45. 1. 34.
    45. 1. 137. § 4. § 5.

[5] Π. 45. 1. 26. "Generaliter novimus turpes stipulationes nullius esse momenti."
    Eod. 27. and 35. § 1.
    Π. 28. 7. 15. "Nam quæ facta lædunt pietatem, existimationem, verecundiam nostram, et ut generaliter dixerim, contra bonos mores fiunt, nec facere nos posse credendum est."

[6] Π. 40. 7. 9. § 2. "Ea enim in obligatione consistere quæ pecuniâ his

præstarive possunt."

[7] Π. 17. 1. 8. 6. "Mandati actio tunc competit quum cœpit interesse ejus qui mandavit; cæterum si nihil interest, cessat mandati actio."
    Π. 19. 2. 32.
    Π. 42. 1. 13. "Neque vani timoris æstimatio ulla est."

[8] Π. 17. 1. 54. "Cum servus extero se mandat emendum nullum mandatum est; sed si in hoc mandatum intercessit ut servus manumitteretur, nec manumiserit, et pretium consequetur dominus ut venditor, et affectus ratione mandati agetur, finge filium naturalem vel fratrem esse; placuit enim prudentioribus, affectus rationem in bonæ fidei judiciis habendam."

An obligation entirely indefinite[1], or resting entirely on the will of the promisor[2], was invalid.

Obligations are certain[3] or uncertain; certain, when the object as to quality and quantity is ascertained, when "ex ipsa pronuntiatione apparet, quod quantumque sit, ut ecce aurei decem, fundus Tusculanus, Homo Stichus, *tritici optimi* modii centum, vini Campani *optimi* amphoræ centum."

They are uncertain when these points are undetermined. "Ubi autem non apparet quid quale quantumque est in stipulatione, incertam esse stipulationem dicendum est[4]," e.g. if things not "fungibiles" "quæ ipso usu consumuntur[5]," are described merely by the name of their species. "Si qui fundum sine propriâ appellatione, vel hominem generaliter sine proprio nomine....dari sibi stipulatur;" or if things consumed by use are bargained for without precise reference to their quality[6]; or when there is an al-

---

II. 27. 3. 1. § 2.

33. 1. 7.

35. 1. 71.

40. 4. 44.

18. 7. 6. 7.

[1] II. 45. 1. 94. "Triticum dare oportere stipulatus est aliquis: facti quæstio est, non juris: igitur si de aliquo tritico cogitaverit, *i. e.* certi generis, certæ quantitatis, id habebitur pro expresso, alioquin. . . . nihil stipulatus videtur."

Eod. 95. "Qui insulam fieri stipulatur ita demum acquirit obligationem, si apparet quo in loco insulam fieri voluerit."

[2] "Nulla promissio potest consistere quæ ex voluntate promittentis statum capit."

II. 45. 1. 108. § 1.

[3] II. 45. 1. 75. "Si qui vinum aut oleum vel triticum quod in horreo est stipulatur, certum stipulari intelligitur."

II. 45. 1. 95. § 5.

Eod. 10. "Certum est cujus species vel quantitas quæ in obligatione versatur, aut nomine suo, aut eâ demonstratione quæ nominis vice fungitur, qualis, quantaque sit, ostenditur."

II. 41. 1. 6.

[4] 45. 1. 75.

[5] Eod. § 1.

[6] Eod. § 2. "Quia bono melius inveniri potest . . . . cum id quod bono melius sit ipsum quoque bonum sit . . . . at cum optimum quisque stipulatur, id stipulari intelligitur, cujus bonitas principalem gradum bonitatis habet."

ternative[1] left to the debtor which of different objects shall be given. The debtor[2] by the delivery of the thing fixes the object; if it rested on the will of either[3], the will being once declared, it was irrevocable.

There may be cases where the exercise of the choice is the condition of the obligation[4]; but where the choice is not a condition, the non exercise of it will not destroy the obligation[5]; or the object may be made to depend on the "arbitrium" of a particular person[6], e. g. "quanti Titius æstimaverit," or "boni viri[7]."

Obligations are indivisible or divisible.

"Et harum omnium quædam partium præstatio-

See the distinction between an imperfect and an uncertain stipulation, II. 45. 1. 105; and II. 23. 3. 69. 4. "Gener a socero dotem arbitratu soceri certo die dari, non demonstratâ re vel quantitate stipulatus fuerat: arbitrio quoque detracto, stipulationem valere placuit....dotis etenim quantitas pro modo facultatum patris et dignitate mariti constitui potest."

[1] II. 45. 1. 75. § 8. "Utcunque is qui sibi electionem constituit....potest videri certum stipulatus...qui vero sibi electionem non constituit incertum stipulatur."

Eod. 112.

[2] II. 40. 9. 5.

[3] "Stichum aut Pamphilum, utrum hæres meus volet, Titio dato; si dixerit hæres Stichum se velle dare, Sticho mortuo liberabitur; cum autem semel dixerit hæres utrum dare velit, mutare sententiam non poterit."

II. 30. 84. § 9.

[4] "Si servus aut filius familias ita stipulatus sit, illam rem aut illam

utram ego velim, non pater dominusve sed filius servusve destinare de alterutrâ debet."

II. 45. 1. 141.

[5] II. 45. 1. 141. § 1.

[6] II. 17. 2. 75. "Si coita sit societas ex his partibus quas Titius arbitratus fuerit, si Titius antequam arbitraretur decesserit nihil agitur."

Eod. 76. "Arbitrorum enim genera sunt duo; unum ejusmodi ut sive æquum sit sive iniquum parere debeamus....alterum ejusmodi ut ad boni viri arbitrium redigi debeat."

II. 19. 2. 25.

[7] II. 18. 1. 7. "Neque enim debet in arbitrium rei conferri an sit obstrictus."

II. 19. 2. 24. "Si in lege locationis comprehensum est ut arbitratu domini opus approbetur, perinde habetur ac si viri boni arbitrium comprehensum fuisset....nam fides bona exigit ut arbitrium tale præstetur quale bono viro convenit."

II. 50. 17. 22.

nem recipiunt, veluti cum decem dari stipulamur; quædam non recipiunt, ut in his quæ naturâ divisionem non admittunt, veluti cum viam iter actum stipulamur[1]."

The true meaning of the division of obligations into divisible and indivisible is not, that in either case the creditor can be compelled to accept partial fulfilment of the contract, but that with his consent a partial fulfilment of the contract is *possible*. The case where Titius has engaged to pay 100 aurei is to be decided precisely on the same principle as the case in which Titius had bound himself to allow a servitude. So in the case of a divisible obligation where there are several debtors, each may pay pro ratâ; whereas in the case of an indivisible obligation the rule is different.

Suppose a man entitled to a servitude died leaving several heirs, each heir might, if interrupted in the exercise of his right, institute proceedings and recover the pecuniary value of his share : "sed verius est omnibus in solidum competit actio, et si non præstetur via pro parte hæreditariâ condemnationem fieri oportet[2]."

[1] II. 45. 1. 2. § 1.
II. 8. 1. 11. "Pro parte dominii servitutem acquiri non posse vulgo traditur."
II. 46. 4. 13. 1.
II. 45. 1. 2. § 2. § 5. Eod. 4. eod. 72. "Ex his igitur stipulationibus ne hæredes quidem pro parte solvendo liberari possunt.....et ideo si divisionem res promissa non recipit, veluti via, hæredes promissoris singuli in solidum tenentur."

II. 45. 1. 85. pr. § 2. "Operis effectus in partes scindi non potest. § 3.....quodsi stipulatus fuero...et unus ex pluribus hæredibus me prohibeat, verior est sententia existimantium unius facto omnes teneri."
[2] II. 8. 5. 4. § 3. "Quia non facit inutilem stipulationem difficultas præstationis."
II. 45. 1. 2. § 2.

As a general rule, demands that rested on a
"facere," as contradistinguished from a "dare,"
were indivisible: "Item puto ut si quis faciendum
aliquid stipulatus sit, ut puta fundum tradi, vel fos-
sam fodiri, vel insulam fabricari, vel operas, vel quid
his simile, horum enim divisio corrumpit stipulationem[1]."

The subject of Obligations is scattered widely
over the different books of the Roman Law, but the
elementary rules on this subject are to be found
under the head De pactis, De oblig. et act., and De
verb. obl. in the Pandects and the Code.   Under
this head it is that the most numerous relations
which affect the interests of men as members of
society are to be found.   The liabilities which the
laws on this subject regulate recur every instant.   To
frame them the Roman jurist had recourse to principles long hidden under the rubbish of Gothic legislation; or if they were here and there discernible,
rather serving to illustrate the absurdities by which—
where nature was too powerful for the legislator—they
were encumbered, than to quicken the corrupt mass by
their vivifying energy.   These principles were those
of conscience illuminated by the progress of reason,
and the study of jurisprudence, in other words, of
refined and perfect equity, which in every civilized
country but England have triumphed over the caprice
and absurdities of the dark ages, and have been the

[1] Π. 45. 1. 2. § 5=72. pr. eodem.
Π. 35. 2. 80. § 1. "Sed et si opus
municipis hæres facere jussus est, in-
dividuum videtur legatum, neque enim
ullum balneum aut ullum theatrum
aut stadium fecisse intelligitur qui ei
propriam formam, quæ ex consumma-
tione contingit, non dederit."

15

harbingers, in civil suits at least, of humanity and of right. To extract from the precious volumes in which these rules are contained, a series of rules which might constitute a body of elementary learning invested with the precision and authority of law, was the object of Domat and Pothier in their immortal works, as well as of the great jurists who drew up the Code Napoléon, which, were not political freedom the first of blessings, might atone for its destruction. But these masters of jurisprudence never imagined that their compilations could supersede the study of the Roman Law. Ill, said they[1], would he understand the disposition of the Civil Code with regard to Contracts, who was to look at them in any other light than as the general rules of equity, all the ramifications of which must be traced out in the Roman Law: there it is that the science of what is just and what is unjust is most perfectly developed, and there it is that every one must look for instruction who wishes to make any progress in that science, or who shall be entrusted with the charge to defend or to execute the laws recorded in our Code.

It is impossible to foresee, and therefore to regulate by a special law, all the different forms which contracts may assume[2]. But among the Romans law

---

[1] Locré, Vol. VIII. p. 313.

[2] *Instit.* 3. 13. The Twelve Tables use the word nexus. La Serna, *Derecho Romano comparado con el Español*, Vol. II. p. 115.

The Institutes pass from the right *in* the thing to the right *to* the thing. The former real, the latter personal; the former absolute, the latter relative; the former in rem, the latter ad rem; the former not necessarily implying the existence of any other ingredient, but the person holding the right, and the thing over which the right is exercised; the latter requiring a passive as well as an active

alone had a coercive power.   So they define an obligation "Juris vinculum quo necessitate astringimur alicujus rei solvendæ, secundum nostræ civitatis jura[1]."

The fear of multiplying litigation deterred the
authors of the Twelve Tables from making this attempt. They provided the means of enforcing certain contracts which were most essential to society,
these were called "nominati."   But as the relations
of men with each other multiplied, it became necessary to extend the law's coercive power. The grand
maxim (which is slowly thawing the prejudices even
of English legists), that it is "contra naturalem
æquitatem unum cum alterius jacturâ et detrimento
locupletiorem fieri," compelled the performance of
a contract by one party, when it had been fulfilled
as far as in him lay by the other. Thus the "contractus innominati," as they were called, because
they were not designated by any special name, were
recognized and enforced by law.

They were comprised under four classes[2], to one

subject of the obligation. Such is the
doctrine, which if not formally stated
by the Roman jurists, is logically de-
ducible from the texts they have left
us, and which has been accepted by
all but writers on English law, who
have invented a jargon peculiar to
themselves, based on notions utterly
incoherent, confused, unworthy of
rational creatures, but of course leading to an incredible amount of litigation, and therefore long carefully
cherished "that the law might be an
art," instead of what it ought to be,
and never has been among us—a
science.

[1] But see II. 46. 1. 16. § 4.   "Naturales obligationes non eo solo æsti-

mantur si actio aliqua earum nomine
competit, verum etiam cum soluta pecunia repeti non potest; nam licet minus proprie debere dicantur naturales
debitores, per abusionem tamen intelligi possunt debitores." He alone is
in the strict sense a debtor, "a quo
invito exigi pecunia potest."

II. 50. 16. 108. As to "secundum
nostræ civitatis jura," see Donellus,
12. c. 1.

"Est contractuum nominatorum
origo quibus legum Romanarum con-
ditores vim astringendi dederunt, sub
certo nomine, quo veluti signo secer-
nerentur ab alteris quibus eadem vis
tributa non est."

[2] II. 19. 5. 5.

15—2

or other of which every contract must belong[1] ; "do ut des," "facio ut facias," "do ut facias," "facio ut des[2]."

These contracts were executed when there was a "causa" or a "nomen[3]"—" si in alium contractum res non transeat subsit tamen causa eleganter Aristo Celso respondit esse obligationem." But if there was neither "causa" nor "nomen," the "pactum" was "nudum."

"Causa[4]" does not mean the motive to a contract, as every pactum, "nudum" qr not, must have one, but the partial execution of the contract by the act of one of the parties to it, "quæ sumpsit effectum datione vel facto."

[5]The "causa" gave rise to the division of contracts, into those which were valid by mere consent, and those which required some act or formality to make them binding.

The first class were *consensu*. The second were subdivided into those established (1) re, as by de-

---

[1] "Encore y en a-t-il une de superflue." Maleville, *Analyse*, Vol. III. p. 10.

[2] II. 2. 14. 7. 2. So if Caius emancipated his slave, on condition that Titius should emancipate his, and after the slave of Caius had been emancipated, Titius refused to fulfil what he had promised, "in hâc quæstione totius ob rem dati tractatus inspici potest."

II. 19. 5. 5. "Necessario sequitur ut ejus fiat condemnatio quanti interest mea servum habere quem manumisi." Eod. § 5.

[3] II. 2. 14. 7. 1, 2.

[4] "Omnis conventio habens proprium et legitimum nomen vel causam, id est dationem aut factum, ea contractus est : quæ vero neque certum

nomen habet neque in effectum cœpit deduci aliquâ datione vel facto ; hæc est pactum." Huber, Vol. I. p. 283.

[5] "Emptio venditio, locatio conductio, mandatum societas." Zeno added to these a form of the emphyteusis, *Inst.* 3. 22. Theoph. Par. § 3. § 1. c. 1. h. t.

II. 2. 14. 7. "Ideo autem istis modis consensu dicimus obligationem contrahi quia neque verborum neque scripturæ ulla proprietas desideratur sed sufficit eos qui negotia re gerunt consentire."

II. 2. 14. 7. "Mutuum, indebitum commodatum depositum pignus." Verbis. "Verbis obligatio contrahitur ex interrogatione et responsione cum quid dari fierive nobis stipulamur."

livery, (2) verbis, the stipulatio, (3) litteris[1], that depend for their validity on some writing.

With regard to consensual acts, it should be observed, that if the parties to one agree that until a formal document is drawn up embodying its terms before a proper officer, such contract shall be incomplete. A document so prepared is requisite to make it binding. Such is the effect of the celebrated law "Contractus," in the Code, 4. 21. 17.

The Romans distinguished three kinds of obligation, and the accuracy of this distinction is obvious. These were, (1) Natural. (2) Civil. (3) Natural and civil.

1. A purely natural obligation is that which cannot be legally enforced. Such were the obligations contracted by an impubes, by a master towards his slave, by a father towards his unemancipated son[2].

Though these obligations could not be the ground of a civil action, they were not wholly without civil consequences, *e. g.* the "pledge" given for their execution might be retained. The money paid on account of one could not be recovered; it might be the basis of a guarantee[3].

---

[1] Gaius, *Inst.* 3. 128. 134. Vat. *Frag.* § 329. Cod. de prob. This had become almost obsolete before the time of Justinian.

[2] Instit. de contr. Empt.

"Naturalis obligatio non omnis in pari pretio habetur, quibusdam enim lex opitulatur, aliis nullam pari tribuit; quæ hujus sunt generis vel neglexit omnino vel enervavit. . . .obligationes quas enervat, sunt pupilli majoris in-fantia, nam infans plane non tenetur filii familias mutuam pecuniam accipientis mulieris fide jubentis."

"Quod pupillus sine tutoris auctoritate promiserit et solverit ejus repetitio est, *quia nec* stipulanti *naturâ debet.*"

II. 12. 6. 13, and 26. § 12.

[3] II. 16. 2. 6. "Etiam quod naturâ debetur venit in compensationem." La Serna, *Derecho R.* II. 116.

2. A purely civil obligation[1] is one on which an action may be brought, but which may be encountered by a peremptory exception[2]. Such is one that is founded on an iniquitous sentence, or extorted by violence.

3. The natural and civil obligation[3] is that which rests alike on positive law and equity: "Quo necessitate astringimur alicujus rei solvendæ secundum nostræ civitatis jura;" he ought to have added, says Maleville, "et æquitatis."

This last class of obligations was divided into civil and prætorian. Civil obligations[4] were those which were drawn from a law, a plebis scitum, a senatus consultum, the constitution of a prince, or the interpretation given to any of these written laws by the juris consulti, to whom the task was assigned "jura condere."

Prætorian obligations were those enforced by the authority of the prætor, according to the exigencies of the case, and the rules of natural equity; such were the pecunia constituta, hypotheca, the obligation arising from the oath.

Another division of obligations is into those

---

[1] sc. "Quæ legum subtilitate duntaxat nititur, æquitate destituta naturali, quæ propterea parit actionem, sed per exceptionem quam suggerit æquitas eliditur." Huber, Vol. I. p. 281. "Exempla passim occurrunt." "Qui metu coactus vel dolo deceptus promisit jure civili obligatur." Huber, Vol. I. p. 282. Inst. de except. § 3.

[2] II. 13. 5. 3. "Quæcunque per exceptionem perimi possunt in compensationem non veniunt."

II. 16. 3. 14.

[3] "Obligatio quæ civilis simul et naturalis est sine exceptione actionem producit efficacem, eaque a Justiniano duplex traditur civilis et Prætoria." Huber, Vol. I. p. 282.

[4] "Is qui honoraria actione non jure civili obligatus est constituendo tenetur."

II. 13. 5. 1. 8.

II. 15. 3.

2 Inst. de oblig.

3 Inst. de jure nat.

which are principal, and those which are accessory.

Accessory, are those claims which the plaintiff
can enforce, which were not the original object of
the contract.

The leading claim of this kind is that which
falls under the head "ejus quod interest[1]."

The object of every obligation[2] is to secure a
thing or act, of a certain value to the person contracting for it. But the worth of this thing or act
may, independently of the thing or act itself, be the
subject of a legal demand. The estimate of this
value depends on the thing or act, and on the circumstances which belong to it. In this point of view
the estimate may be directed only to the marketable
value of the thing or act in question, " verum rei
pretium." If, however, any loss has been sustained,
compensation for which is asked, the value of the thing
or act to the creditor is to be taken into account,
" æstimatio ejus quod interest," which may exceed or
fall short of the former standard. In this the amount
of positive injury, "damnum emergens," as well as
future loss, "lucrum cessans," were to be considered.

Pecuniary interests[3] alone could be weighed in
such a proceeding. The defendant was responsible
for no damage but that which was naturally, and in
a sense immediately, the consequence of what was

---

[1] II. 27. 3. 1. § 20.
19. 1. 11. § 18.

[2] II. 46. 8. 13.   "Si commissa est
stipulatio ratam rem dominum habi-
turum in tantum competit in quantum
meâ interfuit."
II. 36. 1. 11.

II. 9. 2. 21. § 2.   "Sed utrum corpus ejus solum æstimamus quanti fuerit cum occideretur, an potius quanti
interfuit nostri non esse occisum, et
hoc jure utimur ut ejus quod interest
fiat æstimatio." Ib. 77.

[3] II. 9. 2. 33.

complained of. The loss[1] of profit by payment at
one place instead of at another, was to be estimated
by the judge.

Justinian by a law of the Code provided that
the loss or gain should never be estimated at more
than twice the value of the object[2].

These rules hold when the judge is to estimate
the interest according to the proof furnished by the
plaintiff. But there are cases where, as a punishment
for dolus or contumacia on the part of the defendant,
the plaintiff has the right to fix an estimate by his
oath, "jusjurandum in litem," on the value of his
interest, the only limit being the maximum appointed
by the judge. Such was the proceeding also when
the defendant refused to comply with the decree "ad
exhibendum," or "ad restituendum." But even in
cases of dolus[3], where the sum lost consisted of
monies numbered, or where an event had happened
which rendered compliance with the decree, at first
wrongfully disobeyed, impossible, or the death from
natural causes of the slave ordered to be given up,
the oath of the plaintiff was not allowed.

Obligations were bilateral (sometimes called syn-
allagmatic) or unilateral. Bilateral are those in which
either party may be debtor or creditor.

---

[1] II. 19. 1. 21. § 3.
  13. 4. 2. § 8.
[2] II. 12. 3.
  Cod. 5. 53.
    12. 3. 4. § 1. § 2. § 3.
    4. 3. 18.
    10. 4. 3. § 2.
  Cod. 6. 30. 22. § 14.
  "Interdum quod intersit agentis
solum aestimatur, veluti cum culpa non

restituentis vel non exhibentis puni-
tur; cum vero dolus aut contumacia
non restituentis vel non exhibentis
quanti in litem juraverit actor."
  II. 12. 3. 2. § 1.
  II. 4. 3. 18. § 1.
[3] II. 12. 3. 3. "Nummis depo-
sitis judicem non oportet in litem jusjurandum deferre . . . . cum certa sit
nummorum aestimatio." Cod. 8. 4. 9.

If in a bilateral obligation, one party to it only was *legally* bound, as for instance, if a pupillus had engaged himself without the authority of his guardians, the existence of the obligation rested on the choice of the person not legally liable, and he could not insist on it, without carrying into effect his portion of the contract: "Nec tamen ex vendito quid quam consequitur nisi ultro quid convenerit præstet[1]."

He who endeavours to enforce a bilateral obligation, admits his own liability to it; and if he has not fulfilled that obligation, may be encountered by an "exceptio non adimpleti contractus."

Jurists[2] have distinguished bilateral contracts into those more or less perfectly entitled to the name; e.g. emptio venditio, societas, locatio conductio, belonged to the first class. The duty imposed on either party being alike of the essence of the contract, as in the contract of sale, it is as much the duty of the seller to deliver the thing, as of the buyer to pay the price.

The mandatum, the depositum, are instances of contracts belonging to the second; the obligation of the mandans, and of the person placing the depositum, being subordinate to those of the mandatarius, and the person to whom the depositum has been entrusted.

Unilateral contracts are those in which one per-

[1] II. 18. 1. 34. § 3.
18. 5. 7. § 1.
"Qui pendentem vindemiam emit, si uvam legere prohibeatur a venditore adversus eum petentem pretium exceptione uti poterit." II. 19. 1. 25.
[2] Heineccius, *Prælectiones in Grotium*, Lib. II. Cap. XI. § 3 and 4; Toullier, Vol. VI. p. 19.

son alone is responsible to the other, as mutuum, stipulatio.

The action arising from the principal obligation is "actio directa," that arising from the subordinate one is "actio contraria."

This head of division however has given rise to much criticism, and many difficulties might be urged against it; perhaps the best distinction is that founded on engagements, which are unilateral before acceptance, and bilateral afterwards.

Another division recognised by Pothier, and incorporated with the French Code[1], is that of Contracts, into those which are commutative and those which are aleatorial.

A contract is commutative, when each party to it engages to do or give what is considered an equivalent for the act to be done or given by the other.

A contract is aleatorial, when the equivalent consists in the chance of gain or loss for each of the parties, in consequence of an event still uncertain. Such are all contracts of insurance.

It is not however possible, in questions mingled with the infinite mass of human affairs, always to draw the line with metaphysical accuracy between different classes of contracts.

Strictly speaking, it is clear that aleatorial contracts are also commutative, inasmuch as in them one thing or act is exchanged for another thing or act.

Another division of contracts, and perhaps the

[1] Toullier, Vol. VI. p. 16.

most important of all, is into that "*bonæ fidei*," and "*stricti juris.*"

To put this much exhausted subject in another point of view.

A convention or a pactum may be defined "duorum pluriumve in idem placitum consensus."

A pactum was divided into two kinds, a "pactum nudum," and a "pactum legitimum." A "pactum nudum" was that which depended simply on the agreement of the parties to it, which did not belong to any appropriated form of contract, and which was without the causa.

The causa was the consideration which had led to the agreement; e. g. Caius and Titius agree to exchange books. So long as no step is taken to the execution of the agreement, this is "pactum nudum;" when the exchange has taken place, it is "pactum vestitum."

A "nudum pactum" could only be the basis of a natural obligation; it could not give rise to an action, but it might furnish an exception, that is a sufficient answer to one, based on natural equity.

The "actio præscriptis verbis" is brought when the person who has given any thing requires the other party to fulfil his share of the contract.

The "condictio causâ datâ causa non secuta[1]," when the giver of any thing seeks to recover it, the consideration for which he gave it having failed. This is used for the contracts "do ut des," "do ut facias," not for those "facio ut des," "facio ut facias," which give rise to the action "præscriptis verbis:" here there can

[1] II. 12. 4.

be no "condictio dati," as what is done cannot be undone, nor "pro infecto haberi."

A "conventio non nuda" might belong either to the class of the "nominati" and "certi," or the "innominati" and "incerti," supported by a consideration. Hence the definition, "contractus est conventio habens nomen speciale, aut eo deficiente civilem obligandi causam."

To the class of the "certi" and "nominati" belong all that have an appropriated name and certain character, e.g. "emptio, venditio—locatio, conductio—societas mandatum," &c.

The "incerti" and "innominati" are those to which the civil law has given no name that is certain and specific, but which the civil law recognizes in consequence of some act done which gives them validity. Such contracts are of course almost innumerable, but they may, generally speaking, be comprised under four heads: "do ut des," "do ut facias," "facio ut des," "facio ut facias."

These last contracts gave rise to no action bearing a special name[1], or according to a prescribed form, but to one "præscriptis verbis," or "in pactum."

The "contractus nominati" are established in four ways: re, verbis, literis, consensu.

A contract is said to be established, re, when it is completed, not by mere consent, but actual de-

[1] II. 19=5. 5. § 2. "Cum proprium nomen invenire non possumus descendamus ad eas, quæ in factum appellantur."

II. 19. 5. 1. "Cum deficiunt vulgaria atque usitata actionum nomina præscriptis verbis."

livery of the thing in question. It cannot exist
unless some act has been done or some thing[1] delivered.

---

[1] La Serna, II. 125.
"Subsit tamen causa." II. 2. 14.
7. § 2.
  The word civilis, II. 19. 5. 5. 2,
is redundant, and a proof of the ignorance of the compilers of the *Digest*.

Vinnius, *Quæst.* L. I. 46.
  "Dolus dans causam contractui
bonæ fidei reddit eum jure nullum."
II. de minoribus, 16. § 1.
II. 17. 2. pro socio.   3. § ult.
    4. 3. de dolo malo.   1. 2.

CHAPTER X.

OBLIGATIONS CONTRACTED, RE.

THERE are four contracts which are completed, re :
1. mutuum ; 2. commodatum, 3. depositum, 4. pignus.

Mutuum[1] is a contract "juris gentium," "stricti juris," completed by delivery, according to which a thing for use and in commercio is delivered by the creditor to the debtor, to be his property, subject to the restitution to the creditor at his demand, of a thing not the same, but identically the same in kind and in measure[2].

The mutuum must consist of things that can be weighed and numbered, as wine, corn, money, and that are consumed by use[3].

It follows from the definition, that as the property of the mutuum is transferred to the debtor, the thing is at his risk, and he is liable "si quolibet fortuitu casu quod accessit amiserit."

As the object of mutuum is certain, it gives rise to the "condictio certi."

---

[1] II. 12. 1. De rebus creditis si certum petatur et de condictione. Warnkönig, 2. 199. Cod. 4. 1. Gaius, 3. 90. Pothier, Œuvres, IV. 47. Glück, 11. 460. 12. 1.

[2] "Fungibiles" is a barbarous word used to designate the object of the mutuum, and opposed to "non fungibiles." All things consumed in use, however, are not fungibiles, e. g. the last wine of a rare vintage. La Serna, 11. 126.

[3] II. 121. 11 pr. This definition is not to be taken literally ; it means things of which the value is usually so determined.

Commodatum is a contract of the law of nations[1], *bonæ fidei*, complete by delivery, according to which a person was allowed gratis to use a thing not consumed or destroyed by use for a specified purpose,— the bailee being obliged to restore the same identical thing not worsened to the lender. Complete by delivery, because if the thing be not delivered, there is no contract to a particular definite purpose; if the bailee employed the thing, but to a different purpose, he was liable to an "actio furti."

Herein is the distinction between the commodatum and the depositum and the pignus. If the creditor used the pledge, or the person with whom a deposit was made the deposit, in any way they were guilty of furtum.

"Gratis," because if money were paid for the use, the contract was changed, and became locatio.

"Allowed," because the possession and property in the thing lent was not changed, but continued in the lender for a specified purpose [2]—therefore till the purpose originally assented to by the commodans was accomplished, he could not intempestive recall the loan[3]. The rule applies, "Voluntatis est suscipere necessitatis consummare." Herein the commodatum differed from the preceding[4].

The identical thing must be restored, herein differing from the mutuum.

The commodatum gave rise to a double action, "directa" and "contraria."

---

[1] II. 13. 6. Cod. 4. 23. II. 45. 1. § 1.   mus. *Inst.* 3. 14.
[2] II. 13. 6. 8. Rei commodatæ   [3] II. 13. 6. 17. 3.
proprietatem et possessionem retine-   [4] II. 43. 26. 1. and 15.

The Lex Aquilia also gave an action against
the bailee, if the thing lent had been worsened
by him; it gave the highest value the thing bore,
within thirty days; it could be brought after the
actio commodati; but the actio commodati could
not be brought after that founded on the Lex
Aquilia.

The "actio directa" lay for the proprietor against
the bailee, for the restoration of the thing lent and
unimpaired after the time for which it had been
parted with had expired.

The "actio contraria" was that which lay for the
bailee against the owner;

1. If he did not allow him to use the thing
lent;

2. If he had sustained any damage from the
defect which to the knowledge of the lender existed
in the thing lent, and made it unfit for the purpose
of the borrower[1];

3. To recover the expense of what he had laid
out on the thing borrowed, as the medicine for a
slave.

The bailee was liable for dolus, and culpa lata
levis, and levissima, "quia in commodati sola utilitas commodatarii versatur." "Tantum eos casus[2]
non præstet quibus resisti non possit[3]."

In the absence of "mora" and "culpa," and any
special agreement, he was not liable for accident.

---

[1] II. 13. 6. 18. § 3. "Qui sciens
vasa vitiosa commodaverit, si ibi in-
fusum vinum vel oleum corruptum
effusumve est, condemnandus eo nomine est."

[2] "Vis major," "vis divina," "vis
naturalis," "fatum," "damnum fa-
tale." II. 4. 4. 21. II. 39. 2. 24. § 2.
II. 19. 2. 59. 6. 16. 1. 13. 6. 5. 4.

[3] II. 13. 6. 18 pr.

DEPOSITUM[1].

The Depositum was a contract of the law of nations, *specified* by a particular designation, *bonæ fidei*, complete by delivery, according to which a moveable thing was delivered to be safely and gratuitously kept to be restored to the person who had so deposited it whensoever he required it.

Gratuitously, because if any thing was paid, it was locatio.

To be kept. This is the difference between the depositum and other contracts, as the "*mutuum*," where the property in the thing is transferred.

The "commodatum," where the thing was to be used.

The "pignus[2]," where the purpose was the security of the creditor. It was furtum if the bailee used the deposit without permission[3].

It is to be restored to the person depositing, whensoever he requires it, because the deposit is solely for the benefit of the person making it, and continues his property.

The thing is to be restored in the same condition as when it was deposited, otherwise it is not held the same.

It gives rise to two actions, the *directa* and *contraria*.

"Directa," for the person making the deposit, to recover the thing deposited uninjured.

---

[1] II. 16. 3. Cod. 4. 34. II. 12. 1. 9. § 9. "Deposui apud te decem, postea permisi tibi uti; Nerva, Proculus, etiam antequam moveantur, condicere, quasi mutua tibi hæc posse a'unt: et est verum ut et Marcello videtur: animo enim cœpit possidere."

[2] The difference with the mandatum is pointed out. II. 16. 3. 1. § 11.

[3] *Inst.* 4. 1. § 6.

The "contraria," which lies for the bailee against the person depositing, to recover what the former had expended on the thing deposited.

The person with whom the thing had been deposited was liable for the "dolus," and for the "*lata culpa*," which was held in the same estimation as the "dolus."

But he was not responsible for the "culpa levis," or "levissima," because the contract was solely for the benefit of the person making the deposit; and if he selected a negligent person, it was his own fault.

<h2 style="text-align:center">PIGNUS[1]</h2>

is a contract "juris gentium," specified by a particular name, *bonæ fidei*, complete by delivery, according to which a thing is delivered over to a creditor, and a right to the thing conferred upon him for his security ; that is, when the creditor is satisfied, the same thing, uninjured, may be given back to the debtor.

It gives rise to an "actio directa," which lay for the debtor against the creditor, to recover the thing when the debt was paid.

"Contraria," for the creditor against the debtor, to recover the sum he had expended on the thing.

---

[1] II. 20. 1. II. 44. 7. 1. 6. Cod. 8. 14. Cod. 4. 5. 24. See above for   a detailed account of the pignus, p. 210.

CHAPTER XI.

VERBAL OBLIGATIONS.

A CONTRACT was verbal wherein besides consent a certain form of words was requisite.

VERBAL CONTRACTS.

There were originally three forms of verbal contracts:—

1. The *dotis dictio*, obsolete in the time of Justinian, but mentioned in the rules of Ulpian[1]. "Dos," he says, "aut datur, aut dicitur, aut promittitur." It consisted, according to Cujacius, merely in a solemn promise of the "dos" without question or answer for the acceptance.

2. "Promissio operarum a liberto facta et juramento firmata[2]," often mentioned in the Pandects, though the form of it is not preserved. These were limited to a particular object.

---

[1] Tit. 6. 1. The "dos" "dabatur" *when* it was sealed up and deposited with the augurs. Suet. *Claud.* c. 26. "ritu decies centena dabantur." "Antiquo, veniet cum signatoribus auspex." Juv. 10. 333. "Promittebatur" stipulatione. "Dos Pamphile est decem talenta. Accipio." *Andria*, 5. 4. Plautus, *Trinummus*, Act. 5. sc. 2.

[2] Bruno, *Diritto Civile*, 56. II. 38. 1. 3. and 5. 40. 12. 34.

3. The Stipulatio. This comprised every class of lawful obligation, "quarum totidem genera sunt quot pœne dixerim rerum contrahendarum[1]."

It is thus defined by Pomponius[2]: "Verborum conceptio, quibus is qui interrogatur, daturum facturumve se quod interrogatus est responderit." It might be "pure, in diem, sub conditione[3]."

This was called "stipulatio."

Stipulatio was a form of words, according to which a person replied to a question by saying that he would give a certain thing or do a certain act, e.g.

Promittis—promitto.

Spondes—spondeo.

It mattered not in what language the words were uttered if they were understood by both sides.

Though the form was introduced by the civil law, yet as it was used to establish contracts as well "juris gentium" as "juris civilis," the stipulatio was said to be "juris gentium."

It was made in three ways:

"Pure," i. e. without the addition of any day on condition, in which case its effect was immediate, unless it was of such a nature that the immediate fulfilment of it was impossible—as to build a house, "interdum pura stipulatio ex re ipsâ dilationem capit[4]." "In diem," when a day was annexed: if conditionally, then the action would not be brought on the stipulation till the day had come, e.g. "insulam ante biennium illo loco ædificari spondes? ante finem biennii stipulatio non committitur[5]."

---

[1] II. 45. 1. 5, pr. "pendent ex negotio contracto."
[2] 45. 1. 5. § 1.
[3] Inst. h. t. tit. 15.
[4] II. 45. 1. § 3. Ib. 37. § 13.
[5] 124. ib.

If the stipulator (the obligee) died before the condition happened, his heir could enforce the contract, which was not the case in a conditional legacy.

The reason is, 1st, that in contracts it was not the particular person, but the "res familiaris" of him contracting, that was considered.

2ndly, that the contract was valid from the first moment when it was entered into, but its effect was suspended by the condition.

"In stipulationibus id tempus spectatur quo contrahitur." Π. de v. ob. 78.

If the condition was negative, as "si in capitolium Mucius non ascenderit, decem dare spondes?" it could not be enforced till the death of Mucius, nor could the "cautio Muciana," by which a legacy subject to the same condition could be enforced during the life of Mucius, apply; for it was the stipulator's fault that he allowed such a condition to be annexed to the contract.

The stipulatio gave rise to two actions, the "certi condictio," if the stipulation was definite, the "actio ex stipulatu," if it was not.

The formula of the "condictio certi" was, "si paret dare oportere."

The "incerti stipulatio" was when any indefinite object, such as a horse, was stipulated to be given, or any promise indefinite as to value was made; the remedy was generally adopted of fixing a certain sum as the measure of the value of the promisee's interest.

"In ejusmodi stipulationibus quæ quanti res est, promissionem habent commodius est certam sum-

inam comprehendere, quoniam plerumque difficilis
probatio est quanti cujusque intersit[1]."

More persons than one might be creditors or
debtors by virtue of the stipulation.

The Reus stipulandi was the creditor[2].

The Reus promittendi was the debtor.

Two or more creditors were created, when after
the interrogation had been put by all, the promisor[3] replied, "Spondeo, sive utrique vestrum dare spondeo[4]."

Two or more debtors were constituted, when after
the question had been put, they either answered
jointly, "Spondemus," or each replied, "Spondeo."
If two or more were thus created creditors, each had
a right to the entire thing stipulated for; payment
to one was therefore payment to all, discharge from
one was a discharge from all, and any one might
sue without joining his co-creditors.

If two or more were in this manner made debtors, each was liable for the full amount of the obligation; consequently payment by one enured to the
benefit of all. Of two "rei obligandi[5]," one might
bind himself absolutely and the other conditionally,
"nec impedimento erit dies aut conditio quo minus
ab eo qui pure obligatus est, petatur[6]," according to
Tribonian. By the 99 Novel. c. 1, Justinian gave
of two "rei debendi," the "beneficium divisionis,"

[1] II. 46. 5. 11.

[2] "Omnes quorum de re discepta-
tur."
Festus v. reus. II. 45. 2. 1. "Qui
stipulatur reus stipulandi dicitur;
qui promittit reus promittendi habetur."

[3] I have the authority of Paley for
this word.

[4] "L. Istâc lege filiam tuam sponden
mihi uxorem dare? C. Spondeo." Plautus, Trinum. Act. 5. sc.2.

[5] Inst. h. t. 2. Bruno, Diritto R.
p. 67.

[6] "Ex hujusmodi obligationibus et
stipulantibus solidum singulis debetur,
et promittentes singuli in solidum tenentur." Inst. h. t. Tit. 16. II. 45. 2.2.

except in three cases[1]—if the correus was absent, unable to pay, or had renounced that advantage.

Stipulations were divided into judicial, Prætorian, conventional, and common.

Judicial were those which emanated "ex mero officio judicis." The most important was the "cautio de dolo[2]."

The Prætorian[3], or equitable, were those which emanated "ex mero officio Prætoris." Among these were,

1. "Cautio de damno infecto."
2. "Cautio de legatis præstandis."
3. " Ædilitiæ stipulationes."

The Ædiles could oblige security to be given for certain things, e. g. they could compel the seller to give security that his flock was sound.

Conventionales[4], those "quæ ex conventione utriusque partis concipiuntur."

Communes, in which sometimes "Prætor jubet, interdum judex," such as the

1. Cautio "rem pupilli salvam fore."
2. Cautio "de rato habendo," which the Prætor might require from one who acted as the procurator of another.

A stipulatio might be invalid "ipso jure," on account of the thing stipulated for—

[1] This meaning of the novel is generally adopted, but it has been disputed by learned interpreters, who suppose it only refers to the text of Papinian. II. 45. 2. 11. Reos, &c.

[2] See also II. 10. 2. 10. Another was "cautio de persequendo servo qui in fugâ est." *Inst.* h. t. § 1, where see Theophilus's *Commentary*.

[3] II. 46. 5. 1. Ulpian gives other instances, as "judicatum solvi, rem ratam haberi."

[4] "Sicuti Prætoriæ stipulationes legem accipiunt de mente Prætoris qui eas proposuit sic in conventionalibus stipulationibus contractui formam contrahentes dant."

If it did not exist.

If it was "extra commercium," as a free man, a res sancta, sacra, religiosa, and the Catoniana regula applied to this class of stipulatio, "quod ab initio vitiosum est tractu temporis convalescere non potest."

If any man stipulated for what was his own, "quia quod nostrum est amplius nostrum fieri non potest."

If any man stipulated for the act of another, "quia nemo præstat factum alienum;" but this rule admitted of great exceptions, and might be evaded.

It might be invalid on account of the persons who contracted.

If it was between master and slave, or father and son unemancipated, "ob vinculum potestatis."

"Propter defectum corporis;" neither the deaf nor the dumb could enter into one.

"Propter defectum animi;" a "furiosus," an "infans," a "pupillus infantiæ proximus," came under this category.

The "pupillus pubertati proximus" might contract, "tutore auctore;" and even "sine auctore" he might contract a natural obligation, which would render his surety liable, though the pupil himself was under no obligation, and could even recover what he had paid under it.

It might be invalid, "propter defectum voluntatis seu consensus," if there was no "animus contrahendi," if the stipulator meant one thing, and the person promising, another. But if the thing was agreed upon, an error as to the qualities or substance of it did not destroy the stipulation.

If the condition of the stipulation was impossible or illegal.

This rule did not apply to wills, in which case the condition was disregarded, and the bequest was absolute.

Justinian gave the heir the benefit of a stipulation entered into by the deceased in these words : "Pridie quam moriar," or "pridie quam morieris dare spondes."

He also established such a stipulation as "si navis cras ex Asiâ venerit, hodie dare spondes," which the old law rejected as preposterous.

A stipulatio "cum moriar dare spondes," or "cum morieris," was valid.

A stipulatio "inter absentes," was invalid.

A stipulatio might be invalid, "ratione formæ," e. g. "si, stipuler Pamphilum tu mihi decem promittas," or "ratione causæ finalis ;"

If any one stipulated for another.

In a stipulatio mihi aut Titio dare spondes, the words "aut Titio" were rejected, and the obligation was contracted with me alone.

The exceptions to this rule were, that the father might stipulate for the son, and the master for the servant, so might the "tutor" and "curator," the "furiosi actor," the "civitatis procurator," and others.

SURETIES[1].

The word Sureties may be used in a wide or a contracted sense.

---

[1] Caius, 3. § 115, 116. "Idem dari spondes? Idem fidepromittis? Idem fide tuâ esse jubes?" II. 46. 1.

In a wide sense it means a *mandator*, that is, a person who orders money to be given to another, or a contract to be entered into with another, " fide suâ."

Constitutor[1], is one who simply promises that he will pay a debt due from another man.

Expromissor, is he who exonerates another from an obligation and adopts it himself.

A surety in the stricter sense of the word is he who binds himself by a stipulation for another, not subject to novation; therefore "fidejussio," a surety-ship, may be defined, a verbal contract entered into to fortify the obligation contracted by another not subject to novation.

"Sublatâ principali obligatione fidejussoria au-fertur."

The "mora debitoris" did not exonerate the "fidejussor," but it did not increase his liability[2].

A surety[3] might be annexed to every obligation re, verbis, litteris, or consensu, civil or natural; therefore if a "fidejussor" was annexed to a natural

---

[1] II. 13. 5. 8. II. de unius, 32, § ult.

[2] "Moram rei fidejussori nocere moram rei non augere obligationem." Cujac. ad Afric. Lib. VI. p. 967. II. 13. 4. 8. Consider. II. 46. 1. 68. 1.

[3] "Omni obligationi fidejussor accedere potest." Originally neither the formula Spondes, Spondeo, nor that Fide promittis, Fide promitto, could be employed for obligations that did not consist in dare, nor were they of any avail unless to those that were accessory to verbal contracts. Caius, 3, 119. But with the increasing wants of Roman society it became requisite to give a greater latitude to contracts, and the insufficiency of the formulæ hitherto in use led to the fidejussio, by means of which the formula of stipu-lation might be guaranteed in the Latin or any other idiom not verbal only, but real, literal and consensual, Prætorian, natural and civil contracts, of whatever nature. Caius mentions on the subject of Sponsores and Fide promissores the Apuleian law, 652 A.U.C.; the Furian law, 659; a law the name of which has not been read on the palimpsest of Gaius; the Publilian law; the Cornelian law, 673. Caius, 3. 120.

obligation, even though the principal debtor could not be sued upon it, the surety was liable.

"Illud commune est in universis qui pro aliis obligantur[1]," says Ulpian, "quod si fuerint in duriorem causam adhibiti omnino non obligari placuit eos."

The question whether in such a case the fidejussor is liable still "pro parte," has been, says Bruno, fiercely disputed[2].

But there were natural obligations to which no surety could be annexed, e. g. to ensure the payment of what a prodigal had promised[3].

There could be no surety "causâ litis."

There might be a surety for an obligation "ex delicto" in a civil suit.

If there were several sureties, the law of the Code and Pandects made each responsible for the full amount, and the creditor might choose which of them he would sue.

The surety had three privileges against the debtor:—

1. The "beneficium divisionis," according to which, if there were several sureties, all solvent, the creditor was compelled to demand a share of the debt from each. This was introduced by Adrian.

The "beneficium divisionis" was not "ipso jure," but "ope exceptionis;" therefore if one of the sureties paid the debt without appealing to this privilege, he

---

[1] Π. 45. 1. 8. 7. 10 and 11. "In leviorem causam accipi possunt, in deteriorem non possunt." Instit. h. t. § 5.

[2] Cujacius and Vinnius think he was not. Recit. ad lib. 11. resp. Papin. in l. 9. Π. de usurpationibus. Heineccius, whom Bruno follows, thinks he was. Heineccius founds himself, Π. 17. 1. 33. Π. 13. 5. 1.

[3] Π. 45. 1. 6.

could not recover it either from the creditor or his
co-sureties

But if the surety[1] denied his liability, he was
excluded from the benefit of this privilege.

2.   There was the "beneficium cedendarum actionum[2]," by which the surety sued by the creditor might
make the surrender of the creditor's right of action
against his co-surety the condition of payment; after
payment such a proceeding was of no use.

3.   "Beneficium ordinis," introduced by the later
law, according to which the creditor was obliged to
sue the principal debtor before the surety.

There were three cases in which this last privilege
did not apply :—

1.   If the principal debtor was absent.

2.   If the debtor was notoriously insolvent.

3.   If the surety renounced his privilege.

This privilege could only be employed "ope exceptionis."

If the surety paid any thing for the principal
debtor, he had an action "mandati" to recover his
debt[3].

If he had become surety in the absence of the
surety, so that no "mandatum," tacit or express,
could have intervened, he had an "actio negotiorum
gestorum."

---

[1] II. 46. 1. 10. § 1. "Ita demum
inter fidejussores dividitur actio si non
infitientur ; nam infitiantibus auxilium
divisionis non est indulgendum."

[2] Cod. 8. 41. 3. "Authenticâ præsente."

[3] II. 17. 1. 6. § 2. "Si passus sim
aliquem pro me fidejubere, vel alias
intervenire, mandati teneor; et nisi pro
invito quis intercesserit aut donandi
animo aut negotium gerens erit mandati actio."

CHAPTER XII.

LITTERIS.

THE omission of the contract "litteris" in the enumeration of contracts Π. 44. 7. 1. § 1[1], as well as in the law 2 and 4 of the same chapter of the Pandects and in the chapter "de novationibus[2]," Π. 46. 2. 1. § 1, led many interpreters, among whom are Duarenus, Donellus and Wissenbach, to think the contract a mere innovation of Justinian's. But the passage cited below from the commentaries of Caius proves this to be an error[3], and the "nominum obligatio[4]" referred to in several laws of the Pandects was, as Tribonian says[5], an obligation "litteris."

Justinian substituted the contract "litteris" for the old "contractus chirographarius." The "contractus litteris" was where a person delivered to another a written statement that he had received money from the latter, which he never had received[6], and allowed two years to elapse without retracting

---

[1] "Obligationes ex contractu, aut re contrahuntur aut verbis, aut consensu."

[2] "Illud non interest qualis praecesscrit obligatio utrum naturalis, an civilis, an honoraria, et utrum verbis, an re, an consensu."

[3] " Aut re contrahitur obligatio aut verbis aut litteris aut consensu." See too 44. 72. § 1. and 34. eod.

[4] Heineccius, *Antiq.* b. t. Π. 15. 1. 4. 40; 5. 41. 17.

[5] *Inst.* h. t.

[6] *Inst.* § un. h. t. Cod. de non num. pec. 14. § 1. § 2.

the statement; in such a case he could not plead that
he had never received the money [1].

[1] II. 22. 3. 25. § 3 : " Sin autem
cautio indebite exposita esse dicatur,
tunc eum in quem cautio exposita est
compelli debitum esse ostendere quod
in cautionem deduxit, nisi ipse specialiter qui cautionem exposuit causas
explanavit pro quibus eandem con-
scripsit. Tunc enim stare eum oportet
suæ confessioni nisi evidentissimis
probationibus in scriptis habitis ostendere paratus sit sese hæc indebite pro-
misisse." The whole law, notwithstanding one passage which I suspect
to be an interpolation of the detestable
age of Tribonian (alia simplicitate
gaudens et desidiæ deditus) ought to
be studied carefully. We shall look in
vain in our wilderness of various un-
digested crotchets, called Reports, for
an equally concise and lucid summary
of the rules which ought to govern
the practice of courts in admitting the
contradiction of a written document.
Our absurd doctrine about deeds carefully transmitted from the barbarians
of the eighth and ninth centuries was
unknown to the Roman civilians. See
too L. 'Generaliter,' 14. Cod. h. t.,
and 'In contractibus,' eod.

CHAPTER XIII.

CONSENSUAL CONTRACTS.

THE contracts in which consent alone was requisite are four:—

1. Emptio venditio, 2. locatio conductio, 3. societas, 4. mandatum.

1. Emptio venditio[1] is a contract "juris gentium," with a specific name, "bonæ fidei," established by consent alone for the delivery of a certain thing in consideration of a certain sum of money.

The three essential elements of it are, 1. the consent, 2. the thing (merx), 3. the price[2].

The contract was not cancelled by every kind of error[3].

If the error[4] was one as to the quality, and not the subject-matter, as if inferior wine was sold instead of good wine, the contract held.

If the error was as to the subject-matter, as if lead was sold for silver, the contract was void.

But although the contract in such a case was void, the buyer might bring his action " in id quanti

---

[1] *Inst.* 3. 23. II. 18. 1. Richer, *Jurisprudentia,* 3. 9.

[2] II. 18. 1. § 1 : "Quia non semper concurrebat ut quum tu haberes quod ego desiderarem invicem ego haberem quod tu accipere velles electa materia est .... nec ultra merx utrumque, sed alterum pretium vocatur," &c.

[3] As to error, see post.

[4] II. 18. 1. 14. "Quia in corpore dissentimus nulla emptio est."
II. de Cont. Empt. 9.

interest se deceptum non esse," or to recover what he had paid "condictione indebiti," or "sine causâ."

After the price[1] was agreed upon the contract[2] was complete, though the thing bargained for was not delivered; it was at the risk or for the benefit of the buyer.

The exceptions to this rule were:—

If there was "dolus[3]" in a matter essential to the contract.

If the seller consented to take the risk upon himself.

If the thing sold was a genus, e. g. twelve quarters of wheat, twelve oxen, unless it was sold "per aversionem," in which the risk was that of the buyer.

The merx or thing sold must be in commercio[4].

Future things might be sold; and, in the words of Pomponius, an expectation : "Aliquando tamen," he says, "et sine re venditio intelligitur, cum quasi alea emitur ; quod fit cum captus piscium vel avium vel missilium emitur; emtio enim contrahitur etiam si nihil inciderit—quia spei emptio est." (Π. 18. 1. 39. § 1. and 8. § 1.)

---

[1] Pr. *Instit.* h. t. l. 1. § ult. II. 1. 8. 1. 2. § 1. "Sine pretio nulla venditio est, non autem pretium perficit sed conventio perficit sine scriptis habitam emtionem."

[2] "Necessario sciendum est quando perfecta sit emtio, tunc enim sciemus cujus periculum sit, nam perfectâ emtione periculum ad emtorem respiciet ; ut si id quod venierit appareat, quid, quale, quantum sit, et pretium, et pure veniit, perfecta est emtio." II. 18. 6. 8.

[3] Ulpian says, "Nullam esse emp-

tionem si in hoc ipso ut venderet circumscriptus esset." II. 4. 3. 7.

[4] "Omnium rerum quas quis habere vel possidere vel persequi potest, venditio recte fit, quas vero naturæ vel gentium jus, vel mores civitatis, commercio exuerunt, eorum nulla venditio est." II. 18. 1. 34. 1. See the curious law II. 10. 2. 4, which forbids the judge to meddle "libris improbatæ lectionis, magicis forte, vel his similibus, hæc enim omnia protinus corrumpenda sunt."

Incorporeal things might be sold, as an inheritance, but the sale of the inheritance of a living person was void[1].

Things could not be sold which "in rerum naturâ ante venditionem esse desierint[2]."

"Res sacræ, sanctæ, religiosæ, publicæ et universitatis," could not be sold; if these were bought by one who knew their character, the sale was null; if by one who was ignorant of it, the sale was null, but an action lay for the buyer, "in id quod interest," against the seller[3].

The contract gave rise to a twofold action:—

"Actio empti[4]," for the buyer against the seller.

"Actio venditi," for the price.

The "actio empti" belongs to the buyer and his heir against the seller and his heir when the price has been paid for the delivery of the thing sold, with its fruits and accessories, if they can be delivered; if they cannot, for compensation in their stead.

As to what shall be considered accessories as included in the sale of the principal object, there are several laws in the Pandects which supply fruitful

---

[1] The Roman Law, with the morality so long unknown to ours, says that the man "solicitus de vivi hæreditate," was "improbus." II. 28. 6. 2. § 2. This was certainly not the rule of the Church from the days of Constantine downwards. "Ei qui successit ... quoniam adversus bonos mores et jus gentium festinasset, actiones hæreditarias in totum denegandas esse respondi." Papinian, II. 39. 5. 29. § 2.

[2] II. 18. 1. 15.

[3] "Qui nesciens loca sacra vel religiosa vel publica pro privatis comparavit, licet emptio non teneat, ex empto tamen adversus venditorem experietur, ut consequatur quod intersit ejus ne deciperetur." II. 18. 1. 62. § 1. The old words of the law were "venundare" (venum dare), to put to sale, "venundari" (venum dari), to be put to sale, "mancipare" for things "mancipi." For these were substituted "venire, vendere, distrahere," the first two relating to sales as well of a collective whole (universitas rerum) as of individual objects, "distrahere" to the latter only.

[4] II. 19. 1. Cod. 4. 94.

analogies on this head, e. g. " Qui domum possidebat, hortum vicinum ædibus comparavit, ac postea domum legavit." The hortus was included in the bequest "si hortum domus causâ comparavit, ut amœniorem domum et salubriorem possideret, aditumque in eum per domum habuit, et ædium hortus additamentum fuit[1]," and "ædibus distractis vel legatis ea esse ædium solemus dicere quæ quasi pars ædium vel propter ædes habentur, quasi puteal[2]."

The "actio venditi" is the action accruing to the seller and his heir when the thing has been delivered, against the buyer and his heir for the price agreed upon, with the interest due, and compensation for the expense necessary and useful, and the damage caused by the conservation of the thing.

"Addictio in diem." This is a modification of the contract "empti venditi," which has a special chapter in the Digest[3]. It may be defined a covenant, that if within a given time the seller can find a person who will make him a better offer than the original purchaser the contract shall be rescinded. "Quicquid ad utilitatem venditoris pertinet pro meliore conditione haberi debet[4]." Ulpian takes a subtle distinction between the addictio considered as a suspensive condition or as resolutory of the contract[5]. If the contract was conditional only, i. e. that the bargain should hold unless a better offer came, the buyer was not entitled to the "fructus" nor to the benefit of the "usucapio[6]."

[1] II. 32. 1. 91. § 5.
[2] II. 19. 1. 13. § 31. To 14 and 15 eod. II. 19. 1. 17. Inst. 2. 22. § 3. § 8. § 10. § 26.
[3] II. 18. 2.
[4] II. 18. 2. 5.
[5] II. 18. 2. 2. § 1 and 4. § pr.
[6] II. 18. 2. 4. pr. 18. 6. 8.

"Lex Commissoria." This also is a chapter in the Digest[1].

This may be defined a clause added to the emptio venditio, by which if one of the parties to a contract failed in executing his share of it, it was to be considered as if no such contract had been made. Generally speaking, this clause being added for the benefit of the seller, it was at his option to take or not to take advantage of it. If, as usually happened[2], a particular day was fixed as that before which the act was to be done, the debtor was bound to do the act, and the maxim "dies interpellit pro homine" held good[3].

A clause also might be added by which the seller might, on repayment of the price to the buyer within a certain time, recover the thing sold[4].

The "actio redhibitoria" was the action which the buyer who had been deceived, and his heir, might bring against the seller and his heir to restore the price of the thing sold and the interest on receiving the thing, its produce and accessories[5]. If the thing had been in any degree worsened while in the possession of the buyer, the damage as estimated by the judge ought to be made good to the seller[6]. If several objects were sold together, each contributing to the value of the other, a defect in one justified the actio redhibitoria[7] as to all.

[1] Π. 18. 3.
[2] Π. 18. 3. 2. 18. 3. 3. "Si volet venditor exercebit—non invitus."
[3] Π. 18. 3. 4. § 4. and 8 eod.
[4] Π. 19. 12. 5. Cod. 4. 54. § 2.
[5] Π. 21. 1. 1. and 19. § 5. and 48. § 5.
[6] Π. 21. 1. 23. 25. § 5. § 6.
[7] Π. 21. 1. 23 and 25. § 5. § 6. 34. § 14—38, as one singer of a chorus, a horse of a quadriga, &c.

The "actio quanti minoris," also called "æstimatoria," was that by which the buyer who had been deceived, and his heir, might recover, against the seller and his heir, the difference between the sum he had paid for a thing and the real value of the thing at the time of the sale[1].

The actions "redhibitoria" and "quanti minoris" could not be brought together—nor having chosen one[2], could the buyer have recourse to the other[3].

Rescission of the sale[4]. This was called Læsio. The emperors Diocletian and Maximian established that where the læsio amounted to more than half the just price, the contract might be set aside.

Eviction. Eviction is the loss to the buyer of the thing purchased in consequence of a judicial decree that it belongs to a third party. The seller, though not bound in the strict sense of the word to give the buyer the dominium of the thing sold, was bound to deliver him full and free possession of it, so that he might exercise the rights of ownership and obtain a title by prescription. If the buyer was legally disturbed in his enjoyment of the "merx," he had the "evictionis nomine obligationem" against the seller, who was bound "evictionem præstare," to indemnify the buyer for his loss: neither was it necessary in this action for the buyer[5] to prove a total loss. To establish his claim the buyer was bound to shew,

---

[1] II. 21. 1. § 2. § 6. 17. § 20. 48. § 5.
[2] II. 44. 2. 25. § 1.
[3] Cod. 4. 44. 2 and 8. II. 18. 5.
[4] II. 21. 2. 39. § 2. § 3.

[5] "Sive tota res evincatur sive pars, habet regressum emptor in venditorem." II. 21. 2. 1. and 13. and 53 pr. and 64. § 1. § 3.

1st.   That the action in which he sustained the loss was properly brought[1].

2ndly.   That the sentence was just[2].

3rdly.   That it was not collusive, nor the consequence of his neglect[3].

4thly.   That the cause of the eviction was prior to the purchase[4].

5thly.   That he, the buyer, had given due notice of the claim to the seller[5].   This was "litem denunciare," "auctorem laudare."

The buyer might shew, on the other hand,

That the seller had renounced his right[6];

Had by his own act prevented the buyer from giving him notice;

And that he could not discover the residence of the seller.

As to the time within which the notice should be given, any time not too "prope condemnationem" was sufficient[7].

Locatio conductio is a "contractus jure gentium,

---

[1] П. 21. 24. 2. § 1. § 2.

[2] П. 21. 2. 6. § 1.

[3] П. 21. 2. 29. § 1, "ita si culpâ vel sponte."

[4] La Serva, *Derecho Romano*, 2. 295.

[5] П. 21. 2. 29. § 2. and 55. § 1. and 56. § 4. § 5. § 7. and 63. § 1.

[6] II. 212. 63. pr. and 56. § 5. and 55. § 1. and 56. § 6.

[7] II. 21. 2. 29. § 2. There can be no doubt that this doctrine of the evictio came through the canonists into ours, and was corrupted into the almost incredibly immoral and absurd system of recoveries. For the English judges left out, in their profound indifference to truth, all that the Roman jurist had inserted against collusion, which literally continued till the year 1833, as an integral part of English Law. It was originally fraud and falsehood avowedly enforced by courts of justice for a political purpose. What wonder if the practitioners became demoralized? or how could L. C. J. De Grey gravely say in the face of such a system— "Fraud vitiates the most solemn proceedings of a Court of Justice"? *Duchess of Kingston's Case.*

nominatus," perfect by consent alone, by which a certain sum is given for the use of a particular thing, or the service of a particular person.

It agrees with the emptio venditio, inasmuch as it is bilateral, perfect by consent, and for a settled price. If the price was not fixed, there was no locatio conductio, but a contractus innominatus, for which there lay an "actio præscriptis verbis."

The locatio conductio differed from the emptio venditio, inasmuch as the emptio related to things alone—the locatio, to acts as well as things.

The contract emptio venditio might transfer property.

The contract "locatio" could only transfer the use.

The consideration for the "emptio" could only be monies paid.

That for the "locatio" might be for things that were consumable.

The three essential elements of the "locatio" were consent, price, and something hired.

It gave rise to a double action, "actio locati," and "actio conducti."

The "locati" for the person letting to hire for the price of what he had hired, or the restoration of the thing when the period for which it had been let had expired.

The "actio conducti," that the person hiring might have the full use of the thing hired.

The "conductor" of any *thing* to be used paid money for the hire of it to the "locator." The "conductor" of any thing to be done received it.

The "conductor" of a farm was called "colonus;" of a house, "inquilinus;" of any thing to be done, "redemptor."

The "conductor" was bound to fulfil all he had undertaken to do[1], and besides, whatever was fairly to be inferred from the contract, for it was "bonæ fidei."

The "conductor" was responsible for the "dolus," the "culpa lata," and "culpa levis," not for the "casus fortuitus," nor for the "culpa levissima."

There are two principal objects of "Locatio conductio." First, the "Locatio conductio Rerum[2]." Secondly, the "Locatio conductio Operarum[3]." It is a consensual contract, when, Paulus tells us, it is "naturalis," and "omnium gentium."

The essence of the contract on the part of the "locator" was to take care "conductori frui quod conduxit licere." The "locator" was also required to replace the "impensæ necessariæ[4]" and "utiles," and to answer for "omnis culpa[5]."

The "conductor" was bound to pay the sum agreed upon after the expiration of the stipulated time, even if he had derived no benefit from it, unless the use of it had been destroyed either through the fault

---

[1] *Instit.* 4. 6. 30. "In bonæ fidei judiciis libera potestas permitti videtur judici, ex bono et æquo æstimandi quantum actori restitui debeat."

[2] *Instit.* 3. 14. § 2.

[3] Gaius, 3. § 147.

"Quoties autem faciendum aliquid datur locatio est." II. 19. 2. 22. § 1.

[4] II. 19. 2. 55. 1. 61.

[5] "Si quis dolia vitiosa ignarus locaverit, deinde vinum effluxerit, tenebitur in id quod interest, nec ignorantia ejus erit excusata; et ita Cassius scripsit. Aliter atque si saltum pascuum locasti in quo herba mala nascebatur; hic enim si pecora vel demortua sunt, vel etiam deteriora facta, quod interest quæstabitur, si scisti, si ignorasti pecuniam non petes." II. 19. 2. 19. 1.

of the locator, or an extraordinary ("extra consue-
tudinem¹") misfortune; "vis cui resisti non potest,"
"vis major." Under this last, invasions of enemies,
loss by fire, wanton injury inflicted by a passing
army, and plunder by bands of robbers, were included. The loss must be considerable², and if
several years were included in the contract, the gain
of one year might be set off against the loss of an-
other³. In all these cases, the conductor might claim
not entire immunity, but "remissionem pro ratâ⁴."
At the expiration of the term the "conductor" was
bound to restore the thing in the state to which
reasonable use would bring it, and to make compensation for injury occasioned by a "culpa." In the
absence of any stipulation to the contrary, the conductor might sublet what he had hired. If nothing
was said at the expiration of a term⁵, the law implies
the assent of the hirer to the continuance of the original contract. How long the "relocatio tacita"
was to last is a much disputed question⁶.

In the "locatio conductio operarum" it was a
rule that where a work was to be undertaken, as a
whole, by the conductor, i.e. where he contracted for

---

¹ II. 19. 2. 15. 2. 25. 6. "Si ex-
ercitus præteriens per lasciviam aliquid abstulerit."

² "Vis major non debet conductori
damnosa esse si plus quam tolerabile
est, ut si cæsi fuerint fructus; alioquin modicum damnum æquo animo
ferre debet colonus."

³ Ib. 15. 2.

⁴ Ib. 15. 7.

⁵ "Qui ad certum tempus conducit,
finito quoque tempore colonus est: intelligitur enim dominus quum patitur

colonum in fundo esse, ex integro lo-
care, et hujusmodi contractus neque
verba, neque scripturam utique con-
siderant, sed nudo consensu conval-
escunt; et ideo si dominus finire cœperit
vel decesserit, fieri non posse Marcellus
ait ut locatio redintegretur, et est hoc
verum." II. 14. h. t.

1. 13. 11. "Hoc enim ipso, quod
tacuerunt, consensisse videntur."

See Glück, 17, p. 278.

⁶ "Si tale opus fuit ut probari deberet." Eod.

the entire execution at a fixed price, everything was
at his risk until the "arbitrium[1]" was pronounced[2],
unless the work deserving the "approbatio" was
destroyed by a "vis major[3]," when the loss fell upon
the "locator." So if a work was to be performed of a
certain measure, until the admeasurement was made
it was at the risk of the "conductor," supposing that
in either of these cases any delay in obtaining the admeasurement, or the "arbitrium," could be ascribed
to the fault of the "locator."

The conductor[4] was at all times responsible for
dolus, and, until the arbitrium, for culpa[5].

END OF THE "LOCATIO CONDUCTIO[6]."

The "locatio conductio" came to an end when
the hired object ceased to be; or when the time of
hiring had expired; though after that it might be
continued by a tacit understanding on both sides;
by the exercise of a right, specially vested in either
party, to put an end to the contract in a certain
event, e.g. delay in payment of the hire, abuse of

[1] The "arbitrium domini" was the "arbitrium boni viri." II. 19. 2. 24.

[2] II. 19. 2. 36. "Opus quod aversione locatum est, donec approbetur conductoris periculum est."

[3] "Si priusquam locatori opus probaretur vi aliquâ consumtum est, detrimentum ad locatorem ita pertinet si tale opus fuit ut probari deberet." Ib. 37.

[4] "Inita approbatio dolo conductoris facta." II. 19. 2. 24.

[5] "Qui columnam transportandam conduxit, si ea dum tollitur aut portatur aut reponitur fracta sit, ita ad periculum præstat si qua ipsius eorumque quorum operâ uteretur culpâ acciderit; culpa autem abest si omnia facta sunt quæ diligentissimus quisque observaturus fuisset." Eod. 25. § 7.

[6] II. 19. 2. 9. § 1; 12; 13. § 11; 54. § 1; 56; 19. 2. 25. § 2; 27; 60.

II. 39. 2. 27. § 1; 28; 33. "Inquilino non datur damni infecti actio, quia possit ex conducto agere si dominus eum m'grare prohiberet."

the thing hired, &c.; by the obstruction offered by the locator to the use of the thing hired; by circumstances that hindered the use of it; or by a well-grounded fear of danger that would come from the further use of the thing.

These circumstances might rescind, but did not destroy, the effect of the contract while it lasted.

The dolus put an end to the contract and all its consequences[1].

The sale of the thing hired by the locator did not terminate the contract.

Closely resembling the "locatio conductio," and therefore placed under the same head by Justinian, was the contract called "emphyteusis."

Emphyteusis[2] was a contract of the civil law, by which immoveable property was consigned to a man for ever on this condition, that so long as he paid a certain sum for its enjoyment it should not be taken from him.

For some time it was disputed whether the contract was not rather venditio, inasmuch as it was for ever, than locatio, which gives a transient right[3].

The Emperor Zeno created, however, a special contract, and gave it the special name "emphyteusis."

If the thing lost part of its value, the loss fell on the "emphyteuticarius;" if it lost all its value, on the owner; whereas in the contract of locatio,

[1] II. 19. 2. § 23 ; 60. § 4.

[2] See above as to emphyteusis, p. 147. Cod. de jure emphyt. l. 1. The word was not introduced till the lower empire. Caius, 3. § 145, from which text that of Justinian is taken, speaks of the "ager vectigalis."

[3] In most cases, hence "jus perpetuarium," " conductores perpetuarii." But see Cod. 6. 3. 3.

rent was excused on account of sterility and other accidents. The reason of the difference was, that the money paid by the colonus was a compensation for the use and profit; whereas the money paid by the emphyteuticarius was a recognition of ownership.

The third consensual contract was "societas." This was a contract "juris gentium, nominatus, bonæ fidei," perfected by consent, contracted between two or more for sharing gain and loss in a lawful pursuit or avocation.

Lucrum was what remained after deducting the expenses; damnum, what was wanting.

Societas differed from communio, because it was made by consent, whereas communio was the result of accident, between co-heirs or joint legatees.

Societas might be "universal" or "particular." Universal, which included every thing, even without delivering the property of each partner vested in his associate. "Quum specialiter omnium bonorum societas coita est, tunc et hæreditas et legatum et quod donatum est, et quaquâ ratione acquisitum, communioni acquiretur[1]." Particular was that which did not include all the property, but was instituted for a particular purpose, such as the purchase of oil, wine, &c.

In the absence of any special agreement the share of each socius was equal.

The opinion of Sulpicius was adopted by the

----

[1] II. 17. 2. § 3. So the dos, ib. 65. § 16. 66 ib.: still enough was to be left to bear "onera matrimonii."

Roman Law, holding against the opinion of Quintus Mucius, that an agreement for a societas according to which one partner gave money, and the other labour only, was valid.

The societas gave rise to an action "pro socio," on behalf of any "socius," not to an "actio contraria," each "socius" being a "dominus."

The "socius" was responsible for the "dolus," the "culpa," "lata" and "levis," but not the "culpa levissima."

The "societas" might be dissolved several ways:—

By the death of the "socius."

When the object for which it had been entered into was accomplished, or the time had come to an end.

By the confiscation of the property of one "socius" to the "fiscus," in which case the "socius" was held to be dead for the purposes of the "societas."

By the "cessio bonorum" of one "socius."

By the "renuntiatio" of one "socius." This was peculiar to this contract; the general rule being that a perfect contract could not be abandoned. But the "socius" could not renounce in such a way, or at such a time, as to procure for himself an unfair advantage, e. g. when he had just succeeded to an inheritance; if he renounced "dolo malo;" he set free his colleagues, but was bound himself, and became "damni particeps," "lucri expers."

The fourth species of the contracts completed by consent is "mandatum."

The "mandatum" is a "contract nominatus," perfected by consent, "bonæ fidei," by which a special commission is given by one man and accepted by another to be transacted gratuitously.

It may be established in several ways:—

1. For the benefit of the person giving the "mandatum" only; as if I give you the "mandatum" to buy me an estate.

2. For the sake of the "mandatarius" only, which is mere advice, and for which, unless fraudulently given, the "mandans" is not responsible.

3. For the sake both of "mandans" and "mandatarius;" as if I give you a "mandatum" to lend money at interest to my "procurator."

4. For the benefit of the "mandans" and an "extraneus."

5. For the sake of the "mandatarius[1]" and another: "Veluti si tibi mandemut Titio sub usuris credas."

It gave rise to a double action, "directa" and "contraria."

"Directa," for the "mandans" against the "procurator."

"Contraria," for the "procurator" against the "mandans," to recover the expense incurred by the procurator in fulfilling the "mandatum." The "mandatarius" must not exceed the limits of the "mandatum;" e. g. if a man is commissioned to buy an estate at a certain price, and he buys it for a larger

---

[1] Π. 17. 1. 2.

sum, he can only recover the amount to which he was limited.

In this contract, contrary to the usual rule, the procurator was responsible for the dolus, and every, even the levissima culpa, and was only exonerated from the casus fortuitus.

The mandatum might be terminated in three ways:—

1. By the revocation of the mandatum, *re integrâ*.

If it was recalled, "re non integrâ," the mandatum was at an end, but the mandatarius might recover the expense he had incurred.

2. The mandatum was terminated by the death of the mandans, or of the mandatarius[1].

By the death of the mandans, because the will that gave authority was at an end; but if the mandatarius in ignorance of the death executed the commission, he might bring an action "ex æquo et bono" against the heir.

3. The mandatum was terminated by the death of the mandatarius, because the mandans relied in his choice on the qualities of a particular person.

As the contract was brought to an end by the revocation of the mandans, so was it by the renunciation "re integrâ" of the mandatarius. But if the "res" was no longer "integra," the mandatarius, unless prevented by ill health or inevitable accident, was bound to finish what he had begun.

---

[1] II. 17. 1. 26. "Mandatum solvitur morte, si tamen per ignorantiam impletum est, competere actionem utilitatis causâ dicitur."

CHAPTER XIV.

QUASI CONTRACTUS.

THE "quasi contractus" is a transaction carried on by a tacit agreement between the parties, and without any express consent or agreement, and which gives rise to an obligation strictly analogous to that resulting from a contract.

There are five special "quasi contractus," the "negotiorum gestio," the "tutelæ vel curæ administratio," the "rei communio," the "hæreditatis acquisitio," and the "indebiti solutio."

The "negotiorum gestio" is the voluntary management of another man's business without his mandatum.

It gives rise to two actions, the "directa" and "contraria."

The "directa," for the dominus against the "negotiorum gestor," to give an account of what he has done.

The "contraria," for the negotiorum gestor against the dominus, to repay the sums he has laid out for the benefit of the latter in the administration of his affairs.

The "negotiorum gestor" was bound to give "exactissima diligentia."

The "administratio tutelæ" was a "quasi contractus."

It gave rise to an "actio directa" for the "pupillus," when the tutela had expired, against his "tutor," in which the tutor was responsible for the levis, not for the levissima culpa; it being sufficient that he should apply the vigilance of a diligens paterfamilias to the affairs of his pupillus.

The tutor was not only responsible for the loss incurred by his maladministration, but for the gain not acquired and that might have been won.

The "actio contraria" lay for the "tutor" against the "pupillus," to recover the sum spent by the "tutor" in the administration of his affairs.

The Code laid it down that all the goods of the tutor were ipso jure hypothecated to the pupillus. So were the goods of the step-father[1] who married the mother of the pupillus, until he had given his accounts of the "tutela."

The "rei communio," as if the same thing had been bequeathed to two persons, was a quasi contractus, and gave rise to an action; if, for instance, one of the two had laid out money on the thing, or had received the profit of it.

If it was a particular thing, it gave rise to the action "communi dividundo;" if it was the "communio hæreditatis," to the "actio familiæ erciscundæ[2]."

The "consortes" in such a case were bound to employ the same diligence they used in their own affairs, and no more, "quia eos res non consensus socios facit."

The hæreditatis acquisitio was a "quasi con-

---

[1] L. unicâ 1 Cod. de Rei uxoris actione. L. 20. Cod. quando mulier tutelæ officio fungi possit.

[2] II. Familiæ erciscundæ, 25.

tractus," because by accepting the inheritance the hæres obliged himself to pay the legatees.

The legatees therefore had an action against the heir "quasi contractus." This was "in personam," but the legatee, if a "certum corpus" had been bequeathed to him, had also an action against any possessor for the thing "in rem."

The "actio hypothecaria" also lay against any possessor of the things belonging to the inheritance.

The "indebiti solutio" was also a "quasi contractus" if it happened from ignorance of fact, not of law.

Whether money paid "per errorem juris" could be recovered has been matter of much dispute.

The man who, pretending to be a creditor, received what was not due to him, committed a "furtum," and was liable "actione furti."

DE RESCINDENDA VENDITIONE[1].

A sale might be set aside for the reasons just stated, for causes which gave rise to the "actio redhibitoria," for want of free consent, and for excessive injury to one of the parties. What should amount to this "immodica læsio" was left to the arbitrium of the judge[2], till by a rescript[3] of Diocletian and Maximinian the injury was fixed as what must amount to one half of the price, leaving it however at the

---

[1] II. 18. 5. Cod. 4. 44. Merlin, *Répertoire Lésion.* Cod. Nap. 1674—1685. Pothier, *Contrat de Vente,* 331.

[2] II. 23. 3. 12. 17. 2. 79. 16. 3. 2.

"Si Nervæ arbitrium ita pravum est ut manifesta iniquitas ejus appareat corrigi potest per judicium bonæ fidei."

[3] Cod. 4. 44. § 2. § 8.

choice of the buyer to pay the remainder of the sum,
and keep his purchase[1].

ACTIO PRO SOCIO[2].

The "socius" was bound to exercise the same
"diligentia" in the affairs of the society that he did
in his own: he was liable to pay interest on money
belonging to the partnership that he had employed
for his own purposes. The share of loss arising from
the insolvency of one socius was to be equally divided
among his partners. No partner could claim a share
in the illicit gains of another[3]. But he might call
on the partnership to share the loss of an unjust
sentence. In a "societas omnium bonorum" the
partner was bound to fling the damages he had recovered in an action, "ob injuriam sibi factam vel
lege Aquiliâ," into the common stock[4].

The societas was ended by the expressed dissent
of any one of its members, but that dissent must
not be expressed under circumstances leading to the
inference of bad faith. For instance, in a "societas
omnium bonorum" a socius could not extricate himself from its obligations by renouncing it the moment

---

[1] The doctrine, however, must be
taken in conjunction with the rules,—
"Nemo videtur fraudare eos qui
sinunt et consentiunt," and "quod
quis ex culpâ suâ damnum sentit non
intelligitur damnum sentire." II. de
reg. princ.

The French have fixed it at nine-
twelfths. Locré, Vol. XIV. p. 173:
"Ce serait donc evidemment auto-
riser le dol et la fraude que de refuser
l'action rescisoire dans les cas d'une
lésion aussi considérable que celle qui

est énoncée dans le projet de loi," &c.;
i. e. nine-twelfths. This appears too
often the effect, and sometimes almost
the purpose of the law.

[2] 52. § 17. § 18. h. t.

[3] " Prævaluit enim culpæ nomine
teneri eum (sc. socium), culpa autem
non ad exactissimum diligentiam diri-
genda est; sufficit enim talem diligentiam in rebus communibus adhibere
socium qualem suis rebus adhibere
solet."

[4] 16. h. t.

an inheritance had fallen to him. The effect of such conduct was "a se quidem liberare socios suos, se autem ab illis non liberare[1]."

The effect of the renunciation of one was to break up the partnership. If the remaining partners chose to continue in partnership, it was a new one into which they entered[2].

In the case of an absent partner the renunciation did not operate to his loss till the intelligence reached him: it might to his advantage, as all he gained in the interval was his own, while the renouncing partner was found to take his share of loss; and if the renouncing partner met with any loss, it fell exclusively upon himself[3].

A "pactum ne abeatur a societate[4]" was not binding, neither did an agreement "ne intra certum tempus abeatur" confer any advantage on the partner who would insist upon it.

Besides this termination of a partnership by the will of one of the members[5], it might without their will be terminated by the death, the "maxima or media capitis diminutio" of a member, by the destruction or change of character in the subject-matter of the partnership, or by action when the "causa societatis" was altered by a "stipulatio," or a judicial sentence.

A partnership could not be made binding on the heir of a partner, it being a maxim, "societatem non posse ultra mortem porrigi[6]." The farmership of

[1] II. 17. 2. 65. § 3.
[2] Inst. 3.
[3] II. 17. 2. 17. § 1.
[4] 17. 2. 14. 16.
[5] 68. § 10. 65. h. t.
[6] 65. § 9. h. t.

the taxes was, according to the genius of the fiscal rules under the empire, an exception to the rule[1]. But in ordinary partnership the heir was bound to go through with what the deceased had begun, and was responsible for "dolus[2]" and " culpa lata."

When the term agreed upon was ended[3], the partnership expired.

COMMUNI DIVIDUNDO[4].

THE "societas" gave rise to a reciprocal obligation among the partners, the object of which was the division of the partnership property, the contribution to it of whatever might be due from, and the compensation which might be due to, any of the partners. All this was accomplished by the "actio communi dividundo," which lasted so long as the communio. After that had ceased the "præstationes personales" might be enforced by an "utilis actio."

This action extended to all cases where, whether by virtue of partnership or not, several persons had a property in a common object[5].

---

[1] 59. 63. § 8. h. t.

[2] " Hæres socii quamvis socius non est tamen ea quæ per defunctum inchoata sunt explicare debet." 40. h. t.

[3] " Quod si tempus finitum est liberum est recedere, quia sine dolo malo id fiat." 65. § 6. h. t.

" Societas coiri potest vel in perpetuum, id est dum vivunt, vel ad tempus, vel ex tempore, vel sub conditione." 1. pr. h. t.

[4] II. 10. 3. II. 10. 3. § 3. *Inst. de Off. Judicis*, 4. 17. § 5. II. 43. 18. 1. § 8. II. 10. 2. 36.

II. 10. 3. 6. § 1 ; 11; 14. § 1.

[5] II. 10. 3. 2.

ACTIO FINIUM REGUNDORUM[1].

When disputes arose between the possessors of "prædia rustica" as to the boundaries of their property, they were settled by the "actio finium regundorum," which either fixed the precise limits; or, if that could not be done[2], divided the land in dispute, which was looked upon as common property among the litigants. Hence the affinity of this action to that which we have just considered[3]: it is, as has been already stated, the peculiarity of the "finium regundorum," the "familiæ erciscundæ," and the "communi dividundo," that each person stood in the light of plaintiff and defendant at the same time.

DE CONDICTIONE CAUSA DATA CAUSA NON SECUTA[4].

In a general sense "condictiones" meant any personal actions. In a special sense the denomination was applied to extraordinary remedies, resting for their basis, not on any civil transaction, so much as on a principle of natural equity recognized by the Civil Law. Hence they are said to be "juris gentium." They may be deduced from the natural principle of justice, so repeatedly laid down in the Pandects, that no one should gain an unjust profit

[1] Law of the Twelve Tables. Cic. de Leg. 1. 18.

[2] II. 10. 1. "Finium regundorum actio in personam est licet pro vindicatione rei est." 1. h. t.

[2] II. 10. 1. 2. § 1 ; or assigned

entirely new limits, "si per aliam regionem fines dirigere judex velit potest hoc facere." Inst. 4. 17. 6.

[3] 10. h. t.

[4] II. 12. 6.   Cod. 4. 5.

by another's loss[1]. The texts quoted in the note are the landmarks of this jurisprudence[2]. "Hæc condictio," says Papinian, "ex bono et æquo introducta quod alterius apud alterum sine causâ deprehenditur revocare consuevit."

The "condictio causâ datâ causâ non secutâ" was a personal action, by which a person could recover that which he had given for a lawful, expressed, and future object, if that object was not accomplished, with its fruits and consequences, "cum omni causâ."

To maintain this action it was necessary,

1st, that something should have been substantially parted with by the plaintiff[3];

2dly, that it should be given for an object[4];

3dly, that the purpose should be stated in express terms, or implied from the nature of the transaction;

4thly, that the cause should be lawful and possible[5];

---

[1] II. 44. 7. 5. § 3. Gaius, 3. 91. § 1. Instit. 3. 14. 1; 3. 27. 6.

II. h. t. 26. 3. "Indebitum," &c.
    64. "Si quod," &c.
    65. "Indebitum est non tantum," &c.
    32. 3. "Qui hominem," &c
"Ad quod taxi ubique in decisionibus respexerunt." Boehmer, p. 327.

II. 12. 1. 3. "Propius est ut obligari te existimem non quia pecuniam tibi credidi, &c....sed quia pecunia mea ad te pervenit, eam mihi a te reddi bonum et æquum est."

[2] 12. 6. 1. 14, 1. 15, 1. 66, 1. 65, 4. "Quod ob rem datur ex bono et æquo habet repetitionem veluti si dem tibi

ut aliquid facias nec feceris." See particularly II. 12. 4. 3. § 7, where Celsus, "naturali æquitate motus," allows money to be recovered, and II. 12. 4. 5. § 3.

[3] "Substantially."

II. 12. 4. § 10. "Nihil interest utrum ex numeratione pecunia ad eam sine causâ an per acceptilationem pervenerit." Ib. 9.

[4] II. 12. 6. 52. "Damus aut ob causam aut ob rem, ob causam præteritam......ut etiam si falsa sit causa repetitio ejus pecuniæ non sit. Ob rem vero ut aliquid sequatur quo non sequente repetitio competit."

[5] II. 12. 5. 8.

5thly, that the expected result should not have followed either through the delay or fault of the receiver, or through a change of purpose on the part of the giver before any damage had accrued to the receiver[1].

If the event was frustrated by the fault of the giver, there was no "repetitio."

If the event was frustrated by accident, as if the slave whom you had received money to enfranchise died before the time had expired within which he was to be manumitted, the money given could not be recovered[2]. On this principle the cases are decided, cited Π. 12. 4. 5. § 3, 4.

CONDICTIO OB TURPEM CAUSAM.

The "condictio ob turpem causam" was a personal action by which that which had been given for a reason disgraceful to the receiver alone, might be recovered by the giver.

1. The cause of giving must be disgraceful, it must be "ex *turpi causâ*." "Turpis causa[3]" is defined in the quotation below from Ulpian.

2. The turpitude must be that of the receiver only who was bound to restore unjust profit; and as

---

[1] Π. 12. 4. 5. pr. "Si pecuniam acceperis ut Capuam eas, etc. Cum liceat pœnitere ei qui dedit, procul dubio repetetur id quod datum est, nisi forte tuâ intersit non accepisse te hanc pecuniam."

[2] Π. 12. 4. 3. § 3.
     12. 4. 5. pr. § 2. § 3.
     12. 6. 64. § 3. "Ei qui indebitum repetit et fructus et partus restitui debent deductâ impensâ."

[3] Π. 50. 16. 42. "Probra quædam naturâ turpia sunt quædam civiliter et quasi more civitatis, ut puta furtum adulterium naturâ turpe est, enimvero tutelæ damnati hoc non naturâ turpe est, sed more civitatis." Tacitus, *Ann.* 2. 85: "More apud veteres recepto qui satis pœnarum adversum impudicas in ipsâ professione flagitii."

the liability was founded on natural equity, it extended to the heir.

Nor was the accomplishment of the object for which the money had been given any defence, as appears from this passage[1]: "Si vestimenta utenda tibi commodavero, deinde pretium ut reciperem dedissem, condictione me recte acturum responsum est, quamvis enim propter rem datum sit et causa secuta sit tamen turpiter datum est."

If there was turpitude on both sides, what was given could not be recovered.

"Ubi et dantis et accipientis turpitudo versatur non posse repeti dicimus[2]."

So money given to a woman for immorality could not be recovered[3]. Sometimes the money so given was forfeited to the state[4].

The "condictio" for what was given for a reason not consistent with justice was sometimes called "condictio sine causâ." So the rubric of the Code is, "de condict. ex leg. et sine causâ vel injustâ causâ."

In a strict sense the "condictio ob injustam causam" was to recover what had been given, for a reason clashing with the rules of natural equity, recognized by Roman jurisprudence, though in conformity with the strict letter of the law. Acts "contra jus" and acts "contra bonos mores" are sometimes opposed to each other[5].

---

[1] II. 12. 5. 9. pr.

[2] II. 12. 5. 3 and 8.

[3] "Quod meretrici datur repeti non potest ut Labeo et Marcellus scribunt, sed novâ ratione, non eâ quod utriusque turpitudo versatur sed solius dantis, illam enim turpiter facere quod sit meretrix, non turpiter accipere cum sit meretrix."

[4] II. 24. 1. 28.

[5] II. 30. 112. § 3, and the noble law of Papinian.

The "condictio indebiti" is a personal action arising from an obligation of natural equity, in which money not due, paid by mistake, is claimed as if it had been a loan.

This arises from natural equity[1]; it is numbered among the "quasi contractus" in the Institutes[2]. Not only therefore may the person who has paid the money employ this remedy, but he who is injured by such payment may have recourse to it[3], and might recover all that the receiver had gained. "Scilicet quod bonæ fidei possessor in quantum locupletior factus est tenetur[4]."

A debt due by the law of nature, if paid though by mistake, could not be recovered. "[5]Si quod dominus servo debuit manumisso solvit, quamvis existimans se ei aliquâ actione teneri, tamen repetere non potest quia naturale agnovit debitum." So money[6] paid "pietatis causâ" could not be recovered. "Mulier, si in eâ opinione sit ut credat se pro dote obligatam quicquid dotis nomine dederit, non repetit, sublatâ enim falsâ opinione relinquitur pietatis causa ex quâ solutum repeti non potest."

II. 28. 7. 15.
II. 47. 10. 15. § 2. § 5. § 6.
[1] "Nam hoc naturâ æquum est neminem cum alterius damno fieri locupletiorem." II. 12. 6. 14. "Indebiti soluti condictio naturalis est." Ib. 15. "Hæc condictio ex æquo et bono introducta quod alterius apud alterum sine causâ deprehenditur revocare consuevit." II. 12. 6. 66.

[2] I. de oblig. quæ quasi ex contr. § 6.
[3] II. 12. 6. 2. § 1. "Si quid ex testamento solutum sit quod postea falsum, vel inofficiosum, vel ruptum apparuerit, repetetur," etc.
[4] Ib. 3. Ib. 65. § 3.
[5] II. 12. 6. 64. II. 12. 6. 26 pr.
[6] II. 12. 6. 32. § 2.

What was intended as a pure gift could not be recovered[1]. Thus there was no "condictio" for money given in consideration for past services, even though such services had not been rendered. "[2]Damus ob causam aut ob rem; ob causam praeteritam veluti cum ideo do quod aliquid a te consecutus sum, vel quia aliquid a te factum est, ut etiamsi falsa causa est, repetitio ejus pecuniae non sit." So if a debtor privileged as to amount, e. g. the husband liable only to the extent of his means, or as to time, as a debtor not bound to pay before a certain time, chose to waive his privilege, the sum paid could not be recovered[3].

But if the transaction was one reprobated by the Law (as in the instance of a ward paying money due on a stipulation without the sanction of his guardian), the rule did not hold, and the money might be recovered[4].

If the law gave a perpetual defence, for the sake of protecting the class to which a person who had paid money belonged, money paid by mistake under such circumstances might be recovered: but if the defence was given from detestation of the creditor, "in odium ejus cui debetur," as the "senatus consultum Macedonianum[5]," money paid by the father in such a case, notwithstanding the defence provided by the law, could not be recovered.

---

[1] "Cujus per errorem dati repetitio est, ejus consulto dati repetitio est." II. 50. 17. 53.

[2] II. 12. 6. 52.

[3] II. 12. 6. 9 and 11.

[4] II. 12. 6. 40 and 41. II. 16. 1. 8. § 3.

[5] "Si quidem ejus causâ exceptio datur cum quo agitur solutum repetere potest......ubi vero in odium ejus cui debetur exceptio datur peram solutum non repetitur." II. 12. 6. 40.

The rule was that where a person who might avail himself of a perpetual exception[1], paid money in ignorance of such an exception, he might recover it; but when being aware of such a defence he chose to waive it, he could not recover what he had deliberately paid.

What was given in consequence of a reason recognized by the law could not be recovered[2]; for instance, money paid in obedience to a legal sentence, as a compromise, &c.

The burden of proving that the money paid was not due, rested upon the person asserting that it was not due, "Qui enim solvit, nunquam ita resupinus est ut facile suas pecunias jactet," unless the defendant denied that he had received the money, in which case, when that fact was proved, the burden of proving that the money was so paid, was duly shifted upon *him*, and it became *his* task to exonerate himself from the presumption raised against him, by the denial of the truth: "Per etenim absurdum est eum qui ab initio negavit pecuniam suscepisse, postquam fuerit convictus eam accepisse, probationem non debiti ab adversario exigere[3]."

---

[1] II. 12. 6. 26. § 3. "Indebitum autem solutum accipimus non solum si omnino non debeatur sed et si per aliquam exceptionem perpetuam peti non poterat, quare hoc quoque repeti poterit nisi sciens se tutum exceptione solverit." II. 12. 6. 44.

[2] II. 42. 1. 56. "Post rem judicatam vel jurejurando decisam vel confessionem in jure factam nihil quæritur." II. 12. 6. 65. "Et quidem quod transactionis nomine datur, licet res nulla media fuerit, non repetitur, nam si lis fuit hoc ipsum quod a lite disceditur causa videtur esse. Siu autem evidens calumnia detegitur, et transactio imperfecta est, et repetitio dabitur."

[3] II. 22. 3. 25. The whole of this admirable law, which forms so painful a contrast to the proceedings in our courts of justice, should be carefully thought over by the student.

It is enough for the person suing to prove that he did not owe what he has paid; and unless he made the payment in behalf of another, a "condictio" would always lie for an error[1]; in fact, for an error in law it might be brought to save from loss, not to procure gain. "Error facti ne maribus quidem in damnis vel compendiis obest, juris autem error nec fœminis in compendiis prodest; cæterum omnibus juris error in damnis amittendæ rei suæ non nocet[2]."

If the receiver took the money, knowing that it did not belong to him, he was guilty of theft, and liable to the "condictio furtiva." Such a person therefore was not liable in this form of action.

The condictio might be "certi" or "incerti:" "certi," where a definite thing or sum was sought; "incerti," where the object was to establish a right, or recover possession erroneously parted with[3].

Lapse of time was no bar to such a proceeding[4].

A difference was made between the cases where the same amount[5] was sought, as in the "mutuum," or where the identical object parted with was demanded, supposing it either to exist, or to have been fraudulently destroyed or lost; if it had ceased

---

[1] II. 12. 6. 31. "Is qui plus quam hæreditaria portio efficit per errorem creditori caverit, indebiti promissi habet condictionem." II. 12. 6. 44; which is thus reconciled with the law, 19. 1. ib. "Quamvis debitum sibi quis recipiat, tamen si is qui dat non debitum dat, repetitio competit."

[2] II. 22. 6. 7 and 8.

[3] II. 13. 1. 18. "Quoniam furtum

sit cum quis indebitos nummos sciens acceperit."

[4] II. 12. 6. 12. II. 12. 6. 15.

[5] II. 22. 1. 38. § 2. "Fructus quoque repetere debeo." II. 12. 6. 7. II. 12. 6. 26. § 12. II. 12. 6. 65. § 8. "Si servum indebitum tibi dedi, eumque manumisisti, si sciens hoc fecisti tenebris ad pretium ejus."

to exist without the dolus of the defendant, he was exonerated.

The "condictio sine causâ" used in a special sense might be employed in three cases.

1st. When the transaction in consequence of which the defendant received what he is required to restore was altogether null[1]. Instances of this are given in the fifth law under this head, where Papinian says that the "dos" given in consideration of an illegal marriage might be recovered, as the cause was not so much dishonourable as null. "Respondi, non tam turpem causam quam nullam fuisse."

2dly. The "condictio sine causâ" lay when something had been given in the expectation, and under the condition, of a compensation, which compensation was never forthcoming. If a person gave an engagement to pay a certain sum of money in consideration of a loan, and the loan was never made, he might recover the engagement. "Nihil refert," says the Digest, "utrumne ab initio sine causâ quid datum sit, an causa propter quam datum sit secuta non sit[2]."

3dly. This remedy might be used when the legal cause, in consideration of which the thing had been given, had ceased, and therefore the defendant could not in conscience retain what had been given to him. "Si fuit causa promittendi quæ finita est, dicendum est condictioni locum fore," and "constat id donum posse condici alieni quod vel non ex justâ

---

[1] II. 12. 7. 5. "Magis in eâ specie nulla causa dotis dandæ fuit; condic-

tio igitur competit."
[2] II. 12. 7. 1. § 2. § 3. II. 12. 7. 2.

causâ ad eum pervenit vel redit ad non justam causam."

Ulpian puts the case of a person losing the clothes he had undertaken to clean[1], and paying, as he was obliged to do, the value of them to the owner. The clothes being afterwards restored, can he recover the money he has paid in this form of action? That he could bring an action "ex conducto," there is no doubt. Ulpian is of opinion that he can, "quasi sine causâ datum putamus condici posse: etenim vestimentis inventis quasi sine causâ datum videtur[2]."

I have cited below[3] another instance of the concurrence of the "condictio sine causâ" with the "actio ex contractu," in the case of a ring given "arrhæ nomine." The difference between the "actio ex contractu" and the "condictio sine causâ" is, that in the latter only the money paid can be recovered, whereas the former was in the alternative, either to repay the money, or restore the thing paid for. This appears from the text cited below[4].

CONDICTIO FURTIVA.

The "condictio furtiva" lay for the owner against the thing, and his heirs, for the restoration of the

---

[1] "Lavanda." Some critics read "lævanda."

[2] II. 12. 6. 2.

[3] II. 19. 1. 11. §6. " Et secutâ emtione pretioque numerato et traditâ re si annulus non reddatur? et Julianus diceret ex emto agi posse; certe etiam condici poterit, quia sine causâ apud venditorem est annulus."

[4] II. 13. 6. 17. § 5. "Rem commodatam perdidi et pro eo pretium dedi, deinde res in potestate tuâ venit. Labeo ait contrario judicio aut rem mihi præstare te debere, aut quod a me accepisti reddere."

thing stolen, with fruit and interest. The action was
anomalous, as the formula in all other "condictiones"
was "*dare* oportere," the word "dare [1]" supposing
that the thing sued for is not yet the property of
the plaintiff; whereas such a property in the person
suing is the foundation of the "condictio furti."
Justinian says that this was introduced "odio furum."
It was no answer that the thing had ceased to be "in
rebus humanis[2]," as in that case the thief was liable
for the value. The "condictio" was destroyed by
the restitution, or the offer of restitution, of the
things stolen, and by a "novatio[3]."

CONDICTIO EX LEGE.

The *condictiones ex lege* were established on equitable grounds to meet cases growing out of a new
law for which no formula had been provided. Sometimes they were called "actiones in factum præscriptis verbis;" sometimes "condictiones." "Si
obligatio lege novâ introducta sit nec cautum eâdem
lege, quo genere actionis experiamur, ex lege agendum est," says Paulus[4].

[1] *Instit. de actionibus*, 4. 6. § 14. "In furtivâ re soli domino condictio competit." II. 13. 1. 1.

[2] II. 13. 1. 8. 13. 1. 7. 13. 1. 20. "Videtur qui primo invito domino rem contrectaverit semper in restituendâ eâ, quam nec debuit auferre, moram facere."

[3] II. 13. 1. 14. § 2. "Bove subrepto," &c. II. 13. 1. 17.

[4] L. unica. II. 13. 2. "Quod ex his causis (sc. u. aut m.) debetur per condictionem quæ ex lege descendit petitur." II. 48. 5. 28. "Sunt jura, sunt formulæ de omnibus rebus constitutæ ne quis aut in genere injuriæ, aut ratione actionis errare possit; expressæ sunt enim ex unius cujusque damno, dolore, incommodo, calamitate, injuriâ, publicæ a prætore formulæ ad quas privata lis accommodatur." Cic. *pro Roscio Comœdo*, § 8.

CONDICTIO TRITICARIA[1].

The following passage from a great writer will justify my silence on this action. Ger. Noodt passes it over with this remark, "Non assuetus alios docere quod ipse non intelligo."

NEGOTIORUM GESTIO.

The management of another person's affairs without his authority, might give rise to an obligation between the person who had so managed them and the person in whose interest he had acted.

The "directa negotiorum gestorum actio," which was given to the "dominus," required nothing but the dealing of the other party to the obligation with the affairs of the "dominus" for its support.

To support the "contraria" of the "gestor" it was requisite to shew, 1st, that the "gestor" had undertaken the task, not "pietate" or "amicitiâ ductus," but with a view to profit; 2ndly, that it was not against the prohibition of the "dominus;" and 3rdly, that what had been done was "utiliter[2]," for the benefit of the dominus. The general rule was that the "negotiorum gestor," inasmuch as his interference was unauthorized and spontaneous, answered for the "dolus" and the "culpa," and in some cases for the "casus:" but where the interference had

---

[1] "Memoria teneo omnia de hac condictione tradita a Tituli hujus interpretibus, sed expensis omnibus diligenter adeo nihil probare mihi permisi ut contra sæpe sum miratus tam secure tractari actionem cujus nemo non modo usum ac nec nomen ad probabile explicando duxit, tantum abest ut quisquam utrumque aut alterun. sit ex solido consecutus." Noodt, *Op.* Tom. II. p. 305. II. 13. 3.

[2] II. 3. 5. 10. §. 1.

saved the dominus from manifest loss, the gestor was responsible for the "dolus" and "culpa lata" only.

The "gestor" might be responsible for what he had left undone, as well as for what he had done, inasmuch as his interference had prevented perhaps the interference of others; hence he had to pay interest on what was due from him to the dominus, the necessary expense he had incurred deducted.

There were certain cases where the "gestor" of another man's affairs could not bring the actio "negotiorum gestorum," e. g. the "funeraria actio," and the action arising from the "in possessionem missio." A creditor put into possession of the goods of his debtor could not be looked upon as a "negotiorum gestor," inasmuch as the administration of the property was for his own benefit. There lay an "actio in factum" for and against him framed by analogy to the "negotiorum gestorum actio directa et contraria," the creditor being responsible for the "dolus" and "culpa lata."

CURA BONORUM [1].

It is sometimes necessary for the public interest that the commonwealth should appoint a person or persons to watch over an estate.

Where this was done, not on account of any personal defect in the proprietor, the person so appointed was called "curator bonorum."

[1] Π. 4ᵌ. 7.
37. 9.
3. 5.

The necessity for such interference arose where property was to be administered for a body of creditors. Application being made to the prætor, he appointed as curator the person recommended by the majority of the creditors[1].

If the heirs to an estate were uncertain[2].

If the heir was not born, the "curator ventris" might fulfil the duties of a "curator bonorum," or a special "curator bonorum" might be appointed[3].

And a curator might be appointed in cases where the proprietor of the estate was absent, "ne in medio pereat[4]."

The "curator bonorum" could not, unless in cases of extreme necessity, be appointed against his will[5].

He could only sell what, if not sold, would perish[6].

In the case of more persons than one exercising the functions of a "mandatarius," each was responsible "in solidum," so long as more than the value of the debt was not recovered.

On the other hand[7], the "mandans" was bound to make compensation to the "mandatarius" for the expense he had incurred in executing the commis-

---

[1] Π. 42. 7. 2. § 3.
　　27. 10. 5. 9.
[2] Π. 42. 4. 3. eod. 8 and 9. c. 17.
[3] Π. 27. 10. 8.
　　37. 9. 1. § 17, 18.
[4] Π. 26. 1. 6. 4.
　　42. 4. 6. 2.
　　4. 6. 15.
　　53. 4. 4. 4.
[5] Π. 42. 7. 2. § 3.
　　50. 4. 1. § 4.
[6] Π. 26. 7. 48.

50. 4. 1. 4.
[7] *Inst.* 1. 13. *Dig.* 26. 1. 1. Caius, *Inst.* 196. § 1.

"Ut enim tutela sic procuratio reipublicæ ad utilitatem eorum qui commissi sunt, non ad eorum quibus commissa est, gerenda est." Cic. *de Off.* I. 25.

"Quia neque scire neque decernere puer hujus ætatis potest magis quam furiosus."

Π. 29. 2. 9.

sion, together with the interest, to liberate him from all obligations incurred on his behalf, to make good his losses, casualties excepted. The "mandatarius" could enforce these rights by the "actio mandati contraria" against several "mandatarii," "in solidum." To avail himself of this remedy the mandatarius was bound to prove that he had not exceeded the limits of his contract, or that if he had done so, he had made good the excess, and that he had fulfilled, or was ready to fulfil, his undertaking. To prove that he had completed the purpose the mandans had in view, was unnecessary.

The relation between the "mandans" and the "mandatarius" ceased, 1st, by the termination of the affairs the latter was appointed to execute;

2dly, by the revocation of the "mandans," which might be tacit, and implied either from his undertaking the affair himself, or entrusting the task to some one else ;

3dly, by the renunciation of his duty on the part of the "mandatarius" communicated to the "mandans[1]." But the revocation and renunciation must be timed properly.

TUTELA[2].

"Tutela" is a power given or allowed by the civil law[3], exercised for the protection of a free citi-

---

[1] "Consilii non fraudulenti nulla obligatio est; cæterum si dolus et calliditas intercessit, de dolo actio competit." II. 50. 17. 74.

[2] II. 26. 6. 2. § 4.
4. 4. 7. § 2.
Inst. 1. § 23. "Inviti adolescentes curatorem non accipiunt."

[3] "Ei cujus pater in potestate hostium tutorem dari non posse palam est, sed si datus sit an in pendenti sit datio quæri potest, et non puto dationem valere, sic enim post patris regressum cecidit in potestatem atque si nunquam pater ab hostibus captus esset. Immo curator substantiæ dari debet." II. 26. 1. 6. § 4.

zen unable from his tender years to protect himself.

If the deceased father[1] had not declared his choice, the "agnati," or paternal kindred of the nearest degree, were compelled to act as guardians.

The "impubes" alone could be "in tutelâ;" after that age, if necessary, his affairs might be placed in the hands of a "curator," but the "tutor" was appointed independently of his will; the "curator," on the other hand, unless "in litem[2]," could not, generally speaking, be given to him against his will.

A "tutor" could only be given to a "civis Romanus sui juris," therefore a "tutor" could not be given to one whose father, though alive, was in captivity[3]. In such a case a "curator substantiæ" was appointed.

Some persons were naturally, and some legally, disqualified from being "tutores[4]."

The naturally disqualified were the insane, the prodigal, the minor, the blind, the dumb, the deaf.

The legally disqualified[5] were the slave, the "deportatus," the soldier, women, (the mother and grandmother excepted, if of full age, and renouncing the Sen[tm]. Velleianum, and a second marriage), the creditor or debtor of the "pupillus." All others, "filii familias" not excepted, might be "tutores."

The "tutela" might be given by will, by law, by

[1] II. 26. 5. 21. § 2. Cod. 5. 4. 7.
L. un.
   II. 26. 10. 3. § 12.
     27. 1. 6. 17.
     26. 5. 21. 6.
  Nov. 72. c. 4.
     72. c. 2.

[2] II. 50. 17. 60.
[3] II. 17. 1. 20. § 1.
[4] II. 3. 5.
[5] II. 3. 5. 8. § 3. " Ita tamen ut is qui prohibuit ex nullâ parte neque per socium neque per ipsum aliquid damni sentiat."

the magistrate. The first was called "testamentaria," the second "legitima," the third "dativa." The first was preferred to the second, and the second to the third. The father or grandfather alone could appoint a tutor. The father could not appoint a "tutor" to one emancipated, nor the mother to any child.

The person appointed must be "idoneus," free, that is, from the impediments above enumerated[1]. But a person might be appointed who was not "idoneus," if he might become so; and this condition, whether expressed or not, was understood as annexed to his nomination, if the testator knew his incapacity; otherwise, if he did not. The "tutor" might be appointed by a will or a valid codicil. If the will was disputed on behalf of the pupil, the tutor named in it required confirmation. If there was a delay in entering upon the inheritance, a "tutor" was named by the magistrate during the interval. A "tutor" might be appointed absolutely, conditionally, for or from a particular time, the magistrate appointing one for the interval. A "testator" using the words "filiis" and "filiabus" was understood to include posthumous children, not grandchildren, in the expression; but if he used the word "liberis" he was taken to mean grandchildren[2]. Even however if he used the word "filiis," the will might furnish

---

[1] The law of Paulus. II. 26. 2. 21. "Testamento tutores dari possunt cum quibus testamenti factio est" is to be taken negatively, *i. e.* none can be appointed tutores unless with whom there is a "testamenti factio." Thus only a "civis Romanus" could be appointed, not a "servus" nor a "deportatus;" but it does not mean that all with whom there was a "testamenti factio" could be appointed, as this would include the "surdus, prodigus, &c." Donellus, Vol. II. p. 29.

[2] II. 6. 2. 5 and 6.

ground for supposing that he meant to include grandchildren[1]. He who inserted his own name as "tutor"
was excluded from the office by Sen^{tm}. Libonianum;
but where the will of the testator declaring him
"tutor" was unequivocally in his own hand, Papinian
allowed him to be added to the other tutors as "curator[2]." The assignment of a tutor was of no effect, unless it was clear for what child or children he was so
appointed. If a testator appointed a tutor "filiis,"
the expression did not include a son of whose existence he was ignorant, on the principle so long disregarded in our law, "voluntas ergo facit quod in
testamento scriptum valeat." If the testator gave
the "tutela" to a slave of his own, unless a contrary
intention appeared in the will, the bequest gave the
slave his freedom. The slave of another might be
named "tutor," "si liber erit," or "cum liber erit."

The confirmation[2] of "tutores," which was requisite in all cases where they were not "jure dati," was
vested in the chief magistrate, the prætor at Rome,
the proconsul or præses in a province: a "tutor" was
"jure datus," where he was named "a quibus oportet,
quibus oportet, quomodo oportet, et ubi oportet." If
any of these ingredients were deficient, they might be
supplied by the authority of the magistrate.

The "legitima tutela" prevailed when, for whatever reason, there was no testamentary "tutela." The
"legitimi tutores" were those called by law to the "tutela" and to the inheritance; setting aside the case
of freedmen, the old law gave the "tutela" in such a

---

[1] II. 50. 16. 220. "Filii enim appellatione sæpe et nepotes accipi, mul-
tifariam placere."
[2] II. 26. 2. 29.

case to the nearest "agnatus." The "agnatio," and therefore the "tutela," was destroyed by the "capitis diminutio," even the "minima." It is sufficient for the purpose of this treatise to say that Justinian[1] provided that the "onus tutelæ" and "successionis emolumentum" should go together.

The "dativa tutela[2]" took place where neither the "testamentaria" nor the "legitima" existed. The appointment was made by the principal magistrate within his jurisdiction. The "legatus proconsulis" was empowered by a special law to exercise this power, and so were other magistrates: but as a general rule it could not be delegated: "Nec mandante præside alius tutorem dare poterit." Justinian, with the wretched superstition that was blended with vanity and flagitious wickedness in his character, gave this authority to bishops—at that time as corrupt a body as any class on earth. In the absence of the usual magistrate it was given to the majority of decurions.

The appointment[3] of a tutor by a magistrate was "ex officio." To facilitate the election of proper persons to discharge this trust, the Roman Law established the "petitio tutoris" or "curatoris[4]." The duty of preferring this "petitio" was incumbent on those who if the minor died intestate would be his

<hr/>

[1] Novell. 118. c. 5. Inst. de legit. Pat. tut.

[2] Inst. de Atil. tutore. De Tutor. et Curat. dat.

[3] II. 26. 6. 4.

[4] II. 26. 6. 2.

"Mater enim expellitur a legitimâ filii hereditate quasi existens indigna accipere legitimam hæreditatem negligens ei constitui tutorem, et non solum si non petierit sed et si. . . . petierit eum qui dimitti poterat, deinde dimisso eo vel abjecto alium non petierit rursum vel ex studio malos petierit." II. 39. 17. 2. § 23 and § 43.

"'Confestim' autem ni erit accipiendum ubi primum potuit, id est prætoris copiam habuit huic rei sedentis . . . . ita tamen ut nullo modo annale tempus excederet." II. 37. 17. 2. § 43.

heirs. They were bound to prefer it within a year, under pain of losing what they would otherwise have inherited if the minor died before he could make his will.

With the exception of the mother[1] and grandmother, every one not disqualified for the office of tutor might be compelled to accept it.

Persons in the situations stated below were exempted from this necessity:—

Persons holding certain offices[2].

"In consilium Principis assumpti."

"Quibus Princeps curam alicujus rei injunxit donec curam genuit."

Absence in the service of the state for a year after the return of the person employed, "qui qualitercumque publicæ plebis Romanorum gratiâ absentes fuerunt, anni habent vacationem post reversionem."

Ecclesiastical office[3].

"Romæ docentes. Philosophi. Oratores. Grammatici. Medici[4]."

"Milites qui honeste compleverunt militiæ tempus."

Poverty.

Sickness such as disqualifies the invalid from managing his own affairs.

Age of 70.

Three tutorships imposed by law.

Three, four, or five children, as the parent happened to be a Roman, Italian, or provincial.

[1] *Inst.* 1. 25.
II. 27. 1.
Cod. 5. 62.
[2] *Inst.* h. t. § 3.
II. 29. 1.
[3] Cod. de Epis. et Cler. 1. 3. 52.
[4] II. 27. 1. 6. § 1—12.

Being a member of certain corporations.

" Mediocritas et rusticitas[1]."

" Si quis se dicit domicilium non habere ubi ad tutelam datus est[2]."

" Capitalis inimicitia " between the father of the " pupillus " and the " tutor," or reasonable ground for supposing that the testamentary tutor was appointed out of spite, " ut supponatur debito et negotiis[3]."

Litigation between the " tutor " and " pupillus," " de omnibus bonis aut plurimâ parte eorum."

The " tutor " might be released from the " tutela " when undertaken on account of absence[4] in the service of the state.

Being made a councillor of the prince.

Poverty and sickness.

Change of domicile with permission of the ruler.

From the moment[5] of his appointment as tutor being made known to him, the tutor was responsible for the duties of that office, " ex quo scit se tutorem datum si cesset tutor suo periculo cessat."

Immediately on his appointment[6] he was bound (1) to draw up an inventory[7], (2) to find sureties (unless testamentary) " rem pupilli salvam fore."

The " tutela " might end either by the emancipation of the " pupillus," or the termination of the

---

[1] II. 27. 1. 6. 19.

[2] II. 46. 2.

[3] II. 27. 1. 6. 17.

[4] II. 44. 11. 2.
      27. 1. 12. 1.
      27. 1. 10. 2.
Cod. 5. 64. 1.
II. 1. 25. *Inst.* h. t. § 2.

[5] II. 26. 7. 1. § 1. Eod. 98. 2.

[6] " Tutor qui repertorium non fecit quod vulgo inventarium appellatur, dolo fecisse videtur, nisi forte aliqua et justissima causa allegari possit an id factum non sit." II. 26. 7. 7.

[7] II. 46. 6. Cod. 5. 42. *Inst.* 1. 24. II. 26. 3. 3.

tutor's trust.   With regard to the first category the
reference[1] in the note will be sufficient.   With regard
to the second, the main causes were—

Supervening incapacity, such as "capitis diminutio," in certain cases[2].

Resignation legally accepted.

Removal by formal complaint (suspecti postu-
latio[3]), or by the interference of authority.

Removal might be on account of "dolus" or
"culpa ;" and if this reason was stated in the decree,
the "tutor" was infamous.

Incapacity or negligence not amounting to the
above-mentioned "culpa," in which case the "tutor"
was not infamous.

The main duties of the "tutor" related to the
administration of the property of the "pupillus," and
the care of his health and education[4].   These duties
were not exercised without control.   The "tutor"
was under the immediate inspection and liable to the
peremptory interference of a superior, sometimes the
prætor, sometimes another dignified magistrate[5].

---

[1] *Inst.* 1. 22. 26.
   Cod. 5. 60.
   5. 43.
   II. 26. 10.

[2] II. 26. 4. 5. § 5.
   4. 5. 7.

[3] II. 26. 10.   "Consequens est ut
videamus qui possunt suspectos pos-
tulare, et sciendum est quasi publicam
hanc esse actionem, hoc est, omnibus
patere. Quinimo et mulieres admittun-
tur, sed hæ solæ quæ pietatis necessi-
tudine ductæ ad hoc procedunt, ut
puta mater, nutrix quoque et avia
possunt, potest et soror," &c.

II. 26. 10. 7. 1—3.
   3. 5. 13—17.
Instit. 1. 26. § 5, 6.

[4] II. 27. 2.   "Ubi pupillus educari
vel morari debeat et de alimentis ei
præstandis."
   Cod. 5. 49.

[5] II. 27. 9. 5. 12.
   26. 5. 27.
"Pupillo qui tam Romæ quam in
provinciâ facultates habet rerum quæ
sunt Romæ, Prætor, provincialium
Præses, tutorem dare potest."
   II. 27. 2. 1. 3. 5.

The "tutor" was responsible for "dolus" and "culpa" and the lack of such "diligentia" as he employed in his own affairs[1]. He was "domini loco[2]." He was bound to sell perishable things, and not to suffer loss by unnecessary delay[3]. So he was bound to collect debts, and to discharge those, even if due to himself, which bore "graviores usuras[4]."

The "auctoritas tutoris[5]" was requisite to give the act of the "pupillus," unless manifestly for his own advantage, a legal and binding character. The "auctoritas" was a sanction given by the "tutor" when the act was done, and thus forming part of the act: "Tutor statim in ipso negotio præsens debet auctor fieri post tempus aut per epistolam auctoritas ejus nihil agit:" it could not be interposed by the tutor for his own benefit[6], unless where such benefit was merely collateral, and a consequence of some advantage of the "pupillus."

The "tutor" was bound to take care that the property of the "pupillus" brought its reasonable and natural return. He was not bound to seek extraordinary profit; but if such profit was made, it was for the benefit of the "pupillus," not his own[7]. Six months

[1] II. 27. 3. 1. "In omnibus quæ fecit tutor cum facere non deberet, item in his quæ non fecit rationem reddet hoc judicio præstando dolum et culpam et quantam in rebus suis diligentiam."
Gaius, I. 190. 192.
[2] II. 26. 7. 27.
[3] II. 26. 7. 7. § 1.
[4] II. eod. 7. § 1. 9. § 5.
15 and 50.
[5] II. 26. 8. 8 and 9. § 5.

26. 8. 1.
[6] II. 26. 8. 1. "Quanquam regula sit juris civilis in rem suam auctorem tutorem fieri non posse, tamen potest tutor proprii sui debitoris hæreditatem adeunti pupillo auctoritatem accommodare, quamvis per hoc debitor ejus efficiatur; prima enim ratio auctoritatis ea est ut hæres fiat; per consequentias contigit ut debitum subeat."
[7] II. 26. 7. 3. § 2 and 7 and 15.
5 pr. 7. § 11.

were allowed him after first undertaking the office, and two months in the ordinary course of it, within which "laxamentum temporis [1]" he was required to invest monies received for the "pupillus," or, unless he could shew that a safe investment was impossible, to pay the regular interest for them.

The "tutor" was not allowed to make gifts for his "pupillus," unless they were of such a character (e. g. the support of a mother or sister, or the remuneration of a master,) as no one could with propriety dispute. I quote the law as one among the many admirable proofs of wisdom abounding in this chapter of Roman jurisprudence. "Cum tutor non rebus duntaxat sed etiam moribus pupilli præponatur, in primis mercedes præceptoribus non quas minimas poterit, sed pro facultate patrimonii pro dignitate natalium constituet, alimenta servis libertisque nonnunquam etiam exteris si hoc pupillo expediet præstabit, solennia munera parentibus cognatisque mittet [2]."

This outlay he might make without the consent of the "pupillus;" beyond this limit, however honestly the outlay might be made, "servanda arbitrio pupilli est."

The "tutor" might sell with the sanction of the prætor, and acting *bonâ fide,* the property of his pupil. If he acted *malâ fide* in the transaction, it was altogether void: "Nam tutor in re pupilli tunc domini loco habetur cum tutelam administrat non

---

[1] This rule was foolishly altered by Justinian, but modern nations have disregarded his law. Novell. 72. 6. 8.

[2] II. 26. 7. 12. § 3.

cum pupillum spoliat[1]." He was liable to restore
fourfold the value of any property of his "pupillus"
that he had clandestinely appropriated; but he
might buy openly and *bonâ fide* what was sold by a
fellow-tutor, or any one with proper authority, though
belonging to the "pupillus."

Two things were requisite for a valid alienation
by the "tutor" of the estate of the "pupillus."

1st, a "justa causa," i.e. pressing necessity.
"Prætori enim non datur liberum arbitrium dis-
trahendi res pupillares, sed ita detur si æs alienum
immineat[2]."

2nd, "Decretum Prætoris," or superior magistrate.

If the "pupillus" did not choose to sue the "tutor,"
an action lay for him "in rem," in which he asserted
"obreptum esse Prætori[3]." In such an action it lay
upon the defendant to prove the "decretum" and the
purchase: "quia a pupillo emit probare debet tutore
auctore, lege non prohibente se emisse[4]." The defendant, if the plaintiff's demand was fraudulent in
fact, might employ the "exceptio" that the "pupillus" was "lucrum captans ex damno alieno[5]," or
he might prove that the plaintiff had ratified the
contract after attaining his majority[6], or that five
years had elapsed since he had obtained majority,
during which the transaction had been unimpeached[7].

Out of the obligation between the "pupillus" and
"tutor" arose, after the "tutela" was ended, the "actio

[1] II. 41. 4. 7. § 3.
[2] II. 27. 9. 5. § 14.
[3] II. 27. 9. 2.
[4] II. 6. 3. 13. § 2.

[5] II. 27. 9. 13.
[6] Cod. 2. 46. 2.
[7] Cod. 5. 74. 3.

tutelæ," having for its object every part of the tutor's administration. No "tutor" could be "aneclogistos," i. e. free from responsibility; not even the express will of the father could give irresponsibility to the tutor he appointed, on the great and salutary principle, "nemo jus publicum remittere potest[1]."

In cases of "dolus" and "culpa," the "pupillus" was allowed a "jusjurandum in litem." In case of embezzlement by the guardian, the "actio rationibus distrahendis[2]" might be employed instead of the "tutelæ actio," in which double the value of the property might be recovered. The "tutor" had a "contraria tutelæ actio" for the reimbursement of his expenses[3].

The claim[4] to which the "tutor" was liable might be preferred against his sureties: so were the "affirmatores," or those who had declared the "fidejussores" idonei.

If any one without being a "tutor" acted as one, he was liable to a "pro tutelæ actio[5]."

The "pupillus" had the "tutelæ actio subsidiaria," or "utilis," when compensation could not be obtained from the "tutor" against the authorities who had failed to exercise sufficient care in the appointment, to the full amount for which the tutor was responsible. "Eadem in magistratibus actio

---

[1] Π. 26. 7. 5. § 7.

[2] Π. 27. 3. 1. § 19.
Eod. 4.

[3] Π. 27. 4. 1.   Contrariam tutelæ actionem. "Prætor proposuit induxitque in usum ut facilius tutores ad administrationem accederent scientes pupillum quoque sibi obligatum fore ex suâ administratione."

[4] Π. 27. 7. 5.
Eod. 4. 3. "Eadem causa videtur adfirmatorum, qui scilicet cum idoneos esse tutores affirmaverint, fidejussorum vicem sustinent."

[5] Π. 29. 5.

datur quæ competit in tutores[1]." This responsibility
did not extend to the prætor or the higher magistrates[2].

The "tutela" came to an end by the death either
of the "pupillus" or the "tutor," and when the former
had attained the age of puberty[3], fixed by Justinian
at fourteen. According to the ancient law, which
was gradually modified, women were subject to perpetual tutelage of parents, guardians, or husbands[4].
Justinian[4] allowed them (probably in the interest of
the clergy) to manage their own affairs at eighteen.

CURATIO BONORUM[5].

The specific difference between the "curator" and
the "tutor" was, that the first object of the former was
the care of the property, and the first object of the
latter was the care of the person[5]. Incapacity for the
management of property might arise from youth or
incapacity[6]. Now there were two kinds of "curatio,"
the "data" and the "legitimata." By the law of the
Twelve Tables, the curatio of the prodigus, or furiosus,
was given to the agnati. The "curator" was granted
at the request of the "adolescens[6]:" it was the duty
of the "tutor" to admonish the "pupillus" to demand

[1] II. 27. 8. 9.
Instit. 1. 24. 2.
[2] II. 27. 8. 1. § 1.
[3] *Inst.* 1. 22.
Cod. 5. 60.
II. 4. 4. 1.
[4] Cod. 2. 45. § 2.
[5] Ulpian, *Regulæ*, 12. § 2.

The Lex Lætoria, or Lectoria, or
Plætoria, established majority at 25.
Plautus calls it "quinavicenaria."
The text of this law has not reached
us.
[6] II. 26. 6. 2. § 4. 'Ωs δέον ἄλλον
αὐτῷ μὴ αἰτεῖν ἀλλ' αὐτὸν ἑαυτῷ.

a "curator¹." A co-litigant or a debtor might require the "adolescens" to appoint a "curator²." A "curator" might be appointed in the case of protracted absence³, "cura bonorum absentis," and in particular cases of an inheritance, "cura hæreditatis jacentis," "ventris nomine," "ex Carboniano⁴ edicto," and in the case of judicial sequestration⁵.

¹ II. 26. 7. 5. § 5.
² II. 4. 4. 7. § 2. "Permittitur etiam . . . . . debitori compellere adolescentes ad petendos sibi curatores."
³ II. h.t. 34.
II. 24. 1. 3. § 12.

⁴ II. 46. 3. 106—108. L. U. Cod. 4. 4.
⁵ II. 24. 3. 22. § 8. X. De sequestratione possessionis et fructuum. 2. 17. Clem. 2. 6. 2. 8. 7. 34. 30. 3. 6. 49. 1. 21. § 3.

CHAPTER XV.

PARTIES TO AN OBLIGATION[1].

THAT two persons are necessary to the existence of an obligation, as debtor and creditor, is obvious.

But the facts out of which an obligation arises may so shape themselves that there may be more than one person with the right of enforcing it; on the other hand, there may be more than one person responsible for its fulfilment.

1. The general rule is in such a case that each obligation is split into so many several engagements as there are parties to it, e.g. if Caius promises to pay Titius and Mævius 100 aurei, it is the same as if he had promised to give fifty aurei to each; or if Titius and Mævius promise to pay 100 aurei to Caius, it is the same as if each engaged to pay him fifty. "Quum tabulis esset comprehensum illum et illum centum aureos stipulatos neque adjectum ita ut duo rei stipulandi essent virilem partem singuli stipulari videbantur; et e contrario quum ita cautum inveniretur tot aureos recte dari stipulatus est J. C. spopondimus ego, A. et C. D. partes viriles deberi, quia

---

[1] *Inst.* 3. 18. 17. II. 45. 2. Cod. 8. 42. Donellus, *Op.* 9. 12. 55. Ribbentrop, *Lehre von der Correal Oblig.* Gottingen, 1831. Savigny, *Ob. Recht.* Vol. I. p. 136. Puchta, p. 350. Vangerow, Vol. III. p. 94, &c.

non fuerat adjectum singulos in solidum spopon-
disse[1]."

2. In such a case the obligations are contempo-
raneous but not identical, or the exceptional case is
possible that the same obligation may be indivisible
as concerns each of several debtors or creditors. Each
may have a right to exact, or be obliged to discharge
the whole of it. Payment by one of the several
debtors is a discharge for all; payment to one of the
several creditors in like manner extinguishes the
obligation as to the rest.

The Romans designated the persons thus bound
up in one as "duo rei[2]," technically "credendi," if
they were creditors; "debendi," if they were debtors;
or in case of an agreement by "stipulatio," "duo rei
stipulandi, promittendi." The expression "correus"
is used once in the Pandects[3] to denote this relation,
and has furnished the phrase for modern jurists.
The same state of things is also indicated by the
expression, "in solidum obligari[4]."

3. The third case is where the obligations have
a common origin, as, first, where several creditors
have each a right to recover the whole. "Idem ait
Neratius ex unâ injuriâ interdum tribus oriri injuriarum actionem, neque unius actionem per alium

[1] Π. 45. 2. 11. § 1. § 2.

[2] Π. 4. 2. 14. § 15. II. 26. 8. 55.
§ 1.
 Π. 4. 8. 34. "Si duo rei sint
aut credendi aut debendi." II. 45. 2.
"De duobus reis constituendis."

[3] Π. 34. 3. 3. § 3. "In solidum
debetur." II. 45. 2. 2. *Inst.* 3. 16. 1.
II. 14. 1. 1. § 25. "Si plures navem

exerceant cum quolibet eorum in solidum agi potest." II. 46. 1. 52. § 3.
II. 17. 1. 60. 2.

[4] II. 47. 10. 1. § 9. II. 47. 10. 18.
§ 2, and II. 26. 8. 55. § 1. "In aliis
furibus ejusdem rei pluribus non est
propterea cæteris pœnæ deprecatio
quod ab uno jam exacta est."

consumi; ut puta uxori meæ filiæ familias injuria facta est; et mihi et patri ejus et ipsi injuriarum actio incipiet competere."

2dly. Where the obligation becomes divisible, as where there are several heirs of the same debtor or creditor.

The creditor[1] might, if he pleased, instead of treating one of his debtors as responsible for the sum due "in solidum," sue them severally. But if he was unwilling to do so, the beneficium divisionis could be obtained only by the epistola D. Hadriani[2], which at first extended only to sureties, but was afterwards extended to all debtors, with the exception of those who were responsible for a "delictum." "Nec enim ulla societas maleficiorum, vel communicatio justa damni ex maleficio est[3]."

The question[4] how far and in what cases a defendant was liable who had paid the whole debt, not arising from a "maleficium," in the absence of any special agreement, does not appear to me very clearly settled. Modestinus says distinctly that one "fidejussor," who being sued had paid the whole, could not recover a share from his co-surety, or the creditor, if the "actiones" were not "cessæ" to him[5].

---

[1] II. 45. n. 3. § 1=h. t. II. 46. 1. 51. § 4. II. 30. 8. 1.

[2] Gaius, 3. 121. II. 46. 1. 26. *Inst.* 3. 20. 4.

[3] 27. 3. 1. § 11. § 12. § 14. II. 3. 5. 30. Novell. 99. II. 19. 2. 47.

[4] II. 35. 2. 62. 3. 5. 30. 27. 3. 1. § 13. 9. 3. 4. "Sed si cum uno (in solidum) fuerit actum, cæteri liberabuntur." II. 19. 2. 47.

[5] II. 46. 1. 39. Cod. 8. 41. 11. Cod. 8. 40. 2.

CHAPTER XVI.

SENATUS CONSULTUM MACEDO-NIANUM.

THE Senatus Consultum Macedonianum, passed to protect "filios familias" against the usurer Macedonianus, was a valid bar to an action of mutuum. The bar or "exceptio" might be pleaded by the father, the son, and the surety, for the benefit of the son.

The Senatus Consultum Macedonianum ceased to be applicable if the loan had been advanced "in necessarias causas;"—if the father[1] had ratified the debt, or it had been contracted with his knowledge, "tantum sciente patre,"—or even when acquainted with his son's purpose refrained from expressing his dissent, "debet pater continuo testationem interponere contrariæ voluntatis;"—if the creditor had reasonable ground for ignorance that the debtor was a "filius familias."

[1] II. 14. 6. 19. "Exceptionem, S. M. nulli obstare nisi qui sciret, aut scire potuisset filium familias esse eum cui credebat."

CHAPTER XVII.

INSURANCE.

In the form of a wager this contract was not unknown to the Romans, as appears from the laws "si navis ex Asiâ venerit[1]," and " dare spondes si nec navis venerit." Emerigon[2] says that a desire to find in the Roman law what it does not contain has led commentators into discussions on this subject more likely to fatigue than to enlighten the understanding. That such a contract might have been enforced by the Roman law is evident, because the object of it was legitimate and the "causa" determined. "Habet in se negotium aliquod, ergo civilis actio oriri potest[3]." The Roman Law contains many texts involving the principle of the Contract of Insurance, i. e. guarding against risk[4]. But as Emerigon[5] says, "il était enveloppé sous une forme commune et générique," it had not assumed a specific shape. Maritime questions were decided by the Rhodian[6] Law.

---

[1] II. 45. 1. 63.
[2] Emerigon, Vol. 1. p. 10. Valin, *Prolégomènes*, tit. 6, *des Assurances*.
[3] II. 19. 5. 15.
[4] II. 19. 5. 2 : 13. § 5.
II. 1. 6. 3. 1, § 35.

II. 2. 14. 7, § 15.
[5] II. 2. eod.
[6] II. 14. 2. 1. Questions of average in 9 eod. ἐγὼ μὲν τοῦ κόσμου κύριος, ὁ δὲ νόμος τῆς θαλάσσης.

CHAPTER XVIII.

LEX RHODIA DE JACTU.

THE owners of goods embarked on board a vessel, and flung into the sea for the sake of lightening[1] it, have a claim against owners of goods on board the same vessel not flung overboard, for "contributio pro ratâ" to their loss. "Omnium contributione sarciatur quod pro omnibus datum est."

The rule applied if the goods had been transferred to a boat for the same purpose[2].

If in such a case the ship was lost, no claim could be made by the owners whose goods had perished with her, on the owners of goods placed in the boat, "quia jactus in tributum nave salvâ venit[3]."

On the same principle, if the ship sank, or was cast away, every one might save what he could belonging to him without liability to contribution "tanquam ex incendio[4]." If goods were flung over-

---

[1] "Demissæ navis damnum collationis consortio non sarcitur per eos qui merces suas ex naufragio liberarunt." L. 5. ib. Again: "si conservatis mercibus deterior facta sit navis aut aliquid exarmaverit, nulla facienda est collatio, quia dissimilis earum rerum causa est quæ navis gratiâ parantur et earum pro quibus mercedem

aliquis accepit." Eod. 2. Vide 6. eod.

[2] Eod. 3. 11.

[3] 4 eod. : "itaque si vicenum merces duorum fuerint, et alterius aspergine decem esse cœperint, ille cujus res integræ sunt pro vicenis conferret, hic pro decem."

[4] Eod. 2.

board and the ship escaped that danger, but perished afterwards, the owners of goods retrieved by divers were liable to contribute to the loss of the owners on the first occasion[1], but not to those on the second. So if the ship was ransomed from pirates, all goods were liable to contribution; but the loss of what the pirates actually carried away fell upon the proprietors of those goods only[2]; no claim could be made by them for compensation against him who had ransomed his property, "quod vero prædones abstulerint eum perdere cujus fuit nec conferendum ei qui suas merces redemerit." That loss only was common which was incurred to escape a common danger. So if the mast was struck by lightning[3], no claim could be made by the owner of the ship for compensation from the merchandize on board the vessel; for if the smith breaks his hammer or his anvil, the person who has hired him to do the work in performing which the accident has happened is not liable: "nam et si faber incudem aut malleum fregerit, non imputaretur ei qui locaverit opus." But if the mast has been cut away to avoid a common danger, or if the loss had been incurred at the request of the owners of the goods, the shipowner could claim contribution "si voluntate vectorum vel propter aliquem metum in detrimentum factum sit hoc ipsum sarciri oportet," and "quum arbor aut aliud navis instrumentum removendi communis periculi causâ dejectum est, contributio debetur." The owners of goods flung into the sea, if they had

---

[1] Eod.

[2] Π. 14. 2. 3. 3.

[3] 6 eod.

agreed on a price for the freight, had an action " ex
locato" against the magister of the ship, and he had
an action " ex conducto" for contribution against those
whose goods had been preserved. The "magister"
was not responsible for solvency of the passengers.

The freighters had an action " ex locato " against
the "magister" who had ventured upon a river without a pilot, in consequence of which the ship was
lost ; and if he had undertaken to deliver the goods
by a certain time, and was unable, whether from his
own fault or not, to fulfil his engagement. If you
hired a ship of 2000 amphoræ "aversione," you must
pay to that amount, whatever be the number of
amphoræ you actually put on board ; otherwise if
you only hire space for a particular number.

The owner of the ship saved was on the principle
stated liable to contribute in proportion with the
rest. " Placuit omnes quorum interfuisset jacturam
fieri conferre oportere—itaque dominus navis pro
portione obligatum esse."

No compensation was due for freemen who had
perished. " Corporum liberorum æstimationem nullam fieri posse."

CHAPTER XIX.

GENERAL VIEW OF THE LAW AS TO ERROR.

ERROR is incompatible with consent, and if it attaches to the substance of a contract annuls it. The general rule is stated thus: "In omnibus[1] negotiis contrahendis sive bonâ fide sint sive non sint si error aliquis intervenit ut aliud sentiat (puta) qui emit, aut qui conducit aliud, qui cum his contrahit nihil valet quod acti est." An error[2] as to the identity of the object destroyed the contract, "quia in corpore dissentimus emptio nulla est[3]." "Si Stichum stipulatus, ego de alio sentiam, tu de alio, nihil actum erit." But an error affecting only what was collateral to the contract did not annul it[4]: as if it was agreed to purchase an estate with the slave Stichus, and the purchaser by Stichus meant one man, and the seller another, the contract nevertheless was valid. Error as to the name, if the thing was ascertained, was immaterial[5]. The contract was invalid if at the time of making it the thing contracted for had ceased to exist: "arboribus quoque vento dejectis vel absumptis igne dictum est emptionem fundi non videri contractam esse si contemplatione illarum arborum velut

---

[1] II. 44. 7. 57.
   II. 50. 17. 116. § 2 : "non videntur qui errant consentire."
[2] II. 18. 1. 9.

[3] II. 451. 83. 1. and 137, § 1.
[4] II. 18. 1. 34.
[5] II. 44. 7. 9. 1.
   II. 5. 1. 86.

oliveti fundus comparabatur sive sciente sive ignorante
venditore, sive autem emtor sciebat vel ignorabat
vel uterque eorum hæc obtinent quæ in superioribus
casibus pro ædibus dicta sunt[1]:" e. g. if it was agreed
to purchase two slaves for a certain sum, and one
was dead, the contract did not hold as to the other[2].
If the thing contracted for was partially destroyed,
the value of what was left determined the validity
of the contract.   If half the value, or the principal
part of the thing contracted for remained, the contract could be enforced, and the loss[3] adjusted by
the "arbitrium boni viri."   Error as to quality,
i. e. the sourness of wine, if the object was agreed
upon, did not vitiate the contract, but if meaning to
buy wine I bought what was not bad wine, but
vinegar, "ab initio acetum," the contract was null[4].
In the case first put, the buyer though the contract
was not void had an action "ex ædilitio edicto" against
the seller.   Error as to the price or quantity of the
thing sold made the contract void.   Error as to the
property, if a man ignorantly bought what was his
own[5].   But if a man thinking himself the proprietor
of what belonged to another, sold it, or thinking

---

[1] II. 18. 1. 58. Cujacius, 4. 244,
Quæstiones Papinianæ: "Sine re videtur contracta venditio si ea res quæ
veniit majori ex parte perierit ante
venditionem, sed si pars dimidia per-
manserit et dimidia perierit, vel si minor pars, venditio consistet, quia non
intelligitur periisse domus cujus pars
major superest aut dimidia......cogitur
igitur solvere pretium rei quamvis non
sit integra res sed......bonus vir arbi-
trabitur ut diminuatur pretium."

[2] II. 18. 4. 1. and 7. 2.   Cujacius,
10, p. 244, Quæst. Papin.
    II. 18. 1. 44.
       18. 1. 15.
[3] II. 18. 1. 57.
[4] II. 18. 1. 10 and 14.
       18. 1. 9. 2.
    The text II. 18. 1. 9. 2. has given rise
to much dispute.
[5] "Suæ rei emptio non valet." II.
18. 1. 16.

what he dealt with belonged to another when in fact it was his own, sold it, in both these cases the contract was valid[1].

An error as to the nature of the contract annulled it: "non satis autem est dantis esse nummos, et fieri accipientis, ut obligatio nascatur, sed etiam hoc animo[2] dari et accipi ut obligatio constituatur."

Error as to the person, where the quality or relation of the person was a main ingredient of the contract annulled: as in the case of a donation, if supposing that I have given to Caius I have given to Titius; or if supposing that I have agreed with Zeuxis to furnish me a picture[3] I have agreed with some one else; but where this is not the case, as in buying and selling, or hiring and letting to hire, error as to the person is of no more importance than error as to the name. A contract[4] did not fail because the motive which led one of the parties to make it was erroneous; but if a person paid money imagining that he was obliged to pay it when in fact he was not so bound, the money might be recovered. The detestable doctrine of our law, that money paid under a mistake as to the law cannot be recovered, had of course no place in the system built up by Caius and Papinian. This topic will be considered more fully in the "condictio indebiti." The law gave no remedy to supine ignorance[5].

---

[1] II. 17. I. 49.
    41. I. 35.
    18. I. 15. I.
[2] II. 2. I. 15.
    5. I. 2.
[3] II. 12. I. 18.
    44. 7. 3, § I.
    3. 5. 5.

18. I. 9.
12. I. 18.
41. I. 36.
[4] II. 19. I. 5, § I.
    12. 7. 3.
Code Nap. 1131.
Pothier, *Oblig.* § 42, § 43.
[5] II. 18. I. 15, § I.

CHAPTER XX.

ÆSTIMATORIAN CONTRACT[1].

If Caius delivered an article estimated at a fixed sum to Titius that it might be sold by Titius—Caius had the " æstimatoria actio præscriptis verbis" to enforce his rights against Titius. In this action the Judge was bound to consider[2] the peculiar character of the transaction, and the principles by which it was to be determined. It might partake of the nature of a "mandatum" or of a "commodatum," but if it was simply a bargain according to which the Receiver bound himself to restore the thing or its value, the risk lay upon him, and this was presumed when his accommodation had been the moving cause of the contract.

---

[1] Puchta, p. 464.

II. 19. 3. 1.

" Actio de æstimato proponitur tollendæ dubitationis gratiâ: æstimatio autem periculum facit ejus qui suscepit, aut igitur ipsam rem debebit incorruptam reddere aut æstimationem de quâ convenit."

[2] II. 12. 1. 11: "Rogasti me ut tibi pecuniam crederem; ego cum non haberem lancem tibi dedi......ut eam venderes......quod si lancem......sine tuâ culpâ perdideris......utrum mihi an tibi perierit quæstionis est. Mihi videtur Nervæ distinctio verissima existimantis multum interesse venalem

habui hanc massam necne, ut si venalem habui mihi perierit......quodsi...... hæc causa fuit vendendi ut tu utereris, tibi eam periisse et maxime si sine usuris credidi."

II. 19. 5. 17. 1: "Si margarita tibi æstimata dedero: ut aut eadem mihi afferres aut pretium eorum, deinde hæc perierint ante venditionem, cujus periculum sit? et ait Labeo, quod et Pomponius scripsit, si quidem ego te venditor rogavi, meum esse periculum, si tu me, tuum—si neuter, nostrum; sed duntaxat consensimus, teneri te hactenus ut dolum et culpam mihi præstes."

As in this case the property was transferred to him, the contract resembles that which has been just considered.

LIABILITY OF MASTERS OF SHIPS, INNS, TAVERNS[1], &c.

The Roman law exercised a special control over this class of persons, as great trust was of necessity reposed in them, and the opportunities for fraud which they possessed were numerous—" Maxima utilitas est hujus edicti quia necesse est plerumque eorum fidem sequi et res custodiæ eorum committere." They were bound to restore or make good the things entrusted to them unless in the cases of "naufragium," "vis Piratarum," "vis major," or a special contract[2].

The law applied to those who received travellers as a trade, not in the case of one "qui hospitio repentino recipitur." It appears from the Law referred to in the note[3], that the keeper of an inn could not refuse to admit travellers; therefore though responsible for the act of regular inmates, he was not responsible for the act of casual guests.

---

[1] II. 4. 9 : "Ait Prætor, nautæ caupones stabularii quod cujusque salvum fore receperint nisi restituant in eos judicium dabo."

[2] II. 4. 9. 7 : "item si prædixerit ut unusquisque vectorum res suas servet neque damnum se præstiturum, et consenserint vectores, prædictioni non convenietur."

[3] II. 47. 5. 6. The rule is very clear; but the Germans have tried to involve it in doubt and darkness. Huschke, *tüb. krit. Zeitschrift*, 3. 22. Gluck, 6, § 493.

See the case of Coggs and Bernard Smith, *Leading Cases*, Vol. I., remarkable because the gleam of a principle is to be traced in the text, and is established in Mr Smith's note, p. 184, though it is clouded by the subsequent comment.

WORK AND LABOUR[1].

He who has obtruded upon another service without any specific promise of remuneration, cannot enforce a claim to it. But if the case falls under this category, that he is a person accustomed to receive pay for such services as he has rendered, and that the persons receiving them knew him to be such a person when he accepted them, he may without any promise bring an action "præscriptis verbis" for his reward. This rule held with regard to the services of physicians, midwives, proxenetæ, &c.

DUTY OF NOURISHING[2].

This may rest on contract, bequest[3], or delictum, or relationship[4].

In consequence of this last head, parents or children, through every direct degree in the ascend-

---

[1] II. 19. 5. 22.

II. 50. 13. 1. 3.

The passage in which Ulpian is supposed to attack Christianity, enumerating the different artists and professional persons who might claim a remedy. He says, "Medicos fortasse quis decipiet etiam eos qui alicujus partis corporis...sanitatem pollicentur, ut puta si auricularius et non tamen si incantavit si imprecatus est si, ut vulgari verbo impostorum utar, exorcizavit, non sunt enim ista medicinæ genera, tametsi sint qui hos sibi profuisse cum prædicatione affirment."

4 eod. "An et philosophi professorum numero sint? et non putem, non quia non religiosa res est, sed quia hoc primum profiteri eos oportet, mer-

cenariam operam spernere. Proinde ne quis quidem professoribus jus dicat, est enim res sanctissima civilis sapientia." I have quoted the law at some length, as it is conspicuous even in the Digest for gravity of language and elevation of sentiment: very different is that of the Code. 4. 3. l. un.

[2] II. 9. 47: "Cum liberi hominis corpus ex eo quod dejectum effusumve quid erit, læsum fuerit, judex computet mercedes medicis præstitas cæteraque impendia quæ in curatione facta sunt, præterea operarum quibus caruit aut cariturus est, ob id quod inutilis factus est."

[3] II. 33. 1. II. 34. 1. 14. 1.

[4] II. 25. 3.

ing and descending lines, were bound "pro modo facultatum" in case of necessity reciprocally to support each other. The crime of the descendant might exonerate the ascendant from this obligation. "Trebatio denique Marius rescriptum est merito patrem eum nolle alere qui eum detulerat[1]."

The mother was bound to support illegitimate children. The obligation did not extend to brothers and sisters.

EVICTION.

The remedy under this head lay for the buyer when he was deprived of the thing he had bought by a valid legal sentence. It was necessary to establish the "auctoritas," i.e. for the buyer's right, that the loss should have been sustained by a formal contract, not by any compromise nor by accident, nor by an unjust decree; that the cause of the eviction must precede in point of time the right of the buyer; and that he should be deprived of the thing bought or a part of it by the eviction, "quoties res ita amittitur ut eam habere non liceat propter ipsam evictionem."

The "auctoritas" did not hold where the buyer bought a chance, or knew the thing he bought to be

---

[1] II. 25. 3. 5. 11. As to children of concubines and all recognized illegitimate children, see c. 5, x. de eo qui duxit in *Matrim.* 4. 7.

Novell. 117. c. 7. Nov. 89. 15.
Novell. 89. c. 12. 4. 6.
Definition of victus.

II. 50. 16. 43. 44.

Ib. 234, § 2: "Verbum vivere quidem putant ad cibum pertinere sed Ofilius ad Atticum ait his verbis et vestimenta et stramenta contineri, sine his enim vivere neminem posse."

the property of another, or a pledge, or lost the property in it by his own fault or negligence, or by any act to which his loss of the enjoyment of what he had stipulated could be ascribed, or by any failure on the buyer's part to fulfil his contract, nor where there was a special contract that the seller should not guarantee against the eviction—which contract however could only prevent the recovery by the buyer of the double value, not of the price of the thing. It was no answer to the buyer in this action, if after eviction the seller offered to replace him in possession[1] of the thing from which he had been evicted.

The liability of the vendor was regulated by the stipulation, which was usually "in duplum" if there was no precise sum mentioned; he was liable for the value of the thing, and "ex naturâ ex empto actionis hoc quod interest[2]."

CONTRACTS OFTEN GRAFTED ON THE EMTIO VENDITIO.

In diem addictio[3].

The "in diem addictio" was an agreement that if a better offer should be made within a certain time the seller might refuse to complete the contract, or cancel it if completed.

---

[1] "Emtori post evictionem servi quem dominus abduxit, venditor, eundem servum post tempus offerendo quo minus præstet, quod emtoris interest non recte defenditur."
Π. 21. 2. 67.
Π. 44. 4. 15.

[2] Π. 21. 1. 60.
19. 1. 11, § 14, § 15, § 18.
[3] 18. 2: "In diem addictio ita fit, Ille fundus centum esto tibi emtus nisi si quis intra Kalendas Januarias proximas meliorem conditionem fecerit quo res a domino abeat."

Any thing[1] that increased the advantage of the seller was a better offer, e.g. that the price would be paid at a more convenient place.

If the sale was perfect[2] the thing sold was at the hazard of the buyer, if conditional, at that of the seller.

If better conditions were offered[3], to accept them or not was at the option of the vendor, and the buyer might, if he pleased, adopt those conditions[1], and renew the contract.

HOW OBLIGATIONS ARE EXTINGUISHED.

The "vinculum" of an obligation might be destroyed "ipso jure," or rendered useless by a perpetual exception granted to the person liable to it.

Obligations were cancelled[5] "ipso jure" by payment, "solutione," set off, "compensatione," by novation, "novatione," by confusion, "confusione," by the destruction of the thing, "rei interitu," by what was inconsistent with their existence, as "acceptilatio," "contrario consensu," "rei restitutione," and the death of those who were parties to them.

The exceptions which prevent an obligation from being enforced are "pactum ne petatur," "transactio-

[1] Eod. 4. 6.
5. "quicquid ad utilitatem venditoris pertinet pro meliore conditione haberi debet."
[2] Π. 18. 6. 8: "Necessario sciendum est quando perfecta sit emtio, tunc enim sciemus cujus periculum est; nam perfecta emtione periculum ad emptorem respiciet."
[3] Π. 18. 2. 7 = 8: "necesse autem habebit venditor meliore conditione allatâ certiorem priorem emtorem facere, ut si quid alius adjicit ipse

quoque adjicere possit."
[4] Π. 18. 2. 4, § 4.
eod. 16.
eod. 6. pr.
[5] Π. 18. 3. 4: "Si fundus lege commissoriâ venierit, hoc est ut nisi intra certum diem pretium sit exsolutum, inemtus fieret," &c.
Eod. 4, § 4.
Π. 18. 6. 4.
41. 4. 2, § 3.
18. 3. 4.
18. 3. 4, § 2.

nis," "jurisjurandi," "rei judicatæ," "in integrum restitutionis," and when the creditor ceased to have any interest therein.

"Solutio," strictly speaking, is when the debtor has done what he promised that he would do.

Tutors and curators might, without the authority of a magistrate, discharge what was owing from their ward, and him who was under their "curatio."

A stranger might make payment for a debtor without his knowledge, and even against his will; but in such cases the stranger could not recover from the debtor what he had paid; there being no right of action "mandati," or "negotiorum gestorum," or "nominis cessio."

The payment must be made with the intention of exonerating the debtor, otherwise it gives rise to another right of action, as "nominis venditio."

Payment may be made to the creditor who has the administration of his own affairs to his procurator or tutor. Payment made to the "pupillus" only exonerates the debtor in so far as the "pupillus" is thereby "locupletior factus."

Payment made to any one but the creditor is not sufficient, unless it has been paid to one who had been, and whom the debtor still supposed to be, the "procurator" of the creditor.

Or, if the money so paid is "in rem versa creditoris[1]," or the transaction is ratified by him. Or to the person whose name is inserted in the agreement "veluti siquis stipuletur sibi aut Titio[2]." And

II. 46. 3. 58. Eod. 61 : "Quoties id quod tibi debeo ad te pervenit et tibi nihil absit, nec quod solutum est, repeti possit, competit liberatio."
[2] II. 46. 12, § 2, § 3, § 4.

this although the creditor forbid such payment, "quia certam conditionem habuit stipulatio, quam immutare non potuit stipulator."

The promise must be literally performed. The creditor cannot be forced to receive any thing different from that he has contracted for, "aliud pro alio invito creditori solvi non potest[1]." The creditor cannot be compelled to accept part of the price, but may retain the thing sold till the whole is paid[2]. The debtor had till the last moment of the day mentioned to pay his debt; if no day was mentioned, the debt was due immediately.

If no specific place in which payment shall be made was agreed on, the debtor so long as he was not "in morâ," might pay where he pleased, after he was "in morâ." The option was the creditor's.

COMPENSATIO. SET OFF[3].

A "compensatio" must be an obligation valid by the civil or natural law immediate and unconditional, and of the same nature as the obligation it is employed to extinguish.

No obligation therefore that could be barred by an "exceptio" was a set off.

A set off was not allowed[4],

1. "Where possession which had been taken by violence was to be restored."

2. In the case of a deposit.

The old law did not allow the set off in the

---

[1] II. 12. 1. 2, § 1.
[2] II. 19. 1. 13, § 8.
[3] II. 16. 2 : "Debiti et crediti inter se contributio." Eod. 6. 7.

[4] Eod. h. t. 14, § 2. 14, § 1.
Pothier, "Spoliatus ante omnia restituendus." 625, § 2.

"strictis judiciis," unless where there was room for the "exceptio doli."

CONFUSIO[1].

This was where the rights of debtor and creditor were blended together.

NOVATIO[2]

was where a new debt was substituted for the old one which was extinguished. "Cum ex præcedente causâ ita nova constituitur ut prior perimatur," are Ulpian's words.

It mattered not what was the character of the preceding contract, or why it was binding. The effect as to the prior obligation was the same as the "solutio;" the sureties and pledges for the original debt became free, and interest on it ceased.

"PER IN CONTRARIUM ACTUM[3]."

Here the rule "quibus modis acquirimus iisdem[4]," or "contrarium actio, amittimus, quibuscunque modis obligamur, iisdem in contrarium actis liberamur," applies. Thus "re integrâ," a consensual contract is destroyed when the consent is revoked; a real contract, by the restitution of the thing, a "verborum obligatio verbis." This is the "acceptilatio," which was the annihilation of a debt by the admission in formal words of a fictitious payment.

---

1 Gaius, 4, § 61, § 63.
2 Gaius, 2, § 38, § 39.
  3, § 176, § 179.
  II. 46. 2.
3 Gaius, 3, § 169.
  Inst. 3. 29, § 1.
  II. 46. 4.
4 II. 50. 17. 153.

"QUOD EGO TIBI PROMISI HABESNE ACCEPTUM?"

"HABEO."

This exonerated the debtor and his sureties, and had the same effect as the "solutio[1]."

By the old law, an obligation not resting on the stipulatio could not be cancelled by the acceptilatio, until the stipulatio had by novation been substituted for it; and Aquilius Gallus invented a form to overcome this technical obstacle, which is to be found in the Digest and the Institutes[2].

An acceptilatio could not be conditional[3].

Besides these methods an obligation might be extinguished, "ipso jure," by the destruction of the object; for "impossibilium nulla est obligatio."

By the death[4] of one of the parties where the action did not pass to the heir, or where the personal services or benefit of the deceased were the object of it; as in the case of a painter or an architect; and when what the debtor contracted to give has already come "ex causâ lucrativâ" to the creditor; "nam duæ causæ lucrativæ in eandem rem et personam concurrere non possunt[5]."

Obligations were destroyed by "exceptio."

PACTUM NE PETATUR

is an agreement between debtor and creditor that what is due shall not be sued for.

Thus though the obligation exists, "ipso jure,"

---

[1] "Solutionis exemplo." II. eod.

[2] II. 46. 4. 18, § 1.
Inst. h. t. § 2.

[3] II. eod. 5.

[4] e. g. "Societas mandatum operis conductio et operarum locatio precarium." II. 38. 11.

[5] II. 46. 7. 17 = 19.

the debtor may bar the creditor's demand by the "exceptio doli," or "pacti conventi."

This agreement might be inferred from the conduct of the creditor; as if he gave back to the debtor his "cautio," or bequeathed him the "chirographum."

" Pactum ne petatur[1]," might be for ever, or for a particular time[2]; it might be "in rem," as if the creditor agreed generally not to sue, or " in personam," as if he agreed not to sue a particular person as a " fidejussor." It did not follow because the name of a person was introduced that the "pactum" was "personale," "plerumque enim persona pacto inseritur non ut personale pactum fiat, sed ut demonstretur cum quo factum pactum est."

It was provided by an exceptional law[3] from respect to the memory of the dead, that if the heirs of an estate liable to debt agreed " ante aditam hæreditatem," with the majority of the creditors, to accept a portion of their debt in lieu of the whole, such an arrangement was binding upon all.

The majority[4] was reckoned by the amount of the debt; if the debts were equal, by the number of creditors; if both were equal, the side prevailed of him " qui dignitate præcellit;" if the dignity was equal, " humanior sententia a Prætore eligenda est."

The other exceptions are the transactio—jusjurandum præscriptio—res judicata—conditio expleta,

---

[1] II. 2. 14 : Noodt, Vol. I. 397.
Toullier, Vol. VII. 320. 341.
Glück, 4. 219.
Warnkönig, Lib. 3. c. 3. ff. 1.
[2] " La remise réelle et la décharge personelle." Pothier, 616. 617.
II. 214. 7, § 8.

[3] II. 2. 14. 10, § 1.
2. 14. 7, § 19.
17. 1. 58, § 1.
40. 4. 54, § 1.
42. 8. 23.
[4] 2. 14. 8.

and the want of any interest in the fulfilment of the
obligation on the part of the creditor. The "transactio" and "jusjurandum" may be discussed elsewhere. The "res judicata," as "pro veritate accipitur," was a complete exoneration of the debtor, as
it extinguished even the natural obligation[1]: and
if the debt was afterwards paid by mistake, the
money might be recovered. "Præscriptio," on the
other hand, destroyed the action, not the debt.

If the debt[2] was not to be sued for in a certain
event[3], the creditor who sued for it, notwithstanding
that event, might be repelled, "exceptione pacti
conventi," or "doli mali."

Every obligation ceased when the creditor had
no longer any interest in the fulfilment of it;
e. g. if, notwithstanding the neglect of the mandatarius, the mandans had sustained no injury; "si
nihil deperierit nulla actio est."

[1] II. 42. 1. 56.
 12. 6. 43.
 20. 6. 13.
[2] II. *Inst.* 3. 15. 3.
 II. 44. 7. 44, § 1, § 2.
 45. 1. 56. 4.

[3] See the reasoning II. 45. 1. 97. § 1.
"Quid enim meâ interest id a te fieri
quod si non feceris æque salvam pecuniam habiturus sum?"

CHAPTER XXI.

LAW OF WILLS. PRÆCOGNOSCENDA.

SUCCESSIO MORTIS CAUSA.

IF property be considered, succession is either universal, that which is given "in universitatem juris," or singular, that which confers the property in a specific object.

It is either "inter vivos[1]," or "mortis causâ;" in the latter case it is called succession.

The universal succession "mortis causâ" is inheritance, which signifies, if taken in the sense of the right of the heir, the right of succeeding "in universum jus" of the deceased[2]. The inheritance so succeeded to stands in the place of the deceased. "Hæreditas non hæredis personam, sed defuncti sustinet[3]." In it are comprised all that the deceased has left[4], as well corporeal things, though "extra commercium," as incorporeal, and whatever gain or loss accrued to the inheritance after the death of the deceased[5].

---

[1] Brissonius de verb. signific. voc. succedere, successio, successores.

[2] "Hæreditas nihil aliud est quam successio in universum jus quod defunctus habuit." II. d. R. T. 62. de V. S. 24.

[3] II. de acq. Hær. 34.

[4] "Hæreditas etiam sine ullo cor-

pore quis intellectum habet." II. 5. 3. 50.

[5] "Item non solum ea quæ mortis tempore fuerunt, sed si qua postea augmenta hæreditati accesserunt venire in hæreditatis petitionem, nam hæreditas et augmentum recipit et diminutionem." II. 5. 2. 20, § 5.

Of this succession there are two kinds — the direct and indirect (fideicommissaria). The heir succeeds directly: if he is ordered to give the inheritance to any one he is termed "fiduciarius[1]." The "fideicommissarius," the person in favour of whom the trust is left, succeeds indirectly " quasi hæres."

The "successio singularis," that which confers the property in a specific object[1] is (1) "per legatum[2]," by means of a legacy; (2) "per fideicommissum singulare," by means of a special trust[3]; (3) "per mortis causâ donationem[4]," and "mortis causâ capionem[5]."

"Successio civilis" is of two kinds; either according to the will of the deceased, i.e. testamentary; or according to the law, i.e. "ab intestato."

The power[6] which enables man after he has disappeared from the earth to control the enjoyment of its surface, and its produce, is emphatically the creature of positive institution. The law of nature obliges the father to nourish his children during his life, and to provide if he can for their support after his death. There it stops: the manner in which his property shall be distributed, the period

---

[1] II. 36. 1. 67. 3.

[2] Florentinus defines legatum, "delibationem hæreditatis quâ testator quod universum hæredis foret alicui quid collatum velit."

[3] Ulp. Gr. 25, § 1.

[4] II. 39. 6. 32.

[5] II. 39.'6. 8. 11. 18.

[6] La Serva, in his admirable work *Derecho Romano*, defines inheritance as "reemplayo de unas personas en los derechos de otras." Vol. I. 363.

Instit. Lib. 2. tit. 10—25.

Caius, 2. 97. 98. 99. Lib. 3. tit. 1—9. 100.

II. 28—38.

Cod. libb. tit. 1—50. Novell. 115. 118. 127.

Gaus, "Erbrecht," in *Weltgeschichtlicher Entwickelung* (warped to the Hegelian view, but a work of uncommon merit), see especially Vol. II.

Donellus, Lib. 6—8. Lib. 9. c. 1—4.

of time during which his will shall regulate that
distribution, the rules and conditions in conformity
with which his inheritance shall be enjoyed, depend
altogether upon the assistance and pleasure of society,
and until society was established never could have
existed. Consequently, the civil and not the natural
law is the standard to which alone the jurist must
appeal when he examines this most comprehensive
and eminently artificial chapter of human legislation. There is no topic on which the jurisprudence
of different nations so widely differs, no head of
private law with which the political state of society
is more immediately and intimately connected. A
fundamental change in the law of descent would
in our own country most assuredly, and in most
others, draw after it a change in the form of our
government, and give society a widely different
aspect[1].

According to the Roman law the death of an
individual possessed of property gave certain persons, by his command if he had made a will, by
command of the law if he had died intestate, the
right or the duty of filling up the place he had left

[1] There are four principal objects in
every code of Laws which are not
within the scope of ordinary rules, and
the basis of which must necessarily be
adapted to the form of the government of the nation for which the code
is made. These are paternal authority, the contract of marriage, successions, and testaments. There are two
others of great interest, but which
have a narrower scope, and are concentrated almost entirely in commer-
cial matters; these are the contract of
loan and mortgages. "Pour le régle-
ment de toutes les autres transactions
de la vie humaine il n'y a qu'à suivre
la droite et simple équité; mais pour
celles dont je viens de parler il faut
s'élever au dessous de la routine ordi-
naire, et fixer ses regards sur la forme
et la situation de l'état auquel on veut
donner des lois." Maleville, *Analyse
Raisonnée du Code Civil*, Vol. II. p. 170.
Montesquieu, L. 27.

vacant, and of assuming towards all mankind, so far as property was concerned, the character of his representative. The person occupying this position was called "hæres." The assemblage of rights and liabilities with which he was so invested was called the "hæreditas." The Roman Law allowed the deceased to bequeath to those who were not the "hæres" certain shares, called "legatæ," which were to be taken from, and which depended for their validity upon, the inheritance in the strict and legal sense. With the law therefore of inheritance, the law regulating these shares of the inheritance is in strict connexion; and afterwards with the progress and refinement of society other rights grew up, and particular persons, under particular circumstances (the deceased having violated those conditions on which the society to which he belonged enforced obedience from its members to his will), might invoke the aid of law to give them the inheritance or a share of it, even against the will (cruelly or capriciously exercised) of the deceased. This right so recognized will form another head of our inquiry (Bonorum possessio contra tabulas).

That if a valid will had been left it disposed of all belonging to the testator, was a fundamental doctrine of Roman jurisprudence. "Nemo," said the civilians, "pro parte testatus, pro parte intestatus decedere potest." Hence it followed that if the will omitted the mention of certain portions of the estate, the portion so omitted went to the heir, or heirs if there were more than one, and not to those who would have succeeded in case of an intestacy.

Another principle was, that no one could leave more than one will. The arrangement in the Institutes inverts the natural order, and treats of succession "ex testamento," before that "ab intestato." Thus it appears that according to the Roman Law, death, though it destroyed all the rights of the deceased that arose from his public rank, or domestic condition, did not affect his property, with regard to which a legal, immediately took the place of the physical personality. His property considered as an integrally judicial whole, was called succession, in the objective meaning of the word; a name repeatedly exchanged in the Roman laws with that of "hæreditas," "patrimonium defuncti," "bona defuncti," "universum jus defuncti," and sometimes that of "familia." The austere and exclusive character of the early Roman law is ineffaceably stamped on this portion of jurisprudence. All that the son represented being absorbed by the father, his death left no chasm, and it was not necessary that the community should create a legal personality to fill his place. When the head of the family died, the reverse happened. For he personified all things, sacred and profane, of the domestic society of which he was the head.

SUCCESSION AB INTESTATO.

According to the law of the Twelve Tables, the first order of heirs were the "sui hæredes," i.e. children unemancipated at the time of the father's death. Emancipated children were not called to the succession. Daughters were called with sons to the succession in equal shares, as children did not succeed to the mother; and husband and wife succeeded each other only when there was no other heir; the estate of the daughter sooner or later returned to the family from which she was descended.

After the "hæredes sui" came the "agnati," or male relations, excluding maternal relations, emancipated children, the mother of the deceased, and the daughter's children.

If there were no "hæredes sui" or "agnati" the succession devolved on the relations through the female side—the "cognati."

By the law of the Twelve Tables daughters were called to the succession with sons; but the evils and corruption caused by leaving so much wealth in the power of women were so great that the Voconian law limited the amount to which they could succeed in any case, even when the deceased was their father and had no other children.

Such was the order of successions "ab intestato;" but the right of bequest, to which the Romans clung with great tenacity, broke down these legal barriers, and destroyed the original equality which it had been the object of the legislature to establish.

As the manners of the Roman softened, the exclusion of emancipated children from the paternal inheritance was considered unjust, and the Prætor, the organ of real equity, admitted them to their share of the patrimony.

By the "senatusconsultum Tertullianum" mothers were admitted to the inheritance of their chil-

dren, by the "senatusconsultum orphilianum" children were admitted to the succession of their mother.

Increasing luxury and false refinement triumphed
over the Voconian law, and the daughter's children
were admitted to the succession of their maternal
grandmother; first, with the reservation of a fourth
for the "agnati," and finally for the entire estate.

At last Justinian, by the 118 and 127 Novells,
abolished all distinction between the "agnati" and
the "cognati," and called to an equal share of the
inheritance the relations by the male and the female
side, the descendants of sons, and the descendants of
daughters. The laws which make this change be-
tray, as might be expected from the age in which
they were established, the most entire ignorance both
of the general principles of jurisprudence, and of the
political object which the laws he abrogated had in
view.

The order in which heirs were called to the succession "ab intestato" was the following:—

1st. The lawful children of the deceased male
and female, whether by the same or different mothers, to the exclusion of all other relations.

If in the first degree, they succeeded "per capita;"
if these were grandchildren, the succession was distributed "per stirpes:" the grandchildren, howeve.
numerous, taking no more than their father or mother would have taken had he or she been alive.

The representation in the direct descending line
continued to the remotest link; and what has been
said of grandchildren applies also to great grandchildren, &c.

2nd. In the failure of the descending line those in the ascending line succeeded according to the proximity of degree, and not on the principle of representation; the father and mother, or either, excluding the grandfather and grandmother, paternal or maternal, and they the great-grandfather.

In the event of claims by the ascendants in the same degree, but of different lines, the succession was equally divided between the two lines; one progenitor in one line if alone taking an equal share with several who might belong to the other.

3rd.   Collaterals.

Failing descendants and ascendants the succession was given to collaterals, according to the proximity of degree, with two exceptions, the one derived from the principle of representation, the other from the double tie.

The principle of representation, that is of putting one person in the place of another, gave the children of brothers and sisters an equal share with their uncles and aunts, all such children taking only the share that their father or mother if alive would have inherited.

By the doctrine of the double tie the brothers and sisters of the whole blood excluded those of the half-blood, whether uterine or consanguineous.

Neither of these rights of representation or of double tie extended beyond the children of brothers and sisters.

They prevailed only when the children of different brothers and sisters competed with the brothers and sisters or uncles and aunts of the deceased;

otherwise the children of different brothers and sisters, though the members sprung from the respective stocks was different, divided the succession "per capita."

So when the children of different brothers and sisters, some of the half and some of the whole blood, came to the succession "jure suo," without any competent relations in the higher degree, the privilege of the double tie ceased, and the succession was distributed among them "per capita."

Such was the system that the barbarous hordes who overthrew the Roman empire, and who may still be said to be in great measure the legislators of our attorney-governed, and in that sense most unpractical country, found established in Western Europe.

There were eight degrees of the "bonorum possessio" by the old law.

1. "Unde liberi," according to which the "sui hæredes" and emancipated children were called to the succession of their father or grandfather, "ab intestato."

2. "Unde legitimi," giving the succession to the legitimate heirs; e.g. the "agnati, patroni, mater, liberi," who by law, a senatusconsultum, or the constitution of the prince, had a right to it.

3. "Unde decem personæ," giving the succession of an emancipated son "non contractâ fiduciâ" to ten persons. These were the father, mother, grandfather, grandmother (paternal and maternal), the son, the daughter, the grandson, the granddaughter, brother and sister.

4. "Unde cognati," by which the cognati, there being no heirs or agnati, were called to the succession.

5. "Tanquam ex familiâ," by which failing the patron and his children, the agnati of the patron were called to the freedman's succession.

6. "Unde patroni patronæque liberique eorum," given to the patrons of each sex and their children.

7. "Unde cognati manumissoris."

8. "Unde vir et uxor," by which failing the agnati and the cognati, the patron, his children and agnati, the husband was called to the possession of the wife, and the wife to that of the husband.

Of these the Emperor Justinian removed four:

The " Unde Decem personæ."

The "Tanquam ex familiâ."

The " Unde patroni patronæque et liberi eorum."

The " Unde cognati, manumissoris."

If the external form of wills was considered, they were divided into public and private by the Roman Law.

Private wills were written or nuncupatory. The ingredients required for the validity of both were—

1st. That the will should be made or pronounced "uno contextu[1]" without interruption.

---

[1] "Uno contextu actus testari oportet."

II. qui test. fac. 21. § 3.

"Nec vero nocet interruptio quæ necessitate superveniente fit suspenso interim testandi actu." Cod. qui test. fac. 28.

Inst. de Test. Ordin. § 3.

Pauli Sentent. 3. 4. 10.

II. qui test. fac. possit: " In testamentis quibus rogati adesse testes de-

bent ut testamentum fiat, alterius rei causâ forte rogatos ad testandum non esse idoneos placet...si tamen ante testamentum certiorentur ad testamentum se adhibitos, posse eos testimonium suum recte perhibere."

Inst. de Testam. Ordin. 6...9. Vinnius *ad loc.*

II. qui test. fac. pot. § 18.

20. § 6.

20. § 2.

22

2ndly. The presence of seven witnesses[1], with regard to whom it was necessary—first, that they should be specially invited to witness the transaction; secondly, that they should all at the same time be in presence of the testator.

3rdly. That they should be present voluntarily.

4thly. That they should be competent, that is, labouring under no legal or natural disability to act as witnesses when the will they attest is made. Such were madmen, the deaf, blind and dumb; those who had not attained the age of puberty, and prodigals, slaves, criminals who had incurred the sentence of deportation, or the loss of the testamenti factio; the filius familias, with regard to the testament of the father; the paterfamilias, with regard to the testament of the son; the brother unemancipated with regard to the will of a brother, subject to the same parent; the heir, the person over whom the heir could exercise the "patria potestas."

The peculiarities of a written will were—

1. The writing of the testator, whether he subscribed it only in the presence of seven witnesses, or being unable to write, employed an eighth witness for that purpose; or wrote himself every word of the testament, which is an holograph.

2. The signature of each witness in his own hand, and his seal affixed to the instrument[2].

---

[1] "Legatariis et fidei commissariis quia non prius successores sunt, testimonium non denegamus." 20. eod. 27.

[2] Cod. de test. 28. § 1. § 29. eod. *Inst.* 4. de test. ord. II. eod. 30. 22. 4 and 5: "Singulos

testes qui in testamento adhibentur proprio chirographo adnotare convenit quis et cujus testamentum signaverit." *Inst.* de test. § 5.

"Alieno quoque annulo licet sig-

If the testator wrote a holograph will, and declared it to be his will in the presence of the witnesses, and placed it in a cover, if the witnesses signed and sealed that in which the will was so deposited, it was sufficient. Otherwise, in the case of a testament not a holograph, unless the testator signed it in the presence of the witnesses before he placed it in the covering.

Nor did it matter in what language or on what substance the will was written, nor whether the witnesses did or did not understand the language in which it was written.

The essence[1] of a nuncupatory will is that the testator declares his will in the presence of the witnesses, and in a voice which they can hear.

PUBLIC TESTAMENTS.

These testaments were made in the presence of the sovereign, or of an appointed magistrate, and witnesses were not required for their validity.

There were two kinds[2] : one was made on petition to the prince and with his permission ; another was deposited by the proper magistrate among the public archives.

---

nare testamentum." II. qui test. fac. possit 22. § 22: "Possint omnes uno annulo signare testamentum." Cod. 22. § 7: "signatas tabulas accipi oportet et si linteo quo tabulæ involutæ sunt signa impressa fuerint."

II. 37. 1. 6. § ult. eod. 4.

Inst. de test. ord. 12.

"Non tamen intelligentiam sermonis intelligimus...nam si vel suum percipiat quis cui rei adhibitus sit sufficere."

II. qui t. f. p. 20. § 9.

[1] II. 28. 2. 21.

"Ut exaudiri possit...non ab omnibus sed a testibus."

Cod. de test. 21. § 2. 26. eod.

Inst. de test. ad § 14.

[2] Cod. de test. 19.

Can. cap. 10. X. de test. gave validity to a will signed in the presence of the clergyman of the parish and two witnesses.

CHAPTER XXII.

CODICIL[1].

ANY one who had the right to make a will might make a codicil. And therefore, like wills, they were written or nuncupatory.

Codicils were made either as appendages to a will, or when there was no will.

Codicils without a will were said to be "ab intestato." The basis on which they rested was the good faith of the heir. And therefore any heir was bound to their fulfilment.

Codicils, however, that were appendages to a will, whether written or nuncupatory, followed the fate of the will[2].

They might be confirmed, or not confirmed, by the will; if confirmed, they were taken as part of the will[3].

They might be confirmed[4] whether they were

---

[1] History of Codicils given in the *Institutes*.

[2] II. 29. 7. 16. § 1.
"Quicumque ab intestato successerit locum habeat codicilli."

[3] "Quaecunque in his scribuntur perinde habentur ac si in testamento scripta essent." II. 35. 5. 25.
"Testamento facto etiam si codicilli in eo confirmati non essent, vires tamen ex eo capient." II. 29. 7. 16. § 3.

[4] Cod. de jure codicill. I. III.

"Si ex testamento hæreditas adita non fuisset, fidei commissum ex hujusmodi codicillis nullius momenti erit."
II. 29. 7. 16. § 3.
The forms of confirmation, 45. 5. 56. II.
"Si quos codicillos reliquero valere volo," or "si quid tabulis aliove quo genere ad hoc testamentum pertinens reliquero, ita valere volo." II. 29. 7. 18.

made before or after the will which confirmed them,
" in præteritum," or " in futurum."

Codicils, like testaments, were public or private.

Public, such as, like wills, were authenticated by
the sovereign or the magistrate.

Private, such as were attested by five competent
witnesses[1], and if written, subscribed by them; if they
were confirmed by the will, witnesses were not
necessary to their validity. The seals of the witnesses, and the subscription of the testator, were not
required.

An heir[2] could not be directly made, or disinherited by a codicil; but a " substitutio " might be
supported[3] " per fidei commissum."

A testator might make several codicils[4].

[1] Cod. 1. ult. 3 de eod.
C. H. 4. 4. 1.
[2] *Inst.* de codicillis, § 2. § 3.

[3] II. 36. 1. 76.
[4] "Codicillos et plures quis facere
potest." II. 29. 6. § 1.

CHAPTER XXIII.

LAW OF WILLS *(continued)*.

THE will of the testator must be certain and fixed. Therefore a will leaving to such persons as Titius shall select is invalid, "quod alieno arbitrio permissa est[1]."

But a will made by one (testamentarius) at the suggestion and according to the dictation of the testator is valid; nor is the bequest invalid which leaves a choice or selection to a particular person.

In the case of a blind person[2], besides the seven witnesses, a tabularius who wrote under their eyes the will of the testator, or if the tabularius could not be found, an eighth witness was requisite.

Peculiar privileges were conceded to soldiers by the Roman Law in making a will. They were released from the necessity of observing any formality: "Militibus quoque modo velint et quo modo possunt testamentum facere concessum esse[3]," was

---

[1] "Nam satis constanter veteres decreverunt testamentorum jura per se firma esse oportere."

[2] Cod. L. VIII. qui test. facere possunt.

[3] II. 29. 1. 40.

the maxim of the Roman Law. To enter into the details of these peculiar provisions would be of no utility; they will be found under the head of the digest to which I have referred.

The institution of an heir being the basis of the Roman Testament, it is important to consider who might be instituted heirs.

Any one might be instituted an heir who had the "testamenti factio" with the testator.

Slaves as well as freemen might be appointed heirs. The slaves of strangers as well as of the testator—the slaves of the testator with those of strangers without emancipation. The "*Peregrinus*," the "filii perduellium," apostates, and heretics, were without the "testamenti factio[1]."

An heir could not be appointed "litis causâ[2]."

1. The code forbad the parent or child of an incestuous intercourse to be the heirs of each other.

2. It forbad the party to a second marriage to inherit more than the portion bequeathed by the testator to the children of the first. Natural children, where there were legitimate children, could inherit only a twelfth share of the property.

By the old Roman Law an "incerta persona," such as a corporation, could not be appointed heir. Neither could a posthumous child. But the later law allowed the nomination of an "incerta persona,"

---

[1] Cod. I. 7. L. III. de apostatis.
Cod. 9. 8. 5. § 1. ad Leg. Jul.
[2] "Imperatorem litis causâ hæredem institui invidiosum est." II. 28. 6. 91.

Cod. de incertis nuptiis, 5. 5. L. VI.
Nov. 89. cap. ult.
Cod. de secundis nuptiis, 5. 9. L. VI.
Cod. 5. 27. 2. de nat. lib. Nov. 89.
Gaius, 2. 238 or 242.

who could be ascertained[1]. Thus the poor of a particular place[2] might be named as heirs. The posthumous child[3] was by degrees acknowledged.

The right of the testator to make a will, and of
the heir to take under it (i. e. "testamenti factio"),
depended upon two periods—the one at the time
when the will was made, the other at his death.
During the interval between the will and the devo-
lution of the inheritance the absence of the right
was of no significance.

A bequest to a person incapable of receiving it
was null, and was distributed among the heirs.

The strictness of the old law as to the nomination
of the heir was gradually relaxed.

Justinian allowed the appointment of the heir in
the midst of a will, and declared that if instead of the
words "Titius hæres esto," "Titium hæredem esse
jubeo," other words were employed from which the
will of the testator could be inferred, it was sufficient.
So the reference to a document in which the name of
the heir was written was sufficient.

If it did not clearly appear who the person
intended by the testator was, the will was invalid[4].

Any mark[5], however, by which he could certainly
be discovered was enough, and if the person was

---

[1] *Inst.* 2. 20. § 25. de legatis.
Cod. 6. 48.

[2] Cod. de episcop. et clericis, 1. 3.
24. 49.

[3] II. 28. 2. 29.

[4] II. 28. 5. 62. § 1.
"Quoties non apparet quis hæres

institutus sit, institutio non valet,"
etc.

[5] "Nemo dubitat recte ita hæredem
nuncupari posse hic mihi hæres esto,
quum sit coram qui ostenditur."
II. 28. 5. 58. ib. 1. § 4.
35. 1. 72. 8.

ascertained, an error in the name or false description was of no importance [1].

None but soldiers could leave a will disposing of a portion of their property.   In an ordinary will the testator must distribute all that belonged to him. If a special exception was made it was disregarded. [2]So if one or more were declared heir or heirs of particular portions of property, the limitation was disregarded, as it would have clashed with the testator's purpose which was clear.

An inheritance could not be given to take effect on or from a particular day: in such a case the limitation was disregarded, and the bequest considered absolute[3].

A testator might institute any number of heirs as well as a single heir[4], but he could not institute more than one heir "pro solido."

The Roman inheritance was divided into twelve ounces[5], all of which composed the integral "as," by which the whole was represented; the ounce[6] therefore was the twelfth part, the sextans or two ounces the

---

[1] "Si quis nomen hæredis quidem non dixerit sed indubitabili signo eum demonstraverit." 28. 5. 9. § 8. Even in abuse: "filius meus iniquissimus male de me meritus hæres esto." Ib. 48. § 1.

[2] II. 28. 5. 74: "Si ita quis hæres institutus fuerit excepto fundo," "excepto usufructu." "Perinde erit jure civili ac si sine eâ re hæres institutus esset."

[3] "Servanda est enim testantis voluntas, et cum certum sit eum hæredem nominasse, pro non scripto habetur id quod cum institutione congruere

nequit." II. 49. 17. 19. § 2.

[4] "Hæreditas ex die vel ad diem non recte datur, sed vitio temporis sublato manet institutio."
II. 28. 5. 24.

[5] 4 Inst. h. tit.
II. De Reg. Juris. 141, § 1.

[6] II. 6. 8.
    21. 2. 39, § 2.
    31. 1. 21, § 1.
"Paterfamilias distribuere hæreditatem in tot partes potest quot voluerit, sed solemnis assis distributio in duodecim uncias fit." II. 28. 5. 13, § 1.

sixth part, the quadrans or three ounces the fourth
part, the triens or four ounces the third part of the
whole, the quincunx was five ounces, the semis six
ounces or half, the septunx was seven ounces, the bes
(bis triens) eight, the dodrans, or the as from which
the quadrans had been deducted, nine, the dextans
ten, being the as from which the sextans had been
deducted, the deunx eleven, being the as from which
one ounce had been deducted.

The testator might subdivide the inheritance into
as many portions as he thought proper.

Heirs named conjunctively were taken to make
up a single heir.

This conjunction might be,—

1. Re, as "Titius et Mævius ex parte dimidiâ
hæredes sunto[1]."

2. Re et verbis, as "Titius hæres esto, ex
parte dimidiâ[2]. Teius ex parte dimidiâ, ex quâ parte
Teium institui ex eâdem Sempronius hæres esto."

3. Verbis, as "Titius hæres esto. Gaius et Mævius ex æquis partibus hæredes sunto."

If a person is named as heir, and no particular
portion of the inheritance is assigned to him[3], he
takes that part of the whole "as" which is undistri-
buted; if there are several in the same condition, the
part undisposed of is distributed among them, "ea
enim pars data intelligitur, quæ vacat[4]." If the

___

[1] Π. 50. 16. 142. Paulus says, "tri-
plici modo conjunctio intelligitur; aut
enim re, aut verbis et re, aut verbis
tantum."

[2] Π. 28. 5. 15. "Conjunctim hos
Teium et Sempronium videri institu-
tos sic fiet ut Titius semissem hi duo
quadrantes ferant."
Π. 28. 5. 66.

[3] *Inst.* 14, § 6.

[4] "Qui sine parte heres institutus
est vacantem portionem vel alium
assem occupat." Π. 37. 11. 12.

whole "as" should have been exhausted, leaving an heir or heirs unprovided for, the inheritance is turned into two asses (dupondius fit)[1]. Otherwise it is if after the whole "as" has been distributed the testator adds an heir, by the phrase "ex reliquâ parte hæres esto[2];" for as there is no reliquum the last-mentioned takes nothing.

So if the double "as" was exhausted, the inheritance was broken into three.

If part of the inheritance[3] was undisposed of, it was distributed among the heirs in proportion to their shares. If part was wanting to make up the portion assigned, each heir submitted to a proportionate loss. If the testator appointed Teius his heir, "ex his partibus quas ascripsi[4]," and he had in fact not assigned him any share, Teius took nothing, but if he used the word "ascripsero," and did not assign any portion, Teius took an equal share with the other heirs[5].

If the testator wrote "Caius aut Titius mihi hæres esto[6]," Justinian decided that "aut" should have the sense of "et."

The appointment of an heir may be absolute or conditional. An impossible condition is considered as if it did not exist, and therefore the appointment or bequest to which it is annexed is absolute; nor does it matter whether the condition is impossible

---

[1] "Si asse expleto alium sine parte hæredem scripserit in alium assem veniet, aliter atque si ita scripsisset expleto asse ex reliquâ parte hæres esto, quoniam quum nihil reliquum est ex nullâ parte hæres institutus est." II. 28. 5. 19. 3.

[2] II. 28. 5. 87.
[3] Ib. 81.
   II. 28. 2. 13.
[4] II. 28. 5. 2.
[5] "Si voluntas defuncti non refragatur." Ib.
[6] Cod. 6. 38. 4.

from physical or from moral causes, as contrary to the laws and morality.

The condition of taking an oath was unlawful. But if the act which the testator enforced by an oath was lawful[1], the heir might be compelled to do it.

Conditions inconsistent with freedom of marriage were invalid[2]; but the condition prohibiting marriage with a particular person might be enforced. A condition that the person should be divorced[3], or should always fix his domicile in a particular city, was invalid[4].

Inconsistent conditions[5] were looked upon as unwritten, e. g. "Si Titius hæres erit Teius hæres esto."

"Captatory[6]" conditions were void, e. g. "I leave Titius heir for the same portion of my estate that he shall leave me of his;" but a bequest, "I leave Titius my heir for the same portion of my estate that Mævius has left me of his," was valid[7], as referring to the past, not anticipating the future.

Immoral conditions were considered by the Roman jurist as impossible[8]: "Nam quæ facta lædunt pietatem, existimationem, verecundiam nostram et ut generaliter dixerim contra bonos mores fiunt, nec facere nos posse credendum est."

The paramount rule[9] of interpreting conditions

---

[1] Π. 35. 1. 26.
[2] Π. 38. 7.
[3] II. 7. 8. 8. 1.
[4] Π. 35. 1. 71, § 2.
[5] Π. 35. 1. 16. 50. 17. 188.
[6] "Captatorias institutiones non eas Senatus improbavit quæ mutuis affectionibus judicia provocaverunt, sed quorum judicium confertur ad secretum alienæ voluntatis." II. 28. 5. 70.
[7] Ib. 71. Bynkershoek de Captat. Instit. 1. 429. II. 28. 7. 20, § 2. Π. 28. 5. 29.
[8] Π. 28. 7. 15.
[9] Π. 35. 1. 19.

was to ascertain the will of the testator: "in conditionibus," says Ulpian[1] emphatically, "primam vicem
voluntas defuncti obtinet eaque regit conditionem."
If in the same will after an heir had been conditionally appointed, he was appointed absolutely,
the latter sentence prevailed, "plenior est enim
quam prior[2]."

Whensoever the heir took the inheritance, his
succession dated in law from the death of the testator[3].

If the heir was unable to fulfil the condition
within a certain time, e.g. if it had been left to him
on condition that he should be chosen consul, the
prætor might distribute the estate among the creditors[4].

The heir appointed[5] "in diem certum," or "incertum," might recognize the possession of the estate
at once, and distribute it "secundum tabulas."

In the case of wilful and affected delay, the
prætor might fix a time within which the inheritance
should be taken.

One form of the conditional appointment of an
heir was the substitutio, by which one person was
put in the place of another.

This was either (1) vulgaris, (2) pupillaris, or
(3) quasi pupillaris.

"Titius hæres esto, si Titius hæres non erit
Sempronius esto," was a "vulgaris substitutio."

Any one who had the right of making a will,

---

[1] The very last thing formerly considered in English jurisprudence.
[2] II. 28. 5. 67.
[3] II. 29. 2. 54.
[4] II. 28. 5. 23, § 1.
[5] II. 28. 5. 23.

might substitute in this manner. And any one might be substituted who had the "testamenti factio" with the testator.

The same causes which would prevent the direct heir from taking, e.g. his death in the lifetime of the testator, or the non-fulfilment of a condition, would prevent the substitute.

The "pupillaris substitutio" appointed another heir in the event of the death of the original heir, the son being the descendant in potestate of the testator, before he attained the age of fourteen, or of the daughter before she reached that of twelve years[1].

The "pupillaris substitutio" could only be made by the father or grandfather of children in their power, or who would have been in their power, had they not been posthumous. The grandfather could only appoint a substitute for his grandchildren, for so long as they did not fall under the power of the father on his grandfather's death.

The "pupillaris substitutio" might be made for disinherited children, if the ground of their disinheritance was valid.

No one could thus make a will for his children without making one for himself. If, therefore, his own will was invalid, so was that made for the son.

If the heir was extraneous, i.e. if he could choose whether he would accept the inheritance or not, and refused to take it, the substitutio pupillaris fell to the ground; if he was "suus," whether he took the

---

[1] *Inst.* de Pupill. subit. § 8.
Being the child, or in certain cases grandchild, of the testator; and in the event of the death of such person before the age of fourteen if a male, or if a female twelve.

paternal estate or not, the pupillaris substitutio was established.

The effect of the "substitutio pupillaris" was to confer upon the person substituted the property of the impubes, and of the testator, in the event of the death of the impubes. Nor could the substitute separate the inheritance of the impubes from that of the parent, but was obliged to accept or reject both. This disposition might exclude the legitimate successors, even the mother and brother of the "impubes," "quia pater ei hoc fecit [1]."

The *substitutio quasi pupillaris* [2] was introduced from motives of humanity, and not to strengthen the paternal authority; it was finally settled by Justinian. It was the institution of an heir by the parent in the place of his insane children, if they died without recovering possession of their faculties. The heirs so appointed must be first the children of the "mente captus." If he had no children, his brothers or sisters. If there were none extranei, and he might be substituted for any child emancipated or not provided, the "legitima portio" was left to the original heir or heirs.

The condition of succession was that the original heir should die insane. The substitutes succeeded to all the property of the "mente captus:"

---

[1] II. de inoff. Test. 8, § 5.   [2] L. 9 Cod. de impub. et al. substit.

CHAPTER XXIV.

PROGRESS OF TESTAMENTARY LAW.

THE old Roman Law gave the testator an absolute power to dispose of his property by will, "uti legâssit super pecuniâ tutelâve ejus rei ita jus esto," are the words of the Twelve Tables.

In the process of time, however, this power was circumscribed. The children of a citizen were called " necessarii hæredes," and they were considered as having a right to the succession. Still the father might deprive them of that right either by disinheriting in express words, or by passing them over without mention in his will[1].

Gradually the rule was established that a child " necessarius hæres " must be disinherited by express words. A will in which the unemancipated son was not named either as heir, or as excluded from the inheritance, was invalid.

The same rule was at last applied to an unborn child, if on his birth he would be a "necessarius hæres." If the unemancipated son was named, but the other sui hæredes were not mentioned, the will

[1] Cic. 1. 38. *De Orat.*

was valid, but the unnamed "necessarii hæredes" were entitled to a share of the estate with the written heirs: to half, if the heirs were "extranei"; to a single portion for each unmentioned heir, if they were necessarii.

The civil law[1] required no notice of emancipated children, but if they were passed over in silence, the prætor gave those of both sexes "contra tabulas bonorum possessionem." This was given to the children of emancipated children.

At length the power was given to a child who had been by name disinherited to appeal to the centurions to set aside the will as inofficious, as if the testator when he made it was insane. Actual insanity was not asserted, but the groundless exclusion of a child placed the will on the same footing as if it had emanated from a person of unsound mind. The right of making this complaint extended to parents, children and brothers[2].

As the ground of the complaint was that nothing had been left to the persons aggrieved, the cause was removed if a certain portion, which came to be called "portio legibus," "debita," or "legitima," and was (from analogy to the Falcidian law, enacted for the protection of the heir against excessive legacies) finally fixed at one-fourth of the shares to which the persons would have been entitled if the deceased had died intestate was bequeathed to them. This continued to be the law till the days of Justinian.

Justinian[3] abolished all difference between the

---

[1] II. 37. 4. Gaius, 2, § 135.   [3] Cod. 6. 28. 4.
[2] Pliny, *Ep*. 1.

necessity of mentioning sons and daughters, in so far as the necessity of mentioning them in the will was concerned.

Secondly, he abolished the "querela inofficiosi testamenti," if any part of the inheritance had been left to those who had a right to the "legitima portio." He enacted[1] that the deficiency should be made good.

By the eighteenth Novell the proportion of the portio legitima was increased.

Still greater changes were made by the third and fourth chapters of the 115th Novell[2].

The "necessarii hæredes," or persons whom it was necessary to appoint heirs, unless there was a reason valid in law for their exclusion, were, according to the law as finally framed, the relations in the ascending or descending line.

The exclusion of the "hæres necessarius" was by express words, or by omission.

That by express words was the formal declaration of the testator in his will that he did not wish the person named to be his heir.

It could be done only where the hæres was necessarius, and where the exclusion was complete, by suitable words, in the will, not the codicil.

---

[1] Just. 2. 11, § 3.

[2] Novell. 115. c. 3.

"Non licere parentibus, patri, vel matri, vel aviæ proavo aut proaviæ suum filium aut filiam vel cæteros liberos præterire aut exhæredes facere in suo testamento...nisi forsan probabantur ingrati et ipsas nominatim ingratitudinis causas parentes suo inser-

uerint testamento." c. 4. Sancimus "non licere liberis parentes suos præterire," &c. Before this last law the necessarii hæredes were "jure civili sui hæredes." II. de injusto rupto, irrito, testamento, 17.

"Jure prætoris omnes emancipati." Inst. de lib. exhær. 3. § 7. eodem.

The "hæres" was "præteritus[1]," who was neither named as heir, nor disinherited by appropriate words, e.g. if he was disinherited conditionally[2].

The testator might disinherit the "necessarius hæres" from motives of hostility or kindness, "odio," or "bonâ mente:" "multi[3] non notæ causâ exhæredant filios nec ut eis obsint sed ut eis consulant." To establish the will in either case it was requisite that the exclusion proceeded "ex justâ causâ."

The "justæ causæ exhæredationis quæ ex odio fit" were fourteen, so far as descendants were concerned[4]:—

1. If they had raised their hands against the parent.

2. If they had inflicted on them a grave and scandalous injury.

3. If they had by poison or otherwise endeavoured to take away their lives.

4. If they had accused them before a court of justice, and thereby exposed them to suffering.

5. If it could be proved that they had endeavoured to prevent them from making a will.

6. If they had allowed a parent to remain in captivity without making an effort for his or her release.

7. If they had neglected a parent during the time of his or her insanity.

---

[1] *Inst.* de hæred. quæ ab intest. defer.

[2] 28. 5. 64 sub fin.

[3] Π. de lib. et posth. 18.

[4] Pauli recept. Sentent. Novell. 115, § 3. § 4. 5. 16. § 2.

Π. de hæred. instit. 44.

de Lege Falcid. 41, § 8.

"Liberi testamento patris præteriti sunt qui neque hæredes instituuntur neque ut oportet exhæredati sunt." *Inst.* de hæred. quæ ab intest. defer.

8.   If not being the children of persons engaged in such pursuits, they had, against the will of their parents, become actors or gladiators, and persevered in such an occupation.

9.   If they had become heretics.

10.   If the son had accused the father or mother of a capital crime (murder excepted).

11.   If the son consorted with malefactors or was a malefactor.

12.   If he had unlawful intercourse with his stepmother or the concubine of his father.

13.   If the son did not become surety for his father when he was imprisoned.

14.   If the daughter, when the father was willing to marry her with a dowry, became a prostitute for money.   But the daughter of 25 years, if her parents delayed to marry her, could not be disinherited for mere want of chastity, nor for marrying any freeman without the consent of her parents.

These were the "justæ causæ" for the parent to disinherit the child.

Those for the child towards the parent were eight.

1.   If the parent had given up the child to suffer capital punishment.

2.   If it could be proved that they had endeavoured to destroy the child's life by poison or in any other manner.

3.   If the father had been guilty of illicit intercourse with his daughter-in-law or the concubine of the son[1].

---

[1] Cujacius, 4. 96. "Si filius suus testamento patris præteritus est, testamentum est ipso jure nullum; quod si filius emancipatus testamento patris

4.   If the parent had endeavoured to prevent the child from making a will.

5.   If they had neglected the child when insane.

6.   If they had not redeemed them from captivity.

7.   If they became heretics.

8.   If either parent had administered poison to the other.

The exclusion of a brother or sister was valid unless some "turpis persona" was instituted heir.

The causes of disinheritance "bonâ mente" were[1], when there was reason to fear if the "necessarius hæres" was disinherited that it would turn to his injury; e. g. if the son being still impubes was passed over, and an heir appointed "per fidei commissum" who was requested to consign the inheritance to him at a proper age; or if the testator bequeathed to his son who was mad or prodigal the means of support, and appointed the grandchildren his heirs.

With regard to the form[2] of disinheriting a "necessarius hæres," it was necessary,

1st.   That the cause of exclusion should be inserted in the will.

2ndly.   That the cause should be real and capable of proof.

---

præteritus est, valet quidem testamentum sed rescinditur beneficio Prætoris, datâ bonorum possessione contra tabulas, quæ tamen intra annum petendum est."

[1] "Si quis non malâ mente parentis exhæredatus sit sed aliâ ex causâ, exhæredatio ei non nocet." II. de bon. jibert. 12, § 2.   27. 10. 16, § 2.

Cod. de inoff. Test. 25.

[2] "Si ita eum exhæredaveris, quisquis mihi erit hæres filius exhæres esto, ut Julianus scribit, hujusmodi exhæredatio vitiosa est."   II. de lib. et post. 3. § 2.   Cujacius, *Obs.* 17. 38.

"Nominatim exhæredatus filius et ita videtur—filius meus exhæres esto, si nec nomen ejus expressum sit, si

3rdly. That another heir should be appointed. In the case of descendants it was requisite, 1st. That they should be excluded by name, or by a certain designation of the person. 2dly. That the disinheritance should be absolute, not conditional. 3dly. That it should extend to the whole inheritance. 4thly. That it should be in the proper place[1], and that the person excluded should be "a toto gradu submotus[2]."

As to the institution of an heir, it was requisite, first, that the heir should either by express nomination or in any other way be certainly designated.

If the designation was certain[3], a mistake in the name, or a false description, or abusive words accompanying the nomination, did not impair it.

But an error as to the person overthrew the will[4].

An heir might be appointed by reference to another document in which he was described[5].

The appointment of an heir might be absolute or conditional[6]. He could not be appointed heir from a

---

modo unicus sit ; nam si plures sunt, sibi benignâ interpretatione potius a plerisque respondetur nullum exhœredatum esse."

[1] II. de lib. et post. 3. § 1. Ib. 13. § 2. de bon. poss. c. t. 18.

[2] II. de lib. et post. 3. § 2. eod. 3. § 3. § 4. § 5.

[3] Cod. de test. 15 ; cod. 29.

II. de hær. instit. 9, § 8, " si quis nomen quidem hæredis non dixerit sed indubitabili signo eum denuntiaverit quod pene nihil a nomine distat valet institutio." II. eod. 48. § 3.

"Dum de eo qui demonstratus est constet, institutio valet."

" Illa institutio valet, filius meus

ineptissimus male de me meritus, hœres esto." II. eod. 48, § 1. Averanius, *Interpret.* 5. 13.

[4] " Quoties volens alium hœredem scribere alium scripserit, in corpore hominis errans, placet neque eum hœredem esse qui scriptus est quoniam voluntate deficitur, neque eum quem voluit quoniam scriptus non est." II. eod. 9.

[5] II. eod. 36. 77.

[6] *Inst.* 2. 14. 9: "diem adjectum haberi quo supervacuo placet et perinde esse ac si jure hœres institutus esset." II. 28. 7.

Ib. jus.

certain day or at a particular time : in such a case
the appointment was taken absolutely: "Incertus
dies in testamento conditionem facit[1]."

BONORUM POSSESSIO[2].

An accurate knowledge of this doctrine is essential for any one who wishes to understand the Roman
law of succession[3]. Ulpian says, "Bonorum possessionem ita definiemus, jus persequendi retinendive patrimonii sive rei, quæ cujusque cum moritur fuit."
This was a Prætorian remedy introduced in some
cases to mitigate and in others to strengthen the ancient positive law, by adapting it to the temper and
exigencies of a more refined period.

The persons whom the Prætor invited to the inheritance were not heirs, for the Prætor could not
make an heir; but those who were by him appointed
in the place of heirs, and thence called "honorarii
successores." "Prætor bonorum possessorem hæredis
loco in omni causâ habet[4]."

As he who took the succession by the civil law
was called "hæres," he who took it by the Prætorian law was called "bonorum possessor." He
was neither hæres nor dominus, but a substitute for
both. The Pandect says, he is "vice hæredis," and

---

[1] Π. de condit. et dem. 74. eod. 1.
§ 1. 30.
[2] Π. 43. 1. Pothier, *Analyse.*
Averanius, Vol. 1. p. 148.
It resembles "possessio bonorum"
nothing but name; it is an incorporeal right (jus).
[3] Warnkönig, § 3. 222.
"Die Grundlage des Romischen·

Erbrechts ist die successio per universitatem die bei jeder Erbfolge ange-
nommen werden muss, und neben wel-
cher alle andere Rechts verhältnisse,
als blosse nebens acten erscheinen."
Savigny, *System,* &c. 8. 296.
[4] Π. 50. 17. 117. Π. 2. 37. 4. 3.
Oratio in Verrem, 3. Cujacius, Vol.
VIII. p. 1.

like him shares in all the advantages and disadvantages of the inheritance. His possession was rather legal than physical, and if there were no corporeal object of inheritance, was said to be "agnita[1]." The "bonorum possessio" could be given to no one against his will, and it devolves only upon him to whom the Prætor has assigned it. It was twofold, edictalis and decretalis.

The edictalis[2] was an ordinary proceeding conferred "de plano," without investigation by the Prætor. The decretalis was an extraordinary proceeding, after the cause had been heard, by a formal decree. It was twofold, one given "Ventris," the other called "Carboniana:" "Ventris," when after the death of her husband the woman declared herself pregnant; "Carboniana," from the Carbonian edict, when a controversy was raised as to the "status" of an impubes. The inquiry was delayed till he had reached the age of puberty, and in the mean time the "bonorum possessio" was granted, as if no such dispute existed. The edictalis was granted by the Prætor in analogy with the rule of the civil law in conferring inheritances; for the "bonorum possessio" was of two sorts and might either be granted where a will had been made "ex testamento," or in the case of intestacy, "ab intestato[3]." In the case where a will had

---

[1] "Agnitio bonorum possessionis multum differt ab aditione hæreditatis." "Inter cætera illud est multo maximum discrimen quod bonorum possessio agnosci potest per tutorem nomine pupilli." Averanius, Vol. I. 148.

[2] Cujacius, Vol. VIII. p. 7: "quod manat ab ipsâ lege."

[3] "Bonorum possessionis beneficium multiplex est, nam quædam bonorum possessiones competunt contra voluntatem, quædam secundum voluntatem defunctorum, nec non ab intes-

been made, it might be either "contra tabulas," rescinding the will of the testator, or "secundum tabulas," establishing it. In the case of intestacy, different people were called to the inheritance, according to the degree of their relation to the deceased.

In order to prevent the evils that might ensue from leaving the succession vacant, the Prætor[1], by the successorian edict, fixed a period within which those whom he called to the inheritance were to determine whether they would accept it. "Idcirco propositum est ne bona hæreditaria vacua sine domino diutius facerent et creditoribus longior mora fieret. E re igitur Prætor putavit præstituere tempus his quibus bonorum possessionem detulit," etc. Gaius[2] puts the whole matter under our eyes; and as the passage illustrates the admirable wisdom, and the vigilance with which the law guarded against technical error and misuse, I shall translate it. "We have also," he says, "in certain formulæ, fictions of another kind, as when he who succeeds 'ex edicto,' to the 'bonorum possessio,' pleads as fictitious heir; for as he succeeds to the place of the deceased by the prætorian and not the strict law, he has not the direct actions, and neither can say that what belonged to the deceased is his own, 'suum esse,' nor that was due to the deceased 'dare sibi oportere,' in his 'intentio,' i. e. the changing part of the formula. Therefore he sup-

---

tato habentes jus legitimum, vel non habentibus propter capitis diminutionem; quamvis enim jure civili deficiant liberi qui propter capitis diminutionem desierant sui hæredes esse,

propter æquitatem tamen rescindit eorum capitis diminutionem prætor."

[1] II. 37. 46. § 1.
[1] II. 38. 14.
[2] 4. 34. *Instit.*

poses himself the heir, and the formula is so conceived. If he, the plaintiff, were the heir of the deceased, and in *that* case could claim the field in dispute as his 'ex jure quiritium,' or in case of a debt,
if in *that* case M. N. ought to pay him ten thousand
sesterces."

A question sometimes arose whether the heir
or the "bonorum possessor" was to be preferred; this
depended on the class to which each belonged in
the successorian edict; when the heir, if he was in
the inferior class, might be compelled to restore the
property[1] of the deceased to the bonorum possessor,
or if he sued for them, be repelled by the "exceptio
doli."

"Bonorum possessio" is defined "jus persequendi
retinendive patrimonii quod cujusque cum moreretur
fuit." It is called "jus[2]" to distinguish it from the
actual "possessio bonorum," a merely physical fact;
"persequendi," that is, of obtaining it if possessed
by another; "retinendi," that is, by exceptiones, if
demanded by another.

It was introduced to aid those whom the civil
law had overlooked, that is, the "liberi emancipati,"
because they were not "sui hæredes." They were
relieved by the provision "unde liberi."

The cognati who were passed over by the civil
law, were relieved by the "unde cognati."

The "bonorum possessio contra tabulas[3]" was

[1] II. 37. 4. 13. 15.
[2] Cod. de acquirenda possessione.
[3] II. 37. 2. 4. § 3. *Inst.* de exhæredat. lib.
"Emancipatos liberos jure civili ne-

que hæredes instituere neque exhære-
dare necesse est, quia non sunt sui hæredes; sed Prætor omnes tam feminini
sexus quam masculini si hæredes non
instituantur exhæredari jubet. Viri

given (1) to "emancipated children," not mentioned
in the father's will; if they had been by name disinherited, their remedy was the "querela inofficiosi
testamenti." (2) To the "sui hæredes," who had been
passed over; for though they had a remedy by the
civil law, the "bonorum possessio" might enable
them to prevent the written heir from obtaining
"bonorum possessionem secundum tabulas."

This was given to emancipated children if passed
over or disinherited by the will of the father, or to a
more remote relation in the ascending line, as also to
the Patronus and his children, if passed over in the
will of the freedman[1]. The persons claiming were
called to the succession in the same order as they
were called by the civil law. The whole right of
the written heir was transferred to him who was so
called. Therefore the person formally disinherited
could only assert his right by the "querela inofficiosi testamenti." Under the bonorum possessio the
"substitutio pupillaris," and the legacies of the substitutio were upheld[2], and the fidei commissa, "hoc
est liberis[3] et parentibus[4] uxori nuruique dotis nomine legatum," and so were the "mortis causâ
donationes."

The "sui" and "necessarii hæredes[5]," i.e. heirs

lis sexus nominatim—feminini vero inter cæteros, quia si neque hæredes in-
stituti fuerint neque ita ut diximus
exhæredati permittit eis Prætor contra tabulas bonorum possessionem."
§ 4. cod. § 12. cod.

[1] II. 37. 2. 4. § 1.
[2] II. 28. 34. § 2: "Etiamsi contra

patris tabulas bonorum possessio pe-
tita sit, substitutio tamen pupillaris
valet, et legata omnibus præstanda
sunt quæ a substitutione data sunt."
[3] II. 35. 5. § pr.
[4] II. 35. 5. § 3.
[5] II. 38. 16. 1. § 4.
Inst. 3. 1—6.

without their choice or knowledge, were children in the first degree natural or adopted.

Grandchildren of the son who had ceased to be in their father's power.

Posthumous children who would have been "in potestate" of the testator had they been born during his life. And the wife "in manu instar filiæ."

The "capitis diminutio" in any degree took away the "jus sui hæredis;" but it might be recovered by postliminium, the "restitutio in integrum," and adoption.

The grandson of a father[1] disinherited was a "necessarius hæres."

The Prætor[2] gave the children the "beneficium abstinendi," the right, that is, of renouncing the paternal inheritance. The effect of such a determination on the part of the heir was that the inheritance was dealt with as if the "suus" was not his father's heir.

The "bonorum possessio secundum tabulas" was given sometimes to the written heir in a will properly attested, but by the civil law defective.

1. Sometimes where the will had been cancelled by the birth of a posthumous child, and the child had died in the testator's life-time, but the testator made no other will, the will was invalid, but the

---

[1] "Interdum filii familias et sine aditione acquirunt hæreditatem his in quorum sunt potestate, ut puta si nepos ex filio exhæredato sit hæres institutus, patrem enim sine aditione faciet hæredem et quidem necessarium."

[2] Gaius, 2. 158—160.
Instit. 2. 19. 1—3.
II. 28. 8. 7. pr. 28. de jure deliberandi, 11. 1. 12.

II. 29. 2. 6. 5.

Prætor distributed the inheritance according to its provisions, "secundum tabulas."

2. To heirs properly named in the will in order to obtain possession more easily by the Prætorian authority, without any corporeal act.

The right to take the inheritance was limited by the capacity of the person claiming it.

The Roman Law established several grounds of disqualification, which it would be superfluous now to specify. But it required that the heir at the time of the testator's or intestate's death, be either in the world or on his way to it — "natus" or "nasciturus," born or conceived.

Artificial persons, churches, corporations, eleemosynary institutions, might succeed by special privilege.

RIGHT OF SUCCESSION.

The old law, as I have stated, called the Agnati only to the succession.

After this had been mitigated and expanded by a series of laws, or the intervention of the Prætor, all the established[1] rules were superseded by the

---

[1] According to the old law the "sui hæredes," those whom the death of the owner made "sui juris," came first; then the nearest agnati extending among women to sisters only; then in early times the Gentiles. Pauli, sent. 4. 8. Gaius, 3. 1—17. Ulp. tit. 26. *Instit.* 3. 1. 16. II. 38. 16. 3. 1.

"Quod Scipio Orfilus et Vetius Rufus consules verba fecerunt de filiorum successionibus in maternis bonis,

aliisque rebus quæ Imperator Cæsar divi Antonini filius Marcus Aurelius Antonius, et Lucius Aurelius Commodus filius Augusti Maximique principes oratione sua complexi sunt.

" De ea re quid fieri placeat, de ea re ita censuerunt.

"Ut sine in manum conventione matris intestatæ hæreditas ad liberos pertineat, tametsi in aliena potestate sint.

" Ut filia simul cum filiis succedat

118th Novell., which substituted a simple rule of succession, based on relationship only, setting aside altogether the privileges of the agnatus, and placing emancipated and unemancipated children on the same footing. The right so given extended without distinction of sex to all degrees of relationship.

NATURAL CHILDREN[1].

As far as the mother and the relations on her side were concerned, the illegitimate child was on the same footing as the legitimate.

matri et liberi vulgo quæsiti cum legitimis.

"Utque illi omnes omnibus consanguineis et agnatis ipsius matris præferantur.

"Si nemo filiorum eorumve quibus simul legitima hæreditas defertur volet ad se eam hæreditatem pertinere jus antiquum erit.

"Quæ judicata transacta finitave sunt rata maneant.

"Fuisse etiam aliquid cautum de servis manumissis patet ex paulo Recept. sent. lib. 4. tit. ult. Nempe.

"Ut si testator non proprio nomine, sed certâ aliquâ demonstratione, servum designasset, nihilominus liber existeret." Meermann, *Thesaurus.* Rauchini *Tractatus de succ. ab intestato*, Vol. III. p. 200.

"Quod Tertullus et Licinius sacerdos coss.

"11. Constantini lex de agnatis cum matre concurrentibus.

"12, 13. Senatus consulti Tertull. capita Jure Gallorum sublata.

"14. De ascendentibus quatuor regulæ.

"In senatu verba fecerunt de his

quæ Imperator Cæsar Adriani filius, T. Aurelius, Antoninus Pius, Augustus Maximusque princeps oratione sua complexus est de iis rebus quid fieri placeat, de iis ita censuerunt.

CAP. I.

"Ut mater ingenua trium liberorum jus habens, libertina quatuor, ad bona filiorum filiarumve admittatur intestato mortuorum, licet in potestate parentis est.

CAP. II.

"Ut præferantur matri liberi defuncti, qui sui sunt, quive suorum loco sunt, sive primi gradus, sive ulterioris.

CAP. III.

"Ut etiam pater defuncti ei anteponatur non tamen avus, aut proavus.

CAP. IV.

"Ut frater consanguineus defuncti matrem excludat, soror autem consanguinea pariter cum matre admittatur."

[1] "Proconsul naturali æquitate motus omnibus cognatis promittit bonorum possessionem, itaque etiam vulgo quæsiti liberi matris et mater talium liberorum item ipsi fratres inter se ex

With regard to the father they had not the full rights of cognati.

Legitimatized children were put afterwards on a level with those born in wedlock[1].

The order in which relations according to Justinian's law were called to the succession is the following. Each preceding class excludes that which follows.

1.   Children and children's children, descendants of every degree.

2.   Ascendants. Parents, brothers and sisters of the whole blood. Those of the nearest degree precede the others. Fathers and mothers precede all others in the ascending line. Illegitimate children though of the same parents' rank with the half-blood.

Children of brothers and sisters take the place of their parents[2].

3.   Brothers and sisters of the half blood, and their children, according to the same rule as that which governs the succession of children of brothers and sisters of the whole blood.

All other collateral relations without distinction

hâc parte bonorum possessionem petere possunt quia sunt invicem inter se cognati." II. 38. 8. 2. Our legislator, not "naturali æquitate motus," said that the bastard being "nullius filius," should inherit neither from father nor mother (Cruise, 3. 319), and could have no heirs but his own children, and then, with a wisdom and in a dialect all his own, dilates upon the case of "bastard eignè et mulier

puisnè..." See also on a rational system, II. 38. 8. 4. § 2. II. 38. 8. 2. § 4. and 10.

2 Cod. 5. 27. 10.

Novell. 89. § 8.

[1] Si filii sint legitimi, II. 4. 17. 2. 8. 14. 15.

[2] The 3 cap. of the 118 Novell was altered by the 1st cap. 127 Novell in this respect.

as to the whole or the half blood, the nearer class excluding the more remote[1].

Thus was established first the "successio ordinum," so that one class was called after another to the succession, and then the succession graduum, by which the descendants of those belonging to the class succeeding stood in the place of their ancestors.

This was a change in the old system, for Gaius tells us, " In legitimis hæreditatibus successio non est[2]."

The division of the property among those entitled in their own right was " per capita," among those representing another, " per stirpes."

The law, contrary to the genius of the feudal system, did not look to the origin of the property unless in one case, that of a second marriage, when the "dos," or "donatio propter nuptias," was kept untouched for the children of the first[3].

If there were no relations[4] entitled to succeed, the survivor of two married people might succeed, by applying for the " bonorum possessio unde vir et uxor."

If the deceased[5] left no legitimate children, and no wife, Justinian gave his natural children, if acknowledged by the father, a sixth part of their father's inheritance; one share of which went to

---

[1] 118. 3. § 1.
[2] Gaius, 3. 12.
Paulus, 4. 8. 23.
Ulpian, 26. 5.
II. 38. 15.
   38. 9.
Cod. 6. 16.
[3] Nov. 22. 22—26.

Nov. 2. 1. 2. 4.
Cod. 5. 9. 6. 1.
[4] The law (A. D. 537) Nov. 53, c. 6, was altered by the law 117, cap. 5. (A. D. 541.)
[5] Nov. 18. c. 89.
   c. 13.
The English judges disinherited a

their mother, and the father had a right to a corresponding share in the inheritance of his children[1].

FALCIDIAN LAW.

The Falcidian Law[2] is a plebiscitum passed by
Publius Falcidius, tribune of the people, A.U.C. 714,
providing that a fourth part of the goods of the
testator free from all burdens should be given to
the heir, or if there were more heirs than one, to
each of them.

The period for estimating the value of the estate
was the death of the testator. If after that time
and before the inheritance had been entered upon,
the estate was increased or diminished, this in no
way affected the right of the heir to whom "omne

posthumous child; "on an appeal to
the House of Lords this judgment was
reversed, against the opinion of *all* the
judges, who were much dissatisfied."
Cruise, Vol. II. p. 251. In consequence,
the 10 & 11 W. III. c. 16, was passed,
like many others, to restore the trace
of reason and humanity which had
been effaced. See the provisions in the
Will act, 1 Vict. c. 26. § 29, especially; 7 W. IV. c. 9; and see page
374 infra.

[1] II. 38. 16. 6. "Lex 12 Tabularum
eum vocat ad hæreditatem qui moriente eo de cujus bonis quæritur in rerum naturâ fuerit." 7. eod. "vel vivo
eo conceptus est quia conceptus quodammodo in rerum natura esse existimatur." *Inst.* 3. 1. 8. II. 38. 81. § 8.
II. 28. 3. 6. "Verum est omnem post-
umum qui moriente testatore in utero
fuerit si natus sit bonorum possessionem petere posse." II. 37. 11. 3. *Inst.*
3. 9.
 Cod. 6. 24. 12.

Cod. de episcop. 1. 3. 49.
Cod. de SS. eccles. 1. 2.
Cod. de hæred. *Instit.* 8: "Collegium *nisi* speciali privilegio submis-
sum sit hæreditatem capere non posse,
dubium non est."
 [2] Inst. de lege Falcidiâ, 2. 22.
II. 35. 2.
Cod. 6. 50.
Gaius, 2. 224—227.
Pauli sententiæ, 3. 8.
Paulus, lib. sing. ad Legem Falci-
diam, "Lex Falcidia lata est quæ primo capite liberam legandi facultatem
dedit usque ad dodrantem," abrogat-
ing the L. Furia and the L. Voconia
which limited the amount of legacies:
"Quicunque civis Romanus post hanc
legem rogatam testamentum faciet is
quantum cuique civi Romano pecuniam jure publico, dare legare volet.
Jus potestasque esto dum ita detur
legatum ne minus quam partem quartam hæreditatis eo testamento hæredes capiant."

commodum, vel incommodum," of the inheritance appertained.

The Lex Falcidia applied only to legacies; but the principle was extended to "fidei commissa," whether created by will, or "ab intestato."

To "donationes mortis causa," by a law of Severus.

And "donationes inter virum et uxorem," confirmed by death.

Before the Lex Falcidia was applied, deduction was made of the debts due from the testator and of the funeral expenses.

Of the value of slaves emancipated by the will.

The Lex Falcidia did not apply to the will of a soldier:

Nor, by a law of Justinian, thoroughly characteristic of the gross superstition of that prince, and of the avarice of the clergy, to legacies for pious purposes :

Nor if the heir paid the legatees in ignorance of the law ; otherwise, if it was in ignorance of fact :

Nor if the heir entered upon the inheritance without making an inventory :

Nor if the testator expressly forbad the application of it.

The heir could enforce his right under this law by " rei vindicatio."

" Indebiti condictio."

" In factum actio."

" De dolo actio."

" Interdictum quod legatorum."

He might require security to be given him for the repayment of a legacy in cases of doubt.

FIDEI COMMISSUM[1].

"Fidei commissum" was that which had been so left by will to any one as to oblige him to give it to another person.

It was universal when the entire inheritance[2], or an aliquot part of it, was to be so delivered; singular, when any thing else was the object of such a bequest.

Any one who could make a will might bequeath a "fidei commissum" even to a person with whom, with regard to the thing bequeathed, he had not the "testamenti factio[3]."

The "fidei commissum" of a slave, or a "filius familias," was valid if àt the time of their deaths they were emancipated.

The task of fulfilling a "fidei commissum[4]" might be imposed on any one who derived any benefit from the inheritance, by the will of the testator, as well on those who were the object of a "mortis causâ donatio[5]," as on those to whom any thing was given in fulfilment of a condition[6]. So if imposed on the "hæres hæredis" it was valid[7].

---

[1] "Augustus rerum potitus consulibus quotannis delegavit jurisdictionem, ut de fidei commissis auctoritatem interponerent." *Inst.* de fidei c. hæred. § 1. ib. 10.

Ulpian, Fragment. tit. 25. § 1.

"Ex 12 tabulis tantummodo ratæ fuerunt supremæ voluntates directis atque imperativis verbis conceptæ, juris igitur vinculo non astricta fidei commissa, quippe precario modo relicta."

[2] Voet. 36. 2.

[3] II. 30. 40. "Sed si res cujus commercium legatarius non habet, per fidei commissum relinquatur, puto æstima-

tionem deberi." 114 eod. § 5. II. 32. 11. 16. Vinnius differs.

[4] "Damnari hæres potest ut alicui donum extruat aut ære alieno cum liberet." Pauli sent. recept. 3. 6. § 10.

[5] II. 32, 1. 1.

[6] "Cui statu liber pecuniam dare jussus est is rogari potest ut eandem pecuniam alicui restituat." II. 30. 96. § 4.

[7] II. 32. 5. § 1. ib. 6.

"Si quis non ab hærede vel legatario sed ab hæredis vel legatarii hærede fidei commissum reliquerit, hoc valere benignum est."

But it could not be imposed on one who derived no benefit from the will, or who derived a benefit accidentally, not from the settled purpose[1] (certo judicio) of the testator. The person liable to such an obligation might be requested to give one thing in exchange for another, but not more than he had himself received[2]; and if he accepted the testator's legacy he might be asked in exchange to give up something of his own[3], even though the legacy was of inferior value.

If no particular person was designated in the will as he on whom the burden of the "fidei commissum" should devolve, all the heirs were liable each in proportion to his share of the inheritance.

If the heirs were enumerated, the burden was divided equally among them, without reference to their respective shares. It might be left in any part of the will or codicil[4], or *vivâ voce* in the presence of at least five witnesses.

"Fidei commissa" are divided by the interpreters into absolute and conditional.

A "fidei commissum[5]" might be established by a transaction "inter vivos," as is proved by the re-

---

[1] "Qui fortuito non judicio testatoris consequitur hæreditatem vel legatum, non debet onerari, nec recipiendum est, ut cui nihil dederis eum rogando obliges." II. 32. 6. 1.

[2] "Si centum legatis duplum restituere rogatus sit ad summam legati videbitur constituisse.' Ib.

[3] Eod...."Enimvero si pecuniâ acceptâ rogatus sit rem propriam quamquam majoris pretii est restituere non est audiendus legatarius legato per-

cepto, si velit computare, non enim æquitas hoc probare patitur." Ib.

[4] *Institut.* 2. 23. 10. l. ult. Cod. de fidei commissis. Voet. 36. Lib. 1. ult. inst. de Fidei comm. Hæred.

[5] II. 32. 37. § 3. Pater emancipato filio, etc.

Ib. 30. 77. Si pecunia, etc.

Ib. 16. 3. 26. Publia Mævia, etc.

Cod. dedonati quæ sub modo, 2. "si rerum."

markable law cited[1]. In this case, the person for
the benefit of whom the trust was given had an
"actio utilis[1] ex æquitate" against the trustee.

A "fidei commissum[2]" might be tacitly left, that
is, implied from the language of the testator, e. g.
"mando tibi hæres ne testamentum facias donec
liberos susceperis," might be construed as a trust
to the heir not to alienate the inheritance. So
where a testator requested his wife not to leave
any portion of his inheritance to her brothers, adding that there were the children of her sisters to
whom she might leave, it was held that on her
death intestate the sister's sons were entitled to the
property; or if the testator used in his will words to
this effect, "se credere," "se scire," "se existimare,"
"futurum esse ut hæreditas vel res Sempronio restituatur[3]." If the words were addressed to the heir
it was a tacit trust[4]; so was a request to the son that
the land might descend to his sons[5]. The distinction was of course narrow; for instance, a direction
to Titius to give to a third person, "si voluerit," was
not a trust; but a direction to give "si fueris arbitratus, si putaveris, si æstimaveris, si utile tibi fuerit

---

[1] II. 36. 1. 9.

Vinnius, tract. de partis, cap. 15.
§ 11. § 12.

[2] II. 36. 1. 74.

II. 31. 88. 16.

"Testamentum aut non jure factum
videtur ubi solemnia juris defuerunt
aut nullius esse momenti quum filius
qui fuit in patris potestate prætentus
est, aut rumpitur alio testamento, ex
quo hæres existere poterit; vel agna-
tione sui hæredis, aut in initum con-

stituitur non aditâ hæreditate." II. 28.
3. 1.

[3] II. 30. 1. 115: "Etiam hoc modo
cupio des, opto des, credo te daturum;
fidei commissum est."

[4] "Rogo te fili ut prædia quæ ad te
pervenerint pro tuâ diligentiâ diligas
et curam eorum agas, ut possint ad
filios tuos pervenire."

[5] II. 32. 11. § 9: "Licet non satis
exprimunt fidei commissum sed magis
consilium," etc.

visum vel videbitur," was a binding trust, "non enim plenum arbitrium voluntatis hæredi dedit[1]." In short, a tacit trust was upheld as often as it appeared to be a corollary from the words of the testator.

The Roman Law[2] enabled a testator to do by means of a trust what he could not do by a direct proceeding.

Considered in itself a request to my heir to make Titius his heir, was invalid, because it interfered with the liberty of testamentary disposition. Considered as a trust, it might be enforced.

A request in this form was valid[3]: "Peto cum morieris licet alios quoque filios susceperis Sempronio nepoti meo plus tribuas in honorem mei nominis."

One of the most usual conditions under which a "fidei commissum" was left, was this, "si gravatus hæres sine liberis moriatur," in which case if the person burdened with the trust, did not die childless the trust was void.

One child was enough to destroy the condition, even if the expression was "sine liberis;" so was a child "in utero matris," a grandchild, or great grandchild[4].

This condition was sometimes understood; for instance, if Titius left his son, then childless, his estate, requesting the son on his death to give it

---

[1] II. 32. 11. § 7.

Mantica, *de Conject. Ultimæ Volunt.* p. 247. Lib. 6. tit. 14. § 24.

[2] 36. 1. 17. II.

II. 30. 114. § 6. § 7.

[3] II. 31. 76. § 5.

II. 31. 77. § 25.

[4] "Non est sine liberis cui vel unus filius, una filia est." II. 50. 16. 148.

"Si quis prægnantem uxorem reliquit non videtur sine liberis decessisse." II. 50. 187.

to Mævius, the son was only bound by the bequest in the event of his dying childless, "conjecturâ
pietatis[1]."

But if the son of the testator was known by his
father to have children, the condition was not implied[2].

A "fidei commissum" might be left "familiæ"
for ever. Under the name "familia" were included
not only all relations, but if they failed, the son-in-
law and daughter-in-law[3]. In the event of such a
bequest the inheritance went to each successively as
he would have taken it in the case of an intestacy; if
the actual holder sold it, without compulsion, the
"fidei commissi petitio" devolved upon those who
were to succeed him in their order. If the sale was
compulsory, the purchaser held it during the life of
him who sold it.

If the testator merely forbad the alienation of
the estate, without assigning any reason for the prohibition, or naming any person for the benefit of
whom it was intended, the prohibition was void,
"quasi nudum præceptum[4]."

The fiduciary heir might retain what was called
the Trebellian fourth, from analogy to the share
given by Falcidian Law. The Senatusconsultum
Trebellianum was enacted in the time of Nero, and

[1] "Quum avus filium ac nepotem
ex altero filio hæredes instituisset a
nepote petiit ut si intra annum trigesi-
mum moreretur hæreditatem patruo
suo restitueret; nepos liberis relictis
intra ætatem suprascriptam vitâ decessit, fidei commissi conditionem pietatis conjecturâ respondi defecisse."
Π. 35. 1. 102. What a contrast to
our law! See page 367, supra.

[2] Cod. de instit. et substit. l. generaliter b.

[3] L. ult. Cod. de verbor. signific.
Π. 31. 69. § 4.
Π. 29. 7. § 3.
Meermann, *Thesaurus,* Vol. VII. p.
625. T. F. de Retes.

[4] Π. 30. 114. § 14.
32. 38. § 4. ib. 93.

transferred all actions for and against the fiduciary heir to the beneficial owner: "*omnes actiones quæ jure civili hæredi et in hæredem competerent, ei et in eum cui ex fidei commisso restituta esset hæreditas darentur*[1];" but as it often happened that the heir refused "*adire hæreditatem*" from which he could derive no benefit, and thus wills were cancelled, the Senatusconsultum Pegasianum under Vespasian provided that any heir called upon to restore the inheritance might deduct a fourth part from it for his own benefit, and if he then refused[2], might be compelled to undertake the trust by accepting the inheritance. All that the heir received under the will was reckoned into the fourth. The heir who "*coactus adiit hæreditatem*" lost his right to the fourth[3].

The testator might fix, subject to what has been here stated, the person who should be the trustee, the time and manner of the restitution, and the amount to be restored. He might require the heir at his death to give to another what remained of the inheritance, a bequest which confined the heir's power of spending the principal to three-fourths of the inheritance, and obliged him to find security for the remaining portion.

[1] II. ad sc. Trebell. 1. 1. § 4. ib. *Instit.* de fidei c. Hær. § 4.
The Trebellian was in fact the Pegasian fourth.

[2] II. 29. 4. 17: "Si quis omissâ causâ testamenti omnino eam hæreditatem non possideat excluduntur legatarii, nam liberum cuique esse debet etiam lucrosam hæreditatem omittere, licet eo modo legatos libertatesque intercidunt, sed in fidei commissariis hæreditatibus id provisum est, ut si scriptus hæres adire nollet hæreditatem, jussu prætoris adeat et restituat."

[3] Gaii *Instit.* 253—257.
Inst. h. t. § 4—7. 10. Cod. de fidei comm. 6. 42. 29. Novell. 108. § 1.
II. 36. 1. 54: "Pro ratâ patrimonii quod hæres habuit."
II. 36. 1. 58.

The person[1] for the benefit of whom the inheritance was burdened with a trust, either conditional,
or to take effect on a future day, might demand
security from the trustee, and unless it was obtained,
take possession of the bequeathed property; or if the
trustee had ceased by his own contrivance to possess
the property, or neglected for six months to give
security, he might take the property of the trustee,
applying[2] the income first to the payment of the
interest, then of the principal due to them.

This right[3] of demanding security might be destroyed, by the words of the will, by the conduct of
the legatee, or from the nature of the bequest.

By accepting the inheritance, or taking possession of the bequest, the obligation of the party
burdened became complete. If he gained nothing
from the inheritance he was responsible for the
"dolus" and "lata culpa," only otherwise for the
"levis culpa[4]." He who was required to restore the
inheritance was responsible[5] only for the "culpa dolo
proxima," not for the "levis et rebus suis consueta
negligentia[6]." An action lay for the legatee against
the person so burdened by the testator.

Justinian enacted several laws for the particular
benefit of "pia corpora[7]."

---

[1] Π. 36. 3. Ib. 4.

[2] Π. 36. 4. 5. § 16. § 21.

[3] Π. 2. 14. 46: "Pactum inter hæredem et legatarium factum ne ab eo
satis accipiatur...validum esse constat."

    Π. 36. 4. 18.

        36. 4. 1. § 2.

        36. 4. 1. § 9. § 10.

[4] Π. 30. 108. § 12. 30. 85.

[5] Π. 36. 1. 22. § 3.

[6] *Inst.* de oblig. quæ ex contractu,
§ 5.

    Π. 44. 7. 5. § 2.

[7] Cod. de episc. et cler. 46. § 4.

    Nov. 131. c. 12.

    Inst. de art. § 19. & 26.

LEGACIES. RIGHT OF THE LEGATEE.

The legatee could not by his own unauthorized act take possession of his legacy.

If he did so without the sanction of the heir, the heir had the "interdictum quod legatorum[1]" for restoration of the thing taken, or compensation for his loss.

The person obliged to pay the legacy might sue the legatee for restitution of any profit beyond his right that the legatee had acquired, and for recovery of what the heir had laid out on the legacy for the benefit of the legatee[2].

Any one who could name an heir could leave—any one who could be chosen an heir could take—a legacy[3].

The "Catoniana regula[4]" established the rule that a legacy which would have been invalid, if the testator had died the moment after making his will, could not, whenever he died, be valid.

But this rule was not universal, e. g. it did not include conditional legacies.

Legacies might be bequeathed by testament or by codicil[5]. The form was the same, except that in the codicil five witnesses were sufficient; neither was

---

[1] Π. 43. 3. quod legatorum. Cod. 8. 3.

[2] Π. 30. 70. § 1. 116. § 4. 58. 61. *Inst.* de Lege Falcidiâ. Π. 35. 2.

[3] Π. 28. 5. 59. § 4.

[4] Π. 34. 7. 30. 41. § 2. "Ad conditionalia Catoniana non pertinet." Π. 34. 7. 3.

Π. 34. 7. 1. § 1. § 2: "Si tibi legatus est fundus qui scribendi tempore tuus est, si eum vivo testatore alienaveris legatum tibi debetur quod non deberetur si testator statim decessisset."

[5] Π. 29. 7. Cod. 6. 36. *Inst.* 2. 25.

Π. 29. 7. 6: "Codicillos et plures quis facere potest et ipsius manu neque scribi neque signari necesse est."

it requisite that the codicil should be written in the hand or authenticated by the signature of the testator[1].

The person burthened might be the heir, he who stood "loco hæredis," or he who derived any benefit from the testator's will.

He was only liable to the extent of the benefit he derived. If no person was specified as the person bound, the heir or heirs were taken to be meant in proportion to their share of the inheritance; if the heirs burdened were specially named, each person named paid the same sum[2].

He was said to be "honoratus" by the bequest to whom in making it the testator intended an advantage[3]. The benefit might be indirect, as if the "honoratus" were to take a benefit on an heir's accepting an inheritance or a legatee a bequest; or direct; or it might be "mortis causâ capio." In all cases[4] the person whom the testator intended to

[1] II. 31. 33.

"Legatorum petitio adversus hæredes pro partibus legatariis competit."

[2] II. 30. 54. § 3.

30. 124.

"Si pars hæredum nominata sit, viriles partes hæredes debent."

[3] "Plerumque evenit multorum interesse id quod relinquitur, verum testatorem uni voluisse honorem habitum, et est hæc sententia Marcelli verissima."

II. 32. 11. § 20.

11. § 21. § 22. eod.

49. 4—6.

30. 69. 2.

[4] "Si testator quosdam ex hæredibus jusserit æs alienum solvere, non creditores habebunt adversus eos actio-

nem, sed cohæredes quorum interest id fieri, nec solum hoc casu alius habet actionem quam cui testator dari jussit, sed alio quoque, veluti si filiæ nomine genero aut sponso dotem dari jusserit, non enim gener aut sponsus sed filia habet actionem cujus maxime interest." II. 30. 60, § 2. 34, § 3, § 4.

"Consequenter quæritur cur et ille socius pro legatario habeatur cujus nomen in testamento scriptum non est, licet commodum ex testamento ad utrumque pertineat si socii sint: et est verum non solum eum cujus nomen in testamento scriptum est, legatarium habendum, verum eum quoque qui non est scriptus si et ejus contemplatione liberatio relicta esset."

"Filio pater quem in potestate re-

benefit was the substantial legatee, e. g. if the testator, meaning to confer a benefit on his daughter, ordered that in her name dower should be paid to his son-in-law. But the "mortis causâ capio" did not give to him on whom it was conferred the rights of a legatee[1].

The "mortis causâ capio" included in its widest signification legacies, "nam quicquid propter alicujus mortem obvenit mortis causâ capitur[2]."

If a special legacy[3] were bequeathed to one of several heirs, or to an heir, he might claim it though he did not accept the inheritance (prælegatum percaptio); if he did accept the inheritance he was only entitled to contribution "pro ratâ" from his coheirs. The "prælegatum" was considered as cut off from the rest of the inheritance[4].

Any thing, corporeal or incorporeal, specific or universal (as a flock of sheep), whether the property of the testator or not, might be the subject of a legacy. If the thing bequeathed was the property of a third person, the heir, if he could not obtain the specific object, was bound to give its value to the legatee. The only restraint was that the thing bequeathed should be a subject of lawful contract. Thus a legacy was useless which bequeathed what was sacred, or a free man.

tinuit hæredi pro parte institutâ legatum quoque reliquit, durissima sententia est existimantium, denegandam ei legati petitionem si patris abstinuerit hæreditate, non enim impugnatur judicium ab eo qui justis rationibus noluit negotiis hæreditariis implicari."

II. 30. 87.
[1] II. 29. 4. 8.
[2] II. 39. 6. 8.
[3] II. 30. 34. 11. § 12. eod. 116. § 1. II. 30. 17. § 2. 30. 18. 30. 87. 30. 91. § 2. 32.
[4] 32. eod.

The bequest of what belonged to another[1] was only valid if the testator knew that the thing so bequeathed was not his own, "non si ignoraverit[2]." The burden of shewing the testator's knowledge, generally speaking, was on the legatee[3].

But if the bequest was to some near connexion, or a wife, the burden was shifted according to the maxim, "quod factum est cum in obscuro sit ex affectione cujusque capit interpretationem[4]." The rule did not apply where the thing bequeathed was the property of the heir.

In cases where the owner asked an extravagant price, or where feelings of natural affection stood in the way of the bequest, the judge might "officio" exercise an equitable discretion[5].

If the thing bequeathed was burdened with a debt to the knowledge of the testator[6], the heir was bound to redeem it, in the absence of any express direction which left no room for conjecture[7].

Another case arose when the legatee during the life of the testator had become the owner of the thing bequeathed. A distinction was made between the case where it had been acquired "titulo oneroso[8]," or "titulo lucrativo."

---

[1] Cujacius ad Leg. 34. ff. d. v. o.
7. *Inst.* de Leg. eod. § 3.
II. 30. 14.
[2] II. 31. 67. 8.
"Nam succurrendum est hæredibus ne cogerentur redimere quod testator suum existimans reliquit."
[3] Cod. h. t. l. 10: "Verius est ipsum qui agit, id est legatarium, probare oportere scivisse alienam rem probare defunctum."

[4] II. de reg. j. § 168.
[5] II. 30. 71. § 3.
[6] II. 30. 57.
[7] II. 32. On the principle, "Cum in verbis nulla ambiguitas est, non debet admitti voluntatis quæstio."
[8] II. 30. 108. § 4.
"Causæ onerosæ, emptio, permutatio, transactio, dos—causæ lucrativæ donatio, legatum, fideicommissum."
II. 30. 34. § 1.

In the first hypothesis he might recover the value of the article from the heir, in the second he could, because it is a principle "duas lucrativas causas in eundem hominem et in eandem rem concurrere non posse."

If the same thing[1] was bequeathed to the legatee by two wills, A and B, and, in conformitywith the wish expressed in A, it had already been delivered to him, he could not sue the heir under B for the price.   But if he had received the value only of the thing bequeathed under will A, he might sue the heir under B for the thing itself: "Ejusque rei ratio evidens est quod eadem res sæpius præstari non possit eadem summa volente testatore multiplicari potest."

The legacy of a thing not yet existing was valid, e. g. of the child of a slave, or the produce of land. "Inest autem conditio legati, veluti cum legamus quod ex Arethusâ natum est, hæres dato[2]."   But the bequest was not technically conditional: a bequest to the legatee of what already belonged to him was of no value[3], "quia quod proprium alicujus est amplius ejus fieri non potest;" but the legatee might claim from the heir compensation for any sum he had laid out in acquiring the complete enjoyment of what the testator had bequeathed, e. g. if he had bought the usufruct[4], and the testator bequeathed the whole estate, he might claim the sum he had so laid out.

---

[1] "Bona fides non patitur ut bis idem exigatur."

[2] II. 30. 34. §§ 1, 2, 3.

[3] II. 50. 57.

[4] II. 35. 1. 1.

If the testator bequeathed as belonging to another what was his own, the legacy was valid.

LEGACY OF A SUM OR QUANTITY[1].

If a specific sum or quantity of things to be consumed by me was bequeathed without any other limitation, the action lay, even though no such things belonged to the testator[2], or formed any part of the inheritance. But the heir might choose to discharge the legacy[3], furnishing the article of such quality as he chose, provided it were of the kind mentioned in the will. If such things were left without any limitation as to their quantity, all that belonged to the testator alone was comprised in the bequest[4].

A sum[5], or specified quantity, might be left, to be paid at certain recurring intervals, such as "annuum legatum[6]." Such a bequest is not to be confounded with that of a specified sum to be paid at intervals. Every bequest of a rent may be considered as so many separate legacies to be paid respectively at each returning period.

The "alimenta" or "cibaria legata[7]" were looked

[1] II. 36. 2. 28. *Inst.* 2. 20. 18.
II. 30. 21. 33. 6. 33. 9. 34. 2. 33. 10. 30. 79. 1. 30. 65. 4.
[2] II. 30. 8. 33. 5. 33. 3.
[3] "Cum certum pondus olei non adjectâ qualitate legatur, non solet quæri cujus generis olei uti solitus fuerit testator, aut cujus generis oleum istius regionis homines in usu habeant, et ideo liberum est hæredi cujus vellet generis oleum legatario solvere."
[4] II. 3. 3. 6. 7.

[5] II. de annuis legatis, 33. 1: "Cum in annos singulos legatur non unum legatum esse, sed plura constat." II. 36. 2. 10.
[6] II. 36. 2. 20: "Exonerandi hæredis gratiâ." As to the way in which the "quarta Falcidia" was calculated in such a case, see II. 35. 2. 45 = 73. § 4. 1. § 16. 55. 3. § 2.
[7] II. 34. 1.
Computation, II. 35. 2. 68.

upon in the same light as the rent, except that the right to them ended with the life of the legatee— "constat enim alimenta cum vita finiri[1]."

GENERIC LEGACY[2].

If a thing not destroyed by use, the class including which alone was named, as a house, was bequeathed by the testator, and such a thing formed part of the testator's property, the bequest was valid, and as a general rule the choice of it lay with the legatee: if no such thing belonged to the testator, and the class to which the object belonged alone was mentioned, the legacy was invalid. "Derisorium est legatum."

LEGACIES OF RIGHTS OVER REAL PROPERTY.

The testator may transfer to a legatee his right (jus) over what belongs to another. "Pignus, emphyteusis, superficies[3]." "Quia[4] aliquod jus in eo, is qui legavit habet, valet legatum[5]," "via," "ususfructus[6]," "quasi ususfructus[7]," so an estate might be left to Titius, and the usufruct of that estate to Sempro-

---

[1] II. 2. 15. 8. 10.

[2] II. 30. 1. 7 t.
Inst. 2. 20. § 22.
II. 23. 3. 69. § 4.

[3] II. 43. 18. 7: "Sed et tradi posse intelligendum est ut et legari et donari possit." De superficiebus. *Inst.* de servitut. 2. 3. § 4. ib.
  2. 4. § 1.

[4] II. 30. 71. 5. 86. § 4: "Valet legatum si superficies legata sit ei, cujus in solo fuerit, licet is dominus soli sit, nam consequetur ut hac servitute libe-

retur, et superficiem lucri faciat." II. 33. 2. 2. 4. II. 33. 3. 2.

[5] "Fundum communem habentibus legari potest via." II. 33. 3. 1.

[6] "Omnium praediorum jure legati potest constitui ususfructus ut haeres jubeatur dare alicui usumfructum." II. 7. 1. 3: "Ususfructus cujusque rei legari potest et aut ipso jure constituetur aut per haeredem praestabitur." Pauli sentent. 3. 6. II. 7. 5. 1.

[7] Sc. "earum rerum quae usu consumuntur." II. 7. 51.

nius, in which case the "jus accrescendi[1]" did not generally arise[2].

OPTIONAL LEGACIES[3].

The choice of giving to the legatee one of different objects may be bequeathed to the heir. In such a case the choice once formally announced was irrevocable[4], "quum autem semel dixerit hæres mutare sententiam non poterit;" or the choice between different objects might be given to the legatee, and in the absence of any direction[5] it was presumed to rest with him as to personality, not as to land[6].

If a general legacy was left of one among several objects, neither the best nor the worst of the class were to be chosen[7]. The right of option went to the heir[8] of the legatee; if there were several heirs, the exercise of it was decided by lot. A period might be fixed within which the choice given must be exercised[9]. If an option was left between two things, one given absolutely, the other conditionally, the time for making the option did not arrive "pendente conditione[10]."

---

[1] II. 7. 2. L. 2. 3: "Si deducto usufructu proprietas legetur."
[2] "Usufructus non portioni sed homini accrescit." II. 44. 2. 14. § 1. II. 7. 2. 33. II. 7. 2. 10.
[3] II. 33. 5.
[4] II. 30. 1. 84. § 9. § 11.
[5] II. 30. 1. 34. § 14: "Si ita Titio legetur, &c. et in arbitrio ejus esse, &c;" "quoties servi electio datur legatarius optabit quem velit." II. 32. 5. 2.
[6] *Inst.* 2. 22.

[ ] II. 30. 1. 37. § 1.
[7] II. 30. 1. 37: "Legato generaliter relicto veluti hominis Cassius scribit id esse observandum ne optimus vel pessimus accipiatur."
[8] II. 33. 5. 19. *Inst.* 2. 20. § 23. II. 36. 2. 12. § 7.
[9] II. 33. 5. 8: "Decernendum est a prætore nisi intra certum tempus optaveris petitionem tibi non datum iri."
[10] II. 36. 2. pr. 25. pr. 16. L 14.

25

But if in such a case the death of the legatee destroyed one alternative, the other perished, and the legacy fell to the heir[1].

---

[1] The law, which is worth reading, will be found II. 36. 2. 14. 1.

CHAPTER XXV.

LEGACIES.

UNIVERSAL LEGACY[1].

An universal legacy is a bequest requiring the restitution of the inheritance of the testator, or an aliquot portion of it. Effect was first given to such a "fidei commissum[2]" by the "senatus consultum Trebellianum," by transferring the actions against the heir to the benefitted person, "in eos quibus ex testamento fidei commissum restitutum fuisset." The heir charged to fulfil such a trust was called "hæres fiduciarius," the person for the benefit of whom it was bequeathed, "hæres fidei commissarius." The "Senatus consultum Pegasianum" compelled the heir to accept the inheritance, even if suspected, at the desire of the benefitted person, and transferred the actions "ei et in eum qui recipit hæreditatem[3]," in

---

[1] *Inst.* de fidei commissariis hereditatibus, 2. 23.

II. 36. 1.

Cod. 6. 49.

[2] II. 36. 1. 1. § 1. § 2. According to the old law there existed a "legatum partitionis," a "partitio legata," desiring the heir to share the inheritance in certain proportions with another. Gaius, 2. 254; *Inst.* 2. 23. § 5; Ulp. 25. 15. It is mentioned historically in the passage cited from the *Institutes*.

[3] As to the case where the trustee died before the testator, see II. 29. 1. 14.

like manner as the "Senatus consultum Trebellianum." Such a bequest might be made in the form
of a command or an entreaty[1].

If an ancestor enjoined the grandson to whom
he left a portion of the inheritance to restore that
portion to his the grandson's uncle, after his the
grandson's death, the trust was understood to fail
if the grandson had children. "Fidei commissi
conditionem respondi defecisse conjectura pietatis[2],"
said Papinian. When the "hæres scriptus" was requested[3] to give the inheritance to another, when
he chose, "quum volet," this was equivalent to the
words "post mortem."

The inheritance might be given, and the trust
fulfilled[4], either "re ipsâ," or by implication from the
acts of the trustee. The "fiduciarius" was responsible for the "culpa dolo proxima[5]," and negligence
beyond that which he displayed in the management
of his own affairs, "rebus suis consuetâ negli-
gentiâ[6]," after he had incurred "mora" for the profits.
If the trust was to give back "quicquid ex hæreditate meâ superfuerit," at the death of the trustee
"fiduciarius," this gave the trustee the right of

---

[1] Π. 36. 1. 19: "To rogo," &c. "nec
verba spectantur senatus consulti sed
sententia quibuscunque verbis dum
testator senserit ut hæreditas sua restituatur."
    II. 36. 1. 78.
    II. 31. 1. 69. 36. 1. 17.
        31. 1. 77. § 25.
        88. § 16.
[2] If the English judges in Equity
had read this law, English jurispru-

dence would have been spared the
scandal of decisions which the Wills
Act has at last swept away! II. 35.
1. 102: "conjectura pietatis" is a
phrase unknown to those to whom
England assigned the task of interpreting disputed wills.
[3] II. 32. 1. 41. § 13.
[4] II. 36. 1. 37.
[5] II. 36. 1. 22. § 3.
[6] II. 36. 1. 18. 27. § 1. 44. § 1.

disposing as he pleased of three-fourths of the estate; but of the fourth[1] only in case of extreme necessity.

The heir[2] is entitled, until the time of fulfilling the trust has arrived, to administer the property, and to take the profits. He may require compensation for the expenditure he has incurred and release from obligations. But the most important of his rights was his claim to an integral fourth of the testator's estate[3], or of his share in it, which he might, if necessary, deduct from the property of which he was required to make restitution.

This right arose with the application of the Falcidian law to " fidei commissa," by the "Senatus consultum Pegasianum[4]."

In the fourth were included[5] all the profits he had derived from the inheritance, e.g. the produce of what he was called upon to restore before the time of restitution.

A bequest " conditionis implendæ causâ[6]" to the heir was not included in the fourth.

The consequence of the " restitutio" by the "fiduciarius" was that the " fidei commissarius," or object of the testator's liberality, stood in the place of the heir altogether, if he obtained the whole inheritance; partially, if a part only was to be his. "Factâ in

---

[1] II. 36. 1. 54. Novell. 108. c. 1.
32. 70. § 3.
71. 72.
[2] II. 36. 2. 19. § 2. 22. § 3.
II. 12. 6. 40. § 1, where the heir rebuilt the house burnt down before the trust was due. II. 30. 58. 60. II. 36. 2. 36. 69.
[3] Inst. 2. 23. 5. 9. Gaius, 2. 254.

[+] II. 36. 2. 27. § 10. 64. § 3.
[4] A. U. C. 827.
A. D. 74.
[5] II. 35. 2. 91.
"Res quæ ab hærede alienatæ sunt in quartam imputantur hæredi." II. 36. 1. § 3. 22. 2.
[6] II. 35. 2. 30. § 1. 86.

fidei commissarium restitutione statim omnes res in
bonis sunt ejus cui restituta est hæreditas, etsi nondum earum rerum nactus fuerit possessionem[1]." He
could enforce his rights by means of the "utiles
actiones," or the "fidei[2] commissaria hæreditatis
petitio," even against the "fiduciarius" himself,
and he was liable to the creditors.

If the "fiduciarius" refused to accept the inheritance, the "fidei commissarius" might compel him
"quia poterit fieri ut hæres institutus nolit adire
hæreditatem...prospectum est ut si fidei commissarius diceret suo periculo adire, et restitui sibi velle
cogatur hæres institutus a Prætore adire et restituere hæreditatem[3]." The other "compulsus" ran
no risk[4] and gained no advantage by the fourth or
by the will, not even "pœnitendo." He might, however, require time for deliberation, and if he then
accepted the inheritance, he was still entitled to
any benefit from it, "nec enim suspectam coactus
adiit sed sponte post deliberationem[5]." If the "fidei
commissarius" took possession of the inheritance
which the heir refused to deal with as "suspecta,"
the former was bound to pay the legacies, which
the heir would have been obliged to pay. In paying
those he might take the benefit of the "Lex Falcidia[6];" but for those legacies which he, not the
heir, was burdened with, he could not. The "fidei

---

[1] II. 36. 1. 63. p. 2.

[2] II. 5. 6.

[3] II. 36. 1. 4.

Instit. 2. 23. 6.

[4] II. 36. 1. 14. § 4.

27. § 2. 14.

43.

45.

55. § 3.

[5] II. 36. 1. 9. 1.

[6] II. 36. 1. 63. 11.

"Si quum suspectam videres hære-

commissarius" being the creature of the testator's favour, could not take in spite of it.

If the bequest was subject to a condition to be performed by the heir, "si neque difficultatem neque turpitudinem ullam habet conditio nec impendium aliquod[1]," he might be ordered to fulfil it; if to give any thing, the fidei commissarius might fulfil it. But if the condition was "turpis," or "difficilis," and the heir refused submission, the bequest fell to the ground, "aperte enim iniquum est, cogi eum explere eam alterius gratiâ." "Plus enim tribui ei qui fidei commissum petit quam testator voluit absurdum est, utique autem testator nisi expleta sit conditio neque scriptum hæredem ad hæreditatem vocavit, neque per hunc illi voluit restitui hæreditatem."

The fidei commissarius[2] might take the inheritance instead of the heir,—

1. When the heir died in the testator's life, without the knowledge of the testator.

2. When the heir died before he had acquired the inheritance.

3. When he refused to accept or to decline the inheritance, in express words.

ADEMPTION OF LEGACIES[3].

Legacies and trusts might be recalled "nudâ

---

ditatem postulante me jussu Prætoria adieris...ita utar legis Falcidiæ beneficio adversus legatarios si tu quoque eâ lege uti poteras et quatenus uti poteras," &c. Cod. 55. § 2. "Aliud est enim ex personâ hæredis conveniri, aliud proprio nomine defuncti precibus astringi."

[1] II. 36. 1. 63. § 7. 31. § 2.

[2] II. 36. 1. 14. 1. § 1. Cod. h. t. 6. 49; and see II. de test. mil. 29. 1. 13. § 4.

[3] Iust. 2. 21.
II. 34. 4.

voluntate;" so if bitter and deadly hatred, "capitales aut vel gravissimæ inimicitiæ," arose between the testator and the legatee, "ademtum videri quod legatum est[1], sin autem levis offensa manet fidei commissum[2]." Where the legacy ademed had been given to Caius in trust for Titius, a question might arise whether Caius was to keep it, which was answered by considering whether Caius had been chosen as a mere vehicle for transferring the estate, "nisi duntaxat ut ministrum elegit," in which case it was taken from him; if not, he was allowed to profit by it.

And as a legacy might be ademed, so it might be transferred. Paulus enumerates four ways of translation, "aut enim a personâ in personam transfertur; aut ab eo qui dare jussus est, transfertur ut alius det; aut quum res pro re datur, ut pro fundo decem aurei; aut quod jure datum est transfertur sub conditione[3]."

---

[1] II. 34. 4. 3. § 11.
31. 1.
[2] II. 34. 4. 31. § 1.

II. 31. 17.
[3] II. 34. 4. 6.

CHAPTER XXVI.

CONDITIONS[1].

THE doctrine of substitutions extends to legacies. A legacy may be given to Caius in the event that Mævius does not take it, or it may be so left that several persons shall take it in succession; the first legatee's death being the condition on which the second legatee takes it; the second legatee's death, that on which the third receives it, and so on. This is the "precaria substitutio," which includes the "indirecta hæredis substitutio." Such legacies are termed successive. One class of them is termed "fidei commissa familiæ[2] relicta," by which the trustee is enjoined to transmit the property to a particular family[3]. Some-

---

[1] Π. 32. 50: "ut hæredibus substitui potest ita etiam legatariis videamus...ut id promittat ille alteri si ipse capere non poterit." 1. cod. 77. § 13. "Volo prædia dari libertis meis; quod si quis eorum sine liberis vitâ decesserit partes eorum ad reliquos pertinere volo." Heineccius, *A. R.* Lib. II. 20—22. § 11—14. Ejusdem, *Instit.* s. 544, 549.
Π. 30. 114, § 17.
Π. 2. 69. 2.
[2] The word "familia" comprises all relations; see II. 31. 69. 4.

[3] "Rescripserunt eos qui testamento vetant quid alienari, nec causam exprimunt propter quam id fieri velint, nisi invenitur persona cujus respectu hoc a testatore propositum est, nullius esse momenti scripturam ...quod si liberis, aut posteris, aut libertis, aut hæredibus, aut aliis quibusdam personis consulentes, ejusmodi voluntatem significarent, eam servandam esse, sed hæc neque creditoribus neque fisco fraudi esse."
Π. 30. 114. § 14. § 18.
31. 69. § 1. § 3. § 4.

times the selection of any particular member of the family is left to the holder.   If the holder refrains from the exercise of this right, or transmits the property to a stranger, the nearest[1] relations of him to the family of whom the bequest is made may claim it, and after them those of the former trustee. If they consent to the alienation, they lose their right, and the trust may be destroyed by the consent of all the members of the family[2].

The "Catoniana regula[3]" did not apply to conditional legacies.

An uncertain day, e. g. if the testator should write, The person who shall be the second living son of Mucius at his death, is a condition; "dies incertus conditionem in testamento facit."   A suspensive condition was valid; and if it could not be fulfilled at once, the heir took "bonorum possessionem secundum tabulas."   If the condition was negative, which could not be determined before the death of the heir, he might take immediate possession on giving security[4] (cautio Muciana) to those who were to succeed in the event of its violation.   The Roman Law held the condition fulfilled if the fulfilment of it had been prevented by the person who was to profit by the non-fulfilment of it[5].   Impossible conditions, among

---

[1] II. 31. 69. § 3. § 4. § 5.

By the 159th, c. 2, the trust came to an end after four generations.

[2] II. 30. 120. § 1.

   31. 77. § 27.

[3] II. 34. 7. 3.

   30. 41. § 2.

[4] "Nunc duæ cautionis utilitas consistit in conditionibus quæ in non fa-

ciendo sint conceptæ; ut puta si in capitolium non ascenderit, si Stichium non manumiserit, ut similibus," etc. II. 35. 1. 7.

[5] II. 38. 7. 3.

"Si ita hæres institutus sim si decem dedero, et accipere nolit cui dare jussus sum, pro impletâ conditione habetur."

which are included those false to the knowledge of
the testator, make a contract void, but are, in a will,
as if they had not been written, leaving the bequest
absolute. So a condition[1] directly left "in arbitrium"
of a third person—obliquely such a bequest might be
valid. Contradictory conditions were void, "ubi
pugnantia inter se testamento juberentur neutrum
ratum est[2]."

With regard to conditions relatively impossible,
if they were impossible before the will they were as
if not written; if they became so afterwards the bequest failed[3].

It was a rule not only that "falsa demonstratio[4]"
did not vitiate a legacy, but that neither did "falsa
causa," e.g. I leave Titius a thousand pounds because
he was my cook, because he transacted my business:
supposing there to be no doubt as to the person,
the legacy is valid, though Titius is not a cook, and
though he never did transact my business.

The Prætor's edict held the condition to take an
oath, void even in a soldier's will.

Before Justinian, "legata pœnæ nomine relicta,"

"Jure civili receptum est ut quoties
per eum cujus interest conditionem impleri fit quo minus impleatur, ut perinde habeatur ac si impleta conditio
esset." II. 35. 1. 24.

[1] "Obtinuit impossibiles conditiones
pro nullis esse habendas." II. 35. 1.
3..

[2] II. 50. 17. 188. "Si conditiones
perplexæ." II. 35. 2. 88. 28. 7. 16.

[3] See II. 35. 1. 31.
72. 4—7. 40. 7. 39. 4.
II. 38. 7. 8. 29. 1. 29. 2.

[4] This illustrates the mistake into
which those have fallen who complain
of the sum left by Napoleon, to a man
because he attempted to kill the Duke
of Wellington, having been paid to
him. According to all rules of jurisprudence the legatee had a right to
the money. Otherwise, if the bequest
had been, I leave it to A. B. *if* he will
kill the Duke of Wellington. - II. 35.
1. 17. § 2. "quod autem juris est in
demonstratione *hoc vel magis est* in
falsâ causâ."

imposing a fine on a person if he did not obey the testator's command, were invalid, as being not so much "in favorem legatarii" as in "odium hæredis[1]." Justinian provided means for enforcing them[2].

Sometimes a condition is implied from motives of humanity[3].

The heir could not be appointed for a certain or after a certain time[4].

As to the opening and proving wills, see references[5].

DE REBUS DUBIIS[6].

The task of interpretation, as it is that which most clearly displays the wisdom of the judge, is that which places in the most conspicuous light the deficiencies of the narrow-minded and illiterate who were at one time raised by the favour of men as narrow-minded and illiterate as themselves to the highest places of the law.

Fruitful as every other head of our jurisprudence is in shocking absurdities, I do not know that (the rank and impudent evils of special pleading always excepted) there is any department of law even among us in which more fantastic tricks have been played, more wanton caprice exhibited, more cruel and systematic injustice inflicted by our tribunals, or in

---

[1] Gaius, 2. 235. II. 34. 6. Jus. 1. 20—36.

[2] Cod. 6. 41. L. U.

[3] II. 35. 1. 102.

[4] L. 2. 14. 9, de hær. instit.

[5] II. 29. 3. eod. 5. Pauli Recept.

Sentent. 4. 6. Cod. 6. 43. 5. 32 and 35. Cod. 87.

[6] Instit. 2. 20.

II. 34, 5. Cod. 6. 38. Richer, Vol. II. 639.

which we have more fully deserved Virgil's description—

"Penitus toto divisos orbe Britannos,"

from sense and knowledge, than in the construction of wills. I do not allude to any living person, but it is no exaggeration to say that if every decision on a disputed will had been the reverse of what it is, society on the whole would have been gainers, and the intention of the testator more frequently fulfilled than it has been. If the object was to make the fortune of attorneys[1], nothing could be wiser than the decisions of English judges, or the system on which they were founded. For they first annexed to plain and ordinary words a meaning totally abhorrent from their usual signification, and they then applied that artificial meaning to the language of wills made without legal assistance[2], although at the very time when they pronounced the interpretation reducing the child to beggary, and missing the much-loved person for whom the testator intended to provide, with a grave pedantry unknown to any other country, they declared that they perfectly well knew the meaning to be altogether different from that which they judicially declared it to be[3]. Far from

---

[1] See the work of a very respectable writer, Wigram on *Extrinsic Evidence*, p. 10. The rules he lays down as those of our law are precisely what, unless the testator has legal advice at his elbow, must counteract his intention. See how completely this illustrates Burke's remark, that for substantial injustice and formal regularity no people ever equalled the English.

[2] "Præsumptiones legum rebus non verisimilibus accommodari non debent," says a great commentator, who as far as England is concerned, might as well have written in Japanese. Mantica, p. 2, § 8. And again "non est aliqua præsumptio in testamento contra quam probatio non est accipienda."

[3] Doe v. Oxenden.

e. g. Doe, Gwillim v. Gwillim, 5 B. and Ad., still law. "The Court

taking into consideration the circumstances of the
testator, as for instance whether he could or did obtain legal advice, the position of his estates, the expressions familiar to him, which the Roman Law en-

is to decide *not* what the testator
intended, but what is the meaning of
the words he has used." But why
does the testator use words (i.e. technical) at all? is it not to declare his
meaning? And if you know his meaning, is not that what you are called
upon to declare? See too Grey and
Pearson, 6, H. of Lords' cases. If
you give to the testator's words a
meaning you know they were not
intended to carry, you must be
wrong — " vocis ministerio utimur."
Why are words important? that from
them we may collect the meaning.
But is there any country but England
where a judge (not bribed) says, I will
reject the end for the sake of the
means, which are only important as
they lead to the end—and I will as-
cribe a sense to the words of the
testator, which reason, humanity,
grammar, custom, instinct, shew he
never intended them to have? These
remarks apply to the class of cases
where the judges have insisted on
construing in a technical, words that
they know the testator to have used
in a popular sense—cases which, for
the honour of human reason be it said,
are confined to English law. Take
the case of Robinson v. Robinson,
1 Burrow, 38, where the devise was
to A. B. for his life, and no longer;
and yet the judges decided in three
courts that the devises extended beyond his life. Or the case, unequalled
for its absurdity and cruelty, but decided according to stint law, of Doe
d. Blackiston v. Hartwood, 10 C. B.
544—which, that my reader may see

the effect of narrowness and pedantry,
I will transcribe. A testator expect-
ing to die speedily left lands to his
wife for her life, and if his wife should
give birth to a posthumous child, to
such child, but if no such child was
born, to his nephew. A child was born
before the testator died. And it was
gravely decided by five human creatures who could read and write, and
understand connected sentences—that
the land went to the nephew—and
that the father disinherited his own
son, whom it was admitted he intended if posthumous to provide for,
because he came into the world while
the father was yet alive. Such is the
effect of allowing attorneys (at second-
hand) to make the law. All commentary on such gross perversion of reason
would be flung away.

But there is another class of cases,
not quite so flagrant, but still absurd
enough, where the judges wilfully close
their eyes against evidence within
their reach which would enable them
to put a right interpretation on the
will they are called upon to expound;
such is the case of Delmare v. Robello,
1 Vesey Senr. 412. 3 Brown, 446. Hamp-
shire v. Pierce, 2 Vesey Senr. 216, where
literally the same evidence was admitted to prove the meaning of the testator in one part of the will, and excluded
from assisting to explain the other,
and Doe d. Oxenden v. Chichester, 3
Taunton, 147. Anstee v. Helms, 4 Dow.
65, 225. Of course, a set of decisions
may be cited irreconcileable with those
in which by dint of the most strained
and subtle distinctions, e. g. Gill v.

forces upon the judges' consideration, they carefully
and elaborately stopped up all these avenues to truth;
or if they sometimes deviated so far into a track of
reason as to admit portions of such material evidence,
it was done in a fashion so thoroughly empirical,
such care was taken to deprecate any notion of decid-
ing the case on principle, such anxiety was displayed
to guard against the possibility of any benefit to society by a breach on the Chinese wall of prejudice and
folly, such doubts were raised, and such alarm expressed by subsequent judges at the attempt, that
reason lost more than she gained by the innovation.
The maxim of the Roman jurist was, "nihil tam
conveniens naturali æquitati quam voluntatem domini
volentis rem suam in alium transferri, ratam habere[1];"
and the rule laid down by him as the basis of rational
interpretation is the direct reverse of that which has
dictated so many cruel decisions in this country,
"nemo existimandus est dixisse quod non mente agi-
taverit[2]."

Shelley, 2 Ross and Mylne, 336,
judges have escaped from being the
instruments of gross iniquity. But
this adds to the confusion and to
the difficulty of making a will in an
ordinary case without legal assistance, which it seems to be the great
object our judges labour to establish,
it being of course that which it ought
to be their special endeavour to prevent. In Langston v. Langston, 2
Clark and Finnelly, 241, the whole
case turned upon the question whether a mistake had been made in
copying the draft of a will by leaving
out a line; and it was insisted that
the judges ought not to look at the
draft of the will, which was produced!
Well may foreigners exclaim at the
state of our jurisprudence. Miller v.
Travers is another instance where the
known intention of the testator has
been defeated. 8 Bingham, 244. Doe
d. Gord v. Weed, 2 M. and W. 129.
Lord Bacon, Reg. 23, explains the
law, but does not justify it; nor can
his doctrine be reconciled with many
of the cases.

[1] II. de don. 1.
[2] II. 33. 10. 7. 2.

Where words were plain, no question as to the meaning of the testator was allowed. "Non aliter," says Marcellus, "a significatione verborum recedi oportet quam cum manifestum sit aliud sensisse testatorem[1]," but where it was manifest, as the object was to give the true interpretation, it was adopted; e. g. "usus" might be used for "usus fructus," "tutela" for "cura"—the meaning of "liberi" and "filii" are explained. There is an admirable law, full of reason and principle, which I shall therefore quote at some length. "Quod vero quis obscurius in testamento vel nuncupat, vel scribit, an post solemnia explanare possit, quæritur, utpote Stichium legaret, cum plures haberet nec declaravit de quo sentiret. Titio legavit cum multos Titios amicos haberet nec declaravit, de quo sentiretur erravit in nomine, vel prænomine, vel cognomine, cum in corpore non errasset— poteritne postea declarare de quo senserit, et puto posse. Nihil enim nunc dat, sed datum significat. Sed etsi notam postea adjecerit legato vel suâ voce, vel literis, vel summam vel nomen legatarii quod non scripserat ad nummorum qualitatem an recte fecerit, et puto etiam nummorum qualitatem posse postea

[1] П. 32. 68.
П. 7. 8. 22.
"Respondi cum in conditionibus testamentorum voluntatem potius quam verba considerari oporteat," &c. П. 35. 1. 101, directly the reverse of the rule ostentatiously asserted in our jurisprudence, "cum verba dubia sunt," says Richer, 639, Vol. II. "vel ambigua ad voluntatis conjecturas confugimus hæ sunt." 1. "Loquentis affectio." 2. "Consue-

tudo regionis." 3. "Singularia personarum et rerum adjuncta."
П. 50. 17. 12. "In testamentis plenius voluntates testantium interpretantur."
П. 50. 18. 220: 84 ib.
П. 26. 2. 6.
The reader will observe that down to this point the cases are provided for by Lord Bacon's rule. Those which follow are the fruitful causes of our chicane.

addi, nam etsi adjuncta non fuisset utique placeret conjunctionem fieri ejus quod reliquit, vel ex vicinis scripturis, vel ex consuetudine patris familias vel regionis[1]."

The first rule then is[2], "ut res magis valeat quam pereat;"another is[3], "benignior sententia præferenda[4]." Another, the rule so ostentatiously violated in our courts, to consider what it is probable (in a case of doubt, it must be remembered) the testator meant. Another his habit of speech[5]—the propriety of language and conduct, as "Si numerus nummorum legatus est neque apparet quales sunt legati, ante omnia ipsius patris familias consuetudo, deinde regionis in quâ versatus est exquirenda est, sed et mens patris familiæ, et legatarii caritas vel dignitas et necessitudo[6]," &c. And where there was an uncertainty as to the person : "Testatoris voluntas si quibusdam argumentis apparebit de quo dixit, adimplenda est[7]." The leaning towards the humane interpretation is well illustrated by the law cited below[8].

---

[1] II. 28. 1. 21. § 1.

See II. 32. 101. 68. II. 34. 5. 13. As to supervening doubts, II. 34. 5. 13. 30. 17. Case of a posthumous child. "Si qua filia mihi genitus hæres ei certum dato, pluribus natis videtur singulis tantum legasse,...nisi evidens sit contraria sententia testatoris." 34. 5. 10.

[2] 34. 5. 12.

[3] 34. 5. 10. § 1. 21.

[4] Ib. 24, and 28. "Secundum id quod credibile est cogitatum." Compare this with the horrible case of Doe d. Blackiston v. Harewood, 10 C. B. 544 ; and see particularly eod. 28, where it is expressly required that

the judge shall ascertain "an nomina servorum dominus nota habuisset."

[5] Eod. 1, overthrowing Doe d. Oxenden v. Winchester, 13. § 1.

II. 33. 10. §. 5. "Propter usum imputatorum si in argento relatum sit candelabrum argenteum argenti esse videtur, *et error jus facit;*" and 34. 2. 33 : "Si ipse solitus fuerit uti quâdam veste...itaque ante omnia dicendum est eam legatam esse de quâ senserit testator."

[6] II. 30. 50. § 3. 32. 75, words construed by will of testatrix. II. 35. 1. 36. § 1.

[7] II. 34. 5. 25.

[8] 34. 5. 10. § 1.

26

Let it not, however, be supposed that the Roman Law, to use the incessant cant of our books, made a will for the testator. Far otherwise. Equally cautious to avoid real error as stedfast in adherence to substantial right, it shrank from decision, as the texts cited below prove, where there was no sufficient ground to rest upon. To it rash presumption was as alien, as what Lord Mansfield called, with becoming indignation, on the bench of justice, the "disgraceful[1] subtleties," by which our reports in his time as in ours are crowded and defaced[2].

[1] I subjoin Sir E. Sugden's description of the state so satisfactory to our judges, and inferior practitioners of English law. It is peculiar to the constitution of this country that the law on the same case is frequently administered differently by different courts; and that not from a contrary exposition of the same rules.

p. 16 eod. "You have now both land and money. I will suppose that you have by your will given your estate to your eldest son, and the money amongst your younger children. You then grant a lease of the land to Thompson, and give him an option to purchase the estate for £20,000 at any time within ten years. You would think, no doubt, that you had secured your estate to your eldest son. But on the contrary, if you die before the end of ten years, and Thompson after your death elect to purchase the estate, the money would go to your younger children, and your eldest son would be stripped of all his fortune.

"A moment's reflection may shew what serious consequences may follow from a neglect on your part; for suppose you purchase an estate with the £50,000 in the funds, which you have given by your will to your younger children, and which constitutes the bulk of your personal property, and should neglect to devise the estate, the money must go to pay for it at the expense of your younger children, who would be left nearly destitute, whilst your eldest son, to whom the estate would descend, would have an overgrown fortune. Distressing cases of this kind are continually happening." Sugden's *Letters on Real Property*, 1st edition.

[2] II. 34. 5. 3. & 4: "Paulus respondit cum nomen fidei commissarii testamento ascriptum non sit, nulli personæ, neque certæ, neque incertæ datum fidei commissum videri, indubitatum est." See 10. 17, 18. eod. See also II. 35. 1. 10. "In his quæ extra testamentum incurrunt possunt res ex æquo et bono interpretationem capere, ea vero quæ ex ipso testamento oriuntur necesse est secundum scripti juris rationem expediri."

LEGACIES[1].

Justinian enumerates four kinds of legacies, which he says formerly were in use:

1. "Per vindicationem." The form of this was do — lego — sumito — capito. This under the old law was the only form that gave the "jus accrescendi[2]."

2. "Per damnationem—hæres meus damnas esto dare" or "dato." By this form the testator might bequeath not his own property alone, but that of other people[3]. See Domat. Vol. II. p. 673. Also he might bequeath things not actually in existence, as the produce of the soil, or the child with which a slave was pregnant.

3. "Sinendi modo." The form was "hæres meus damnas esto sinere Lucium hominem Stichum sumere sibique habere[4]." This, Caius tells us, was wider than the form "per vindicationem," as it enabled the testator to leave not only what belonged to him, but what belonged to his heir, and more limited than that "per damnationem." All that was requisite to make such a bequest valid was, that at the time of the testator's death the thing bequeathed should be in his possession, or the possession of his heir.

4. "Per præceptionem." "Lucius Titius hominem Stichum præcipito[5]." This gave rise to a subtle dispute between the Sabinians and Proculeians, on which it is not necessary to enter. The

---

[1] Just. *Instit.* 2. 20.   Caius, *Inst.*
2. 196.

[2] Caius, 2. 201.

[3] Caius, 2. 203.

[4] Caius, 2. 209.

[5] Caius, 2. 216.

404 ROMAN PRIVATE LAW. [CH.

reader will find the arguments on both sides stated
by Caius, himself a Sabinian[1].

It turned upon the Senatus Consultum Neroni-
anum, which became law between the year 54 and
68 of the Christian era; it provided that every
bequest made in imperfect language should be considered as "per damnationem," or, in the words of
Ulpian, "senatus consulto cautum est ut quod minus idoneis verbis legatum est perinde sit ac si op-
timo jure legatum esset[2]."

These methods were rendered unnecessary by a
law to which Justinian alludes, of Constans and
Constantius[3]; but they still remained, and the words
of the testator, if he did not use the precise form,
were adjusted to that of the form which appeared
most to correspond with his intention. Justinian put
them all upon a level, "nostra constitutio dispo-
suit...ut omnibus legatis una sit natura." This equality, however, as the context itself, in which the action
"in rem" is mentioned, shews, related to the form
only, and not to a difference inherent in the nature
of the thing; e. g. if the testator bequeathed a horse
without saying what horse, or a quantity of any thing,
or freedom from an obligation, or an act to be done
or to be left undone, there could be no translation of
the dominium; so if he bequeathed the property of
another, that property did not pass at once to the
legatee, and the maxim would apply, "nemo plus
juris ad alium transferre potest quam ipse habet."

In the third paragraph Justinian assimilates en-

[1] Caius, 2. 217.   [2] Tit. 24. § 11 of his rules.
                    [3] Cod. 6. tit. 37. l. 21.

tirely all "legata" to "fidei commissa." The fragment of Ulpian in the Pandects, "per omnia exæ-
quata sunt legata fidei commissis [1]," is an interpolation of the compilers, as is evident from Ulpian's
own words in the 24th and 25th Rules.

[2] *The Legata* explained and commented upon in
the Pandects are of several kinds, namely,—

I.   [3]*Annua legata.*

The "annuum legatum" was due at the beginning
of each year; the first year it was absolute; the second, conditional on the life of the legatee. If it was
to be paid at different intervals, "anni bimâ, trimâ,
die," it was nevertheless considered absolute, and that
the intervals were only for the relief of the heir.
Therefore it was due from the moment of the testator's death ; and if the legatee died before the time
of payment, it was due to his heirs. If the testator
made certain lands liable for the "legatum," it was
not due till the produce had been gathered. If the
produce[4] of one year was insufficient, it was to be
supplied from the produce of other more favourable
years.

If the testator left an "annuum legatum[5]" in

---

[1] II. 30. 1. § 1.
[2] *Instit.* 2. tit. 20.
II. 33. tit. 1.
Cod. 6. tit. 37.
[3] A bequest of an annuity is primâ
facie for life only. Savery *v.* Dyer,
Amb. 139. Blewitt *v.* Roberts, Craig
and Ph. 274. As to when it is perpetual, see Letts *v.* Randall, 2 De Gex,
F. and J. Kerr *v.* Middlesex Hospi-
tal, 2. 6. M. and G. 576. Innes *v.*

Mitchell, 9 Vesey, 212. Stokes *v.*
Heron, 12 Cl. and Finn. 161. Yates
v. Madden, 3 Mac. and G. 540.
[4] II. 33. 1. 17. § 2. "Vini Falerni,"
etc.
[5] II. 34. 1. 12. "Paulus respondit
—integra deberi—neque ex eo quod
postea prædia ejus pignoris jure testator obligare voluit, ut ex reditu eorum
alimenta perciperent, minuisse eum
vel duxisse ea quæ reliquerat videri."

the first part of his will, and in the latter part of it charged for the greater security of the legatee certain lands with the payment, though the produce of the lands was not sufficient, the money was nevertheless due.

[1] If a bequest was, Pay to Attia till she marries fifty pounds, this was an "annuum legatum," though "in annos singulos" was not added.

[2] So if the testator leave a certain sum to be given to the decurios on his birthday.

[3] An "annuum legatum" is held to exist where the testator leaves money for one year, and other things, wine or corn, for another.

[4] So a bequest to a person of what the testator had been in the habit of giving him was valid, but it did not include what the testator had given the legatee for his, the testator's, purposes.

[5] If the testator had not always given the same sum, or quantity, and his will fluctuated, the last execution of his will was to prevail[6]. If the testator bequeathed an "annuum legatum" without specifying or leaving any means by which to estimate the amount, if he had already made any gift to the legatee, that was to be the measure of the legacy; if he had not, the rank of the legatee and the wealth of the deceased are to be taken into account; and his bequests to other legatees similarly situated, failing all these indications, it is to be supposed that the testator meant to bequeath alimony. The "an-

[1] II. 33. 1. 17.
[2] II. 23. ib. 24.
[3] II. 36. 2. 11.
[4] II. 33. 1. 10. § 1. § 3.

[5] II. 34. 4. 4.
[6] II. 33. 1. 14.
34. 1. 22.
33. 1. 16—20.

nuum legatum" ceased with the death of the legatee, but not by the "capitis diminutio[1]." "Quia," says Modestinus, "tale legatum in facto potius quam in jure consistit." If however it was left to the heirs, it continued to all his successors[2]; it might be supposed perpetual from the nature of the bequest, as to the priest of a particular temple, or to a college of decurios[3]. The rule was different with regard to the bequest of an "ususfructus" which ended in a hundred years. The principles which govern the "annuum legatum" apply to monthly, daily, weekly pensions.

2.   *Ususfructus[4] et reditus legatum[5].*

If the "reditus[6]" of an estate is left, the annual value of the produce is understood, whether the heir or his tenant collect the produce. The heir might sell the farm so long as he paid the value to the legatee[7]. This is the difference between the bequest of the "reditus" and the "ususfructus." For the owner of the estate of which the "ususfructus" was bequeathed could not substitute the money for the land[8].

[1] II. 4. 5. penult.
33. I. 4.
[2] "Hæredis appellatio non solum ad proximum hæredem sed et ad ulteriores refertur, nam et hæredis hæres et deinceps hæredis appellatione continetur." II. 50. 16. 65.
[3] II. 33. I. 20. I. "datum templo." II. ib. 23.
3. 4. 7. § I.
[4] The English cases, Doe v. Biggs, 2 Taunton, 109. Doe v. Bolton, 11 Ad. and Ellis, 188. Barker v. Green-

wood, 4 M. and W. 421. Doe v. Nicholls, 1 B. and C. 336. Doe v. Field, 3 B. and Ad. 564.
[5] II. 33. 2.
Inst. 2. 20.
Cod. 6. 31.
[6] II. 33. I. 21.
[7] II. 33. 2. 38.
[8] In Doe v. Lakeman, 2 B. and Ad. 30, it was held that a devise of the rents and profits of land was equivalent to a bequest of the land.

Moreover, the usufructuary had a right to a habitation on the land, which the legatee of the reditus had not. The "reditus[1]" might be left with a condition annexed, which the legatee was bound to fulfil. If the condition was that certain games should be exhibited in a town in memory of the deceased, which were not permitted there, the heir did not profit by the circumstance, but the bequest was changed with the assent of the more eminent citizens into some other celebration in honour of the deceased.

In the absence of the express will of the testator the "legatum annui reditus" ended with the death of the legatee[2].

3. *De alimentis legatis*[3].

This, like the "annuum legatum," is considered as a series of separate bequests. It continues, unless an opposite intention is clear, to the death of the legatee. It may be left to one incapable of taking the inheritance. It comprises only, if there is no defined specification, what is necessary for bare subsistence according to judicial discretion. A general revocation of legacies does not, if there is room for doubt, extend to this.

4. *De optione legata*[4].

A legacy may be in the alternative, that is,

---

[1] II. 35. 1. 19.
    23. 4. 20—1.
    30. 1. 1. 12.
    33. 1. 17.
[2] II. 33. 2. 22.
[3] II. 34. 1.
    36. 2. 20.
    35. 2. 68.

34. 8. 3.
34. 1. 6. 7. 21. 23.
33. 1. 14.
[4] II. 33. 5.
    31. 76. § 1.
    32. 34. § 2.
J. de legat. 2. 20. 21.
II. 31. 8. § 2.

giving the legatee his choice among several objects. The testator confers the choice, and the person whom he has selected may transfer his right to another person. The "optio," or "electio legata," is when the right of choosing among several things of the same species is given to the legatee. If without option or specification a thing of a particular class is left to him, he is not to take the best of the kind, nor is he bound to receive the worst. The legatee entitled to choose must select one definite object, not part of one and part of another. The right goes to the heirs of the legatee. A period may be fixed within which he is bound to exercise his right. If a third person is to choose for the legatee, and he dies, or delays his choice beyond a year, the legatee may choose himself.

5. *De dote legata vel prælegata* [1].

The "dos" is said to be bequeathed when it is left under the name of a legacy to the girl or woman about to marry, either by her father, or a relation, or a stranger. Even if the word "dos" is not mentioned, it is taken to be a legatum "dotis nomine," if the testator says that it is to be paid on marriage.

[2]It is conditional if it is left by a stranger not obliged to provide a dos to be paid on marriage, as it implies a tacit condition that the marriage shall take place, and without matrimony there can be no dos: "Dies incertus conditionem in testamento

---

[1] II. 23. 3.   [2] II. 35. 1. 75. 30. 1. 30.

facit;" and if it never comes, the legacy is never due.

If the father leaves his daughter 200 aurei, and pays a hundred for her dos when she marries, the remainder will be due, in the absence of proof by the heir that the father had abandoned his intention[1].

The "dos" is said "prælegari" or "relegari" when the husband who has received it, or the father who has taken it in the name of his son, leaves it again to the wife; it is so described because it really belongs to her, as the "dominium" of the "dos" has always been hers. This may be done by express words, or by implication; by express words, when it is mentioned directly; by implication, when it is mentioned indirectly, and in a sense subordinate to another bequest, as "Titiæ uxori amplius quam dotem aureos tot hæres meus damnas esto dare." So if the husband leaves the wife not the exact things he has received as her dowry, but other property in their stead, even though he does not add that this is to be in lieu of the dowry, yet if the intention is manifest, it is to be so considered.

If the very things constituting the dowry are left, and they perish without the husband's fault, the legacy fails; it is otherwise if the husband leave not the very things, but other property which perishes. Nor does it affect the wife's right in this respect that she brought no dowry, "quia falsa demonstratio legato non nocet." But in this case[2]

[1] II. 30. 1. 84.
II. 31. 1. 22. "Onus enim probandi mutatam esse defuncti volun-

tatem ad eum pertinet qui fidei commissum recusat."
[2] II. 30. 1. 75. § 1. II. 34. 3. 25.

a certain sum or particular things must be specified. Nor does this militate against the rule of Ulpian, that if a testator leaves 100 aurei that he has in the bank of Titius, and he has nothing in the bank of Titius, the legacy fails; for it fails not on account of a "falsa demonstratio," but because there is no such thing in "rerum naturâ[1]." If an estate, which was the "dos," is left specially in the will to the wife, and her dower in general words is afterwards bequeathed to her, it is to be taken as a single bequest.

The husband could not impose any burden upon his bequest of his wife's dowry, unless he had added to it, in which case he might charge it with the additional value.

6.　*Facta legari possunt.*

The testator may also by his will enjoin effectually the performance of certain acts; e.g. he may oblige his heir to rebuild, or exonerate from a mortgage, the house of a legatee[2]—to buy a farm from, or sell one to him[3]. If he has fixed the price, it must be paid or taken, though beyond or below the real value of the object, as the testator had a right to give such an advantage to the legatee[4]. If the testator has not fixed any sum, it must be sold at a fair value, "vero pretio[5]." But the Roman Law did not allow a testator to indulge a boundless caprice: "Ineptas voluntates defunctorum circa sepul-

---

[1] II. 25. 1. 5.
　　31. 1. 77 & 12.
[2] II. 30. 112. § 2.
Inst. 2. 21.
[3] II. 30. 66.

[4] II. 30. 49. § ult. "Quod si certo pretio damnatus sit facere, necesse habebit tanti vendere quanti damnatus est."
[5] § 8. ib.

turam, veluti vestes aut si qua alia supervacua ut in
funus impendantur, non valere Papinianus scribit[1];"
and the same principle applies to what we should
call the law of entail; concerning which I shall cite
at length a remarkable passage. A prohibition to
alienate the property bequeathed was invalid if no
reason was assigned, unless it had been inserted for
somebody's benefit[2]—"nisi inveniatur persona cujus
respectu hoc a testatore dispositum sit." This is a
rule which has never been applied in our jurisprudence, but that might operate most beneficially:
it is, however, far too much power to be left in the
hands of a single judge. Neither could the testator
compel the performance of an act contrary to the
manners and feelings of his country, " si liberos suos
emancipare rogatus fuerit quis, non cogitur hoc
facere, potestas enim patria inestimabilis est[3];" and
Scævola lays it down that the heir cannot be compelled to adopt a stranger[4].

7. *Bequest of mortgaged or pledged property.*

Such a bequest was valid[5]; and if the testator
was aware of the fact, the heir was bound to set free
what had been so left[6]. If the property bequeathed

[1] II. 30. 1. 113. § 5.
[2] "Divi Severus et Antoninus rescripserunt eorum qui testamento vetant quid alienari, nec causam exprimunt propter quam id fieri velint, nisi
inveniatur persona cujus respectu hoc
a testatore dispositum sit, nullius esse
momenti scripturam, quasi nudum præceptum reliquerint, quia talem legem
testamento non possint dicere; quodsi
liberis, aut posteris, aut libertis, aut
hæredibus, aut aliis quibusdam per-

sonis consulentes, ejusmodi voluntatem significarent, eam servandam esse;
sed hæc *neque creditoribus* (compare
the English law before 1830) neque
fisco fraudi esse." II. 30. 1. 114. § 14.
[3] Ib. § 8.
[4] II. 32. 1. 41. § 8; but see II. 35.
1. 92.
[5] Inst. h. t. § 4. § 5.
II. 30. 1. 57.
[6] II. 30. 1. 57.

was mortgaged for its full value, even though the testator was ignorant of the fact, the heir was bound to redeem it, because it must be supposed that the testator meant the legatee to derive some benefit from the bequest. If a farm of which the "usus-fructus" was alienated was bequeathed, the heir was bound to redeem the burden, or to give the value of it to the legatee, subject to the distinction before mentioned as to the testator's knowledge[1]. But the heir was not bound to redeem a servitude[2].

8.   The testator might bequeath incorporeal rights, debts due to himself, or to his debtor, or to any one else, "corpora legari omnia et jura, et servitutes possunt[3];" the legacy of what was due from another was called "legatum nominis."   If the document attesting the debt was bequeathed, this was tantamount to a bequest of the debt itself[4]. If the testator bequeathed to Sempronius the ten aurei which the testator owed to Caius, although the testator owed nothing to Caius, the bequest was valid, "quia falsa demonstratio non perimit legatum[5];" a strong example of a very important principle.   There were cases in which though the testator had obtained payment of the debt during his life, the bequest of the debt was valid—as if the testator had taken the debt to keep as a deposit[6], or

---

[1] Π. 32. 1. 4. ult.
Ib. 30. § 1.
[2] Π. 30. 1. 70. § 1.
[3] Π. 30. 1. 41.
[4] Ib. 44. 5.
[5] Ib. 75. § 1.
[6] "Si rem suam testator legaverit,

eamque necessitate urgente alienave-rint, Mucianus putat fidei commissum peti posse, nisi probetur adimere ei testatorem voluisse—probationem au-tem mutatæ voluntatis ab hæredibus exigendam." II. 32. 1. 12; and see 13. ib. II. 50. 17. 162.

if it had been forced upon him by his debtor, or if he had been compelled by the pressure of strong necessity to exact it, or if he immediately lent it out again; a *fortiori* a "novatio" of the debt did not affect the legacy.

9. *The legatum rei alienæ*[1].

The "legatum rei alienæ" was valid, (1) if the testator knew that the thing bequeathed did not belong to him; (2) if it was made to a "conjuncta persona."

10. [2]The testator might bequeath what belonged to the heir—and whether the testator knew that the thing bequeathed belonged to the heir or not, the heir was bound to give it to the legatee.

11. [3]If a definite sum or quantity of things consumed by use was left without any other limitation, the heir was liable to the legatee, though no such things were in his inheritance; if the quality of the thing so left was not mentioned, it was left to the choice of the heir; if an indefinite quantity of things consumed by use, or if money was left, the heir was only bound to give the legatee what was to be found in the inheritance[4].

---

[1] II. 32. 1. 14.
40. 5. 31.
31. 1. 67.
As to the "conjuncta persona," see II. 342. 10. Cod. h. t. 10. "cum alienam."
[2] II. 31. 1. 67. § 8.
4 Inst. h. t.
II. 50. 17. 149. "Ex quâ personâ quis lucrum capit, ejus factum præ-

stare debet."
[3] II. 33. 6. 5. 3. 4.
II. 33. 6. 1. 2. 3. § 1. 6.
II. 33. 7; and see 30. 1. 51.
II. 33. 10.
II. 33. 9.
[4] On this topic see especially Averanius, *Interpret. Juris.* Tom. II. ch. 21—24.

12. *Legatum generis*[1].

Not specific objects only, but classes of things, may be bequeathed, as a "calendarium." All moveable, all immoveable, goods, "supellex," etc. Difficulties may arise if together with such a general bequest the testator enumerates particular objects. A distinction will arise if the general bequest is first, or if it follows the detail of separate articles: if the class is first stated, and the articles it includes follow, as, I leave Titius my "fundus instructus," and then the slaves or articles are enumerated, a question arose whether the enumeration was "ex abundanti[2]," or intended to limit and restrain the original bequest. The rule in the absence of any clear "indicia voluntatis," which were always carefully to be sought for, is, that if the testator after a general clause enumerates particular articles which he knew to be comprised under that clause, his object was to restrain the original bequest. If the particular objects are first stated, and the general clause follows, it is then to be supposed that the testator meant the bequest to be universal. Sometimes the enumeration of the specific articles is put,

[1] II. 33. 7. 20. II. 33. 10. 9. "Legatâ supellectile cum species ex abundanti per imperitiam enumerarentur, generali legato non derogatur. Si tamen species certi numeri demonstratæ fuerint modus generi datus in his speciebus intelligitur." Papinian. II. 33. 7. 12.
33. 6. 16. § 1. § 2. "dulcia omnia." 34. 2. 32. "Pediculis," &c.
"Mobilibus legatis aurum vel argentum non debetur, nisi de eis quo-

que manifeste sensisse testatorem—possit ostendi." 3 tit. 6, Paulus, Sentent.

[2] " Si quis fundum ita ut instructus est legaverit, et adjecerit cum supellectile vel mancipiis vel unâ aliquâ re quæ nominatim expressa non erat, utrum *minuit legatum adjiciendo speciem*...et Papinianus respondit non videri minutum sed'potius ex abundanti adjectum." II. 33. 7. 12. 46.

to remove all possible doubt. If all the moveables
in a particular place are bequeathed, the legatee is
entitled to those which are accidentally absent, and
not to those which are accidentally present in it.
" Labeonis distinctionem," says Pomponius, " valde
probo, qui scripsit nec quod casu absit, minus esse
legatum—nec quod casu ibi sit, magis esse legatum[1]."[2]

---

[1] II. 32. 4. 86.
[2] For an excellent summary of the
English law on the topics discussed in
this chapter, I may refer to the treatise recently published on the construction of Wills, of Mr F. V. Hawkins.

INDEX.

27

THE END.

CAMBRIDGE: PRINTED AT THE UNIVERSITY PRESS.